TAIWAN

HAWAII

T A I W A N

Nation-State or Province?

SIXTH EDITION

JOHN F. COPPER
RHODES COLLEGE

WESTVIEW
PRESS
A Member of the Perseus Books Group

Westview Press was founded in 1975 in Boulder, Colorado, by notable publisher and intellectual Fred Praeger. Westview Press continues to publish scholarly titles and high-quality undergraduate- and graduate-level textbooks in core social science disciplines. With books developed, written, and edited with the needs of serious nonfiction readers, professors, and students in mind, Westview Press honors its long history of publishing books that matter.

Published by Westview Press,
A Member of the Perseus Books Group

Find us on the World Wide Web at www.westviewpress.com.

Every effort has been made to secure required permissions for all text, images, maps, and other art reprinted in this volume.

Westview Press books are available at special discounts for bulk purchases in the United States by corporations, institutions, and other organizations. For more information, please contact the Special Markets Department at the Perseus Books Group, 2300 Chestnut Street, Suite 200, Philadelphia, PA 19103, or call (800) 810-4145, ext. 5000, or e-mail special.markets@perseusbooks.com.

Typeset in 10 point Minion Pro by the Perseus Books Group

Library of Congress Cataloging-in-Publication Data

Copper, John Franklin.
    Taiwan : nation-state or province? / John F. Copper.—6th ed.
      p.   cm.
    Includes bibliographical references and index.
    ISBN 978-0-8133-4692-2 (pbk. : alk. paper)—ISBN 978-0-8133-4693-9
(e-book) 1. Taiwan. 2. Taiwan—International status. I. Title.
    DS799.C67 2012
    951.249—dc23
                                                        2012031338

10 9 8 7 6 5 4 3 2 1

To Lei

CONTENTS

PREFACE

IN A PREVIOUS EDITION OF the US Central Intelligence Agency's often-cited *World Factbook* there is a list of "independent states," "dependencies," and "areas of special sovereignty." Taiwan alone is in a separate category: "other." The most recent *World Factbook* refers to Taiwan as an "administrative division" and notes that China considers it its twenty-third province. Many international organizations do not mention Taiwan or provide information on Taiwan; some include data on Taiwan under the heading China or the People's Republic of China. However, Taiwan appears in lists of countries or nations of the world in many other publications. Thus whether Taiwan is to be considered a sovereign nation-state or a province of China is uncertain.

Much else about Taiwan is either unique or uncertain or both.

In the past Taiwan was called a "pariah nation"—an authoritarian country diplomatically isolated. But even before it lost that opprobrium Taiwan became widely hailed as a "model country" for its economic (rapid growth with equity) and political (quick but peaceful democratization) "miracles."

Taiwan ranks very high in almost all of the criteria used to measure globalization—trade, foreign investment, travel in and out, and so on. Yet it is the world's most isolated nation (if it is a nation) by other criteria—ranking last in memberships in international organizations and very low in the number of foreign countries that grant it formal diplomatic recognition. Taiwan is the only important nation or "administrative division" not a member of the United Nations.

Taiwan has one of the best militaries in the world. It is often listed as a country capable of building nuclear, chemical, and biological weapons. Yet it would likely survive but a few days or weeks if China were to attack the island and if the United States were to no longer guarantee its security.

Analysts have labeled the Taiwan Strait the world's number one "flashpoint." The world's only superpower, the United States, and its only rising power, China, each with nuclear weapons targeted at the other, appear poised to fight over Taiwan. It is said to be the only nonnegotiable issue between them.

In 1996, they almost went to war over Taiwan. Taiwan proclaimed that, as a democracy, it should decide its future and held its first-ever direct presidential election to underscore this right. Seeing this move as a sign of secession, China conducted intimidating missile tests near Taiwan's shores. In reaction, the United States sent the biggest military force deployed since the Vietnam War to the region. For a while a US-China conflict appeared imminent.

Since 2008 tension in the Taiwan Strait has diminished, even though China's claim to Taiwan has grown more credible with the rapid expansion of its economic and military power and the rapid decline in America's strength in both areas.

Some hope that global opinion or an international organization such as the United Nations will help decide Taiwan's future. Yet there is little reason to think that will happen. Public opinion in Taiwan favors the status quo, but that does not help resolve the question.

Two other salient facts about Taiwan need to be noted: Taiwan is more linked to China commercially than most members of the European Union are to each other. Taiwan's economic health depends largely on China, and most people in Taiwan know this. Political links, however, are weak. Will economics or politics decide Taiwan's future? No one seems to know.

In the following pages the author will examine the background, details, and problems associated with this "other" place. This means looking at its geography, history, society, economy, political system, and its foreign and defense policy with an eye on the issue of whether Taiwan has nation-state status.

Most of the Chinese terms used in this book have been rendered into English script using the Wade-Giles system long used in Taiwan. However, some names are spelled according to the Pinyin system developed in China; it was adopted by Taiwan in 2008 and is being put into use gradually. For personal names, the author uses the spelling that person prefers. The term "Beijing" is used for the capital of China; "Peking" is used to refer to that same city during the historical period when the old spelling was in use. For clarification an alternative spelling is sometimes provided in parentheses.

Throughout this book the US dollar is used in measuring Taiwan's economy as well as in monetary transactions and expenditures unless otherwise specified. Other measurements use the US system, though the metric system is also used along with the US system.

JOHN F. COPPER

ACRONYMS

ADB	Asian Development Bank
APEC	Asia Pacific Economic Cooperation
ASEAN	Association of Southeast Asian Nations
ARATS	Association for Relations Across the Taiwan Straits
BCC	Broadcasting Corporation of China
CAL	China Airlines
CNA	Central News Agency
DPP	Democratic Progressive Party
ECFA	Economic Cooperation Framework Agreement
EPZ	export processing zone
GATT	General Agreement on Tariffs and Trade
GDP	gross domestic product
GNP	gross national product
GSP	Generalized System of Preferences
JCRR	Joint Commission on Rural Reconstruction
KMT	Nationalist Party or Kuomintang
NIC	newly industrializing country
NP	New Party
PFP	People First Party
PLA	People's Liberation Army
SEF	Straits Exchange Foundation
TMD	theater missile defense
TRA	Taiwan Relations Act
TSU	Taiwan Solidarity Union
WTO	World Trade Organization

1

THE LAND AND THE PEOPLE

LOCATED IN THE WESTERN PACIFIC just east of the south-central coast of China, the island of Taiwan comprises most of the land area of the nation known officially as the Republic of China (also called Nationalist China, Free China, the Republic of China on Taiwan, the Republic of Taiwan) but most often referred to as just Taiwan. Taipei is its capital. In the West, Taiwan was formerly known as Formosa. The term Formosa has fallen into disuse, though it has been revived at times by advocates of Taiwan's independence looking for a non-Chinese term for the island. Some Aborigines call for using the word "Kaitagelan" or some other native word for the island, the nation, or both. Chinese leaders in Beijing regard Taiwan not as a nation but rather as territory belonging to the People's Republic of China and refer to the island of Taiwan, the Pescadores, and some other islands close to Taiwan as "Taiwan Province." In the past, the government of Taiwan likewise espoused a one-China policy and claimed sovereignty over all of China, or both China and Taiwan, saying that the government in Beijing was illegal and illegitimate. Subsequently, government officials in Taiwan proclaimed that both Beijing and Taipei possessed sovereignty and spoke of unification at some unspecified time in the future. Others, especially the opposition Democratic Progressive Party (DPP), argue that Taiwan should not be seen as part of China and should be legally independent. Chen Shui-bian, a member of the DPP, became president in 2000 and promptly vowed not to declare independence, but his subsequent statements and actions indicated legal separation from China was his intention. The DPP was

1

soundly defeated in a legislative election in early 2008 and then, two months later, lost the presidency to the Nationalist Party or Kuomintang (KMT). Thenceforth, formally splitting from China seemed to be a losing issue, particularly after DPP's loss in the 2012 election, which party leaders largely attributed to its China policy. The victorious presidential candidate, Ma Ying-jeou, conversely, pledged not to pursue unification. Taiwan's status as part of China (however defined) or not still divides the country's leaders and its population. The political parties and the various ethnic groups espouse different and often clashing views on independence, self-determination, unification, one China versus two, one China and one Taiwan, "Greater China," and so on. Taiwan's leftist or liberal parties favor independence or separation from China; its conservative parties oppose independence and advocate closer ties with China. The Fukienese Taiwanese generally favor independence; the other ethnic groups generally do not, especially the Mainland Chinese. The United States, in whose hands Taiwan's fate ostensibly rests, and many other nations treat Taiwan as de facto independent, but de jure part of China—a seeming contradiction.

Physical Setting

Under the Republic of China's governance is Taiwan, more than a dozen smaller islands, and many islets that surround it and are considered geologically linked to it. Among these islands are the Pescadores (Penghu) Islands, sixty-four in all—nineteen of which are inhabited; Orchid Island (Lan Tao); Green Island (Lü Tao); some smaller islands off Taiwan's eastern coast; the Offshore Islands (the Quemoy and Matsu groups and some other small islands near them); and some islands in the South China Sea. All the territory under Taipei's control is also claimed by the People's Republic of China, which it labels "Taiwan Province"—except for the Offshore Islands, which it regards as a part of Fukien (spelled Fujian in China) Province, and the islands claimed by Taipei in the South China Sea.[1]

Approximately 230 miles long and 85 miles wide at the center, the surface area of the island of Taiwan is 13,814 square miles, about the size of Holland or the US states of Massachusetts, Rhode Island, and Connecticut combined. The Pescadores add another 49 square miles, Quemoy about 68 square miles, and Matsu 10 square miles. If Taiwan and the other territory under the jurisdiction of the Republic of China were regarded as a province of China, it would be the People's Republic of China's second smallest province (the smallest before Hainan Island was made a province in 1988). Taiwan has less than 1/260th of China's land area. Yet if Taiwan were seen as a nation, it would rank above average in population (number 51 of 242 countries) though just below average in land area (number 139 of 249).[2]

The Penghu Islands lie twenty-five miles off Taiwan's west coast, slightly south of the island's center. The Quemoy group (six islands, two of them controlled by the People's Republic of China) is located within shouting distance (at the closest point) of Fukien Province of the People's Republic of China, west of central Taiwan. This island group is situated strategically near the port of Amoy. The Matsu group is located northwest of Taiwan and, like the Quemoy group, is close to the Mainland. It is near the Chinese port of Fuchou (Fuzhou). Both the Quemoy and Matsu island groups are geologically part of China.

The Republic of China also lays territorial claim to some of the Pratas (Dongsha) Islands and Spratly (Nansha) Islands—in fact, the largest islands in both groups—located in the South China Sea, and maintains military forces on islands in both groups. These island groups are small but are strategically located adjacent to important sea-lanes. In addition, ownership may provide the basis for claims on some of 3.5 million square kilometers of ocean territory and undersea minerals, including oil, around the islands. These claims involve Taipei in a territorial dispute with the People's Republic of China, Vietnam, the Philippines, Malaysia, Brunei, and Indonesia.[3] Taipei's position vis-à-vis the People's Republic of China has differed, however, from its disputes with the other claimants. The dispute has not been about whether the islands are Chinese territory but rather about which government has legal jurisdiction. Recently, however, this has changed. In fact, Taipei has made claim to at least part of the Spratly Islands based on Japanese jurisdiction over the islands when Taiwan was part of the Japanese Empire and the islands were considered part of Kaohsiung Prefecture. In mid-2012 Taipei restated its claims, and legislators visited some of the islands in the midst of a heated territorial dispute in the area.[4]

Taipei claims ownership of the Senkaku Islands, or Tiaoyutai (Diaoyutai)—meaning "fishing stage" in Chinese—Islands: eight tiny, uninhabited islets just over one hundred miles northwest of Taiwan. This claim was made in 1971 after the US government agreed to return the Ryukyu Islands, which included the Senkakus, to Japan. The issue grew more intense after UN reports suggested the presence of undersea oil, possibly very large deposits, in the vicinity. Taipei based its claim on the fact that Taiwanese fishermen had been using the islands for some years as a stopping-off place to gather bird eggs and dry their nets. Also, because the islands are geologically part of China's continental shelf and because Taipei claimed sovereignty over all of China, it made an argument based on geography.[5] More recently Taipei has cited the peace agreement with Japan at the end of World War II. Beijing likewise laid claim to the islands.

The United States turned over the islands to Japan without paying much attention to either Beijing's or Taipei's claims. The Japanese government assumed sovereignty over the islands at this time, rejecting both Beijing's and Taipei's positions. The territorial issue remained essentially dormant until 1989, when the Japanese navy chased some of Taiwan's fishermen away from the islands. The next year, Japan built a lighthouse on one of the islands. Subsequently, citizens from

Taiwan organized a protest and put an Olympic torch on one of the islands in the chain. In 1992, China's legislature passed a territorial sea law that declared the islands to be part of the People's Republic of China. In 1996, groups from Hong Kong and Taiwan went to the islands to support Chinese sovereignty over the islands, and one protester was killed. This incident focused global attention on the dispute. China and Japan continue aggressively to make claim to the islands. Taiwan stakes claim to the islands, but not aggressively so.

In the past, advocates of Taiwan's independence proposed the abandonment of Taipei's claim to Quemoy and Matsu so that Taiwan would be more distinctly separate from China and thus legally independent, but they found the public did not support this view. In 2001, Taiwan established the "three mini links" policy that allowed direct trade, travel, and postal links between the islands and the Mainland. Contacts increased markedly as did trade. A bridge will connect Quemoy with China in 2016.[6]

The island of Taiwan is positioned between 21°459 and 25°509 north latitude, which in the Western Hemisphere would be just north of Cuba. The northern part of Taiwan shares the same latitude as southern Florida. The Tropic of Cancer bisects the island just below its center. Taiwan is bordered on the east by the Pacific Ocean, on the west by the Taiwan (Formosa) Strait (95 miles from China at its closest point), on the northwest by the East China Sea, and on the southwest by the South China Sea. To the north, less than 80 miles away, lie the Ryukyu Islands, Japan's southernmost territory—the closest land area to Taiwan. The island of Kyushu (the southernmost of Japan's main islands), however, is 700 miles away, and Tokyo is 1,274 miles distant. Less than 100 miles to Taiwan's south, separated by the Bashi Channel, are the Philippine Islands, though the island of Luzon is 230 miles from Taiwan. East of Taiwan is the great expanse of the Pacific Ocean and finally Mexico. Of the major cities in the region, Hong Kong is the closest to Taiwan—483 miles away. Next in proximity is Guangzhou, which is 564 miles from Taipei. Manila is 705 miles from Taiwan, Seoul is 885, and Beijing is 1,677 miles away.

Taiwan and the Pescadores lie on the edge of the East Asian continental shelf. Thus, to the west of Taiwan, the water (in the Taiwan Strait) is relatively shallow, its depth averaging three hundred feet. The ocean waters off Taiwan's east coast, in contrast, are deep; in fact, thirty miles offshore in the Pacific Ocean, the seabed drops precipitously to a depth of thirteen thousand feet.

Some geologists say that Taiwan was originally part of the Asian mainland. The depth of the water in the Taiwan Strait, the configuration of Taiwan's coastlines, and the age of rocks and their formations on Taiwan's periphery all indicate that the time of Taiwan's birth was not the same as that of the Ryukyu Islands to the north or the Philippines to the south. In addition, the soil, plants, and animal life do not suggest great differences between Taiwan and China.[7] Yet others contend that, because Taiwan has volcanic soil and is part of the long chain of islands extending south from the Alaskan Aleutian Islands, the island's origins are similar to those of Japan, the Philippines, and other islands off the eastern Asian coast that were created by volcanic activity in the Pacific Ocean. The frequency of earthquakes—an average of 160 per year—also makes Taiwan resemble Japan more than South China.[8] This evidence suggests either a more distant time connection, or none at all, to the Asian mainland.[9]

Mountains cover approximately two-thirds of Taiwan's surface. The highest and most rugged are found in the eastern part of the island. In some areas, mountains or mountain cliffs extend right up to Taiwan's eastern shore. Fifty peaks tower near or above 10,000 feet; Yu Shan (Jade Mountain), reaching 13,114 feet above sea level, is the highest. When Taiwan was part of the Japanese empire, Yu Shan was labeled Japan's highest mountain.

Because the Central Mountain Range, which traverses the island from north to south as if it were Taiwan's spine, lies close to the island's eastern shoreline, there are few natural harbors there. Suao Bay is an exception. Keelung harbor, which serves Taipei, is located on the north coast. In contrast, the west coast has good ports—including Kaohsiung, Tainan, and Taichung—and is home to most of Taiwan's population and all of its large cities.

Foothills surround the Central Mountain Range and account for nearly 50 percent of Taiwan's surface area. Around the foothills are sloping tablelands, many terraced for rice cultivation. Below the tablelands stretch plains and then basins. The plains constitute Taiwan's most productive farming areas. On the west coast there are tidal basins and, in some areas, swamps. Elsewhere there are spits and sandbars. On the east side of the island, the mountains turn into foothills and plains much more quickly than in the west, leaving less flatland to be farmed.[10] Although China is not lacking in mountains and foothills, most of its population resides in areas that are relatively flat.

The point of origin for Taiwan's rivers is the mountainous central part of the island. Most of the island's rivers, however, are short and the flows are rapid. Only one, the Choushui, is longer than one hundred miles. Because of this, Taiwan relies very little on river transport. The Tamsui River, less than ninety miles long, flows past Taipei and into the Taiwan Strait; it is considered Taiwan's only navigable river.[11] Unlike China, where water control has been a major concern for centuries and floods have caused untold human suffering and loss of life, Taiwan's rivers do not pose a serious flood menace. They seldom overflow, except during typhoons, and farmers do not depend on them to a great extent for irrigation.

In many respects, Taiwan's geography and topography resemble Japan's (where a feudal system of government evolved) more than China's (where the need to control water and building and maintaining levees and dikes gave rise to a bureaucratic political system). Taiwan, however, is not as compartmentalized as are the Japanese islands. Comparing Taiwan's geography with China's evokes quite contentious views. On the one hand, Taiwan is not very much like most of China: it is an island; its soil is volcanic; its rivers are small; its rainfall patterns are very different. On the other hand, China is a very large nation, and differences in terrain and geography from east to west and north to south are greater than differences between Taiwan and southeastern China.

Climate, Soil, and Natural Resources

Taiwan's climate is subtropical; the very southern tip of the island is tropical. Summers are hot, humid, and long, extending from April or May to September or October. Winters are short and mild, lasting from December to February. During the winter, snow falls in the mountains and occasionally even at some lower elevations in the northern part of the island. Taiwan's climate and weather patterns change considerably, however, with variations in elevation and shifts in the prevailing winds.

The average daytime high temperature on the island is 70 degrees Fahrenheit (21 degrees Centigrade). Although the temperature rises or falls by about 1.5 degrees Fahrenheit for every degree of latitude in the winter, there is little variation in the summer: Keelung's mean July temperature of over 81 degrees compares with 83 degrees at the island's southernmost tip. The fact that Taipei lies in a basin makes the hot summers there similar to those of cities much farther south, such as Jakarta and Bangkok.[12]

Temperature fluctuations during any of the seasons are minimized by the proximity of the ocean; this is only somewhat less true in the central part of the island compared with the coastal areas. The Japan Current, which flows from Southeast Asia past Taiwan and on north, also moderates Taiwan's weather.

Taiwan has abundant rainfall year-round; the mean annual precipitation is 102 inches. The east coast usually receives more rain than the west and the mountains more than the lowlands. Some of the mountains on the windward side of the island (the east) often see rainfall exceeding five inches within a twenty-four-hour period. One odd feature about Taiwan's rain patterns is that the dry season at one end of the island coincides with the rainy season at the other. In the north, the heaviest rains fall between October and March; in the south, it is between April and September.[13]

Agriculture is not much of a gamble in Taiwan compared to other places in the world (including China) owing to the ample and predictable rainfall and because water for irrigation, when needed, can be obtained from small streams, lakes, and reservoirs. The plentiful rain supply also provides Taiwan with hydroelectric power, which in the early post–World War II period was cheap and facilitated the island's industrialization.

The patterns of precipitation in the Pescadores resemble those of the southwest coastal part of Taiwan, except that rainfall is not so much influenced by Taiwan's mountains. Rainfall on the Offshore Islands (Quemoy and Matsu) is like the coastal areas of Fukien Province in China. The islands Taiwan claims in the South China Sea have rainfall patterns like the other islands there and the adjacent Southeast Asian countries.

Located near the Asian landmass but in the world's largest ocean, Taiwan's winds are monsoonal—or periodic—and seasonal. Taiwan experiences none of the strong continental winds, cyclones, and tornadoes common in parts of China. Yet typhoons plague the island, particularly in the late summer and early fall, as they do the Philippines, Vietnam, and other places to the south, the Ryukyu Islands and the main Japanese islands to the north (though they are seldom so strong further north), and the coast of China. These "hurricanes of the east" are among the most severe in the world. When they hit Taiwan—usually in July, August, and September—they often cause damage to buildings and crops.

Taiwan's lowland plains and valleys generally have rich alluvial topsoil because much of Taiwan's land is either volcanic or partly volcanic and thus quite fertile despite centuries of farming. The soil in the uplands and at higher elevations, however, is leached, acidic, and infertile, and it has been subjected to considerable erosion, though it remains rich compared to that of most mountainous areas elsewhere in the world. Because of its good soil and plentiful rainfall, Taiwan's forests have survived extensive cutting for many years and still cover half the island's land surface.

Owing to the variations in soil quality, elevation, climate, and other factors, Taiwan enjoys a diversity of flora. Of its more than 190 plant families and nearly four thousand species, about one-third are considered indigenous. From sea level to about six thousand feet, plants tend to be either tropical or subtropical. Mixed forests of broad-leafed deciduous trees and conifers occupy the higher areas. Conifers grow primarily at the highest elevations.

More than 60 types of mammals have been found in Taiwan, about 45 of which are native species. The largest predatory mammal is the Formosan black bear. Foxes, flying foxes, deer, wild boar, bats, and squirrels inhabit the less populated areas. Taiwan has 330 species and subspecies of birds, just over 30 of which are indigenous. And there are more than 65 species of reptiles and amphibians. Snakes are found throughout the island; 13 species are poisonous. Many of the animals native to Taiwan are not found in China or elsewhere in the region. The plant and animal life on the island generally offers evidence for both Taiwan's early birth and for the view that it was in the past connected to the Mainland.

Taiwan's farmers produce a variety of crops. Rice is the staple, and the two or three harvests each year usually produce high yields. Other grains are less common. Fruits—considered among the best tasting in the world—and vegetables are also important crops. Taiwan has been self-sufficient in most food commodities and in the past exported large quantities of sugar and rice, and more recently sizable quantities of fruits and vegetables and canned foods; but it now imports significant amounts of meat, grains (other than rice), and animal feed. Taiwan has a dairy industry and its farmers raise cattle for meat, but both are new to Taiwan and remain rather small in their economic importance. The nation's fishing industry has been important as a source of employment and food. In recent years, though, because fishermen have had to sail much farther from Taiwan's shores, this has changed. Taiwan's fishermen contract with other nations to fish off their shores. Fish farming has also become common and profitable. Agriculture has shrunk in importance because of industrialization. Also, now that Taiwan is a member of the World Trade Organization (WTO), many farmers' livelihoods are threatened by foreign competition.

Taiwan is not well endowed in mineral or energy resources. Twenty minerals can be found on the island, but none in commercially significant amounts. Coal, which in Taiwan's early history made the island a port of call for merchant ships, was once important to the economy. Although coal was mined until just recently (primarily in the northern part of the island), production was very labor-intensive because the seams are so small.

Gold and copper have been mined in the northern part of the island for a century, although the extraction of neither metal is currently of economic importance. Taiwan has small deposits of sulfur (in the form of pyrite), dolomite (a source of magnesium), and nickel. Marble and a low-quality jade mined in Taiwan are used mostly for vases, jewelry, and other decorative items. Some oil and natural gas have been found, both onshore and offshore, but not in the commercially meaningful quantities once thought possible.[14]

One thing is clear when looking at Taiwan's natural resource base: Taiwan has very little. This means that it must develop another resource: its human talent.

Population

Taiwan's population numbers just over twenty-three million. Given its small area, this makes the island one of the most densely populated places on earth. In fact, the number of people per square mile in Taiwan is nearly double that of Japan and almost five times that of China. If Taiwan were a province of China, it would be its most densely populated one. Furthermore, as more than two-thirds of Taiwan's surface is covered by mountains, the island's real population-to-land ratio should be regarded as even higher than the numbers indicate.[15] The population density of the lowlands surpasses the island's average of more than 1,600 per square mile (635 per square kilometer) by a very large margin. If regarded as a nation-state, Taiwan would be the most densely populated nation in the world after Bangladesh (excluding, of course, some ministates and city-states).[16] And, considering the large mountainous area in Taiwan that cannot be inhabited, Taiwan's population density may be said to exceed even that of Bangladesh.

Taiwan's high population density, however, is of recent origin. In 1940, the island's population was only 5.8 million. An influx of people fleeing the Mainland after the Communist takeover in 1949 and a very high birthrate for a decade and a half after that pushed Taiwan's population to more than 10 million by 1960.

The birthrate in Taiwan in 1952 was 4.66 per 1,000 people annually, one of the highest in the world. In response, in 1964 the government established an official birth-control program to expand population control measures that had been unofficially in effect in the cities for some time. As a consequence Taiwan's birthrate fell to 3.27 by 1965 and by 1980 to 2.34—just about the world average. By reducing the fertility rate by more than 100 percent in twenty years, Taiwan accomplished what it took most Western countries a century to do. After 1980, the birthrate fell to a figure well below the world's average. In 2011 it was reported Taiwan's birthrate was the lowest in the world.[17]

Paralleling the decline in the birthrate, Taiwan's death rate dropped significantly, falling from 18.2 per 1,000 people in 1952 to 5.92 in 2006. Meanwhile, the infant mortality rate dropped from 44.7 per 1,000 to 4.6 per 1,000 during that same period. Hence increases in life expectancy have been extremely high over the past forty-five years. From 1951 to 1991, the life span of Taiwan's population rose from just over 55 (53.1 for males and 57.3 for females) to almost 75 (71.5 for males and 76.9 for females). In 2012 it was 76.2 for males and 82.7 for females—even higher than the life expectancy figures in many European countries and ten years above the world's average.[18]

Owing to the success of Taiwan's efforts to reduce the birthrate, together with dramatic decreases in the death rate, the average age of Taiwan's population has risen markedly since the 1960s. In 1964, 45 percent of the population was under the age of fifteen; just 2.6 percent was over the age of sixty-five. (In the United States the relevant numbers were 30.9 percent and 9.3 percent, respectively.) By 1986, nearly one-third of the population was still under fifteen. Since then, the age of Taiwan's population has increased rapidly. In 1992, only about one-fifth of the population was under the age of fifteen; 6.8 percent of the population was over sixty-five. In 2010, 10.7 percent was over sixty-five.[19]

The problem of aging in Taiwan is thus a serious one and portends to be much more acute in the future. It is forecast that Taiwan's population will peak at just under 23.5 million in 2020 and will fall to 18.4 million by 2060. At that time the proportion of the population over 65 will be nearly 42 percent. There will be just 1.2 people in the working-age population to support one elderly individual. This will mean paying very high costs for government retirement, health, and other expenditures.[20] The government is currently encouraging mothers to have more children. Immigration may help resolve the problem, but its political ramifications are controversial.

The gender ratio of Taiwan's population has also been an issue of concern. Because more of those who fled to Taiwan in 1949, especially the military, were male, the ratio of men to women was quite unbalanced for some time and as a result many men could not find wives. This situation subsequently improved, but in 1964 there were still 109 males for every 100 females. Even today there remains an imbalance of men over women in most age groups. Only in the population over the age of sixty-five are there more females than males. Recently, after seeing the male-female ratio gap close for a number of years, it has increased again for a different reason: in 1985 a law was passed allowing abortions twenty-four weeks into pregnancy in order to prevent the birth of babies suffering congenital defects. This produced a rise in the proportion of male to female babies from 106.7 (versus 100 females) in 1985 to 110.3 in 1991. In other words, the use of scientific tests to determine the sex of babies before they are born resulted in more sex-selection abortions. Very recently, the imbalance has diminished, but it is still a problem.[21]

Because of the imbalance in the sex ratio and owing to the fact that many men perceive Taiwan's women to be too liberated, they seek wives from other countries. In 2003, nearly one in three marriages was with a foreign spouse—87 percent of whom were brides, mostly from China (nearly two-thirds) and Southeast Asia. During the Chen Shui-bian presidency, the government sought to limit the number of foreign spouses in various ways, including restricting their right to vote. (Foreign spouses generally did not favor the DPP.) This resulted in a slight decline in foreign marriages.[22] President Ma Ying-jeou lifted various restrictions on marriages with foreigners, thus ending discrimination against brides from other countries.

After 1949, Taiwan had almost no immigration. A high birthrate and a low death rate caused the population to increase rapidly for a few years. Then a falling birthrate caused it to become static for a number of years. Because of the resulting shortage of young people in the last fifteen to twenty years, Taiwan has attracted immigrant labor to offset a shortage of local workers. Meanwhile prosperity allowed more people to stay out of the workforce to get an advanced education. Many also avoided low-paying and hard labor jobs. Meanwhile high wage rates in Taiwan compared to most other parts of Asia were an attraction to foreign workers. By the late 1990s, there were one-third of a million foreign workers in Taiwan.[23] In 2000, the government moved to reduce the number of employees recruited from other countries. Still the number increased to 424,000 in 2006. Most of these, 69 percent, were guest workers and were supposed to return to their native countries at the end of their contracts.[24] Some sought to stay, and this created controversy when they complained of ill treatment and, on one occasion during the Chen administration, when they rioted over wages not paid, thus exposing serious government corruption.

Not unrelated to this issue is the number of citizens who have gone to China—most to do business or, since Taiwan's economic downturn in 2001, to find jobs. A million or more, perhaps three million, people from Taiwan currently live in China, mostly in the southern coastal areas.[25] Among these, many have settled semipermanently. Many men have found wives in China, some second wives, and a good proportion have children there. This and the rumored large numbers of Chinese from China residing in Taiwan illegally has given rise to concern, sometimes alarm, over Taiwan's "demographic unification" with China.

Still another population issue is urbanization. In 1920, only 4 percent of the people in Taiwan lived in cities with populations of more than a hundred thousand. The proportion changed in 1949 because of the influx of Chinese from the Mainland, who, to a large extent, became city dwellers. Then, in the middle and late 1950s, as a result of land reform and the enhanced productivity in the agricultural sector, people began moving to the cities in large numbers. This process accelerated in the 1960s as factories proliferated in or near Taiwan's large and medium-sized cities. By the early 1970s, Taiwan's population was two-thirds urban.[26]

Urbanization was accompanied by an especially rapid growth of Taiwan's largest cities. In 1952, just over 47 percent of the population lived in cities of more than fifty thousand people. By 1980, the proportion had risen to 78 percent (compared to the world's average of 43 percent)—ranking Taiwan twenty-eighth in the world (higher than Japan, 77 percent, or the United States, 75 percent) in terms of the percentage of the urban population.[27]

Taipei's population, which was less than 326,000 in 1947, grew to more than 1 million by 1966—an increase of 260 percent. Another 1 million people were added before 1974. Other large cities in Taiwan have grown at a similar rate, nearly doubling or tripling in size between 1947 and the mid-1960s, while experiencing high growth even into the 1990s. Taiwan's four largest cities now account for nearly 30 percent of the population and 60 percent of the island's urban residents. Recognizing this trend, five of Taiwan's cities are now classified as metropolitan cities and some have been renamed. New Taipei City's population is currently 3.9 million; Kaohsiung City's is 2.8 million; Taichung City's is 2.7 million; Taipei City's is 2.6 million; Tainan City's is 1.9 million.[28]

Since the mid-1990s, migration to most of Taiwan's large and medium-sized cities has slowed because of urban crowding and other associated problems. Since 1978 Taipei and some other cities have experienced a population decline. Satellite or "urban towns" near Taipei, Kaohsiung, and Taichung were built to reduce the population pressures there.[29] However, many of these have been absorbed with the redrawing of boundaries and the creation of metropolitan cities.

Nearly all of Taiwan's population resides on the island of Taiwan itself: 99.7 percent. The population of the Pescadores is just over ninety thousand; Quemoy is fifty thousand; Matsu is around eight thousand, although the large numbers of soldiers garrisoned on Quemoy and Matsu are not included in these figures. Islands off Taiwan's east coast have even smaller populations; islands under Taipei's jurisdiction in the South China Sea lack civilian populations.

Ethnic Groups

Taiwan's population is made up of four major ethnic or subethnic groups: the Aborigines, two groups of "Taiwanese" Chinese (Fukienese—or in their language Hoklo or Holo—and Hakka), and "Mainland Chinese."[30] The Aborigines are usually seen as ethnically distinct from the Chinese. However, they may or may not belong to a single ethnic group; different tribes are sometimes considered distinct ethnic groups. The three Chinese groups are more accurately described as being different from each other according to their provincial origins and the time they arrived in Taiwan, as well as the language or languages (dialects) they speak, rather than according to ethnicity.

The Aborigines have long been considered to have migrated from Southeast Asia or South China several millennia ago, though some tribes in the northern part of the island might have come from the north—meaning other parts of China or Japan. The languages of the Aborigines resemble Bahasa (the language spoken in Brunei, Indonesia, and Malaysia) in structure and vocabulary. Aboriginal culture for the most part seems to have originated in Southeast Asia, though it obviously evolved considerably in Taiwan. However, it may be that the Aborigines populated Taiwan much earlier and migrated from Taiwan to other parts of Asia, rather than the other way around; some recent DNA studies suggest they are the ancestors of the natives of New Zealand and some of the Pacific Islands.[31]

The government lists fourteen major Aboriginal tribes: Ami, Atayal, Bunun, Kavalan, Paiwan, Puyuma, Rukai, Saisiyat, Sediq, Sukizaya, Thao, Turku, Tsou, and Yami. Other tribes can also be identified, but all are either small or are being rapidly assimilated or both. Some tribes have virtually vanished. Around a tenth of Aborigines do not identify with a tribe. More than one-third of Taiwan's Aboriginal people are of the Ami tribe. All the Aborigines are less urban than the three Chinese groups mentioned above, and, with the exception of the Yami tribe living on the Orchid Island off Taiwan's southeast coast, most reside in the Central Mountain Range area or on the east coastal plain. Although the Aborigines vary considerably from tribe to tribe in physical appearance, they are generally short and have rugged features, with larger noses and eyes than the Chinese. Most are identifiable because of their looks and by tattoos, clothing, and manners.

The Aborigines have long been assumed to be the original inhabitants of the island, though there is no definitive proof of this. In fact, some anthropologists say there were probably people on the island before the Aborigines. Nonetheless, the Aborigines regard themselves as Taiwan's first inhabitants; certainly they populated the island long before the arrival of any Chinese. It is difficult to say when the first Chinese arrived on the island; it was probably around a thousand years ago. It is known that early Chinese immigrants were few in number, and most went to Taiwan only temporarily—for seasonal work or to trade. Major migrations began in the seventeenth century. At that time and after most of the immigrants sought to stay in Taiwan permanently.

When Chinese immigrants arrived, they identified two groups of Aborigines: sedentary groups who lived in the lowland areas and practiced agriculture, and less settled tribes who lived in the mountains and survived by hunting and fishing. The Chinese killed many of the former during frequent armed conflicts and drove many more into the mountains. Many were also assimilated. Now most of the Aborigines are mountain Aborigines.[32] Although all of the Aboriginal population is said to be "acculturated"—speaking the national language and knowing both Taiwanese and Mainland Chinese customs while living amicably under the law—most still reside in the less populated areas of Taiwan, especially the mountains. Many also keep their tribal ways. Some observers see many similarities between Taiwan's Aborigines and Indigenous Americans.

Early Chinese migrants to Taiwan hailed mainly from Fukien (Fujian) and Kwangtung (Guangdong) provinces. They are now called Taiwanese or sometimes "native Taiwanese." They are also referred to as "early arrival Chinese." However, there are two distinct groups of migrants. The Fukien Taiwanese came mostly from the southern part of Fukien Province, especially the area near the city of Amoy. Hakka Taiwanese, or just Hakkas, also came from southern Fukien, but most came from Kwangtung. The migration of both groups was concentrated in specific spans of time; one might say they came in waves. The fall of the Ming Dynasty in 1644 brought a particularly large number of migrants from Fukien Province to Taiwan. Some non-Hakka Chinese from Kwangtung Province were among these early immigrants to Taiwan, but most turned out to be only temporary residents.

There were likely some Hakkas in Taiwan before the first Fukienese arrived, though this is not a certainty and their numbers were in any case small. The Hakkas were a persecuted minority in China, having been driven from their home area in northern China around fifteen hundred years ago. They became itinerants and took up residence in various parts of China. Some writers have likened them to the Jews in Europe. Recent evidence from DNA tests and linguistic studies indicates the Hakka people might have once resided in Mongolia.[33] In any event, many migrated to southern China and engaged in fishing and trading in the coastal areas and from there migrated to the Pescadores and then on to southern Taiwan. Some migrated to Southeast Asia and elsewhere. By about AD 1000, there were a number of Hakka settlements in southwest Taiwan. The last large-scale migration of Hakkas to Taiwan occurred in the late 1860s after the very destructive Taiping Rebellion in China. Because a Hakka led the rebellion, Hakkas incurred blame, resulting in even worse persecution than they had faced before; consequently many fled to Taiwan.

Fukienese, mostly farmers and fishermen, came in such large numbers that they pushed many Hakkas inland, sometimes into enclaves. The Fukienese then inhabited most of the western plain. The Fukien Chinese later called themselves *pen ti jen* (natives) or *ben sheng jen* (local province people); they labeled the Hakkas *ke chia jen* (guest people, which is what Hakka literally means), and they named the Aborigines *shan ti jen* (mountain people).

Notwithstanding this rather long period during which Chinese migrated to Taiwan, as late as the mid-seventeenth century, when the Dutch took control of Taiwan, it is estimated that there were only twenty-five thousand Chinese on the island.[34] It was not until the nineteenth century that the Chinese constituted a majority of the island's population, and even then they occupied considerably less than half of the island's land area. The Dutch encouraged the migration of Chinese to the island, as did the local governments that ruled Taiwan after the Dutch departed. However, the government of China during various periods banned emigration to Taiwan, often under the penalty of death. In addition, for long stretches of time, the Chinese government prohibited women or children from going.

In 1949, when the Communists defeated Nationalist Chinese armies and assumed political control over the mainland of China, another wave of more than 1.5 million Chinese immigrants arrived on Taiwan's shores. Because they hailed from various parts of China, they were known simply as Mainlanders, or *wai sheng jen* (outside-province people). Most, though, came from China's coastal provinces, more from the south than the north (because Chiang Kai-shek's base of support was near Shanghai in southeast China and thus more of his army and government was composed of people from that area). Also, the Communists took control of China from the north and isolated much of the west, keeping the people there from escaping.

Taiwan's population today is grouped as follows: Mainlanders, around 14 percent; Taiwanese, slightly more than 84 percent (the Hakkas make up 10–15 percent); and Aborigines, around 2 percent. The birthrate is slightly higher among the two groups of Taiwanese mainly because they are more rural and less educated than the Mainland Chinese. The death rate is higher among the Aborigines. These and other population trends, however, have not greatly affected the ethnic ratio in Taiwan.

The early Chinese who immigrated to Taiwan did so mostly because of poverty, difficult conditions at home, and the prospects for a better life in Taiwan. Most emigrated for the same reasons Europeans left for America—except that few, if any, went to Taiwan because of religious persecution. Like the Europeans who flocked to the New World, most Chinese who settled in Taiwan severed ties with their homeland. For some time, as noted above, even when Taiwan was ruled by China, it was illegal for Chinese to emigrate, and those who did were punished, sometimes severely, if they returned to China—another reason the move was considered permanent by those who went to Taiwan. Few maintained or tried to reestablish broken family ties. Such efforts were banned during the Japanese period and after 1949 until the late 1980s.

The Mainland Chinese who fled to Taiwan in 1949 did not generally consider the move permanent. They hoped that the Nationalist Chinese military could regroup and counterattack and that the mainland of China could be liberated from the Communists, after which they would return home. After a while, most Mainlanders began to call Taiwan home and gave up any serious thought of going back to China. Their resignation to living permanently in Taiwan was at first more evident among younger and more successful Mainlanders, but after years of separation, Taiwan's miracle economic growth, and lagging growth in China, most Mainlanders came to view Taiwan as home.[35]

By the mid-1980s, more than half the Mainland Chinese population of Taiwan was born on the island. At that time, of the total population of the Republic of China, less than 6 percent was born in China.[36] As a result, it seemed that, at least as reflected in Taiwan's demographics, ties between Taiwan and China were weakening fast. At the time, however, people from Taiwan began visiting China in large numbers, and economic links grew. Soon most Chinese residents of Taiwan, both Taiwanese and Mainland Chinese, began to think differently about ties with China.

Culture

Taiwan's culture, for the most part, is of Chinese origins. It was brought to Taiwan by early Chinese immigrants from Fukien and Kwangtung Provinces and, after World War II, from various parts of China. It contains elements of both regional cultures as well as the national culture in China.[37] The Chinese from Fukien and the Hakka Chinese brought cultures with them that were different from each other in many ways, though both reflect their southern coastal and rural origins. As stated earlier, Aboriginal culture may have been transplanted to Taiwan from somewhere else or it may have largely evolved in Taiwan. Whatever their origins, Aboriginal customs influenced Chinese culture in Taiwan, although the predominant influence was the other way around. Nonetheless, the customs and culture of many Aboriginal groups, especially those of the mountain Aborigines, remain intact. Missionaries and scholars from China and the West, as well as merchants from throughout East Asia and later from Europe and the United States also influenced Taiwan's culture. Additionally, Japanese culture had a strong influence on the mix during Japan's rule of Taiwan, while the United States has had a major cultural impact for the past sixty-plus years.

Western cultural influence came to Taiwan through early missionary activities and in a host of other ways during the period of Dutch colonial rule, however brief, in the seventeenth century. Japan had a major effect through the imposition of its language and educational system on Taiwan during the Japanese colonial period. But many other facets of Japanese culture are to be found in Taiwan, among them music, art, literature, culinary skills, religion, and martial arts. During the Japanese period, Western influence continued to find its way to Taiwan, but it was largely filtered through Japan. Then, as a result of war between China and Japan, which started in 1937, Tokyo restricted Taiwan's contacts with China; thus, Chinese culture, albeit well rooted in Taiwan, was cut off from its source.

With the transfer of political control over Taiwan to the Republic of China in 1945 came a marked increase in Chinese influence and what may be called a Chinese cultural revival. The Nationalist government, especially after moving to Taiwan in 1949, sought in a variety of ways to propagate traditional Chinese culture. Because the political leadership considered acculturation a necessary process to be applied to the population in Taiwan after half a century of Japanese control, the government sponsored cultural activities of various kinds. In fact, specific efforts were made to eradicate Japanese cultural influence. Anti-Soviet and anti-Communist themes were also in evidence and reflected the government's views and Taiwan's international status. Yellow journalism, pessimism, and defeatism were seen as bad for the society and were thus discouraged or banned. Chiang Kai-shek's personal cultural interests, which included Chinese calligraphy, classical painting, opera, and folk arts, had a strong influence.

The government promoted cultural change in large part through the Ministry of Education. In the early 1950s, the ministry launched a project to preserve the Chinese classics, and it subsequently sponsored cultural organizations and various awards. The Nationalist Party supported many cultural activities while the central government financed national museums, the National Central Library, concert halls, and Chinese opera theaters. The Taiwan Provincial Government budgeted funds for libraries, fine arts museums, and music halls in all counties and large cities. The Ministry of National Defense took an active role in encouraging cultural pursuits in the military. Besides efforts to expand social and political control, considerable government funding of cultural pursuits is explained by the fact the Constitution mandates that 15 percent of the national government's budget be used for education and culture.

Although culture was to a considerable extent manipulated by the government for political reasons in the years after 1949, this influence did not discourage the freedom of cultural expression unless it was considered subversive or in poor taste. Nor did the government's claim that it was the preserver of Chinese culture mean that Western ideas were unwelcome (except for pornographic materials and pro-Communist writings). In fact, Western—especially US—influence in Taiwan in the 1950s and 1960s (unlike in China) was very evident: schools of thought such as symbolism, surrealism (especially among Taiwan's poets), existentialism, Freudianism, modernism, and sometimes even nihilism appeared in public debate and in local publications. Popular Western movements in art and literature also influenced Taiwan's local culture as many Western words and concepts became part of the language spoken in Taiwan—a marked contrast to the situation in the People's Republic of China.

In the 1970s, cultural developments in Taiwan reflected pragmatism (generally attributed to rapid economic growth), nationalism, nativism, and realism. Western influence increased markedly in the 1970s and thereafter as Taiwan's economic development became more dependent on exports and as more people gained access to Western newspapers, magazines, movies, and music. The culture also mirrored the changing nature of politics in Taiwan, especially as it became more acceptable to expound political ideas and as political and literary writing often merged. Modern scientific thought and new trends in the West had a growing influence on Taiwan's culture.

The 1980s saw the development of informational literature, science fiction, feminism, and the extensions of various trends from the 1970s.[38] Taiwan's growing cosmopolitanism and cultural self-confidence also became more evident. Culture, meanwhile, became less subject to government regulation and more pluralistic in nature. Official support and the encouragement of cultural pursuits continued, however, because the public believed tax money should be spent on advancing culture and the government still sought to maintain some oversight.

Chinese calligraphy, opera, and traditional music and dance currently appeal to the more educated and conservative segments of the population. Chinese opera is popular mostly among older people. Writing Chinese characters as a form of art was traditionally an avocation of the educated class but became more common because Chiang Kai-shek encouraged it and for some time it was included in the civil service exam. Additionally, after 1967, musical education became part of the required curriculum in primary and secondary schools in Taiwan.

Sculpture, which never became popular in China because it was associated with manual labor, gained favor in Taiwan. It reflected traditional Taoism and contemporary political and social themes. Although architecture during the Japanese era followed styles that were either Japanese or culturally neutral, most museums and other cultural buildings are now constructed in traditional Chinese or Western forms.

Many cultural expressions now reflect a "people's culture," although these are also merging with elite norms. Folk art reveals religious themes, whereas cartoons and posters are often political or avant-garde. Photography mirrors Western influence, but puppet shows, especially the traveling type, draw on local rural culture. The decision in 1987 to allow residents of Taiwan to visit China resulted in a surge of Chinese cultural influence of various kinds from the Mainland.

In Taiwan, movies attract large audiences.[39] Taiwan produces classical Chinese movies as well as modern dramas, romance stories, and adventure movies. Taiwan's filmmakers, although in critical disfavor for many years, have recently won various awards for their movies. Films made in Hong Kong and the West, and particularly American films, are popular in Taiwan. Japanese films, banned for some years, are now shown and attract fairly large audiences. Recently, films made in China have become popular. Actors, regarded as low class in the past, now enjoy a decent social reputation. Many have become famous, some have even become social models, and a few have entered politics.

Because literature was discouraged during the Japanese era, Taiwan's writers are generally young and include a higher proportion of women than elsewhere, including China. Common earlier themes among writers were poverty, communism, the differences between the Mainland Chinese and the Taiwanese, and local culture. Now, however, romance and social problems are more common topics, as is Taiwan's sense of identity.[40] Freer expression in recent years, the growth of democracy, and increased foreign travel have broadened the interests and concerns of writers. Western books, like foreign music and movies, are very popular in Taiwan.

Transportation and Communications

Until the late 1800s, Taiwan did not have a transportation or communications network that linked various parts of the island. Roads were local and few were very good. Contacts between people living in different areas were hence limited to places accessible by foot, oxcart, or boat. At the end of the nineteenth century, new roads, railroads, and ports were built, though much more was done under the Japanese. In recent years, new construction in transportation and communications facilities has paralleled Taiwan's rapid economic growth.

For some time, railroads were one of Taiwan's most important means of carrying goods and transporting people. The Japanese built a network of narrow-gauge tracks that served the island well. More and better lines were built during the 1950s. During the 1960s and 1970s, usage increased at a rate of 5–10 percent annually. In the mid-1970s, railroads accounted for nearly half of the freight moved and passengers carried over more than a short distance.[41] After that, usage fell because of competition from other means of transport, especially trucks and buses using the new expressways. At its lowest point, rail travel in the last fifty years accounted for just 10 percent of the country's passengers and cargo.

In recent years, because of highway congestion and the greater comfort and safety that trains provide to passengers, together with faster service brought by better trains and double tracks, there has been an increase in rail travel. In 2006, the rails carried 463,000 passengers. In 2007, a high-speed train that runs at a speed of 186 miles per hour (300 km/h), making the trip from Taipei to Kaohsiung in around ninety minutes (two hours if stopping at all stations), was completed at a cost of $15 billion. It was the first such infrastructure project undertaken by the private sector in Taiwan to improve rail service and make the trains more competitive.[42] In 2010, Taiwan's high-speed trains made sixty-four trips daily and served thirty-seven million passengers, an increase of 14.2 percent from the previous year. The on-time rate (less than five minute delay) was 99.2 percent.[43]

The population of Taiwan has long depended upon roads as its main form of land transportation. Today, when it comes to road quality, Taiwan stands out. Most of Taiwan's roads are paved and there is an extensive system of express highways. In total Taiwan has twenty-forty thousand miles of roads. In 1978, a national expressway, the Sun Yat-sen Freeway (also called the North-South Freeway), was completed. Running almost the length of the island, this highway made it possible to travel between Taiwan's two largest cities, Taipei and Kaohsiung, in less than four hours. After it opened, traffic increased around 11 percent annually for more than a decade. A parallel expressway, the Formosa Freeway, was completed in 2004. Both freeways are on Taiwan's western side, the latter a bit further inland. A new freeway is under construction on the island's east coast. Taiwan's freeways are toll roads, the tolls being adjusted upward at times in order to reduce the heavy traffic flows.[44]

Automobiles were not seen much in Taiwan in the past. In recent times, most automobiles were used as taxis or were company cars. This changed dramatically in the 1970s and 1980s, and by 1999 there were more than 16.3 million motor vehicles in Taiwan (around 10 million of which were motorcycles), up from 5 million in 1980. Now there are 6.9 million passenger cars registered, plus 14.8 million motorcycles.[45] A large portion of this growth came from the individual use of vehicles. This rapid increase in private ownership of vehicles mirrored both Taiwan's prosperity and the reduction of tariffs on imported vehicles. Now more than 50 percent of families in Taiwan own cars. The number of vehicles per capita in Taiwan compares to that of most developed nations; as is the case in other developed nations, the downside of this is serious traffic jams in Taiwan's largest cities.

Still many citizens in Taiwan's cities rely on buses for transportation. Currently Taiwan has nearly 7,000 city buses whose ridership is nearly 811 million annually. In addition there are highway buses: 7,400 in 2010 that had a ridership of 234 million. Plus there are 13,000 tour buses. Many city streets in Taiwan have dedicated bus lanes. In addition to buses Taiwan has 87,400 taxis. Very recently some individuals have given up their cars and use public transport during the week and rent on the weekends or for outings. There are twelve hundred rental car companies in Taiwan.[46]

Taiwan has seven seaports that accommodate oceangoing vessels. Most were modernized and improved during the 1970s. For a while, Kaohsiung, the largest, had the distinction of being the world's third-largest container port (after Hong Kong and Singapore). In 2008, an agreement was reached with China on opening direct shipping. In addition to freight shipments increasing as a result, by 2010 eighty-seven thousand tourists from China visited Taiwan by ship.[47]

Taiwan's merchant marine consists of 278 vessels with a combined tonnage of 2.78 million gross tons. It is one of the world's largest and is still growing in size and importance. Evergreen Marine Corporation, a private company founded in Taiwan, is one of largest container forwarders in the world.[48] Taiwan's shipping industry is large not only because Taiwan is a major trading nation but also because the government fears China might try to blockade or quarantine the island and has therefore encouraged shipping to grow for security reasons.

Taiwan has three international airports. The largest of these is Taoyuan International Airport (called Chiang Kai-shek International Airport before 2006), located outside of Taipei. The other two are Kaohsiung International Airport located near Kaohsiung and Taipei International Airport (also called Songshan Airport) in Taipei. They handle nearly thirty million passengers annually. Taiwan also has fourteen domestic airports. Several foreign international carriers use the international air terminals, as well as Taiwan's flag carrier, China Airlines (CAL), the privately owned EVA Airways, and some other local airlines. Both international and domestic air travel have been growing rapidly.[49]

Traffic in Taiwan's largest cities became congested in the 1980s because of the proliferation of cars and other vehicles. Thus there grew a demand for subways. In the case of Taipei, construction was begun on a subway system in 1988 that was completed in 1996. Its construction was delayed for some time because of the high cost of building such a system in a city that lies in a basin and is gradually sinking. At a cost of $18 billion, it was the most expensive system in the world. It has since its opening been expanded to a total of 62 miles of track and ninety-four stations. It serves 1.5 million passengers on weekdays.[50] A link to Taoyuan International Airport is scheduled to open in 2014. Kaohsiung had a similar, though less serious, traffic problem, and in early 2001 work began on a subway system there. It was plagued by construction problems, accidents, and scandals involving political kickbacks, not to mention riots by foreign workers helping build the project; as a result, its opening date was delayed. Currently it is 26 miles long and has thirty-seven stations. In 2009 Taichung City launched the building of a system that will go into service in 2015.[51]

Postal services, the traditional form of communications, have continued to grow in size and efficiency. There are six or more pickups a day in most of Taiwan's large cities, and this together with the efficiency of Chunghwa Post, the state-owned company that operates postal services, makes it possible to get a letter to another party in the same city within a few hours and to most cities throughout the island the next day. In 2010, Chunghwa Post handled 2.7 billion letters, 6.2

million pieces of express mail, and 26.4 million parcels. That year direct postal services to and from the Mainland were established, after which the company handled cross-Strait services including 8.3 million letters, 95 thousand parcels and 395,500 pieces of express mail.[52]

Telephones came into popular use in the 1960s. During the 1970s, the number of telephones increased eightfold to more than 2.5 million by the close of the decade. Pagers soon became popular and then cellular telephones. In 2007 the number of mobile telephones exceeded landline phones. Chunghwa Telecom landline services and several private companies provide mobile phone services and have saturated the market. Smart phones have recently taken most of the market.[53]

Internet usage has grown very fast in Taiwan in recent years. Residents use the Internet for research, sending and receiving e-mail messages, entertainment, and other purposes. Visitors to Taiwan find online computers easily accessible. Household penetration reached 82.8 percent in 2010. Various business rating services give Taiwan high marks for Internet and related services.[54]

The Media

Knowledge of the media and the profound changes it has undergone is vital to understanding Taiwan's past, its present, and its future. Economic modernization and its side effects, such as affluence, increasing literacy, urbanization, a growing middle class, and higher levels of education, have been the driving forces behind the transition to a new and forceful media in Taiwan. So has Taiwan's political development, including the end of martial law, the growth of political parties, and more.

In the distant past, the common mode of mass communications was to paste written bulletins on walls in public places. During the Japanese period, radio and newspapers became common. Five radio stations operated in Taiwan and companies and individuals began to purchase newspapers. There were nearly a hundred thousand radio receivers in use by the mid-1940s. Both newspapers and radios proliferated in the 1950s and after. In the 1960s television came to Taiwan. Today, Taiwan is modern and up-to-date in communications and has numerous and different kinds of newspapers, magazines, radio stations, television stations, cable TV, and movies.[55]

The Central News Agency (CNA), Taiwan's largest news agency, disseminates news worldwide. In 1990, it became fully computerized and in 1997 added a website that became very popular. In 2010, CNA expanded into video news. CNA has correspondents in all of Taiwan's cities and counties and more than thirty foreign countries. It offers coverage in Chinese, English, and Spanish. Though there are nearly two thousand other news agencies in Taiwan, they are much smaller and, except for some that disseminate economic news, none are very important. The China Economic News Service operated by the *United Daily News* is an exception.[56]

In the past, Taiwan's two largest Chinese newspapers were the *China Times* and the *United Daily News*. Both claimed to be the biggest paper in Taiwan; it is uncertain which actually was. The *China Times* was reputed to be a bit more liberal and the *United Daily News* a bit more conservative. Both publish other papers, including economic and local editions. The *United Daily News* publishes the *United Evening News*; the *World Journal*, which is the most popular Chinese newspaper in North America; and the *Economic Daily News*. *China Times* publishes the *Commercial Times, China Times Weekly*, and *Want Daily*. Today these two papers remain competitive.

In recent years the *Liberty Times* has become Taiwan's largest newspaper, with a ranking of number thirty-five in the world by circulation. (*United Daily News* and *China Times* rank at forty-seven and forty-eight respectively.) The *Liberty Times* favors the DPP. *Apple Daily*, a popular newspaper that tends toward simplifying or sensationalizing its coverage, ranks in the top one hundred in the world and is viewed as one of Taiwan's top papers. The *Min Sheng Pao* also ranks in the top one hundred. *Apple Daily*, which started in Hong Kong, says its ranking would be much higher if newsstand sales, rather than just subscriptions, are counted.[57] Three English dailies have operated in Taiwan—the *China Post, Taipei Times*, and *Taiwan News*—though the *Taiwan News* went to an online version only in 2010. The *Asian Wall Street Journal* and the *International Herald Tribune* are printed and sold in Taiwan and are available in most hotels. The trend in Taiwan has been toward larger papers, and as a result many small and local papers have suffered from declining circulation. Some commercial papers and religious papers have been the exception.

Magazine publishing in Taiwan has an even more interesting history than newspapers and other forms of media. In 1960, Lei Chen, who published the *Free China Fortnightly* for a short time, formed the China Democratic Party (which was an illegal act at the time) and was arrested and jailed. His publication died with him. The founding of the *Taiwan Political Review* in 1975 by Kang Ning-hsiang, some say, marked the beginning of a real political opposition in Taiwan even though the magazine was closed soon after it started publishing. The *Eighties*, another magazine published by Kang and his associates, was more moderate and lasted longer. In 1979, opposition politicians associated with the *Formosa* magazine formed the "Formosa Group" and organized a protest demonstration in Kaohsiung late that year. The gathering turned violent and led to the arrest and imprisonment of several oppositionists who later became DPP leaders, including former Vice President Annette Lu and two former heads of the Democratic Progressive Party. In 1989, the editor of the *Freedom Era Weekly* published a proposed new Constitution; when an arrest warrant was issued, he set fire to the building and died in the blaze. In 2002, police seized the current issue of *Next* magazine when it published a story about government corruption.[58]

Currently Taiwan has a large number of magazines, some of them published by newspapers, some by book companies, and some by individuals. Many of them fail, but more start than close. There are a number of both general interest and specialized magazines. Many magazines focus on social and political conditions, business, and fashion. The *China Times Weekly* and *Next* are well known for news and inside stories, respectively. *CommonWealth* is a popular financial magazine. Various other magazines deal with health issues, computers, and the English language. Because of a better-educated population in the north, magazine sales are much larger there: 60–65 percent of the total. In 2011 there were 8,122 magazines on sale.[59]

Book publishing is also a big industry in Taiwan and continues to grow. Over forty thousand titles are published yearly—a large number considering Taiwan's population. Although foreign books used to be pirated in Taiwan, this is now a thing of the past. Chinese books are sold both locally and in other Chinese-speaking areas in East Asia. A number of publishers have agreements with foreign publishers and copublish English-language books. China, South Korea, Singapore, and Japan have been major purchasers of publication rights of books published in Taiwan. Books are marketed through bookstores and newsstands, while online bookstores have seen a growing business in recent years. In addition to these means of marketing and distribution, Taipei also holds frequent international book exhibits. E-publishing has also become common with around a third of publishers. In 2010 BenQ, a leading Taiwan computer manufacturer, launched its nReader, the first multilingual e-reader sold. The government considers digital publishing very promising and has provided funds and other help to promote it.[60]

Radio stations have proliferated in the last decades. Before 1993, there were only 33 stations; in 2011, there were 171 and more under construction. In the past, radio was devoted to dramatic, cultural, educational, and children's programs. Now radio broadcasts concentrate more on news, traffic, market reports and financial analysis, and talk programs, though music stations are the most popular. Broadcasts are in Mandarin Chinese, Taiwanese, Hakka, and English. Taiwan has private and government-owned services and stations; the most well-known government-owned service is the Broadcasting Corporation of China (BCC). Taiwan also has an English language station, an educational station, and a police radio station. Recently stations have also broadcast in Aboriginal languages as well as in Thai, Indonesian, and Vietnamese. Radio Taiwan International, funded by the government, broadcasts in thirteen languages.[61]

Television began broadcasting in 1962 with the National Educational Television station. Taiwan Television Enterprise followed that same year, and China Television Company in 1969. Chinese Television System began operation in 1971. For some time, opposition politicians complained that the Nationalist Party controlled the television media. To counter this they even established broadcasting systems on ships anchored offshore. Formosa Television began broadcasting in 1997 and represented opposition politicians. Public Television Service followed the next year. Meanwhile, a large number of cable operators started doing business, many of them illegally, including individuals who set up cable operations to serve a large apartment building or a square city block. The practice was brought under control to some extent when the Cable Television Law was passed in 1993. Now sixty-two cable companies compete for customers and around 65 percent of households subscribe. The rate is typically less than $20 per month for ninety channels. As of 2010, 70 percent of cable systems offered digital programming.[62]

Movies are very popular in Taiwan. In the 1950s most came from Hong Kong and Shanghai. Subsequently most movies viewed in Taiwan were made in the United States. As mentioned earlier, Japanese films were banned but this changed in the 1980s. Meanwhile Taiwan developed its own movie industry. It boomed in the 1970s and became one of the largest in the world. Many of its films were love stories, and many of them became popular in Southeast Asia. Taiwan's movie industry then encountered difficult times in part caused by strong foreign competition. Hence fewer movies were produced. Seventeen movies were released in 2001 compared to thirty-five the previous year. There was a subsequent revival, and recently forty films on average have been released annually. In addition to fictional movies, Taiwan companies also produced a large number of documentaries. Films made in Taiwan are now viewed in China and Chinese-made films are seen in Taiwan.[63]

Tourism

After the Chinese government acquired Taiwan from Japan at the end of World War II, it did not welcome foreign tourists to visit the island because of the war on the Mainland with Mao's Communist regime. After 1949, tourism was still discouraged. Tourists, it was thought, would create a security problem. There was little realization that considerable money could be made from tourists and that this revenue would help resolve Taiwan's foreign exchange shortage.

In 1956, Chiang Kai-shek established a new policy regarding tourism. The year before fewer than fifteen thousand tourists visited Taiwan. Subsequently the industry took off, experiencing a growth rate of more than 23 percent annually for the next two decades. In 1976, more than 1 million tourists visited the island. At this time foreign visitors provided Taiwan with considerable foreign currency and were a significant source of employment. In the mid-1980s, however, the rate of growth fell in part as a result of competition from China as a place foreigners wanted to visit and the fact that Taiwan had become expensive. Nonetheless, the number of tourists continued to grow at about 10 percent a year. Almost 2 million visited Taiwan in 1988, and in 2006 Taiwan hosted an estimated 3.75 million tourists.[64]

By far the largest number of visitors to Taiwan was from Japan—more than one-third. Hong Kong was second; the United States was third. Singapore, Indonesia, and the Philippines followed in that order. Australia and several European countries trailed the Philippines. This list did not change much in ensuing years except that the number of visitors from Hong Kong increased significantly. One important change, though, was that more of Taiwan's citizens visited other countries, and in the 1980s outward tourism exceeded the number of visitors from abroad to Taiwan.

Since 2008, there has been a significant increase in tourists visiting Taiwan. This is the product of the government aggressively helping the tourist industry. There has also been a change in origin of the tourists visiting Taiwan in recent years. That is the marked increase in the number of visitors from East Asia, notably China. In 2010, of the 5.6 million tourists Taiwan received, 4 million came from East Asian countries. China accounted for the largest number. Chinese tourists spent an average of eight days and between $230 and $300 per person per day.[65]

In 2008, when Ma Ying-jeou ran for president he proposed allocating a large sum of government funds to increase tourism in Taiwan and said he expected his proposed direct flights to China to attract 3,000 Chinese tourists per day by year's end.[66] In 2010, 1.6 million Chinese tourists visited Taiwan adding $3 billion or 0.72 percent to Taiwan's gross domestic product.[67] In 2011, the number of tourists from China visiting Taiwan increased further with a change in rules allowing them to visit as individuals or families rather than in groups. Tourism will no doubt expand various other ties and mutual understanding between Taiwan and China.

Tourists visiting Taiwan typically go to the National Palace Museum near Taipei to see the world's largest collection of Chinese artifacts, antiques, jade, paintings, and other historical objects. When the Nationalists left China in 1949, they took with them many of the treasures from the best museums in China. At the time, the government in China accused Chiang Kai-shek of "stealing" China's precious possessions. This was subsequently seen as a good thing, however, as many would have been destroyed during Mao's Great Proletarian Cultural Revolution in the late 1960s and early 1970s had the treasures remained in China. Returning the treasures was mentioned during the Chen Shui-bian era if the KMT were to dispose of its assets accumulated at the time, but there was no public support for this. The Chiang Kai-shek Memorial Hall (renamed the National Taiwan Democracy Memorial Hall during the Chen presidency but changed back to its original name later) is also popular. Located in downtown Taipei, it is devoted more to Chinese history and contains the National Theater and the National Concert Hall. Another attraction is Taipei 101—until recently the tallest building in the world.

Taipei's night markets are among the places most frequently visited by tourists; department stores and small shops are favorite places for travelers to purchase local goods. Taipei is often said to have the best restaurants and most varied cuisine anyplace in the world because famous chefs from all over China fled to Taiwan in 1949. Eating places in Taipei, in fact, serve food representing cuisine from nearly all areas of China. There are also many very good Japanese, Korean, and Western restaurants in Taipei.

On the more exotic side is Lungshan Temple in Taipei, one of Taiwan's oldest. Nearby is "snake alley," where one can see local showmen play with poisonous snakes and offer the daring observer the snake's blood to drink (which is said to be good for the health). Visitors can also see habu-mongoose fights (the habu is a poisonous snake similar to the rattlesnake); the mongoose usually wins. In earlier days there were restaurants in the area that served dog, snake, turtle, and other unusual things; some of these eateries can still be found.

North of Taipei is Yangmingshan Park, where there are hot springs, volcanic craters, and waterfalls, as well as a good view of Taipei. South of Taipei, in Wulai, visitors can see waterfalls, mountains, and Aboriginal entertainment provided by the Atayal tribe. In Yehliu, north of Taipei, one can view unusual rock formations made by the wind and the ocean, many of which look like gigantic mushrooms.

In central Taiwan is the famous Sun Moon Lake, one of the most serene places anywhere, according to its many visitors. There is also Ali Shan (Mount Ali), Yu Shan (Jade Mountain), and a giant Buddha statue near Changhua. In the south is Tainan, the island's oldest city, which has forts from the Dutch period and other interesting sights. Also in the south is Kaohsiung, Taiwan's second largest city, and nearby are the island's largest Buddha, Moon World (where the landscape resembles the moon), and some beautiful beaches further south. In eastern Taiwan are Taroko Gorge, a marble-walled cliff, and other spectacular scenery.

Visiting Taiwan at the time of national holidays is more interesting than at other times. The most important one is the Chinese New Year, or Lunar New Year. It comes early in the year, but not on the same date each year, as it is determined by the lunar calendar. The Dragon Boat Festival is held in the summer, followed by Mid-Autumn Festival (or Moon Festival, again according to the lunar calendar), and Double Ten Day (or National Day) on October 10.

Notes

1. For details on Taiwan's geography and the territorial claims made by the Republic of China, see *The Republic of China 1994 Yearbook* (Taipei: Government Information Office, 1994), chapter 1.

2. See "List of Countries by Population," *Wikipedia*, accessed May 20, 2012, http://en.wikipedia.org/wiki/List_of_countries_by_population. The original source is the UN Department of Social and Economic Affairs, Population Division.

3. For details, see Michael Hindley and James Bridge, "Disputed Islands," *Free China Review* (August 1994): 42–47.

4. Jane Richards, "Taiwan Stakes Its Claim on Disputed Isle," *Washington Post*, February 3, 2008, A18; "Lawmakers Visit Dongsha Islands to Highlight Taiwan's Sovereignty Claims," *China Post*, May 11, 2012 (online at chinapost.com.tw).

5. For further details on this controversy, see John F. Copper, "The Fishing Islands Controversy," *Asia Quarterly* (1972/1973): 217–227.

6. "Construction of Kinmen Bridge Begins," *Free Taiwan News Channel*, January 9, 2011 (online at focustaiwan.tw).

7. See Chiai-min Hsieh, *Taiwan—Ilha Formosa: A Geography in Perspective* (Washington, DC: Butterworths, 1964), 2–4.

8. See ibid., 20, regarding the frequency of earthquakes in Taiwan.

9. *The Republic of China Yearbook—Taiwan 2002* (Taipei: Government Information Office, 2002), 25. Also see Hsieh, *Taiwan—Ilha Formosa*, chapter 6, for further details.

10. See W. G. Goddard, *Formosa: A Study in Chinese History* (East Lansing: Michigan State University Press, 1966), x–xi.

11. For a list of Taiwan's rivers and their lengths and watersheds, see *Taiwan Yearbook 2007* (Taipei: Government Information Office, 2007), 14.

12. Daniel P. Reid, *Taiwan* (Hong Kong: APA, 1984), 24.

13. See chapter 4 of Goddard, *Formosa*, for details.

14. See "Taiwan," *Wikipedia* (online at wikipedia.com, viewed March 2008).

15. Taiwan ranks number five in the world in the percentage of its surface covered by forest. See *Asiaweek*, December 7, 1994, 17.

16. Yuen Ching, "Taiwan's Population Density Ranks No. 2 Around the World," *Free China Journal*, September 8, 1995, 4; *Republic of China Yearbook—Taiwan 2002*, 22.

17. "Taiwan's Birth Rate Falls to the World's Lowest," *Voice of America*, August 16, 2011 (online at voanews.com).

18. *The Republic of China 2011 Yearbook* (Taipei: Government Information Office, 2011), 192.

19. Ibid.

20. Ibid., 36–37

21. "Taiwan: Health Agency to Probe High Male Birth Rate in Some Areas," *Central News Agency*, May 15, 2011 (online at cnanews.com).

22. Hungfu Hsieh, "Foreign Spouses Seen Taking up 18% of Marriages in '07," *Taiwan News*, January 21, 2008, accessed January 25, 2008 (online at taiwannews.com).

23. *Republic of China Yearbook—Taiwan 2002*, 347.

24. See *Taiwan Yearbook 2007*, 28, for data on the number of foreign workers.

25. Willy Wo-Lap Lam, "China Wages 'Big Bucks Diplomacy,'" *CNN*, June 19, 2002.

26. "Urbanization at Full Speed," *Free China Journal*, February 17, 1995, 4.

27. *Wikipedia*, citing *CIA World Factbook*, n.d., accessed March 2012.

28. Tomas Clancy, *Countries of the World: The Republic of China* (n.p.: Create Space, 2012), 368.

29. Wen-hui Tsai, *In Making China Modernized: Comparative Modernization Between Mainland China and Taiwan* (Baltimore: University of Maryland School of Law, 1993), 129.

30. For details on Taiwan's ethnic groups and the settlement of Taiwan, see Ronald G. Knapp, ed., *China's Island Frontier: Studies in the Historical Geography of Taiwan* (Honolulu: University of Hawaii Press, 1980), part 1.

31. John Nobel Welford, "Pacific Islands' Ancestry Emerges in Genetic Study," *New York Times*, January 12, 2008 (online at lexisnexis.com).

32. *Republic of China Yearbook—Taiwan 2002*, 27.

33. See Eugenia Yen, "Still Guests After All These (Fifteen Hundred) Years," *Free China Review* (October 1993): 12.

34. James W. Davidson, *The Island of Formosa: Past and Present* (New York: Oxford University Press, 1988), 561.

35. This is demonstrated by various studies and opinion polls. Further discussion on this issue will follow.

36. Wen-lang Li, "Social Change in Taiwan and the Solution to Ethnic Problems," *United Monthly* (May 19, 1987): 2, cited in Hung-mao Tien, *The Great Transition: Political and Social Change in the Republic of China* (Stanford, CA: Hoover Institution Press, 1989), 36.

37. For further details on culture, see James C. Hsiung, ed., *Contemporary Republic of China: The Taiwan Experience, 1950–1980* (New York: Praeger, 1981), part 1. Also see *The Story of Taiwan* (Taipei: Government Information Office, 2000).

38. See *The Republic of China, 1988: A Reference Book* (Taipei: Hilt, 1988), chapter 39.

39. In 1983, Taiwan ranked eleventh in the world in per capita movie attendance. Its rank dropped in subsequent years, however, as videotapes and other forms of entertainment became popular. See *Asiaweek*, December 14, 1994, 18.

40. For details about this and some of the changes in culture mentioned previously, see Thomas B. Gold, *State and Society in the Taiwan Miracle* (Armonk, NY: M. E. Sharpe, 1986), 130–134.

41. For information on the development and status of Taiwan's railroads, see Loren Aandahl, *The Taiwan Railway: 1966–70* (Taipei, 2011), and Loren Aandahl, *The Taiwan Railway: 1971–2011* (Taipei: 2012). Both were published by the author.

42. "Taiwan High Speed Rail," *Wikipedia* (accessed January 25, 2008, online at wikipedia.org).

43. *Republic of China 2011 Yearbook*, 167.

44. Ibid., 164.

45. Ibid.

46. Ibid.

47. Ibid., 169.

48. Ibid., 168.

49. Ibid., 170–171.

50. Ibid., 167.

51. Ibid., 168.

52. Ibid., 171.

53. "Smartphones Take 62% of Taiwan's Mobile Phone Market," *Want China Times*, March 9, 2012 (online at wantchinatimes.com).

54. Ibid, 173.

55. Tien, *Great Transition*, 196–197.

56. *Republic of China 2011 Yearbook*, 208.

57. "World's 100 Largest Newspapers," *World Association of Newspapers* (accessed June 15, 2012, online at wan-press.org).

58. *Taiwan Country Report on Human Rights*, U.S., Department of State Bureau of Democracy, Human Rights and Labor, March 8, 2006 (online at lexis-nexus.com).

59. *Republic of China 2011 Yearbook*, 211.

60. Ibid., 214–215.

61. Ibid., 194–195.

62. Ibid., 216–218.

63. Ibid., 248–250.

64. *The Republic of China 1989 Yearbook* (Taipei: Government Information Office, 1989), 459.

65. *Republic of China 2011 Yearbook*, 261.

66. "Presidential Election: 2008," *Taipei Times*, March 21, 2008, 4.

67. Andrew Jacobs, "As Chinese Visit Taiwan, the Cultural Influence is Subdued," *New York Times*, August 10, 1011 (online at nyt.com).

2

HISTORY

TAIWAN'S PAST IS OFTEN CITED as evidence for both those who advocate that it is part of China, or should be, and those who do not. As noted in Chapter 1, studies of its prehistory suggest links with Southeast Asia, China, Japan, and possibly some other parts of Asia. Early historical records indicate connections with China, but those ties were tenuous. Yet Taiwan's early history does not offer any proof it should be seen as connected to or belongs to any other country. For a brief period in the seventeenth century, Taiwan was a Western colony. It subsequently enjoyed a short span of self-rule before it was governed by China for more than two hundred years and then by Japan for fifty years. At the end of World War II, Taiwan was returned to Nationalist China, but just four years later that government was deposed by the Communists and fled to Taiwan, at which time Taiwan became the home of the Republic of China and, to many people, synonymous with it. For more than twenty years, until 1971 when Beijing obtained the China seat in the United Nations, Taipei represented China in international affairs. Since then, Taiwan has been diplomatically—though not in most other ways—isolated as a result of Beijing's efforts to undermine its claim to sovereignty. Meanwhile, for nearly five decades during the Cold War, Beijing and Taipei were on opposite sides and there were few interactions between them. From the 1960s on, Taiwan's economic success, then its rapid democratization and the growth of a local identity, made Taiwan look quite different from China. Most of its residents perceived that separation was both desirable and inevitable. But, during the past three decades, economic ties with China proliferated, and, with China becoming a formidable economic and military power, this view changed. One might say Taiwan is separate from China politically as a result of democratization, yet booming commercial ties and, to a lesser degree, people-to-people ties in recent years have made the two closer. With the decline of the United States, Europe, and Japan, Taiwan's future likely involves closer ties with China.

Prehistory and Early History

Evidence of human life in Taiwan dates back to the Paleolithic Age, twenty to thirty thousand and possibly fifty thousand years ago.[1] Whether Taiwan's earliest inhabitants were the ancestors of the present Aboriginal population is uncertain. In any event, the Aborigines are the first people known to reside on the island. Anthropologists long believed they hailed from Southeast Asia, perhaps via the Philippines, and are kin to the present-day Malay people who inhabit Brunei, Indonesia, and Malaysia. There are remarkable cultural similarities, and as many as two-thirds of the words in several of the Aboriginal languages are similar to Malay, even though the two peoples have had little or no direct contact in recorded history. There are also similarities in physical characteristics, social organizations, and crafts.[2] However, some scholars say the Aborigines migrated to Taiwan from China, having originally lived in what is now northern Myanmar, and are likely related to the Miao people in South China. They base this argument on the many linguistic and cultural similarities between the two groups and the fact that in the past crossing the Taiwan Strait was much easier than it is today.[3]

An alternative view is that the Aborigines have several origins and that some of their ancestors, perhaps two tribes, migrated from the north, from either Japan or northern China. Some myths seem to link them to one or two minority nationality groups in North China, and there are some cultural similarities with the Ainus, the original inhabitants of Japan. When the Japanese governed Taiwan, they advanced the theory that the Aborigines were of Japanese origin, and some Western anthropologists agreed. Some Mainland Chinese scholars say the Aborigines of Taiwan migrated from southeast China sometime around 1700 BC in search of better land.[4] Still other scholars have suggested connections elsewhere, such as with India.[5] Very recently, researchers, using DNA tests, have connected the Aborigines to the native populations in Australia, to New Zealand's Maoris, and to some inhabitants of the South Pacific islands and advance the theory that Taiwan's Aborigines are Australasians. Related to this view is the belief that the Aborigines migrated from Taiwan to these places not the other way around.[6]

The examination of fossils, pottery, and other artifacts in Taiwan has established some generally accepted information: that the Aboriginal population was fairly evenly distributed throughout the island; that their livelihood came from fishing, hunting, and some shifting agriculture; that land was usually owned in common; and that the political and social systems were tribal. Most Aboriginal groups were patriarchal and patrilineal; some, however, were matriarchal and matrilineal. The Aborigines had contacts several centuries ago with other peoples in East Asia. However, detailed or genuinely historical information about Taiwan's Aborigines does not begin until the seventeenth century when the Dutch rendered some of their languages into a written form.[7]

There is mention of Taiwan in early Chinese records, which is quite natural inasmuch as the island is visible from Fukien Province on a clear day and travel to Taiwan by boat was possible more than two millennia ago. However, Taiwan was not often cited in the early Chinese historical writings that were essentially chronicles of each ruler or dynasty. When mentioned, early court records seem to indicate that Taiwan was not regarded as part of China.[8] This view, of course, was to be expected, because early in its history China occupied only what is today part of North China, and the seat of the Chinese government was, throughout the centuries, usually in the north—a great distance from the part of China now adjacent to Taiwan. Furthermore, throughout most of its history and even in modern times, "China" was defined more by culture than by territory; Chinese governments did not propound the concept of territorial sovereignty or boundaries, as nation-states did in the West.

Before the Han Dynasty (206 BC–AD 222), Taiwan was known in China as the land of Yangchow. During the Han and the Three Kingdoms period that followed, it was called Yinchow. The first official contact mentioned in Chinese historical records was in AD 239: the Chinese emperor at that time sent a ten-thousand-member expeditionary force to Taiwan, apparently to explore the island. This, Chinese leaders in Beijing now say, constitutes grounds for a legal claim to the island based on discovery.[9] But no territorial claim was mentioned in Chinese court records and no follow-up missions were sent. Moreover, at that time Taiwan was referred to as an area "outside the pale of Chinese civilization."[10]

Almost four centuries later, in AD 605, the Sui Dynasty emperor sent a second expedition to Taiwan. The leader of the mission brought back several Aborigines, who were taught Chinese. A more serious follow-up expedition sent six years later, accompanied by an interpreter, brought back considerably more information about Taiwan. Though there were no subsequent visits and this mission ultimately had little impact, it has also been cited as the basis of a Chinese claim to Taiwan.[11]

After this, China sent no official expeditions or missions to Taiwan for some time. Some say this was because China did not seek colonies or the expansion of its territory across the seas. Taiwan's Aborigines, meanwhile, having ceased to be seafaring, initiated few contacts with China. Outsiders visiting the island in ensuing years were mainly pirates from the Ryukyu Islands and areas on the China coast adjacent to Taiwan.[12]

If China's historical visits to Taiwan were infrequent and established neither Chinese civilization on the island nor grounds for a territorial claim, the early migration of Chinese to Taiwan afforded a meaningful Chinese presence there and seems to provide the strongest rationale for a legal claim by China based on history. Yet it is uncertain when the earliest migration of Chinese occurred, whether they were Hakka or Fukienese, or even whether Chinese migrants preceded Japanese settlers on the island.[13] It is thought Chinese farmers and fishermen resided on the Pescadores as early as the seventh century AD; they were certainly to be found on Taiwan before the twelfth century.[14]

By the thirteenth century, there were a significant number of permanent Chinese settlements on Taiwan, and Fukien Chinese were already displacing Hakka from choice land.[15] There were no Japanese or other settlers on the island. If Japanese had migrated to Taiwan earlier—as seems to have been the case—there was no evidence of them at this time. Notwithstanding the number of Chinese communities on the island, the Chinese government apparently did not know much about the emigration to Taiwan or did not consider it important; in any event, no records were kept of it. Also, as was noted in Chapter 1, throughout much of Chinese history, going to Taiwan was a violation of Chinese law. As a result, most who went there did not plan to return to China and did not contemplate claiming the island for China; they simply sought land and a better life in Taiwan.

During the Yuan Dynasty (1263–1368), when the Mongols ruled China, the Peking government's interest in the "eastern and southeastern seas" areas grew, and the Pescadores were brought under its control, though Taiwan remained outside of Chinese (or, more accurately, Mongol) jurisdiction. Moreover, court records indicate that there was still confusion about whether Taiwan was part of the Ryukyu Islands to the north. Further, no mention was made of Taiwan's being Chinese territory or a part of China. The Mongols sought to conquer Japan, an ambition that prompted their expeditions to the Taiwan area. But this had no lasting impact.[16] Meanwhile, Chinese and Japanese pirates and Chinese farmers wrested control of some parts of the western coastal plain areas of Taiwan from the Aborigines. Chinese occupied some of the southwestern parts of the island, and Japanese settlers, who had meanwhile reappeared on the island, held some northern coastal areas.[17]

In 1430, during the Ming Dynasty, the explorer Cheng Ho landed on Taiwan's west coast and made contact with the Aborigines. His visit, however, was inadvertent: he had been shipwrecked there while returning to China from Southeast Asia. He obtained supplies from the Aborigines as well as herbal medicines that were said to have "miracle powers." When he returned to China, Cheng provided the emperor with a written account of his experiences. Thus Cheng Ho's visit is cited as evidence of China's claim to Taiwan. But there were no subsequent visits. In ensuing years, Chinese court chronicles described Taiwan as a "base for pirates."[18] It is also odd that Chinese historical records do not indicate that Cheng Ho, other explorers, or other visitors to Taiwan had contact with Chinese residing there.

Having said all this, however, one must bear in mind that no other country has made a claim on Taiwan based on historical ties, and if one were to do so its claim could not seriously compete with China's. Thus, if history is to serve as the basis for a territorial claim, China has the best case to make. Finally, it is important to note that there was no central political authority on the island historically to justify an argument that Taiwan was self-governing or had the attributes of a nation-state or even something that might have evolved easily into one.

Western and Chinese Rule

The captain of a Portuguese vessel sailing through the Taiwan Strait en route to Japan in 1517 sighted Taiwan and wrote in the ship's log the words "Ilha Formosa," or beautiful island.[19] This was the first Western encounter with Taiwan. But the Portuguese ship did not stop. Just over a century later, in 1622, Dutch forces landed on the Pescadores Islands and established a military presence there. They subsequently used the Pescadores as a base for monitoring ship traffic in the Taiwan Strait and harassing Portuguese trading vessels sailing to and from ports to the north and south. The next year, a local Chinese official signed a treaty with Dutch representatives granting Holland a post on Taiwan and other privileges in exchange for their withdrawal from the Pescadores. Chinese officials at this time suggested that China had jurisdiction over Taiwan but presented no evidence to support this claim.[20]

In 1626, Spanish forces seized Keelung and subsequently expanded their control to Tamsui on the northwest coast. Spanish colonial efforts were facilitated by an isolationist policy adopted by the Tokugawa Shogunate that in 1628 led to the departure of Japanese settlers on Taiwan. Spanish settlers arrived, but Dutch forces drove them out in 1642. Shortly thereafter, the Dutch quelled Chinese opposition to their presence with the help of the Aborigines and established nominal jurisdiction over the entire island.

Taiwan economically and politically became a Dutch colony. It was governed by the Dutch East India Company, which claimed sovereignty over the island for Holland. The company rented land and farm implements to Chinese settlers and introduced oxen to till the fields, enabling the peasants to grow sugarcane and some other cash crops. Dutch East India Company rule led to an expansion of commerce on the island and trade with merchants from China, Japan, and elsewhere in the region. The Company built castles, dug wells, conducted land surveys, created a writing system for the Aboriginal languages, and converted some of the population to Christianity. Though the Dutch East India Company exploited the island for profits, Taiwan experienced significant progress under Dutch rule.[21]

At the beginning of the Dutch period, the Chinese population was small; the Aboriginal population was several times larger. Chinese immigration increased under Dutch rule, however, and more Chinese became permanent inhabitants rather than seasonal workers. Still, most Chinese settlers on the island did not willingly or readily submit to Dutch rule; in fact, they rebelled against Dutch authority in 1640 and again in 1652. Most of the Chinese inhabitants preferred to be governed by China or wanted self-rule.[22]

Meanwhile, China's Ming Dynasty came under threat from the Manchus (a non-Chinese people who inhabited Manchuria). In a last-ditch effort to protect China from a Manchu invasion, Emperor Sze Tsung appointed Cheng Chih-lung, a pirate operating from a base in Taiwan, to command the remnant Ming naval forces. Though successful in winning some important battles, Cheng Chih-lung failed to prevent a Ming defeat, and the Manchus established a new dynasty in 1644, the Ch'ing (Qing), which ruled China until 1911.

Cheng Chih-lung's son Cheng Ch'eng-kung (also known as Koxinga), born in Japan to a Japanese mother, inherited his father's military forces. The Dutch at first saw him as a pirate of little consequence and allowed him to operate in areas in northern Taiwan. They even let Cheng bring large numbers of Chinese, mostly refugees fleeing Manchu rule, to Taiwan to become soldiers, to settle, or both. Cheng was thus able to raise an army of a hundred thousand men and an armada of three thousand junks to fight the Manchus for more than a decade (from 1646 to 1658), at one point nearly capturing the city of Nanking. However, after repeated failures to oust China's Manchu rulers, he was forced to limit his military activities to the coast of southern China.[23]

In 1661, having abandoned his efforts to re-establish the Ming Dynasty, Cheng launched an attack on the Dutch stronghold of Zeelandia, near what is now the city of Tainan. With thirty thousand men, he besieged forts that were defended by two thousand Dutch soldiers. After two years of fighting, the Dutch conceded defeat and reached an agreement with Cheng whereby they were allowed to peacefully evacuate. This brought an end to a generation of Dutch colonial rule of the island.

Cheng Ch'eng-kung subsequently established a Ming-style government on Taiwan complete with a Chinese legal system, a court, scholars, and advisers. Some say he established the first Chinese government on Taiwan.[24] Cheng also promoted Chinese culture and religion. His rule, however, depended on the support of powerful local Chinese families; in this and other ways, his government resembled a feudal system more than it did the Chinese scholar-bureaucratic system. Moreover, because Cheng continued to regard the Manchu government as his enemy, he never established official ties with China.

Cheng successfully encouraged the growth of the Chinese population on Taiwan, and in that way he made the island more Chinese. The Manchus inadvertently helped him in this effort: For a number of years, the government in Peking feared that Cheng might land forces on the China coast. Wanting to preclude local support for him and his armies, it ordered the evacuation of the coastal areas of China adjacent to Taiwan, causing severe deprivation to numerous villages there. Many inhabitants of coastal Fukien Province, bereft of their former livelihood of farming and fishing, fled to Taiwan.

Cheng promoted trade with Japan, the Philippines, Indochina, Siam, and the East Indies. Because Taiwan had several of the busiest commercial ports in East Asia during this time, the island absorbed cultural influences from these contacts and, unlike most of China, became quite cosmopolitan. Still, however, Cheng dreamed of restoring the Ming Dynasty, which he regarded as genuinely Chinese, and making Taiwan part of it.

Cheng's undying desire to drive the Manchus out of China and restore the Ming involved a plan to establish control over the Philippines. On several occasions he sent representatives to Manila to meet with leaders of the Chinese population there. Worried about a rebellion, in 1661 the Spanish rulers massacred ten thousand Chinese inhabitants after which they sent a messenger to Cheng telling him they had killed all Chinese residing in the Philippines. A livid Cheng wanted revenge, but he died two years later, at age thirty-eight—some say of a heart attack precipitated by the news of the slaughter of the Chinese in the Philippines.[25] Cheng no doubt would have accomplished much more, including possibly defeating Spanish forces in the Philippines, had he lived longer. In any event, for his accomplishments, Cheng is acclaimed a hero in Taiwan. Historians in China regard him highly as well for his liberating Taiwan from Western colonial rule—the earliest instance of this in Asia.

After Cheng Ch'eng-kung's death, his son Cheng Ching, whose power base was in Fukien Province, vied with his uncle in Taiwan for the right of succession. The son, with his superior military forces, coerced the armies of his father's brother into surrender. A link between Taiwan and the adjacent area of China was formally established as a result. Cheng Ching, like his father, led several expeditions against the Manchus in his efforts to realize the dream of restoring the Ming Dynasty. But, after four years of failed efforts, he retreated to Taiwan, where he, too, died at a relatively young age.

After Cheng Ching's death, the Cheng house was plagued by palace intrigue and internal dissension. Sensing an opportunity, the Manchu government sent a naval expedition to the Pescadores, where it destroyed the Cheng government's fleet and set the stage for an assault on Taiwan. When Manchu troops landed on the island, local military forces promptly surrendered, ending just over twenty years of Cheng family rule of Taiwan. Summing up the Cheng period, Taiwan was self-governing but wanted ties with China. Some now draw a resemblance to the Chiang Kai-shek era from 1949 to 1975.

From 1683 to 1895, Taiwan was ruled by China. For most of this time—until 1886—the island was administratively part of Fukien Province. Officials assigned to Taiwan, who were mostly Chinese rather than Manchus, were generally lazy, inefficient, and corrupt. They enforced laws and edicts with cruelty and generally disregarded the welfare of the population, prompting numerous uprisings and such political and social instability that Taiwan became known as "the land of rebellion and unrest." From 1683 to 1843, there were fifteen major rebellions against the government.[26] Official Chinese records during this period called Taiwan a "frontier area." Chinese, primarily from Fukien, continued to immigrate to Taiwan, even though during much of this period, specifically until 1732, the government officially prohibited it.

Citing the Peking government's general neglect of the island, not to mention the numerous revolts against Chinese authority, some scholars claim that China did not consider Taiwan to be part of China.[27] One must keep in mind, however, that China was ruled by the Manchus at this time, and they, to some degree, feared the "Chineseness" of Taiwan, especially because it had been a base of anti-Manchu military operations under Cheng Ch'eng-kung. Also, in spite of poor governance, Chinese culture flourished on the island and the Chinese population increased rapidly.

After 1800, a rapid increase in Western commerce in the area and Taiwan's expanding imports and exports again caused Western powers to express an interest in the island. Another reason for the attraction to Taiwan was that, through the publication of several books about Taiwan by European authors, Westerners had learned much more about the island and its presence on the world stage.[28] Finally, at that time ships became propelled by steam engines that burned coal, and Taiwan had coal.

But it was not until the Opium War (that started in 1839) that foreign powers' desires to control Taiwan became seen as a serious matter in Peking, at which time Chinese forces on Taiwan were mobilized. Subsequently, for strategic reasons stemming from Taiwan's possible role as a base of operations in a broader war, the government of China paid greater heed to the island. Though concern over Taiwan on the part of Chinese leaders soon faded, events had generated an opinion among some Chinese officials that the island had strategic value to China, a view that was to be revived later.

In ensuing years, Peking punished officials in Taiwan for mistreating British sailors who ran into trouble with local authorities, fearing London might use these incidences as a pretext for seizing and colonizing the island. In 1854, Commodore Matthew C. Perry urged the US government to establish a presence on Taiwan. A few years later, Townsend Harris, the US representative in Japan, suggested that the US government negotiate with officials in Peking for the purchase of the island. Because Peking consistently refused to accept accountability for difficulties foreign powers encountered in Taiwan, British and US officials concluded that China did not claim sovereignty over Taiwan or the Pescadores.[29] Nevertheless, neither London nor Washington made a decision to colonize Taiwan.

In the late 1850s, Keelung and Tamsui became important ports of call for Western ships. Accordingly, several European countries and the United States set up trading posts and consulates on Taiwan. Japan's contacts with Taiwan increased, particularly after Tokyo incorporated the nearby Ryukyu Islands in 1879. On several occasions, the Japanese government protested the abuse of Japanese sailors shipwrecked on the coast of Taiwan; Peking's authorities, as usual, denied responsibility. Again demonstrating China's lack of attention to Taiwan, in 1869 the heads of several Aboriginal tribes signed treaties with the United States.

China's neglect of Taiwan, however, ended in the late 1880s. When widespread rebellion broke out in southern China, the threat to Manchu rule there prompted some officials in Peking to recognize anew that Taiwan was strategically important. Even the Imperial Court accepted this view after French forces blockaded and bombarded forts on the island during Sino-French hostilities over Indochina. In 1884, the government reorganized its political administration of Taiwan and appointed a capable official, Liu Ming-ch'uan, as governor. Two years later Taiwan was elevated to the status of province.

Chinese rule under Liu Ming-ch'uan was efficient and enlightened. Liu built roads, railroads, and harbors. He improved and modernized Taiwan's economy and strengthened the island's defenses. Taiwan prospered and its population developed better feelings toward China. Liu would have accomplished much more had it not been for jealous colleagues who saw him as a threat and had not the Chinese government recalled him precipitously. Historians in both China and Taiwan regard Liu Ming-ch'uan highly; today, he is one of Taiwan's most renowned figures.

Part of the Japanese Empire

In 1894, China and Japan went to war over their conflicting interests in Korea. Surprisingly to many observers, Japan won and won handily. The Treaty of Shimonoseki that ended the war in 1895 contained, among various provisions, a phrase whereby China ceded Taiwan and the Pescadores to Japan "in perpetuity." Western powers viewed the treaty as legally binding and thus regarded Taiwan's transfer to Japanese rule as legitimate.[30]

When news of the treaty reached Taiwan, local leaders proclaimed independence and established the "Republic of Taiwan"—Asia's first republic. But the effort was ill-fated, and the new republic lasted but several days. Part of the reason was that Taiwan had no central government to organize a meaningful effort to challenge Japan. Likewise, there was no island-wide support for any of the several contending political or military leaders, as the island's population was divided by ethnic and clan differences. Finally, many residents of Taiwan at the time despised the warlordism and banditry that plagued the island and felt that Japanese rule might bring an end to these problems. They also felt that opposing Japan was futile.

The Chinese government in Peking did nothing to aid the resistance. China offered no support—not even recognition. In fact, during a formal ceremony in Keelung shortly after China signed the Treaty of Shimonoseki, an official sent from Peking formally transferred governance over Taiwan to Japanese authorities. Most Chinese in Taiwan gave up hope of help from China, and many expressed bitterness about China's betrayal.[31]

Within three years, the Japanese military was no longer needed to keep order in Taiwan. The international community was somewhat apprehensive about Japan's colonizing effort because other countries wanted to continue to use Taiwan as a port of call. Not yet powerful enough to challenge most Western nations, even in Asia, Japan allowed foreign ships to stop in Taiwan and left open Taiwan's ports to trade and other contacts.

As Japan's first colonial effort, its rule of Taiwan was an experiment and its policies were often inconsistent. Even though Japanese leaders complained about population pressures at home and later rationalized Japan's expansionist imperial policies by claims that it needed more space, it made no effort to populate the island with Japanese people. Japanese leaders regarded Japan (in contrast to its empire) as sacred ground and the Japanese people as descendants of the gods; transplanting them to areas already populated with non-Japanese contradicted these notions. Except for a few farmers, those Japanese who took up residence in Taiwan were either part of the military government or were in business.

Japanese colonial policy may be described as beneficial and progressive on the one hand yet discriminatory and predatory on the other. It was efficient and in many ways enlightened, but it did not lay the groundwork for self-rule, much less democracy. Some observers have described Japan's intent as expansionist and militaristic from the outset, but those claims are difficult to prove.[32] It seems more accurate to say these aims developed later in anticipation of World War II.

Tokyo's first objectives after it acquired Taiwan were to establish order and promote economic development. Both were seen as enhancing the power and prestige of Japan. Warlordism was eradicated, and law and order were established quickly, albeit by harsh means. Decrees issued by Japanese colonial authorities amounted to criminal law and were applied retroactively, sometimes without legal precedent. Tribunals were used rather than civil courts, and capital punishment was employed frequently.

In the economic realm, Japan's first priority was to increase Taiwan's agricultural productivity. Tokyo encouraged the cultivation of rice in the northern part of the island and sugar in the south. Rice was considered a staple, sugar a cash crop. Using new strains of rice and more efficient farming techniques, yields increased rapidly. By the 1930s, Taiwan produced twice as much rice as the population consumed.

Nearly a million tons were exported to Japan annually, as well as about the same amount of sugar—or two-thirds of Taiwan's crop. Food production increased to such a degree that, by the 1920s, the consumption of meat, vegetables, and fruits in Taiwan was higher than that of any province in China and even higher than in some parts of Japan.[33]

Japan also upgraded Taiwan's economic infrastructure. Before 1895, Taiwan had thirty miles of railroad; by 1905 it had three hundred, and seven thousand more were either planned or under construction.[34] The Japanese constructed new roads and harbors, while communications facilities were built or upgraded. In 1903, hydroelectric generators went into service near Taipei, making Taiwan the first place to use electricity in Asia outside of Japan.[35] Electrification spawned small industries, such as glass factories and paper mills, and made possible the mechanization of harbors. Tokyo standardized the monetary system, established banks, and promoted uniform commercial practices, thereby transforming commerce from a barter system to one based on money.

After World War I, Taiwan's economy received a boost when Tokyo banned foreign enterprises from the island. New industries such as textiles, chemicals, and machinery sprang up quickly. In the 1930s, as a result of Tokyo's expansionist policies, the Japanese government began promoting the development of heavy industries in Taiwan. In the process, Taiwan's foreign trade increased markedly. Taiwan's enviable economic growth and modernization not only helped Taiwan's population, but it also served the colonial rulers. The island's economy was linked to Japan's, just as European nations tied their colonies to the metropolis. Before World War II, 90 percent of Taiwan's exports went to Japan. For Tokyo, Taiwan's economic growth was proof of Japan's enlightened colonial policies; for Taiwan, it was very beneficial, though it increased the island's dependency on Japan.

Meanwhile the Japanese improved public hygiene in Taiwan radically. The island, which had been known as the pesthole of Asia, became second only to Japan in the region in terms of sanitation. By the early twentieth century, bubonic plague had been eradicated, cholera was rare, and smallpox was much less widespread. Dysentery and malaria were drastically reduced. All these diseases remained rampant in China.[36] Japanese rule also brought social change. Taiwan's educational system was improved markedly. The island's literacy rate, technological skills, and knowledge of world affairs soon exceeded that of any part of China or, for that matter, any other area in Asia outside Japan. Laws and customs that kept lower socioeconomic groups perpetually in debt were banned. In 1910, the practice of binding women's feet was outlawed.

Political governance was less enlightened. Japanese colonial governance was facilitated by *pao chia* (a system of common responsibility), which divided the Chinese population into groups of one hundred households each and made the head of each group accountable for the behavior of those families under his authority.[37] This person in turn held each family head accountable for the conduct of that family. Informants and severe punishments ensured effective Japanese political control. Important decisions on almost all matters were made in Tokyo. Although policies were somewhat more democratic before the 1930s when the military grasped control of the Japanese government, there was still little evidence that Taiwan was heading toward self-rule or democracy.

The Aborigines proved difficult to control and incorporate into society. The Japanese were generally successful in disarming them and forcing them to give up headhunting, but even as late as the 1940s many were not "pacified" because the Japanese could not effectively police all of the mountainous areas in Taiwan. In fact, strong resistance by the Aborigines to Japanese rule led the Japanese colonial government to ignore parts of central Taiwan.

Japanese policies had other drawbacks. Japan's social policies, although generally progressive, were carried out with little thought or understanding of Taiwanese customs or feelings. Educational policies forced Taiwanese to learn Japanese; neither standard Chinese nor the Taiwan dialect of Chinese was taught in school. Taiwanese students were encouraged to study medicine, engineering, science, and technology-related subjects, but not law, politics, or any of the social sciences. Reflecting their attitudes of ethnic superiority, Japanese officials and most other Japanese in Taiwan sent their children to their own schools and resided in separate areas.

World War II

Japanese rule of Taiwan just prior to and during WWII was not without problems. The colonial government faced a dilemma regarding its philosophy and its style of ruling Taiwan. Many Japanese officials advocated a policy of tough rule, thinking that the population of Taiwan opposed Japanese control. But they also assumed the island should remain a colony of Japan indefinitely. Others considered Taiwan's colonial status to be temporary and pushed for a different approach, called the Formosa Home Rule Formula. Still others proffered a policy called *kominka*, or "assimilation." *Kominka* had official support, but, because most Japanese opposed granting equality to Taiwan's population, an assimilation policy was not realistic and was carried out only halfheartedly.[38]

In 1935, after Lin Hsien-t'ang and his Home Rule Association had for several years advocated the transfer of political power to a locally elected assembly, Tokyo announced establishing an elective government in Taiwan. But this applied only to local government, and Japanese colonial officials retained veto power over important decisions. Still, an election was held, and some democratic change was in evidence. Progress toward more democratic rule, however, was reversed a year or two later when Japanese politics became dominated by the military and as Japan headed for war.

In 1936, Taiwan's colonial governors once again became military officers. The next year, when war broke out with China, martial law was put into effect in Taiwan. Meanwhile, the Japanese navy referred to Taiwan as an "unsinkable aircraft carrier" and began to use it as a military staging area. Large numbers of Japanese troops were stationed on Taiwan and trained there. Many of Taiwan's newly created industries were expanded and prospered as a result of their vital role in supplying the Japanese war machine. In 1941, Taiwan was the site from which Japanese forces launched the invasion of the Philippines and other offshore countries to the south.

Even before 1941, the Chinese population of Taiwan for the most part had forsaken their ties with China and saw little reason to reestablish them. Most supported Japanese rule or at least had accommodated to it. There had been no meaningful protest in Taiwan to Japan's taking and colonizing Manchuria in 1931 or to its war with China, which started in 1937. Those for whom Japan's invasion of China was a problem or those who felt strong ties to China were allowed to return to China. Few did so.

Many Taiwanese worked in war-related industries or in other ways abetted the Japanese war effort.[39] During the war, many Taiwanese volunteered for military service. Their defection rate was low, and there was little or no protest against military life. A large number of Taiwanese fought in combat in China (including in Nanking, where they participated in atrocities against Chinese civilians). According to one source, 207,183 Taiwanese were conscripted into the Japanese military; 30,304 were casualties during the war.[40]

As Japanese forces retreated in the Pacific, the population of Taiwan was readied for US attacks and, eventually, invasion. Taiwanese served in units that prepared to defend the island. As it turned out, however, US forces limited their military actions to the bombing of oil storage depots in addition to infrastructure and military targets. There was no saturation bombing or targeting population centers. In fact, Taiwan was spared the war damage that Japan and many other parts of East Asia suffered. There were shortages of many goods, but, again, Taiwan was more fortunate than most parts of the region.

Toward the end of the war, the US Navy discussed plans for invading Taiwan but soon abandoned the idea. US military strategists possessed few good maps of the island and, more important, realized that the Taiwanese were unlikely to rebel against their Japanese colonial rulers and would instead battle US forces to help defend the island.[41] To avoid the possible embarrassment of fighting local Chinese defenders of Taiwan, the United States instead invaded Okinawa, the largest of Japan's Ryukyu Islands, leaving Taiwan (unlike Japan proper and China) generally unscathed.

Meanwhile, because of Chiang Kai-shek's special role as an ally of the United States during the war, he was afforded the opportunity to request that "territories occupied by enemy forces since 1937 or 1939," as stated in the Atlantic Charter and as suggested by Winston Churchill, also include those lands taken from China by Japan during the Sino-Japanese War. Chiang had not made a serious effort to claim that Taiwan belonged to China before this, as witnessed by the fact that the constitutions written in 1925, 1934, and 1936 did not list Taiwan as a province of China. Moreover, "lost territories" cited in Sun Yat-sen's Three People's Principles included all or parts of Korea, Vietnam, Burma, the Ryukyu Islands, Bhutan, and Nepal; Taiwan was also cited but was accorded no special status.[42]

In any event, it became the policy of the United States and its allies during the war that Japan could not keep its empire, and that policy covered Taiwan. At the Cairo Conference in December 1943, the United States and the United Kingdom reached an agreement with Generalissimo Chiang Kai-shek to the effect that Taiwan would be put in the category of territories "stolen" by Japan and that Taiwan "shall be restored to the Republic of China." This agreement was reaffirmed in the Potsdam Declaration in July 1945 when Japan's defeat was imminent. Yet Taiwan's legal status remained undecided pending the signing of a peace treaty.

In the fall of 1945, the Japanese—one-eighteenth of Taiwan's population—departed the island. This large contingent of Japanese included most officials of the colonial government, the military, the police, businessmen, many professional people, and some farmers. Chiang Kai-shek sent military forces to keep order and officials from the government of the Republic of China to replace the Japanese colonial administration. It was thus assumed that Japan had surrendered Taiwan to Chiang's forces and that the island was to be returned to China; indeed, there was no other logical choice. The Cairo agreement said this (even though it was a wartime declaration and not a formal treaty). Mao's forces were capable of little more than launching guerrilla operations in the interior of China at this time, and, besides, he and the Chinese Communist Party had expressed no interest in Taiwan.

Not too unhappy that Japan was defeated, or at least fully accepting it as reality, Taiwan's population welcomed the arrival of Nationalist Chinese officials. Most of the population was tired of war and looked forward to the end of colonial rule. A large number of citizens wanted democracy and self-rule. Many wanted to restore family ties in China.

Nevertheless, many were apprehensive about Taiwan's future. A small minority in Taiwan advocated independence. A few suggested that Taiwan should become a United Nations trust territory. Some even proposed that Taiwan should become a territory governed by the United States.[43] Others wanted guarantees about the island's future status should it become part of China again. Taiwanese who participated in the surrender ceremony asked for a provision giving "special status" to Taiwan because the island had been a Japanese colony for fifty years and, therefore, was different from China in many ways.[44] The American public wanted its troops to come home while its government focused more on problems in Europe than in Asia. Taiwan was thus destined to share in China's turmoil and civil war.

Part of China Again

On October 25, 1945, subsequently celebrated as Retrocession Day, Taiwan officially became a part of the Republic of China. But Taiwan was not made a province of China as had been expected. Similarly, no efforts were made to establish a democratic government. Chiang Kai-shek appointed Ch'en Yi governor-general and gave him the same kind of near-absolute power the Japanese governors had enjoyed.

Making matters worse, Ch'en, along with many of the Mainland Chinese soldiers sent to Taiwan at the time of the Japanese evacuation, regarded Taiwanese as traitors for not having opposed Japanese rule. Ch'en and his Mainland Chinese administration, as well as the military, also perceived that the Taiwanese had been tainted for fifty years by what they considered inferior Japanese culture. Few Mainland Chinese soldiers or officials spoke Taiwanese, and few Taiwanese spoke the Chinese national language. Although some Nationalist soldiers and administrators hailed from Fukien Province and spoke the dialect from which Taiwanese was derived, even that did not guarantee good communications. In any event, Ch'en wanted Taiwan to "become Chinese."[45]

The Nationalist Chinese government and the Nationalist Party soon came to be seen by many Taiwanese as a carpetbag regime, much the same way that the South in the United States viewed the harsh post–Civil War rule imposed on it. Disappointed that they had little voice in the political decision-making process and finding the Mainland Chinese by no means fair or likable, the Taiwanese came to regard the Nationalist government as no better than its predecessor and, in many important ways, much worse. They had expected better.[46]

More crucial to what transpired than the political and cultural factors were Taiwan's economic well-being, public health standards, and social order, all of which deteriorated dramatically at this time. Nationalist Chinese leaders were preoccupied with civil war in China and did not regard Taiwan's problems as important. Public and even private buildings were stripped of machines, tools, and sometimes plumbing—anything metallic—to send to the Mainland. Food shortages developed when large quantities of grain were commandeered to feed Nationalist armies fighting the Communists. Public health services almost ceased to function, causing outbreaks of cholera and bubonic plague. Rumors spread that Nationalist soldiers had brought these diseases to Taiwan. Public works were allowed to fall into disrepair, and the education system deteriorated badly.[47]

Just as the Mainland Chinese perceived the Taiwanese as traitors lacking Chinese culture, the Taiwanese perceived the Mainlanders as dirty, dishonest, and technologically backward. Stories circulated about Mainland Chinese who stole bicycles and did not know what they were and about others who spent hours staring at elevators they had never seen before. Clearly, Mainland Chinese officials were unable to maintain basic public services, including power plants, trains, and buses, largely because of their lack of technological expertise. The Taiwanese also had to adjust to a new legal system. Nationalist soldiers often claimed ownership of houses and land based on forced occupation; the Taiwanese considered this theft. Other laws were not understood, and many were not enforced.

The ill feelings between the two groups came to a head on February 28, 1947, when plainclothes police officers killed a Taiwanese woman who had been selling black-market cigarettes to make a living. An angry mob formed and threatened the police, whereupon they fired into the crowd, killing four people. Widespread civil disobedience, and what seemed to some to be a rebellion, erupted, an event now known as *er er ba* (or 2-2-8, for the second month, twenty-eighth day).

Most historians blame "evil" Governor-General Ch'en Yi for the incident. But that is too simplistic. Although Ch'en could speak Japanese and Taiwanese, he refused to use either language in conducting affairs of state. He expected Taiwanese to learn Mandarin Chinese, which older Taiwanese could not do easily. He also ruled as a traditional Chinese official—by example rather than by contact with the people. Trying to govern in a moral way, Ch'en sought to maintain social order with only a fraction of the police and troops Japan had employed. And, though he was generally hardworking and principled, many of his subordinates were lazy, corrupt, and incompetent. Another factor was that Ch'en's agenda for Taiwan included creating a socialist economy with considerable state control, which the local population opposed and was clearly a mistake. Finally, instead of taking action to defuse social unrest in early 1947, he temporized. Worst of all, he treated complaints and protest as pro-Communist, even though Taiwanese had virtually no connections with (or even much knowledge of) the Communists on the Mainland or anywhere else.[48]

During the protest or rebellion (there being disagreement about which it was), Taiwanese killed or injured a large number of Mainland Chinese, including many unarmed, innocent civilians. In some instances, they beat or killed anyone who did not speak Taiwanese, including Hakkas. The killing and the virulent opposition to the government looked like a revolution to Nationalist authorities in China, even though what was happening in Taiwan was by no means well organized. On March 8, 1947, a large contingent of Nationalist Chinese troops arrived and used their weapons with little restraint against unarmed Taiwanese. Though official reports of this incident don't mention this, it seems that the troops acted out of vengeance for the killing of their fellow Mainland Chinese. In any event, the Nationalist government felt what happened in Taiwan was an unwanted distraction, one that helped the Communists in China with whom they were engaged in a life-and-death struggle. By the end of March order was restored, but not before thousands of Taiwanese had been killed, including many of Taiwan's potential local leaders.[49]

Chiang Kai-shek briefly turned his attention from events on the Mainland to Taiwan after the February 28 Incident. He removed Ch'en Yi from his post, along with a number of other high officials. He made Taiwan a province, rescinded military rule, and appointed some Taiwanese to top positions in the government. Various government monopoly enterprises were sold, and efforts were made to alleviate unemployment. However, serious damage had already been done to the Nationalist government's credibility, and Taiwanese hatred of both the government and Mainland Chinese would not soon subside.

In ensuing years, seldom was there mention of what happened in February and March 1947. The government's policy was to erase the incident from history and from public memory. However, with democratization in the 1970s and 1980s, and particularly with the end of martial law, opposition politicians began using *er er ba* as a rallying call. The government subsequently changed its stance and, with the help of scholars, launched an investigation into what happened and why. In 1992, a detailed report was published on the incident.[50]

Yet many politicians would not let the issue die, or they sought to exploit it. Taiwan's new political parties and even their factions differed sharply over whether February 28 should be made a holiday or a day of mourning and whether statues or buildings should be built in remembrance. In 1995, on the forty-eighth anniversary of *er er ba*, President Lee Teng-hui, following the erection of a monument in Taipei's New Park, issued a formal apology on behalf of the government to the families of victims. Taipei's mayor, Chen Shui-bian, representing the opposition party, subsequently announced that the park would be renamed "2-2-8 Peace Park" and that February 28 should be "peace day." Lawmakers meanwhile passed a bill to provide compensation to victims' relatives and made February 28 National Memorial Day. In 1997, February 28 was made a national holiday.[51]

After Chen Shui-bian became president in 2000, he and the Democratic Progressive Party used the event in election campaigns and on other occasions to rally his supporters against the KMT. At times this worked well. But the DPP seemed to overreach and appeared unaware that Taiwan's youth did not know of *er er ba* from direct experience and didn't care about it as much as their parents, while to many it did not substitute for good government or astute management of the economy.

Taiwan as the Republic of China

By late 1949, Chiang Kai-shek's Nationalist forces had been defeated in most of China by Mao Tse-tung's (now spelled Mao Zedong) Communist armies. Chiang and a portion of his military and government fled to Taiwan, where they hoped to regroup and counterattack. With that, Taiwan had to absorb more than 1.5 million people at a time when the economy was in dire straits and social conditions were going from bad to worse. This influx of people aggravated an already stressed infrastructure as well as relations between the Taiwanese and the Mainland Chinese. Chiang ordered Ch'en Yi executed in public and purged the government and the Nationalist Party of the most corrupt and incompetent officials. But these actions, although sincere and in many ways effective, had but a marginal effect toward improving relations with the local population.[52]

However, in spite of their dislike of the Mainland Chinese and the government and the fact that Chiang Kai-shek had little credibility internationally, most Taiwanese saw no realistic choice but to accept Nationalist rule. The likely alternative was worse. Few Taiwanese wanted to be governed by the People's Republic of China: communism was in no way attractive, philosophically or otherwise. Moreover, Mao had no organization or base of support in Taiwan, and consequently he had no means of launching an effective movement against Nationalist rule. To "liberate" Taiwan, Mao would have to invade the island, which everyone in Taiwan knew would be a very costly affair in terms of loss of life and property damage.

Mao's People's Republic of China laid legal claim to the island when the Nationalists were defeated (based on the argument that it was a successor government to the Republic of China), even though Mao had earlier spoken of Taiwan as if it were not part of China. In fact, Mao had some years earlier put Taiwan in the same category as Korea and other would-be "friendly territories" on China's periphery. Even in the late 1940s, Mao expressed no interest in Taiwan and made no effort to launch a Communist insurgency movement there, not even after the Japanese left. He apparently believed that the success of his revolution would eventually persuade all of Asia—particularly areas or countries near China—to adopt communism, and in this context territorial issues did not matter.[53]

Conclusions about Taiwan's legal status at the time seemed academic anyway: the island's future would be determined by military force. In fact, in the spring of 1950, Mao formulated plans for an invasion of Taiwan. But, because the Nationalists had taken with them much of the Chinese navy as well as the large ships of the merchant marine, this required using thousands of small boats. In water holes in Fukien Province, Mao trained his soldiers to swim because they would have to reach Taiwan's shore after being dropped from boats a mile out. But many of Mao's troops became infected with a liver fluke found locally in the soil, forcing a delay of the invasion plans by a few weeks.[54] In the meantime, war broke out in Korea. The United States, having abandoned Chiang Kai-shek in January, now reversed course and sent the Seventh Fleet to the Taiwan Strait to shield Taiwan from an invasion.

The Nationalists quickly took advantage of the respite from conflict. With the United States guaranteeing the island's security, Chiang Kai-shek implemented various kinds of political reform to create a more honest and efficient government. In particular, he took steps to rid the government and the ruling party of corrupt, lazy, and incompetent officials. Chiang even organized elections and made other efforts to democratize Taiwan's political system at the local level.

Because of the Korean War and China's role in it and owing to Nationalist China's adamant stance against communism (not to mention the considerable support Chiang and the Nationalists once had, and again enjoyed, in the United States), Taiwan became a valued member of the Western bloc. With the polarization of the world into two camps and because the Republic of China continued to represent China in the United Nations and most other international organizations (which regarded the government in Peking with hostility and vice versa), Taipei was at center stage in the East-West struggle.

In the ensuing months and years, however, the Nationalists' hopes of reconquering the Mainland dimmed. Thus Nationalist leaders began to think of Taiwan as a permanent home. Furthermore, they felt they were needed in Taiwan, where political leadership and administrative talents were lacking. Finally, they saw they had a chance to redeem themselves and prove that their ideology was superior to communism. Meanwhile, many Taiwanese began to realize that their animosity had to be put aside if Taiwan was to survive and prosper. As time passed, this attitude became more and more prevalent.[55]

With the benefit of a period of peace for the first time in more than a decade and with the help of US economic and military assistance, Chiang Kai-shek instituted new plans aimed at promoting economic development. The first, and one of the most important, was land reform. It was a resounding success—so much so that it still provides a model for other countries to study and emulate. Land reform and Taiwan's overall successful economic development plans, both of which were overseen by US aid advisers, made Taiwan a showcase of US foreign aid and improved Taiwan's economic situation as well as the Nationalist government's image in the international community.[56]

Although the United States protected Taiwan from an invasion by Mao's People's Liberation Army (PLA), the US government also sought to prevent the Nationalist Chinese from trying to destabilize Mao's government on the Mainland, from starting a conflict that might drag the United States into a war with China and the Soviet Union, or both. Keeping the two sides apart was not easy. Two crises erupted, in 1954 and 1958, over the Offshore Islands (the island groups of Quemoy and Matsu, which Communist forces had failed to take in 1949 and which remained in Nationalist hands), when the Chinese military bombarded the islands. Mao apparently saw an opportunity to test US resolve. In response, Washington demonstrated its mettle by supplying Nationalist forces on the islands and even threatening to use nuclear weapons against China.[57]

Chiang Kai-shek adopted the position, not unlike that espoused by the United States, that China was a captive of the Soviet Union. In the US government, this attitude persisted until the Nixon administration, even though relations between Moscow and Beijing showed clear signs of strain. Meanwhile, the Nationalist government failed to adjust to a thaw in the Cold War. Some historians in Taiwan, however, contend that changing course at that juncture would have separated Taiwan from China permanently. Others say that adopting a policy of separation, or a one-China, one-Taiwan stance, would have stimulated premature demands for democracy, which would have evoked political instability and ethnic conflict. Those who advocate an independent, sovereign Taiwan say it was an opportunity missed. In any case, the People's Republic of China won the struggle to represent China in world affairs in the 1970s.

Taiwan, however, had been made ready for economic change. By the mid-1960s, after successful land reform and the beginning of its industrialization process, Taiwan was poised for an economic takeoff. In 1964, US aid to Taiwan stopped. Almost simultaneously, Taiwan's economy took off. Over the next two decades, Taiwan could boast of the world's fastest-growing economy. Economists since have observed that US aid helped Taiwan's economic growth get started and that its termination forced Taiwan to stand alone, which it did very successfully. Little more than two decades of Nationalist rule after 1949 made Taiwan more prosperous than it had ever been.

Economic development fostered social progress in manifold ways. Taiwan also became permeated by foreign influence and culture, especially as trade increased and the population and government came to realize that economic prosperity depended on exports. Taiwan, as a consequence, became much more open and cosmopolitan; this happened at a time when China was becoming more inward-looking and increasingly hostile toward the rest of the world. As economic well-being increased, Taiwanese alienation decreased, even though Taiwan was still under martial law.

With economic growth, democracy began to bud. The Nationalist government had for some time encouraged democracy at the local level where the Nationalist Party functioned as an intermediary among hostile Taiwanese factions. Nationalist Party leaders believed they could institutionalize democratic politics and apply it to the central government in the future—but only gradually and when Taiwan was ready for it. The Taiwanese felt that democracy at the local level would eventually work its way to the top. These opposing views did not cause conflict; rather they provided two paths to democratization that could be reconciled.

With economic and political change as well as a better understanding of the world, the myth that the Nationalists represented the people of China and that Mao's government was a temporary outlaw regime could not be sustained, even though Peking's policies threatening Taiwan reinforced the Nationalists' recalcitrance.

At times, it appeared Nationalist Chinese leaders were resigned to, or even advocated, Taiwan's separation from China. Chiang Kai-shek said publicly that realizing the goal of returning to the Mainland "would be 70 percent political." This statement and the Nationalists' inability to oust Mao from power (and they made no serious efforts to do so after the early 1960s) told many observers that the government, privately at least, accepted the reality of two Chinas.[58]

However, the US escalation of the Vietnam War after the Gulf of Tonkin Incident in August 1964 resuscitated the bipolar structure of world politics in Asia and increased US support for Taiwan. Also, in 1965, Mao launched the Great Proletarian Cultural Revolution, which turned politics in China quickly leftward and resulted in the self-imposed isolation of the People's Republic of China for several years. Both played into the hands of those in Taipei who resisted change and new policies.

But the events that gave Taipei a respite from pressures to reform were not to last. In 1969, relations between the governments in Washington and Peking (by now written Beijing) changed course as a result of US efforts to disengage from Vietnam and an escalation of Sino-Soviet border hostilities.[59] A rapprochement between Washington and Beijing, former archenemies, was mutually advantageous and was soon on the agendas of both governments. In 1971, National Security Adviser Henry Kissinger visited Beijing and arranged for President Nixon to go there the next year in what was to become a watershed shift in US-China relations. That same year, largely as a result of the thaw in US-China relations, the People's Republic of China was admitted to the United Nations and the Republic of China expelled. Subsequently, Taiwan's government suffered the loss of diplomatic ties with most of the nations with which it had formal relations, including almost all of the important nations of the world.[60]

In February 1972, President Nixon visited the People's Republic of China, where he signed the Shanghai Communiqué and engaged in talks that anticipated a rapprochement between the two countries while also anticipating the establishment of diplomatic relations. This historic breakthrough in US-China relations was a shock to Taiwan, but it was not as ominous as many in Taiwan had anticipated. Nixon treated the "Taiwan issue" with deliberate ambiguity.[61] The United States did not abandon Taiwan. Although the credibility of the government and the ruling Nationalist Party were hurt, it could have been much worse. Leaders in Taipei did not lose public support at home because they had, after all, engineered Taiwan's miracle economic development. In addition, most observers in and outside of Taiwan took the view that little could have been done to prevent what happened. Clearly, there was no popular desire for Beijing to rule Taiwan.

In April 1975, Chiang Kai-shek's death symbolized the end of the Nationalists' hope of ruling a unified China—if anyone still espoused any optimism about this.

The next year, Mao died, putting an end to the personal duel between two political factions-turned-governments that had been so much a part of China's modern history.

Taiwan Ruled by Chiang Ching-kuo

Following President Chiang Kai-shek's death, Vice President Yen Chia-kan became president of the Republic of China in accordance with provisions in the Constitution. But Chiang Kai-shek's eldest son, Chiang Ching-kuo, premier since 1972 and head of the Nationalist Party, was the de facto ruler (with Yen's cooperation, of course). In 1978, Yen declined to run for re-election when his term as president expired. Chiang Ching-kuo was nominated and elected president.[62]

Chiang Ching-kuo was not schooled in the democratic tradition or representative government. Instead, in his youth, his father had sent him to the Soviet Union, where he joined the Communist Party, supported Leon Trotsky, and married a Russian woman. Nor had he championed political reform during most of his political career in Taiwan. However, he realized the need for Taiwan to shed its authoritarian political system if it was to sustain its rapid economic growth and maintain important political ties with the democratic West.[63] He also understood that only through political change—meaning democratization—could Taiwan heal the wounds of ethnic ill will, parry Beijing's overtures to negotiate unification, and win support from the international community.

Chiang Ching-kuo lived by his convictions. In the early and mid-1970s, he recruited Taiwanese into the party and the government. As president, he launched an anticorruption campaign that was taken seriously by those both in and out of government, especially after he jailed high government officials for corrupt practices—including some of his own relatives. Ordering government offices to publish their telephone numbers and answer citizens' requests and suggestions, Chiang compelled officials to be responsive to the public and act as "employees of the people." The population applauded his actions and supported his efforts to build good government.[64]

CCK, as Chiang was called fondly by many, made frequent visits to the countryside to talk to farmers and ordinary citizens. Privately, he maintained an austere lifestyle, eschewing publicity and praise. His demeanor won him broad respect at home and good press abroad. He became a truly popular president.

But oftentimes CCK had to force political change upon the ruling party and government by edict. In short, he brought democracy to Taiwan by quite disparate means. Many people felt the change CCK implemented was long overdue, having been envisioned by Sun Yat-sen and set forth in the Constitution. Some thought he moved too quickly. Nevertheless, in retrospect most perceived that no one else could have modernized Taiwan's politics as effectively as CCK did.

However, at a critical juncture Taiwan was dealt a diplomatic shock that set back its democratization. In December 1978, President Jimmy Carter, without warning, announced that the United States would sever diplomatic ties with Taipei effective January 1, 1979, and end their defense treaty a year later. President Carter also acknowledged (in negotiations with Beijing) that there was only one China— the People's Republic of China. These actions mirrored a fundamental change in US-China/Taiwan policy.[65] Although Taiwan was inured to difficult situations, loss of official ties with its only important friend and its protector was a severe blow. Some observers at the time said the events were portentous: Taiwan was now illegitimate and isolated in the international community and would be com- pelled to become part of China.

However, altering and in some important ways reversing Carter's China/Taiwan policy, in April 1979 the US Congress passed a law called the Taiwan Relations Act (TRA). The TRA restored relations with Taiwan to a near-official level. Moreover, it included provisions that provided Taiwan with credible US security and eco- nomic guarantees. Beijing, preoccupied by a war with Vietnam while the TRA was being debated and reluctant to disturb its new and valuable relationship with the United States, reacted to Congress's action with only token protest. Later, how- ever, Deng Xiaoping made calculated efforts to undermine the legislation. He also declared that he would not renounce the use of force against Taiwan—a position still held by the Beijing government today.[66]

Losing diplomatic relations with the United States made CCK even more deter- mined to press ahead with democratization. Meanwhile, opposition forces became more active when they saw how grim Taiwan's diplomatic situation had become. They thought that only profound political change, meaning rapid democratiza- tion, would save Taiwan from being isolated and then absorbed by the People's Republic of China. The opposition's efforts throughout 1979 climaxed in Decem- ber with a protest demonstration in the southern city of Kaohsiung that resulted in widely publicized violence. At that point, public opinion, which had previously supported the activists' proposed reforms, shifted in favor of the government be- cause most citizens feared chaos. The government jailed some of the demonstra- tions' leaders but negotiated further democratic change with others. Reforms discussed included revising Taiwan's election law and reaching some gentlemen's agreements between the government and the opposition so that an orderly but competitive national election could be rescheduled.

As a result, in 1980 Taiwan held an unprecedented election. Whether it was "democracy from the top down," as some observers said who thought it was Chi- ang Ching-kuo's creation, or from the bottom up, as the opposition suggested, is difficult to say; it was both. Some observers noted Taiwan was rebuffing Beijing's overtures to negotiate reunification by pushing democratization. In any event, the election reflected Taiwan's rapid evolution away from an authoritarian, one-party political system toward real democracy.

In 1983, Taiwan held its second national democratic election. Again the KMT performed well. Some critics said it should have, given its advantages in talent, money, and control of the media. Others said the opposition was too radical and, furthermore, had not learned the art of campaign politics. As a consequence of this second democratic national election, Chiang Ching-kuo and the Nationalist Party became more confident and more willing to continue democratic reform.

In 1984, CCK was re-elected president of the Republic of China, even though questions lingered about his health. He picked a new vice president, Lee Teng-hui, who was seen as highly competent, loyal to CCK and the Nationalist Party, and also committed to democratic reform. Lee was soon considered CCK's heir. Because Lee was Taiwanese (though Hakka), his rise seemed to mark the beginning of the power transition from Mainland Chinese to Taiwanese. Seen in retrospect, it was.

In early 1986, at a Nationalist Party's Central Committee meeting, CCK called for several major reforms in government. These included restructuring the parliament, getting rid of martial law, and allowing new political parties to form. In October, in a widely heralded interview with Katharine Graham, owner of the *Washington Post*, President Chiang repeated—some say formalized—these promises. This paved the way for the first two-party election ever held in Taiwan. In December of that year, the newly formed Democratic Progressive Party (DPP) vied with the ruling Nationalist Party for seats in the Legislative Yuan (the lawmaking body of government) and the National Assembly. Performing well in spite of genuine competition while nominating mostly Taiwanese candidates, the Nationalist Party again burnished its image and expanded its mandate to rule Taiwan. It was clear that the days of a one-party dictatorship in Taiwan were over and that the Nationalist Party could lead a democratic nation.

Meanwhile, President Chiang announced that none of his relatives would hold a position of political prominence after his death. He also took steps to ensure that the military would not play a significant political role in Taiwan after his demise. Instead, Vice President Lee Teng-hui was being groomed to become president. Other Western-educated leaders, many of them young by Chinese standards, were promoted to top positions in the government and in the ruling party. In July 1987, Chiang Ching-kuo seemed to put the final touches on political modernization by abolishing martial law. At the same time, trying to ameliorate ethnic differences, CCK noted that he had lived in Taiwan for forty years and should, therefore, be counted as Taiwanese.[67]

When President Chiang terminated martial law, the public did not strongly believe that it should end. Many felt it contributed to social stability and economic growth and should be kept. However, the Western media gave this decision more applause than it had given anything else President Chiang had done, which markedly improved both CCK's and Taiwan's global image considerably. The termination of martial law did have a salutary effect on the exercise of civil and political rights and made Taiwan's media free from military oversight and censorship. A few months later, CCK ended the ban on travel to China by Taiwan's citizens, thus paving the way for economic and other contacts between Taiwan and China that would grow and have a lasting impact.

In retrospect, one of the most salient questions about the Chiang Ching-kuo era is: Did CCK engineer the separation, or further split, of Taiwan from China? He had always advocated a one-China policy. His roots were in China. Yet he brought democracy to Taiwan and that furthered separation. Some say he sought to create a model for China and saw democratization in China as the key to bringing the two together again.

CCK's biographers treat him as a great leader who understood the times and who acted with integrity and with the interests of the citizens of Taiwan at heart.[68] Future historians will no doubt see him as the leader who launched Taiwan's "political miracle" and kept Taiwan's "economic miracle"—launched by his father— on track. Recent public opinion surveys indicate he is Taiwan's most highly regarded president.

Taiwan Under Lee Teng-hui

When Chiang Ching-kuo died in January 1988, Vice President Lee Teng-hui succeeded him as president according to the Constitution and CCK's wishes. At an emergency meeting of the Nationalist Party, Lee was also made temporary head of the ruling party. However, "old guard" members of the party aligned against Lee to block him from assuming too much power. They feared that Lee, who was Taiwanese, would threaten Mainland China, would advance Taiwanization, and threaten mainland Chinese rule. On the other hand, they could not dispute Lee's competence or the fact that he was CCK's chosen successor. A motion to have a rotating party head was voted down, and Lee became the party's undisputed leader.[69]

Lee symbolized an end of the Mainland Chinese minority's hold on political authority. Yet his leadership did not dampen the spirits of the opposition (mostly Taiwanese), who perceived that the speed of democratization was still too slow. Interest groups and new political parties were also seeking a bigger role in the democratization process. So, too, protest had become part of Taiwan's political process. In May 1988, farmers took to the streets to demonstrate, as other groups had been doing at the rate of about 150 per month. Seventeen hours of riots resulted in extensive property damage and injuries to more than five hundred people. This typified the new political climate in which Lee Teng-hui had to operate.[70]

A few months later, the Nationalist Party held its Thirteenth Party Congress. Lee was officially elected chairman of the party, enabling him to further consolidate power. Lee was popular, and the democratization of party rules accomplished at the meeting worked in his favor.[71] Yet these changes meant that he did not have the kind of control over the party that CCK had and that party infighting and factional struggles were going to become serious problems. After the party congress, President Lee picked a new cabinet. For the first time, the majority was Taiwanese. Lee, however, chose the popular Lee Huan, a Mainland Chinese, to be his premier, thereby keeping a balance of Mainlanders and Taiwanese at the top.

Soon after this, President Lee and the Nationalist Party backed new laws to retire members of Taiwan's democratic bodies of government who were elected on the Mainland and subsequently frozen in office or replaced by appointment, the so-called elder parliamentarians. In March 1990, although challenged briefly by the duo of popular Taiwanese politician Lin Yang-kang and Chiang Wei-kuo (Chiang Kai-shek's second son and CCK's half brother), Lee Teng-hui was elected in March 1990 to a new six-year term. Those who opposed him did so for a variety of reasons, saying that he was dictatorial, that he was advancing democracy and Taiwanization too fast, and that he had difficulty filling CCK's shoes. His supporters said his detractors were simply opponents of democracy. In any case, Lee's popularity remained high.[72]

In May 1989, Taipei supported (though not with money, weapons, or material help) the student-led democracy movement in China. The massacre in Tiananmen Square that followed in June damaged China's global image severely. Yet Taiwan did not reduce its growing ties with China, realizing that trying to isolate China was neither feasible nor in consonance with the New World Order. Many perceived Taiwan and China alike were members of a "Greater China," or Pacific Rim bloc, in an era of global economic blocs.[73]

In early 1991, Taiwan embarked on a new Six-Year Development Plan, which its leaders hoped would catapult Taiwan into the top twenty nations in the world in per capita income by the end of the century. In April, Lee lifted restrictions on civil and political rights, and in so doing, he positioned Taiwan to democratize even faster. In December, after the elder politicians agreed to retire, the electorate picked delegates to a new National Assembly. This was Taiwan's first nonsupplementary—or plenary—election. The Nationalist Party performed well, receiving, according to some observers, a democratic mandate it had never before enjoyed. The scope of the victory also aided President Lee and his party in their efforts to make further constitutional changes and extend reforms into the realm of systemic change.

The following March, the National Assembly met to amend the Constitution. Delegates to the National Assembly would henceforth serve for four years, the Control Yuan would become a semijudicial body, and the provincial governor and the mayors of Taiwan's two metropolitan areas would become elected officials. Other reforms followed, including the abolition of the Taiwan Garrison Command, which had been responsible for censorship and tight control of the population and was a symbol of past repressive government.[74]

Its push for reform notwithstanding, the Nationalist Party did not perform well in the Legislative Yuan election in December 1992. The party was divided along ethnic lines and over the issue of relations with China. Some said the KMT's problems were President Lee's fault. Yet his popularity did not suffer. Lee subsequently formed a new cabinet and replaced the Mainland Chinese premier, Hau Pei-tsun (who had succeeded Lee Huan and with whom he had been in considerable disagreement), with Taiwanese Lien Chan.

Meanwhile, a political rapprochement between Taipei and Beijing appeared increasingly likely. President Lee had formally ended the state of war with China in 1991, investment funds from Taiwan were pouring into China in large amounts (surpassing even those from Japan and the United States), and people were crossing the Taiwan Strait in large numbers to visit and to do business. In April 1993, Taiwan and China held preliminary but official talks to normalize relations. Called the Koo-Wang talks, these negotiations resolved some problems that were part of the five decades of hostility between the two sides.[75]

In August, the Nationalist Party held its Fourteenth Congress amid party infighting and concern about future election defeats. Factionalism had become a serious problem; in fact, several members of the nonmainstream faction of the party, a group made up mostly of Mainland Chinese who perceived that President Lee supported an independent Taiwan, left the party to form the New Chinese Party (later renamed the New Party). As a result, President Lee increased his control over the KMT, even though party rules had been changed so as to give increased authority to members of the party who were elected to high office, notably legislators, some of whom competed with Lee for influence in the party.[76]

In 1994, the Republic of China's Constitution was amended again. One amendment provided for the direct election of the president and vice president (instead of election by the National Assembly). Following this, in early 1995 President Lee announced that he would be a candidate. In March 1996, the electorate gave Lee another term in what was Taiwan's first popular election of its president. The event was widely acclaimed by the media in Taiwan and abroad to be the first such election of a chief executive in five thousand years of Chinese history. Lee had indeed made a mark in history.

Meanwhile, in June 1995, as part of Taiwan's (created by Lee) "pragmatic diplomacy," Lee made a controversial trip to the United States at the invitation of his alma mater, Cornell University. The visit incensed Chinese leaders in Beijing who, in the midst of a leadership succession, ordered missile tests in the Taiwan Strait. Beijing conducted even more provocative tests, including the firing of missiles armed with live warheads close to Taiwan's two biggest ports during the lead-up to Taiwan's 1996 presidential election. In response, President Clinton dispatched two aircraft carriers, each with accompanying ships, to the area, thereby putting Washington in a face-off position with Beijing. Needless to say, ongoing talks between leaders in Beijing and Taipei were put on hold.[77]

The direct presidential election was a victory for Lee and Lien Chan (Lee's vice presidential running mate), the ruling Nationalist Party, and democratization in Taiwan. But Taiwan's political system remained under stress. To resolve systemic political problems that resulted from multiparty politics and an increasingly pluralistic society, President Lee convoked a National Development Conference in December. Delegates recommended more constitutional changes, some of which were made in mid-1997. One of them, the virtual elimination of the provincial government, was the most debated. James Soong, Taiwan's first elected governor (in 1994), tendered his resignation in displeasure after the conference. Lee and Soong became enemies, and this, together with crime and corruption worsening, caused Lee's image to suffer.

The United Kingdom's transfer of Hong Kong to the People's Republic of China in July 1997 created another problem for President Lee. According to leaders in Beijing, Taiwan was next. President Lee rejected Beijing's reunification proposals and its "one country, two systems" formula for uniting China. He asserted that Taiwan was not a colony and could, moreover, defend itself. Subsequently, the resounding defeat of the Nationalist Party in local elections in November gave the opposition Democratic Progressive Party (which called for Taiwan's independence) jurisdiction over more than 70 percent of the population at the local level.

Taiwan weathered the storm of the so-called Asian economic meltdown in 1997 and experienced quite normal economic growth in 1998, though its currency floated downward a bit. In the meantime economic problems elsewhere provided Taiwan with better opportunities for investment in the region. Economic stability, among other factors, explained the Nationalist Party's good performance in the December 1998 election. The ruling party made gains in the lawmaking body of government, and Ma Ying-jeou recaptured the Taipei mayorship for the KMT from the opposition DPP's Chen Shui-bian.

In 1999, President Lee, during an interview with a German radio station, stated that relations with China had to be considered as state-to-state relations or special state-to-state relations. Some observers said that Lee was in essence declaring Taiwan legally independent, although others said he was simply explaining what was obvious. Lee may have been responding to President Bill Clinton's "three no's" (no two Chinas; no one China, one Taiwan; no to Taiwan's joining international organizations that assume statehood for membership) statement made when he visited China in 1998. In any event, leaders in Beijing were incensed at Lee's proclamation and harshly criticized him. Some said China-Taiwan relations were deeply and perhaps permanently scarred as a result.[78]

Chen Shui-bian's Taiwan

In March 2000, Taiwan held its second direct presidential election. President Lee Teng-hui was in his midseventies and had held the nation's highest office for twelve years. He decided not to run again. Chen Shui-bian of the opposition Democratic Progressive Party won the election and was inaugurated the fifth president of the Republic of China in May. Chen was made from a different mold than past presidents—young, from a poor family, having never held a position in the national government, with no foreign experience, and more.[79]

How Chen won is also telling. President Lee supported his vice president, Lien Chan, for the ruling Nationalist Party nomination. Lien was eminently qualified; indeed, his experience easily exceeded that of the other candidates. Born into a famous local family, Lien had earned a PhD in political science at the University of Chicago. He returned to Taiwan and, a few years later, became the youngest minister in Taiwan's history. He served in several cabinet positions, was governor of Taiwan, premier, and vice president. Lien was Taiwanese but had close contacts with Mainland Chinese in the party and the government. Notwithstanding the many factors that favored Lien, Taiwan by this time had evolved into a popular mass democracy, and Lien was not so much a man of the people.

James Soong was, and his popularity ratings were much higher than Lien's. Soong was also highly qualified: a PhD from Georgetown University, name recognition from several years of heading the Government Information Office, and experience as the party's secretary-general. He was also the first-ever elected governor of Taiwan. Soong wanted the nomination and, like many others, felt he should get it. But President Lee opposed it. Some said that Lee didn't want a non-Taiwanese president, but others cited different reasons. In any case, Lee prevailed and Soong ran as an independent, which divided the conservative or KMT vote.

During the early months of the campaign, Soong's poll numbers were better by a large margin than those of either Chen Shui-bian or Lien Chan. But, as the election approached, a KMT legislator released information (many thought upon Lee's order, though Lee denied this) indicating Soong had diverted party money into his own bank accounts and to those of his relatives when he was party secretary-general. Though he was later exonerated, the charges severely hurt Soong, who had a reputation for honesty. Soong was further handicapped by lack of a party, a good campaign organization, and money.

A divided KMT played into Chen Shui-bian's hands. The DPP was not split: Chen won the nomination of his party without difficulty, and his party was more unified than usual. Chen also ran a masterful campaign. He handled controversial issues deftly. Most important, he played down his previously strong stand for independence. His party and his campaign team exploited ethnic politics, the KMT's corrupt image, and the split between Lien and Soong. Finally, Chen convinced many voters that a change in ruling parties would bolster Taiwan's democratization.

Down the stretch, some noted business leaders announced their support for Chen, as did Nobel Prize winner Lee Yuan-tseh, who headed Taiwan's most famous think tank, Academia Sinica. Chinese leaders in Beijing, including the premier, publicly attacked Chen and harshly warned Taiwan's voters not to vote for the "independence candidate"—meaning Chen. His effort backfired and helped Chen win.[80]

Chen won by a very slim margin. Soong won just over 2 percent less of the popular vote. Lien was a distant third. Had the KMT not damaged Soong's campaign, Soong would have won. Had there been a runoff election (a provision in the constitutions of many nations, but not Taiwan's), Chen would not have been elected president. Soong won the majority of the vote from all of Taiwan's minority ethnic groups (Aborigines, Hakka, and Mainland Chinese). He won the female vote. He won in almost every part of Taiwan except the south. Chen won among the Fukien Taiwanese and by a large margin in the south. After the election, many questioned Chen's mandate.

Not only did Chen not have a strong mandate, his party, the DPP, had never ruled and was by its history and makeup not prepared for that task. After the election, Soong formed a political party called the People First Party (PFP). Many of its members felt Soong should have been president. Despite hard feelings toward the KMT, the PFP joined the KMT to form a strong opposition bloc. Chen's party held only a third of the seats in the Legislative Yuan; thus the new president faced a divided government.

Making matters worse, Taiwan's political system was a mixed one—presidential, parliamentary, and cabinet. Thus, the role of each branch of the government vis-à-vis the other was not clear. Nor were the powers of each well defined. So Chen decided to build a coalition government and made moves in that direction. He gave up his positions in the DPP and appointed members of the KMT to cabinet positions—even his premier, Tang Fei. But Chen didn't consult with opposition party leaders and in so doing showed a lack of leadership while seriously underestimating the opposition. Alternatively he feared the legislature would usurp his powers and saw playing ethnic politics as his way out. In any case, coalition government was soon forgotten.[81]

Differences with the opposition parties worsened. In fact, the mutual hostility came to a head less than six months into Chen's presidency over the issue of building Taiwan's fourth nuclear plant. Chen's party had long opposed nuclear power and had campaigned fervently against it. The problem was that the plant had already been approved by a previous legislature. In response to Chen's decision to nix the plant, the opposition initiated an impeachment proceeding against him but then withdrew it. Chen was embarrassed and his poll numbers dropped precipitously. His saving grace was that the impeachment effort also damaged the opposition. The result was even more intense political polarization, gridlock, and malaise.

The economy promptly went into a tailspin. The country witnessed negative economic growth (almost 2 percent for 2001) and unemployment figures that were higher than most citizens had ever seen. Chen blamed the opposition. He also attributed the downturn to the weak global economy. But many saw Chen's poor management of the economy as the main cause. Meanwhile, many industries, including many of Taiwan's "best and brightest" companies (especially computer and semiconductor enterprises), started moving all or part of their operations to China to take advantage of cheaper labor costs, lower taxes, and fewer regulations and to be closer to a gigantic and booming market. Chen and his supporters were confused about whether to try to stop the exodus.

President Chen proclaimed that he would be able to accomplish more and could resolve many of the country's travails if his party could win the legislative election in December 2001. Former president Lee Teng-hui came out of retirement and formed a new political party, the Taiwan Solidarity Union (TSU), to help Chen. Chen's DPP and the TSU were labeled the green bloc, or pan-green. Both groups resorted to playing on ethnic sentiments during the campaign. DPP campaign strategists even invoked Adolph Hitler's name as a model in some of their campaign advertisements, much to the consternation of many foreigners in Taiwan. The ethnic appeal worked, as did efforts to label the opposition parties as loyal to China and not Taiwan. The DPP increased the number of seats it held in the legislature by a sizable margin while the TSU performed very well for a new party. The KMT performed very badly, but most of its losses were gains for Soong's People First Party, which made a bigger percentage gain than the DPP. Independents and other parties all but vanished. The opposition (the KMT and the PFP) kept its legislative majority.[82]

Chen and his vice president, Annette Lu, won reelection in 2004, but under quite questionable circumstances. Both were shot, though their wounds were superficial, the day before the voting. President Chen ordered the police and the military to remain at their posts, depriving them of the opportunity to vote. Their vote would probably have been for Lien and Soong, who had joined forces to make a strong opposition ticket. This and sympathy voting for Chen and Lu gave them the victory, which the opinion polls, the stock market, and those betting on the election didn't anticipate. The opposition didn't accept the election results and organized public protest demonstrations while challenging the election in court. As a result, political polarization got even worse.[83]

Even before this President Chen had become unpopular in the United States for playing ethnic politics and provoking China at a time when the Bush administration was preoccupied with the war on terrorism. US leaders retaliated by repeating America's one-China policy while warning Chen and even questioning Taiwan's sovereignty. Chen was not allowed transit stops in major US cities when traveling to Latin America and elsewhere, as had been the case early on in his presidency. US State Department personnel generally refused to talk to Chen or anyone in his administration.[84] This hurt Chen's image.

Meanwhile, corruption infected the Chen administration and the DPP. This and an economy that remained in the doldrums in the minds of many citizens, together with President Chen's reputation for poor governance, playing on ethnic ill will, and ruining relations with the United States and China, caused the DPP to lose public confidence. Worse, as legislative and presidential elections approached in 2008, Chen administration officials were under indictment or in jail for corruption, and Chen's wife was indicted for perjury, falsifying documents, and stealing government funds. Chen's son-in-law was convicted of insider trading. The prosecutor said President Chen would have been indicted except that he was protected by presidential immunity. Shih Ming-teh, a former DPP chairman and party hero, launched a mass movement against corruption and against Chen. A million or more turned out at some of his rallies. Chen survived, but his poll numbers fell into the teens, sometimes below.[85] Chen's presidency ended ignominiously.

The KMT Returns to Power Under Ma Ying-jeou

In January 2008, the KMT defeated the DPP badly in the national legislative election. President Chen assumed blame. Chen forthwith resigned as chairman of the DPP, and Frank Hsieh, a former mayor of Kaohsiung and premier for a short time under Chen, assumed the chairmanship of the party. Shortly after that, Hsieh won the party's nomination to run for the presidency in March. President Chen supported someone else. Hsieh picked Su Tseng-chang as his vice presidential running mate. Both generally, but not totally, distanced themselves from Chen.

Ma Ying-jeou, the KMT's candidate, with Vincent Siew his running mate, soundly defeated the DPP's candidates, getting more votes than any presidential election ticket in history. Most observers blamed Chen for the DPP's loss.[86] But the KMT and its pan-blue allied parties were unified and ran a professional campaign focusing on Chen administration corruption while promising better economic times and improved relations with the United States and China. Ma's stellar academic credentials (a law degree from Harvard University), good looks, and reputation for strict honesty also helped.

Ma began his presidency with a clear mandate and a solid majority in the legislature. However, soon after Ma became president the world fell into recession, and Taiwan, being very global and dependent upon exports, was profoundly affected. Thus, although Taiwan's economic downturn was not his fault, Ma's campaign promises to resurrect the economy were noticeably unfulfilled. The fourth quarter witnessed negative growth of 8.36 percent, and the year ended with the gross national product (GNP) having expanded by only 2 percent. The next year, 2009, was even worse. The economy contracted through three quarters, and the year ended with growth in negative territory by 1.9 percent.

Further denting President Ma's reputation, in August Typhoon Morakot hit Taiwan. It was the worst typhoon in the island's recorded history and did tremendous damage in life and property. Ma took the position that local governments should handle the response. Although perhaps a good idea in theory, he was seen as not caring, and the opposition chided him for making a feeble response to the disaster. His credibility suffered, as did his approval ratings as measured in various opinion surveys. All of this seemed the proximate cause for the KMT losing a number of subsequent local and replacement elections.[87]

In 2010 President Ma negotiated an economic agreement called the Economic Cooperation Framework Agreement (ECFA) that increased commercial ties with China, including reducing a number of tariffs and loosening restrictions on investments, tourism, and other economic ties. The DPP led protests against the agreement, even assaulting Chinese representatives who visited Taiwan. The opposition charged it would make Taiwan dependent upon China and lead to political agreements that would "surrender" Taiwan's sovereignty. The public, however, approved of the deal, and it seemed a sensible agreement in view of the fact that otherwise Taiwan would be shut out of trade with Southeast Asian countries as a result of an economic bloc linking China and the Association of Southeast Asian Nations (ASEAN) concluded early in the year, plus the fact that already for several years Taiwan had been exporting more to China (40 percent in 2010) than anywhere else, and the United States, Europe, and Japan were experiencing economic difficulties.

Meanwhile, in late 2009 Taiwan's economy turned around and continued in a rapid growth mode during 2010. In fact, growth in the gross domestic product (GDP) was better than China's. Unemployment declined and incomes increased. The stock market rose. It appeared that Ma and the KMT had made astute choices in fixing the economy.

Regarding the DPP, not long after Ma's inauguration, Tsai Ing-wen, who had served as vice premier under Chen Shui-bian, was elected chairwoman. Tsai had not been close to Chen and was not tainted by his corruption; in fact, Tsai was seen as a clean politician. She also represented a change from previous DPP leaders being a scholar, a newcomer to the party, and female (the DPP having a reputation for male chauvinism). She went a long way in rehabilitating the DPP, including helping it win some local and replacement elections.

In 2010 Tsai was a candidate in the races for Taiwan's metropolitan mayors, city councils, and borough chiefs. She ran for mayor of the newly constituted New Taipei City. She was handicapped because the district had more KMT voters, but the election was close. Though she lost, this did not hurt her reputation or weaken her leadership of the opposition party. In that election the KMT won three of five of the mayorships and was proclaimed the winner of this "midterm" election contest.

On managing foreign relations, President Ma was regarded as having done a good job. Tension with China had diminished sharply, and there was no longer talk of war as there had been during the Chen era. In fact, the Taiwan Strait was dropped from being ranked the number one flashpoint in the world by most observers. As a product of cordial relations with Beijing, Taiwan was able to gain representation in the World Health Organization and lost none of its twenty-three diplomatic partners. Relations with the United States were also good. The tensions that characterized the period before Ma became president were gone. In January 2010 Washington announced an arms deal with Taiwan exceeding $6 billion, though it did not include the advanced F-16 C/D fighters Taiwan wanted.

In January 2012 Ma stood for reelection. His vice president Vincent Siew had contracted cancer, considered himself too old to run again, and declined to do so. Ma selected Premier Wu Den-yi to be his running mate. Tsai, running with Su Jia-chyuan, a former minister of interior and secretary-general of the party, challenged Ma and at times seemed close to winning. In the end, however, Ma and Wu won easily. In fact, they got more votes than Tsai and Su from all ethnic groups, all groups by level of education, women and men, and from voters in both north and central Taiwan. The KMT meanwhile won handily in the concurrent legislative election (the first time the two elections were held together).[88]

The big wins for Ma and the KMT generated talk that the KMT (after winning the two previous important elections) was back in power perhaps semipermanently. Simultaneously the DPP took stock of its losses and admitted it had some fundamental problems it needed to handle. The party, its leaders admitted, did not convince voters it could deal with Taiwan's economic problems. The DPP had a good reputation for governance in local politics but could not convert this to winning on leadership nationally. It lost badly on foreign policy, especially dealing with China and the United States. Because of Taiwan's maturing democracy, independence was no longer a good issue for the DPP and neither was playing ethnic politics, yet its base supported these issues. Thus there was a serious disconnect between forward-looking leaders and the party's base that needed to be resolved.

At this juncture the KMT seemed solidly back in power. Some pundits suggested this was what was natural and that it would last. Others opined that Taiwan would likely experience frequent changes in ruling parties in the future.[89]

Notes

1. This date has been pushed back even further by recent archeological discoveries. See Chen-wen Tsung, "Clues to a Distant Past," *Free China Review* (April 1991): 61.

2. W. G. Goddard, *Formosa: A Study in Chinese History* (East Lansing: Michigan State University Press, 1966), 3–5.

3. See *Area Handbook for the Republic of China* (Washington, DC: US Government Printing Office, 1969), 22, for a discussion of this topic.

4. See Goddard, *Formosa*, 16, 20. Also see James W. Davidson, *The Island of Formosa: Past and Present* (New York: Oxford University Press, 1988), 3.

5. See Chen-wen Tsung, "Building on the Past," *Free China Review* (June 1992): 85.

6. David Barber, "DNA Shows Maoris Came from Taiwan, Says Scientist," *South China Morning Post*, August 11, 1998 (Internet edition), n.p.

7. See Chiao-min Hsieh, *Taiwan—Ilha Formosa: A Geography in Perspective* (Washington, DC: Butterworths, 1964), 131–138.

8. Taiwan was either regarded as an "uncivilized" area, in contrast to China, which was civilized, or an area that was partly civilized and thus a tributary state. See John K. Fairbank, ed., *The Chinese World Order* (Cambridge, MA: Harvard University Press, 1968).

9. This claim was most recently mentioned in a twenty-four-page pamphlet titled "The Taiwan Question and the Reunification of China" (Beijing: Taiwan Affairs Office and Information Office, State Council, 1993), referred to hereafter as China's White Paper on Taiwan.

10. See John K. Fairbank, *The United States and China* (New York: Viking Press, 1967), 13.

11. See China's White Paper on Taiwan. The different viewpoints espoused by China and Taiwan are discussed in John F. Copper, "The Origins of Conflict Across the Taiwan Strait: The Problem of Differences in Perceptions," *Journal of Contemporary China* (June 1997): 199–227.

12. See Davidson, *Island of Formosa*, 3–4. Also see Simon Long, *Taiwan: China's Last Frontier* (New York: St. Martin's Press, 1991), 5.

13. Some Japanese writers have suggested that the Japanese may have been the first settlers. See Shinkichi Ito, "An Outline of Formosan History," in *Formosa Today*, ed. Mark Mancall (New York: Praeger, 1964), 44. Also see Davidson, *Island of Formosa*, 6.

14. See *Area Handbook for the Republic of China*, 22.

15. Ibid.

16. See Davidson, *Island of Formosa*, 4.

17. Ibid., 5.

18. See Long, *Taiwan*, 4.

19. For details on the period of Western colonial influence, see Goddard, *Formosa*, chapters 3 and 4. See also Hsieh, *Taiwan—Ilha Formosa*, chapter 11.

20. See Goddard, *Formosa*, 51.

21. See George M. Beckman, "Brief Episodes—Dutch and Spanish Rule," in Paul K. T. Sih, ed., *Taiwan in Modern Times* (New York: St. John's University Press, 1973)

22. Long, *Taiwan*, 10–11.

23. For details about Cheng Ch'eng-kung's life and accomplishments from quite different perspectives, see Cheng Cheng I-chou, *Cheng Cheng-kung Chuan* [biography of Cheng Cheng-kung], reprinted in Taiwan in Wen-hsien Ts'ung K'an, *Collection of Works on Taiwan Series* (Taipei: Office of Economic Research, 1960); Ch'u Ch'i, *Cheng Cheng-kung* (Wuhan: People's, 1956); and George Phillips, "The Life of Cheng Cheng-kung," *China Review* 13, nos. 2 and 3 (1985).

24. See Parris H. Chang, "Cheng Cheng-kung (Koxinga): A Patriot, Nationalist and Nation-Builder," in Sih, *Taiwan in Modern Times*.

25. See Davidson, *The Island of Formosa*, 52.

26. See Goddard, *Formosa*, 99.

27. See, for example, Wen-hsiung Hsu, "Frontier Social Organization and Social Disorder in Ch'ing Taiwan," in *China's Island Frontier: Studies in the Historical Geography of Taiwan*, ed. Ronald G. Knapp (Honolulu: University of Hawaii Press, 1980). Hsu notes that there was, on average, an incidence of communal strife every 2.7 years during the 212 years of Ch'ing rule.

28. See Chan Lien, "Taiwan in China's External Relations," in Sih, *Taiwan in Modern Times*, 88–89.

29. Joseph W. Ballantine, *Formosa: A Problem for United States Foreign Policy* (Washington, DC: Brookings Institution, 1952), 17. Note that the Chinese government at this time still did not completely understand the concept of sovereignty.

30. See George H. Kerr, *Formosa: Licensed Revolution and the Home Rule Movement, 1895–1945* (Honolulu: University of Hawaii Press, 1974), 27.

31. Ibid., 14.

32. Ibid., 17–20.

33. See Samuel Ho, *The Economic Development of Taiwan, 1860–1970* (New Haven, CT: Yale University Press, 1978), for an analysis of Taiwan's economic development under the Japanese.

34. Kerr, *Formosa*, 88–89.

35. Ibid., 91. See pp. 89–91 for additional data on railroad and other infrastructure building.

36. See Ming-min Peng, *A Taste of Freedom* (New York: Holt, Reinhart and Winston, 1972), 7. Peng notes that China was not concerned about public health problems and that, because so many Japanese soldiers died in Taiwan in 1895, sanitation became a priority for Japan.

37. See Kerr, *Formosa*, 59–61. The *pao chia* system was called *Hoko* in Japanese.

38. See Harry J. Lamley, "Taiwan Under Japanese Rule, 1895–1945: The Vicissitudes of Colonialism," in *Taiwan: A New History*, ed. Murray A. Rubinstein (Armonk, NY: M. E. Sharpe, 2007), 240–242.

39. See Denny Roy, *Taiwan: A Political History* (Ithaca, NY: Cornell University Press, 2003), 52–53; and Tse-han Lai, Ramon H. Myers, and Wou Wei, *A Tragic Beginning: The Taiwan Uprising of February 28, 1947* (Stanford, CA: Stanford University Press, 1991), 38.

40. Christopher Hughes, *Taiwan and Chinese Nationalism, National Identity and Status in International Society* (London: Routledge, 1997), 22.

41. See George H. Kerr, *Formosa Betrayed* (Boston: Houghton Mifflin, 1965), chapter 2.

42. See Hughes, *Taiwan and Chinese Nationalism*, 5.

43. See Kerr, *Formosa Betrayed*, chapter 3.

44. Ibid.

45. Roy, *Taiwan: A Political History*, 60–64.

46. Ibid., chapter 5.

47. Ibid., 173–182.

48. Historians sympathetic to both the Nationalist government and Taiwanese independence blame Ch'en Yi for the difficulties in Taiwan in the late 1940s—even problems that occurred after he was removed from office—because many of his supporters and appointees remained. For example, see Fred W. Riggs, *Formosa Under Chinese Nationalist Rule* (New York: Macmillan, 1952; reprint, New York: Octagon Books, 1972), 45–48. Also see Kerr, *Formosa Betrayed*, chapter 6. For a less harsh treatment of Ch'en, see Lai, Myers, and Wei, *Tragic Beginning*, chapters 3 and 4, especially pages 97–98.

49. The number of Taiwanese killed at this time is a matter of guesswork. Kerr (in *Formosa Betrayed*) puts the number at 20,000. Lai, Myers, and Wei say it is at most 10,000. For some years, government documents indicated that only several hundred were killed. In 1992, the government released a detailed report on the incident and put the number killed at between 18,000 and 28,000.

50. Roy, *Taiwan: A Political History*, 185.

51. See Murray A. Rubinstein, "Postscript and Conclusion," in Rubinstein, *Taiwan: A New History*, 495.

52. See Hung Chien-chao, *A History of Taiwan* (il Cerechio, 2000), 257–259; and Roy, *Taiwan: A Political History*, chapter 4, for different accounts.

53. See Edgar Snow, *Red Star over China* (New York: Random House, 1938), 33–89.

54. See Frank A. Kieran, *The Fluke That Saved Formosa* (Cambridge: Center for International Studies, Massachusetts Institute of Technology, 1954).

55. See Riggs, *Formosa Under Chinese Nationalist Rule*, chapter 4, for an early account of this process.

56. See Neil H. Jacoby, *U.S. Aid to Taiwan: A Study of Foreign Aid, Self-Help and Development* (New York: Praeger, 1966), chapter 17.

57. See A. Doak Barnett, *Communist China and Asia: A Challenge to American Policy* (New York: Vintage Books, 1960), 415.

58. Chiang Kai-shek had long spoken of the "liberation" of the Mainland as partly political. In the late 1950s, after the United States made it clear that it did not want to get involved in a war with China over the Offshore Islands, Chiang began to speak more of the political nature of the task. Some in Taiwan interpreted this to mean that the mission was being given up or at least de-emphasized. In about 1958, Taiwan began making plans for economic growth and diverting its attention from invasion of the Mainland to the development of the island.

59. I believe that the fighting on the Sino-Soviet border and a new administration in the United States brought about a change in US-China relations. Some scholars think the policy change occurred a year or two later.

60. Technically, the Republic of China withdrew from the United Nations, as it said it would do if Beijing received a majority of support from the UN members for its bid to membership. It is generally believed that the United States opposed Beijing's joining the United Nations at Taipei's expense, but, given the situation and the rules of UN membership, there was no alternative. Many US allies voted for Beijing, an indication that Washington had not asked its friends for votes of support for Taipei.

61. For details, see John F. Copper, *China Diplomacy: The Washington-Taipei-Beijing Triangle* (Boulder, CO: Westview Press, 1992), 38–39.

62. See Ray S. Cline, *Chiang Ching-kuo Remembered: The Man and His Political Legacy* (Washington, DC: US Global Strategy Center, 1989), for details on Chiang Ching-kuo's life.

63. See Peter R. Moody Jr., *Political Change on Taiwan: A Study of Ruling Party Adaptability* (New York: Praeger, 1992), 186–187.

64. For details on Chiang Ching-kuo's leadership and political and economic development in Taiwan, see Shao-chuan Leng, ed., *Chiang Ching-kuo's Leadership in the Development of the Republic of China on Taiwan* (Lanham, MD: University Press of America, 1993).

65. In a sense, this represented a reversal in US policy inasmuch as previous US presidents had declared that Taiwan was part of China. President Nixon had stated that this was the view of both sides but didn't set forth a US policy.

66. For details, see Copper, *China Diplomacy*, 67–75.

67. Jaushieh Joseph Wu, *Taiwan's Democratization: Forces Behind the New Momentum* (Hong Kong: Oxford University Press, 1995), 39.

68. See, for example, Cline, *Chiang Ching-kuo Remembered*; and Leng, *Chiang Ching-Kuo's Leadership*.

69. For biographical information on Lee, see Shih-shan Henry Tsai, *Lee Teng-hui and Taiwan's Quest for Identity* (New York: Palgrave/Macmillan, 2005). For information on Lee's presidency in his own words, see Lee Teng-hui, *Creating the Future: Towards a New Era for the Chinese People* (Taipei: Government Information Office, 1993). For a critical assessment of the Lee era, see Wei-chin Lee and T. Y. Wang, eds., *Sayonara to the Lee Teng-hui Era: Politics in Taiwan, 1988–2000* (Lanham, MD: University Press of America, 2003).

70. See Roy, *Taiwan: A Political History*, 178.

71. See John F. Copper, "The KMT's 13th Party Congress: Reform, Democratization, New Blood," in *Modernizing East Asia: Economic and Cultural Dimensions of Political Change*, ed. Cynthia Chenault (Jamaica, NY: St. John's University Press, 1989).

72. For details on the 1990 election, see Tsai, *Lee Teng-hui*, 177.

73. John F. Copper, *Playing with Fire: Looming War with China Over Taiwan* (Westport, CT: Praeger, 2006), 32–35.

74. For details, see Linda Chao and Ramon H. Myers, *The First Chinese Democracy: Political Life in the Republic of China on Taiwan* (Baltimore: Johns Hopkins University Press, 1998), chapters 10 and 11.

75. See Hungdah Chiu, *Koo-Wang Talks and the Prospect of Building Constructive and Stable Relations Across the Taiwan Strait* (Baltimore: University of Maryland School of Law, 1993).

76. See John F. Copper, "The KMT's 14th Party Congress: Toward Unity or Disunity," *American Journal of Chinese Studies* (October 1994): 59–83.

77. For details, see Copper, *Playing with Fire*; and John W. Garver, *Face Off: China, the United States, and Taiwan's Democratization* (Seattle: University of Washington Press, 1997).

78. See Shang Lijun, *China and Taiwan: Cross-Strait Relations Under Chen Shui-bian* (London: Zed Books, 2002), chapter 3.

79. For Chen's autobiography, see Chen Shui-bian, *The Son of Taiwan: The Life of Chen Shui-bian and His Dreams for Taiwan* (Taipei: Taiwan, 2002).

80. See John F. Copper, *Taiwan's 2000 Presidential and Vice-Presidential Election: Consolidating Democracy and Creating a New Era of Politics* (Baltimore: University of Maryland School of Law, 2000).

81. For details, see John F. Copper, "Taiwan in Gridlock," in John F. Copper, ed., *Taiwan in Troubled Times: Essays on the Chen Shui-bian Presidency* (Singapore: World Scientific, 2002), 19–52.

82. See John F. Copper, *Taiwan's 2001 Legislative Magistrates and Mayors Election*, East Asian Institute (EAI) Contemporary China Series 33 (Singapore: World Scientific, 2002).

83. John F. Copper, *Taiwan's 2004 Presidential and Vice Presidential Election: Democracy's Consolidation or Devolution* (Baltimore: University of Maryland School of Law, 2004).

84. See John F. Copper, "Why the Bush Administration Soured on Taiwan," in *U.S.-China Relations: Cooperation and Competition in Northeast Asia*, ed. Suisheng Zhao (London: Palgrave/Macmillan, 2008).

85. For details on corruption in the Chen administration, see John F. Copper, *The Blight of Corruption in the Chen Administration in Taiwan*, Background Brief, East Asian Institute, December 2007.

86. John F. Copper, *Taiwan's 2008 Presidential and Vice Presidential Election: Maturing Democracy* (Baltimore: University of Maryland School of Law, 2008).

87. Thomas B. Gold, "Taiwan in 2009: Eroding Landslide," *Asian Survey*, January/February 2010, 74.

88. John F. Copper, *Taiwan's 2012 Presidential/Vice Presidential and Legislative Elections* (Baltimore: University of Maryland School of Law, 2012).

89. John F. Copper, *The KMT Returns to Power: Taiwan's Elections 2008–2012* (Lanham, MD: Lexington Books, 2013), chapter 5.

3

SOCIETY

TAIWAN'S SOCIETY AND THE CULTURE upon which it is built are basically traditional and Chinese. More specifically, they are rural southern Chinese in origin.
Taiwan also has an elite culture that is somewhat different. Both have evolved considerably in Taiwan—affected by interactions with the Aborigines, the population's
contact with other people in the region, European and Japanese colonization, and
considerable Western influence in recent years, particularly American. Rapid economic growth since the 1960s has given rise to Taiwan's fast-paced democratization, which in turn produced profound social change. Both have given rise to
many of the problems present in Western countries. The breakdown of tradition,
the weakening of the family, alienation, and other pains of a society in rapid transition were and still are evident. Urbanization, crime, youth problems, divorce,
and drug use are all regarded as serious matters. But Taiwan's problems are less
acute than those in most other quickly modernizing or modern countries even
though most citizens view many of these problems with alarm. The strength of
Chinese culture and its strong family tradition have made many social ills less serious. Social change in Taiwan is worthy of study because it has been so rapid and
some of the solutions to its worst problems—and the new society itself—are
unique. The differences in culture among the ethnic groups help explain Taiwan's
diversity and to some extent its colorful and at times raucous politics. Finally, Taiwan's culture and society connect intimately to the issue of Taiwan's identity and
whether Taiwan is essentially Chinese or is different and whether its future is with

China or not. Culturally, Taiwan grew apart from China for many years, though recently, with an increase in cross-strait contacts and China becoming capitalist and to some extent returning to its traditional culture, this trend has reversed course. Some say a "unified culture" is developing as a product of economic integration and declining admiration of the US, Europe, and Japan.

Social Structure and Order

Before the twentieth century, for a number of reasons the various groups of people inhabiting Taiwan had little contact with each other and, therefore, maintained quite distinct social systems.[1] The Aborigines' social systems were tribal, though their social order differed markedly between two broadly defined groups: the mountain Aborigines and the lowland Aborigines. The mountain Aborigines' social structures were more communal and less settled; the lowlanders' social systems were more sedentary and in some important ways resembled those of Chinese agrarian society. However, customs, mores, and social systems varied considerably among the tribes. In social organization, some groups were classless, while others distinguished between the chieftains and the common people or followers. In some tribes, social status was determined largely by age. Most, but not all, were male dominant: patriarchal and patrilineal. Depending on the tribe, married couples lived with a spouse's parents or apart. All of the Aboriginal groups were monogamous.[2]

Today, the mountain Aborigines' social systems are much more in evidence than those of the lowlanders. With the coming of Chinese migration, many lowlander Aborigines were either killed or assimilated by the Chinese; others retreated into the mountainous areas, whereupon they adopted the mountain Aborigines' societal patterns. In addition, the mountain Aborigines resisted change and assimilation more than the lowland Aborigines.[3]

Chinese immigrants brought their customs, mores, and norms to Taiwan—except they did not bring with them the ancient Chinese prejudice against physical work or necessity forced them to abandon that facet of their culture. Nor did education become the basis of elite class status in Taiwan as it had been in China. Social position was founded more on differences in privileges between the rulers and the ruled and the possession or control of arms, wealth, and sometimes positions in secret societies. Taiwan was a dangerous land, of which the Chinese there were constantly made aware by the Aboriginal practice of headhunting. The authority and status accrued by weapons and money translated into a social order and a political system similar to those in feudal Europe and Japan and quite unlike that in China.

Social relations among the Chinese immigrants were, from the onset of their migration to Taiwan, founded on the village, which was typically controlled by one or a few powerful families. Dominant families chose village leaders who regulated land tenure and were responsible for security. Social norms and rules were established and enforced by family elders. The important families controlled large sections of the flat land on the island, including most of the farmland.[4] Thus, a social hierarchy was to a large degree founded on land tenure.

The landlord system that took root in Taiwan several centuries ago eventually evolved into a mixture of traditional feudalism and government-controlled land rights—the latter a product of Taiwan's experience with Western colonialism. Later, landlords subcontracted with cultivators who then hired farm laborers. Some landlords supervised the use of land; others held official government positions, maintaining their authority and privilege in that way. Those who could provide the Chinese population with protection against Aboriginal raids also acquired rights over land. Serfdom did not become part of Taiwan's feudal order, but indentured servitude, male and female, was common. Men worked in the fields, women in the home. Female indentured servitude lasted until the Japanese colonial period when Tokyo abolished it.[5]

The social hierarchy of the Chinese population of Taiwan was patriarchal and patrilineal. Only males were heirs, and as a consequence female children were seen as temporary members of the family and thus were trained in household skills so, at the proper age, they could be married into a friendly and, if possible, rich and powerful household. A family lacking a male child would adopt one, usually an infant, most often from a relative. Alternatively, the family would "adopt" a son-in-law, who agreed that his children would take his wife's family name, but this practice was considered a loss of face for the man and was less common than infant adoption.

Until the age of about four, male and female children were raised together, with few distinctions based on gender. Typically children were given little responsibility until about the age of six. By the age of sixteen, children assumed many adult duties, and by eighteen they were usually working. Although families were large, children were generally treated with considerable kindness and were regarded as precious possessions. The mother was mainly responsible for rearing the children, but grandparents and older siblings also played a role, as did more distant relatives at times.[6]

Authority within the Chinese family was to a large degree based on age, especially when the extended family lived in one house. Respect for elders also extended throughout society. Older people, even when barely able to work, often kept positions in businesses or government because of the social taboo against forced retirement. Elders served as a stabilizing influence in society, though age did not necessarily equate with authority outside the household unless combined with high social class or important business or political connections.

In terms of the social-class hierarchy, working for the government or in education conferred elite status. However, as Taiwan began to develop economically, there was another route to the higher class: commerce. Some scholars thus identify two upper classes in Taiwan: the first, those with an education who constituted a scholar-official class as in China before 1949, and the second, those who found wealth through business. Though both had to adjust to unique modernizing forces in Taiwan, over time they merged to some degree with the impact of money in politics.[7]

In Taiwan—as in China, Japan, and other Asian countries—parents or other relatives arranged marriages. These marriages bonded families, and young men and women frequently had little or no say about the selection of their mates. In fact, it was not uncommon for a couple to have had no acquaintance before marriage; sometimes they had not even seen each other. Young married women were usually subservient to their husbands and to the elders in his family, but their status was no lower and, in fact, was generally higher than that of women in most traditional societies. Married women's status usually increased over time because of the respect for age in Chinese culture.

In terms of social structure, norms, and mores, early on Taiwan was not much different from China. But when the Communists took control of China in 1949, they sought to reconstruct society, and, in the process, they deliberately weakened the family system and redirected the individual's loyalty toward the state and the Communist Party. This had a profound impact on the culture. Nothing similar happened in Taiwan, although the government endeavored to nurture nationalism for the purpose of building the state, and the central role of the family in society suffered somewhat in the process. The modernization processes, on the other hand—especially urbanization, mass education, consumerism, materialism, and Westernization—profoundly affected the family system in Taiwan. These forces of change have been gradual but very strong and have generally favored a weaker family structure and the nuclear family over the extended family. In China, since the death of Mao, the family has to some degree been restored to its central societal role; in this respect, there is convergence with Taiwan.

Ethnic Issues

As noted in Chapter 1, four ethnic or subethnic groups populate Taiwan: the Aborigines, Fukien Chinese (also called Fukienese or Hoklo or Holo), Hakka, and Mainland Chinese (or Mainlanders). There is disagreement about whether the term "ethnic" accurately describes the Chinese groups; some prefer "subethnic" or "provincial." The Aborigines, however, are generally considered "ethnically" different from the three Chinese groups; in fact, they are sometimes said to be a different race from the other three. The three categories of Chinese may be said to constitute groups that are distinct in culture, language, and in some other ways. But the Mainland Chinese are much more heterogeneous and lack most of the qualities of an ethnic or even subethnic group. The three Chinese groups are all

Han people that make up around 90 percent of the population of China. If self-identification by the four groups is considered important, then they constitute discrete groups.

In the past, the Aborigines were severely discriminated against by the Chinese population, because of the danger they posed to the Chinese communities and the strife between the two groups that lasted for centuries. Stereotypes of the Aborigines as headhunters and the associated fear this caused the Chinese lasted long after this practice became uncommon and even extinct. Prejudice against the Aborigines, based on their "primitive" lifestyle and less success in education, business, and the like, as well as their not being Chinese, persists to this day.[8]

Under the Japanese, the Aborigines were kept separate from each other and the rest of the population. Nationalist Chinese policy was to integrate them into Chinese society. It seemed that neither worked. The Aborigines are afflicted with higher rates of unemployment, alcoholism, adolescent prostitution, and various other social ills. Because of this, they have for some time received special education, job training, and other benefits through provisions in the Constitution to help minority groups and the poor. In recent years, social welfare and other such programs to help the Aborigines have proliferated. Still, the Aborigines remain largely outside the mainstream of society and are considered underprivileged. Most do not want to be assimilated. Many view their government's social programs as conferring few real benefits while causing a further cultural breakdown.

The Aborigines may face an even more serious problem. According to government figures, Aborigines living in special communities have a combined population of 512,000—around 2 percent of Taiwan's total population. Their birthrate is slightly higher than the Chinese population, but so is their death rate. Probably one-sixth of Aborigines have permanently or semipermanently migrated to the cities in search of work, compared to 5,000 who lived in cities in 1960 and 30,000 in 1980. The histories of the various Aborigine tribes, which are mainly oral, are being lost; so are their languages, arts, and songs. Some say the Aborigines are heading for assimilation and extinction.[9]

Democracy, on the other hand, has begun to transform the Aborigines into vocal minority groups that have become unified politically. Most Aboriginal organizations advocate policies of separateness so as to preserve their society and culture. Thus their social integration and the obliteration of their culture are not foregone conclusions. Furthermore, the integration and assimilation of the Aborigines are not firm government policies.

The culture and social structure of the Hakka Chinese were unique in China before they migrated to Taiwan. Hakkas long suffered from various forms of prejudice; they were even barred from taking the imperial examination throughout various periods of Chinese history. Inasmuch as the Hakkas had long experienced persecution, they took with them to Taiwan a strong sense of separateness and "clannishness." They retained this because of the dangers of living in close proximity to the Aborigines—closer than the Fukien Chinese who forced the Hakkas from good farmland close to the shore and into hilly less fertile areas. Hakka culture was also affected by their minority status in Taiwan vis-à-vis Fukienese Taiwanese with whom they frequently fought. Notwithstanding the cultural homogenization Taiwan has experienced in recent years, Hakkas self-identity as Hakka, their culture remains different, and many still live apart or in Hakka communities.

Hakka social customs and mores differ in various ways from those of the Fukien Taiwanese and the Mainland Chinese. Hakka women, for example, engage in physically taxing work such as road building, construction, and agriculture. Yet they are typically more passive and self-effacing than other Chinese women. Some observers note that Hakka men favor certain professions (such as railroad jobs, police work, fishing, small business, and trade) because in the past they were unable to acquire good land or lost it to the Fukien Taiwanese. Some say the Hakkas have a stronger family system because of the discrimination they faced both in China and in Taiwan.

Hakkas can be identified not only by their customs but also by their ancestral records and language (or dialect, which Fukien Taiwanese and Mainland Chinese seldom speak). Many Western authors, though, do not distinguish between the Hakkas and the Fukien Taiwanese, simply lumping them together under the term "Taiwanese." This is odd because the two groups have a history of conflict that has resulted in mutual distrust and even hatred. In 1947 during the February 28 Incident, Fukien Taiwanese killed many Hakka, thinking they would side with the Mainland Chinese in the event of a broader conflict.[10]

Hakkas call themselves Taiwanese (since they regard Taiwan as their home and have even fewer familial ties with China than the Fukienese Taiwanese). However, in many respects, they do not consider themselves Taiwanese in the same way the Fukien Taiwanese so. They got along with the Mainlanders better than the Fukien Taiwanese did in the past and, indeed, still do. In various ways, they see themselves as a minority group like the Mainland Chinese. They feel they are culturally and so-cially unique, and many want to remain that way. Recently they have become more conscious of their separate status, and this put them at odds with Fukienese Tai-wanese during the Chen Shui-bian era. One of the serious disagreements between the two groups involved the efforts by Fukien Taiwanese to make Taiwanese the of-ficial language of the country. Government hiring policies were another.[11]

Hakkas probably number two to three million, or 10–15 percent of the popu-lation. Some claim that the figure is closer to the top figure or is even more be-cause many Hakkas lost their identity when they stopped speaking their language or intermarried with Fukien Taiwanese. Hakkas dwell in many parts of China, but they generally do not have significant ties with their island counterparts. Nevertheless, many Hakka, people say, identify less with Taiwan than do the Fukienese Taiwanese and are more cosmopolitan because they identify with and admire Sun Yat-sen, Deng Xiaoping, and Lee Kuan Yew (Singapore's former prime minister), all Hakka.

Hakkas have adjusted to modernization quite well, much better than have the Aborigines. Additionally, although their incomes are lower than other Chinese on average, many Hakka have done well economically. They have also been successful in politics. Former president Lee Teng-hui is Hakka (though he doesn't speak Hakka), as well as Wu Poh-hsiung and a number of other top figures in the Nationalist Party. Tsai Ing-wen is Hakka. Ma Ying-jeou also claims Hakka heritage. In recent years, Hakkas have come to comprise an important voting bloc and have thus increased their political influence at election time. The Democratic Progressive Party has tried to woo their vote, but with little success.

The Fukien Taiwanese brought their social structure and organization with them from China, specifically southern Fukien Province. Their culture was Chinese but differed from that of other parts of China. Fukienese culture, like Hakka culture, gradually changed with the separation from China, numerous contacts with foreign countries, and fifty years of Japanese rule. The Fukien Taiwanese were originally mostly farmers, fishermen, and traders, and, though many still are, increasing numbers of them have entered business—usually family businesses or firms owned and operated by other Fukien Taiwanese. Today, they dominate the business community, and for this reason their socioeconomic status has improved faster than that of any other ethnic group in Taiwan.

The Fukien Taiwanese have also become active politically, early on joining the KMT (including former president Chen Shui-bian), running for office as independents, and applying for government jobs. Many started careers in local government or in law. Their status and influence expanded from the 1970s on to such a degree that they are now the dominant ethnic group in Taiwan politically. The DPP is made up mainly of Fukien Taiwanese. Democratization has clearly favored the Fukien Taiwanese.

Because the Fukien Taiwanese constitute a numerical majority—around 70 percent of the population—they often regard the other ethnic groups as minority groups. As mentioned above, the Fukienese lived apart from and often engaged in conflict with the Aborigines and the Hakka in the past. However, this was overshadowed by ill feelings toward Mainlanders that grew following World War II particularly after the February 1947 "massacre." After 1949, this tension worsened because of the large influx of Mainlanders who fled to Taiwan after the defeat of the Nationalist armies on the mainland. Mainlanders at this time not only arrogated nearly all important positions in the national government and in education but also assumed a higher class status based on cultural and linguistic ties to China. All of this caused resentment among Fukienese.

Though Fukien Chinese trace their ancestry to Fukien Province, until recently few had been there. Like the Hakka, most did not plan to return to China when they left. Years of separation from the mainland have led them to identify with Taiwan and to see the island, rather than China, as their home. Many have come to regard themselves as Chinese only in the limited sense that European Americans see themselves as Europeans. Some Fukien Taiwanese have even made the argument that they are not Chinese. They point out that because women were not allowed to migrate to Taiwan for long periods, many men found Aboriginal wives; thus they are a "mixed race." This point has been used by pro-independence advocates in the DPP in order to assert that Taiwan and China are different places and should be separate. The whole story, however, should include the fact that many Mainland Chinese soldiers found Aboriginal wives in 1949 and after, and that 90 percent of Fukienese and Hakka have some Vietnamese ancestry.[12] In addition, the population of China is comprised of many ethnically "mixed people."

The Mainland Chinese came to Taiwan from various provinces of China after 1945, but most in 1949. The majority were either soldiers or government officials. They represented all parts of China, though a disproportionate number hailed from the south and central parts of China, especially the coastal provinces. Few came from the northern and western provinces. For some time, an inordinately large number of top government officials in Taiwan came from Chekiang (Zhejiang), the province where Chiang Kai-shek was born; indeed, for some years, Mainland Chinese from other parts of China experienced some discrimination— certainly disadvantages—when seeking government jobs. Many say this bias was also apparent in education and other areas.

After they fled to Taiwan, the Mainlanders sought to preserve Chinese traditions. They spoke Mandarin Chinese (which was the national language of China and traditionally the language of the educated) and, compared with the other Chinese groups residing in Taiwan, had greater—or at least more recent—contact with the fount of Chinese culture. As the self-designated protectors of Chinese civilization, many Mainlanders expressed condescending attitudes toward Taiwanese. They emulated their group's elites and/or saw preserving Chinese tradition as a matter of pride or self-identification. In addition, Mainland Chinese made a claim of cultural superiority on the basis of the years of Japanese colonial rule of Taiwan, which "Japanized" the island's population. Because of their experiences at the hands of the Japanese military during World War II, the Mainland Chinese generally disliked or even hated the Japanese. For this reason, when they arrived in Taiwan, they felt that Japanese culture, which many, especially Fukienese Taiwanese, had adopted, should be eradicated as quickly as possible.

Taiwanese do not espouse such an attitude, and many, especially higher class Taiwanese, speak of the period of Japanese colonization as better than the periods of "Chinese colonization" before and after that. Many perceive that Japan ruled

Taiwan very well. Many admire Japanese culture. This admiration has been an ethnic "identifier"; indeed, foreigners have often observed that one can discern the difference between the Mainland Chinese and the Taiwanese by their attitudes toward the Japanese and by the presence or absence of Japanese items in their homes.

Mainland Chinese are urban dwellers more than are the other groups, with more residing in Taipei proportionally than anywhere else. In fact, certain districts or suburbs of Taipei are predominantly Mainland Chinese.[13] Recently, Mainlanders have developed a new type of exclusivity that stems from being a minority in the context of Fukien Taiwanese gaining political power. Many, in fact, prefer to live in their own areas.

When they came to Taiwan, many Mainlanders brought wealth with them or had good jobs in the government or elsewhere through family and other connections. They filled most of the official positions formerly occupied by the Japanese, and some took over Japanese businesses. Their education level was higher than that of the other three ethnic groups and that remains so today. The socioeconomic status of Mainland Chinese, however, has fallen over the years because of the success of Taiwanese in business and the failure of public sector salaries to keep pace with those in the private sector. The children of Mainlander families now frequently work at menial jobs; daughters are even employed as bar girls— formerly a profession for Taiwanese. Many regard the retired Mainlander soldiers as the most hapless of any segment of the society, having neither family roots nor economic wherewithal. It is certainly no longer accurate to say that the Mainlanders exploit Taiwanese or that Taiwanese are a disadvantaged or oppressed group. In some important ways, it is just the opposite.

It is crucial to point out that ethnicity was once easily discerned from accent, physical appearance, and even mannerisms; this is no longer so. In fact, now it is often difficult to know the ethnic group of young people without asking.[14] Thus, ethnic differences and prejudices have faded in recent years with amazing speed.

Ethnic barriers have also diminished much faster than most observers anticipated three or four decades ago because of Taiwan's rapid economic growth and the material culture it has created and because virtually all ethnic groups have shared in Taiwan's prosperity. A considerable amount of Westernization has also contributed, as have urbanization and intermarriage. Similarly, government policies have helped, including policies that favored Taiwanese in recruitment and hiring beginning in the 1970s. Finally, almost the entire population of Taiwan— and certainly all its ethnic groups—shared a common desire to remain independent of the People's Republic of China for as long as it was poor and Communist.

Despite all this, ethnic tension increased in Taiwan after the election of Chen Shui-bian to the presidency in early 2000. He appealed to Fukienese voters on the basis of ethnicity and won the election that way. The majority of all other ethnic groups voted more for another candidate: James Soong. Subsequently, Chen and the DPP played the "ethnic card" in order to govern. The three minority groups complained of official bias by the government that favored Fukien Taiwanese. In 2008, Ma Ying-jeou, a Mainland Chinese, campaigned on a platform of healing ethnic relations and won the election by a wide margin. This indicated the electorate—even a lot of Fukienese—had come to disapprove of the Chen government's policies of ethnic divisiveness. Under Ma, Taiwan has experienced greater ethnic harmony.

Languages and Religions

The overwhelming majority of the Chinese (all three groups) and the Aborigines speak Mandarin Chinese, or *kuo yu* (meaning "national language"), which derives from the Beijing dialect in a somewhat similar way as American English comes from British English.[15] There are differences in accent, but this does not prevent Mandarin from being a language nearly everyone can use for at least basic communication. The two Taiwanese groups also speak their own languages or dialects (different languages in the sense that they are mutually unintelligible, though they are very similar, almost identical grammatically and in the written form—Chinese not being a phonetic language but rather one that employs pictographs and ideographs). Most Mainland Chinese, with the exception of the young, know the regional dialect of the province or area that they or their parents came from. Thus, although the Chinese residents of Taiwan often do not understand what others are saying, they do have mediums of communication that enable them to talk to each other. Ease of communicating is also enhanced by Taiwan's high rate of literacy, the difficulty of written Chinese notwithstanding.

The Aborigines speak languages that resemble Malay in structure, and many words are similar. Yet the Aboriginal languages or dialects differ considerably, and the various tribes cannot communicate with others in any of their tongues. The Aboriginal languages were not written until the Dutch period, when they were rendered into an alphabetic form and taught in schools. In recent times, Aboriginal languages have been dying out with modernization, though both official and unofficial efforts have helped revive and preserve them.

Fukien Taiwanese speak Taiwanese, a derivative of the Amoy dialect of Chinese, or Amoy Fukienese, spoken in southern Fukien Province. Most also speak Mandarin Chinese. Hakkas speak the Hakka dialect, which originated in north China but was influenced over the centuries by various dialects in southern China where many Hakkas lived. Most—indeed, nearly all—of the Hakka population of Taiwan also speak Taiwanese and Mandarin. Some Hakkas do not speak Hakka, especially if they grew up in a non-Hakka community or their parents didn't teach them. Some older Taiwanese do not speak Mandarin Chinese but rather speak Japanese.

Many younger Mainlanders speak Taiwanese, especially if they have grown up outside of Taipei. Most Aborigines speak Mandarin Chinese and Taiwanese; some speak Japanese. In short, almost all the Republic of China's people speak two or more dialects or languages.

There are regional accents in both Taiwanese and Hakka. Most Taiwanese, for example, can be identified from their speech as being from the northern or southern part of the island. Older Mainlanders have accents coming from their provincial dialects. Local accents, however, are rapidly disappearing because of social mobility and the influence of national radio and television.

Some differences have evolved in the versions of Mandarin Chinese (called *pu tung hua*, meaning "common language," in the People's Republic of China) spoken and written on the two sides of the Taiwan Strait. These differences resulted from more than four decades of almost total separation as well as from Western influence in Taiwan and the lack of it in China. Another factor is efforts by the government of the People's Republic of China to reform the language. In China, many of the characters have been simplified (sometimes for ideological reasons), whereas the traditional ones remain in use in Taiwan. Words, phrases, and slogans based on Communist teachings or ideology or used in Mao's various campaigns are often not understood by people in Taiwan. Yet with the proliferation of contacts, the increased travel by people from Taiwan to China in the past three decades, more people from China visiting Taiwan, and less censorship on both sides, the number of terms and phrases unfamiliar to people on one side or the other of the Taiwan Strait has decreased rapidly.

Controversies have arisen over language use and policies in Taiwan. When Taiwan reverted to China after World War II, the Nationalist government made Mandarin the official language and tried to discourage the use of all dialects. Taiwanese found it difficult to adjust to this policy because it meant learning a new spoken language. Also, many felt that Mandarin Chinese was being forced upon them, as Japanese had been forced on them fifty years earlier.[16] Government officials, however, perceived this policy was a necessary part of nation-building and modernization.

Because Mandarin Chinese boasts more speakers than any other language in the world and is very useful for reasons ranging from travel and commercial relations to education and research, many Taiwanese and Aborigines have long supported its use in the education system, government, and elsewhere. Opening contacts with China in the 1980s and China's economic boom have amplified this argument. Yet there have also been movements in Taiwan to use Taiwanese and Hakka more. Three decades ago, demands for radio and television programs in Taiwanese began to emerge; demands for Hakka followed and, more recently, the Aboriginal languages.

Currently, many Fukien Taiwanese see the use of their language as an expression of ethnic pride as well as their dominance in politics, thus as mirroring the democratization of Taiwan. Indeed, many Taiwanese politicians make it a point to speak Taiwanese when campaigning and sometimes use it in government meetings. Some Fukien Taiwanese, especially those advocating a separate or independent Taiwan, argue that Taiwanese is a unique language, very different from Mandarin Chinese. It is true that it contains different sounds and that the system of tones is not the same; it is therefore unintelligible to Mandarin speakers. Nevertheless, Taiwanese remains very similar to the dialect of Chinese spoken in southern Fukien Province in China. Also, interestingly, it is structurally much more like ancient Chinese than is Mandarin Chinese. Thus, some say Taiwanese is more Chinese than Mandarin Chinese.

Despite the posturing and occasionally bitter debates about language, there have been no language riots in Taiwan as there have been in some other countries. Though continued controversy over language is likely, Taiwan will no doubt remain a bilingual or multilingual country. The majority of Taiwan's population has been raised speaking more than one language or dialect, and most see an advantage in keeping a multilingual population in Taiwan. Those who have advocated making Taiwanese the sole official language of the country to accord with majority rule have not had much success because Taiwanese is not very useful outside of Taiwan, except for some Chinese communities in Southeast Asia. Furthermore, as Taiwan's dealings with China, commercially and in other ways, continue to expand, Mandarin Chinese becomes increasingly vital.

In addition to Chinese, English and some other Western languages as well as Japanese are taught in the schools from primary grades through college and university, though among various foreign languages English predominates. In fact, English is now compulsory in most grade schools. Many English textbooks are used in Taiwan's colleges and universities, especially in the technical fields. Chinese language texts are generally not as good or are not considered up-to-date. Also, students feel a need to know the vocabulary of their field of study in English so they can attend graduate school abroad or communicate with foreigners in their profession. Citizens who travel abroad frequently also use English in business.

Language is not the only way Taiwan is diverse. So are its religious beliefs and practices. Westerners find it odd when they ask people in Taiwan what religion they adhere to and most mention more than one. This is because Taiwan's religions are not exclusive. Nor have religion and politics become intertwined. Thus religion seldom has been the basis for discrimination, ethnic enmity, or social conflict. Some observers have described Taiwan as a nation of extraordinary religious tolerance. Indeed, it might be the foremost place in the world as far as religious freedom is concerned.[17] Almost all religions are practiced in Taiwan without difficulty or interference.

The Aborigines of Taiwan practice animism, nature worship, and various kinds of sacrifice. They also combine ancestor worship with agrarian rites. Their belief systems are polytheistic and they make no distinctions between gods and spirits. Except for two groups, the Aborigines do not espouse the concept of a god-creator. In the past, some tribes practiced headhunting as a source of religious prestige and to enhance their qualifications for marriage. This, of course, is no longer true.

Chinese migrants brought Taoism, Confucianism, and Buddhism to Taiwan, as well as some other religions. The Dutch brought Protestant Christianity, the Spanish brought Catholicism, and the Japanese brought Shinto. When the Communists captured China in 1949, many religious organizations and their officials as well as ministers and priests fled to Taiwan, thereby adding to Taiwan's religious mix.

The principal religions of Taiwan—by number of followers—are Buddhism, Taoism, Christianity, and I-Kuan Tao (the Religion of Unity). Buddhists are said to number 8.1 million and Taoists 7.6 million. Christians total 903,000 (605,000 Protestants and 298,000 Catholics). There are 845,000 I-Kuan Tao followers. Several other religious groups claim adherents numbering more than 100,000. There are nearly 60,000 people of the Islamic faith in Taiwan, most having come from China in 1949, though Islam was practiced in Taiwan before that.[18] Having said this, there is a major caveat: many say all Chinese are Confucian. But this means espousing Chinese culture, philosophy, and certain ethical principles rather than holding to special religious beliefs, though many people regard Confucianism as a religion.

Taoism is the oldest of the Chinese religions on Taiwan, tracing its origins to the teachings and writings of Lao Tzu, who lived in the sixth century BC. Lao Tzu taught individual freedom, laissez-faire attitudes about government, human spontaneity, living in accord with nature or the Tao (meaning "the way" or "path"), and mystical experience. Taoist teachings became more spiritual in nature in the third century BC, after which Taoism evolved into an organized religion. Central to Taoism's religious side is belief in the attainment of immortality. People who live in harmony with their natural environment, according to Taoist teachings, are able to become immortals. Taoism also incorporates the theory of opposites, or yin and yang, which must be reconciled to strike an essential equilibrium or balance in the universe. During the seventh through the ninth centuries AD, Taoism became the religion of the court in China. Subsequently, it adopted aspects of Buddhism and Confucianism and fragmented into different sects or schools. The *Tao Te Ching* is the classic text or bible of Taoism.

Taoism was brought to Taiwan by the earliest Chinese immigrants and was practiced on the island by the various Chinese communities. During the Japanese period, however, Taoism was suppressed because it was associated with Chinese patriotism and nationalism. As a result, many Taoist temples were reregistered as Buddhist temples. After World War II, Taoism made a revival. In 1950, Chang En-pu, a Taoist priest from China, established a Taoist fellowship while creating a more organized form of Taoism in Taiwan. There are now more than eighteen thousand Taoist temples, more than any other religion, and a large number of clergy in Taiwan, as well as a college, various other schools, hospitals, and a library.[19]

Buddhism originated in India in the sixth century BC from the teachings of an Indian prince, Siddhartha Gautama, who renounced his royal status and lifestyle to search for truth. Better known as the Buddha, he taught the Four Noble Truths: life is suffering, suffering is the result of one's desires, one should control one's desires, and the way to eliminate desire is the Eightfold Path. The Eightfold Path consists of right views, intentions, speech, conduct, livelihood, effort, mindfulness, and concentration. In the second century BC, Mahayana (the Greater Vehicle) Buddhism developed the belief in Bodhisattvas, or enlightened people capable of saving sentient beings, and the idea that attainders of merit (for doing good deeds) would reach a state of release called Nirvana. These ideas were similar to many Taoist beliefs prevalent in China, an affinity that helped Buddhism gain acceptance there.

Brought by early Chinese immigrants, Buddhism became more popular in Taiwan in the late sixteenth century when Cheng Ch'eng-kung built many Buddhist temples and supported the religion in other ways. Some of the temples were also used by practitioners of Taiwan's folk religions, thus giving Buddhism a local flavor. The main Buddhist sect that prospered in Taiwan was Chan. During the Japanese period, when Japanese Buddhists of various sects proselytized in Taiwan and Japanese monks took leading positions in the temples, Buddhist teachings and doctrine changed to resemble Japanese Buddhism in many ways. Moral and disciplinary codes and education were particularly affected. In 1949, many Buddhist monks fled to Taiwan from China and brought with them Buddhist practices and traditions not known previously in Taiwan.

In recent years, Buddhist organizations in Taiwan have been socially active, especially in working with the island's youth. They have also taken an interest in education, even building institutions of higher learning and sponsoring religious programs on television. Taiwan has numerous Buddhist temples. There are also a number of Buddhist seminaries, universities, colleges, orphanages, hospitals, retirement homes, and libraries. In addition, Buddhist organizations have been heavily involved in social welfare. In 1991, Master Cheng Yen, a leading Buddhist priest, received the Roman Magsaysay Award (Asia's version of the Nobel Peace Prize) for his contributions to the society. That same year, the Tzu Chi Foundation raised US$16 million for flood victims in China. In 1996, several Buddhist organizations supported Chen Li-an, son of former governor Chen Ch'eng under Chiang Kai-shek and a devout Buddhist, for president though their help did not prove very useful to his campaign. In March 1997, the Dalai Lama visited Taiwan for five days and met with President Lee; he visited again in April 2001. He visited Taiwan in 2009 after Typhoon Morakot, notwithstanding protests from China.[20]

Confucianism originated in China in the pre-Christian period based on the teachings of Confucius, born in 551 BC. Confucius is said to have edited or written several classic books: *The Book of Songs, The Book of History, The Book of Rites, The Book of Change,* and *The Spring and Autumn Annals.* The ethical teachings of Confucius are recorded in *The Analects* and *The Great Learning.* The metaphysical aspects of Confucianism are found in *The Doctrine of the Mean.* Through their teachings and writings, Mencius and Hsun Tzu, Chinese philosophers who lived two centuries later, contributed to what later became Confucian doctrine.

Confucianism, in its original form, may be said to be more an ethical code or handbook for behavior than a religion. When it became the official ideology—or the Imperial Court's political philosophy—during the Han Dynasty (206 BC–AD 221), it embraced a broad spectrum of ideas, though its central themes were rationalism and worldliness. Confucianism later took on the characteristics of a philosophy and a religion, but this transformation did not overshadow its rational side, nor did it affect the opposing ideas it held about human nature, social order, and the like. For example, Mencius taught that man was basically good, whereas Hsun Tzu was pessimistic. Mencius was democratic, Hsun Tzu legalistic. Confucianism, despite its eclecticism, expresses a unique reverence toward heaven and supports ancestor worship and in these ways is as much a religion as a philosophy.

Confucianism came to Taiwan with the early Chinese migrants, though Chinese officials who came to Taiwan later propagated it more. Thought of as a political philosophy or ethical code for officials, it is also a "people's philosophy" and contributed to ideals about the family and interactions among people. There are Confucian temples in Taiwan, though some say they serve the purpose of honoring Confucius and are not strictly for worship. Over the years, Confucianism incorporated many local religious beliefs in China. It did the same in Taiwan.[21]

Christianity's stature in Taiwan is more a function of its social and political influence than of the number of its followers. Christian missionaries have been actively involved in social-help programs and education, founding a number of schools (both secondary and higher) that are quite influential in Taiwan today. A number of Taiwan's top political leaders have been Christian. Chiang Kai-shek and his son Chiang Ching-kuo were Methodists (though how serious they were has been questioned). Lee Teng-hui is Presbyterian—a denomination that has actively supported Fukien Taiwanese interests and is pro-independence. Taiwan's Christians maintain ties with their home organizations and followers in other countries, thereby adding to Taiwan's cosmopolitanism and internationalism.[22]

There is little difference among the ethnic groups in Taiwan in religious beliefs or practices, though there are more Christians among Mainland Chinese and Aborigines due to Western influence and proselytism. Taiwanese more frequently say they are Buddhist. But, as mentioned, the people and the government in Taiwan are very tolerant of religious beliefs and practices, so what religion (or religions) one espouses is not important. In China, religion has been viewed as a challenge to communism, an "opiate of the people," and a propagator of superstition; thus it has been the target of eradication or suppression. On the issue of religion, there has long been little understanding between the people on the two sides of the Taiwan Strait. On the other hand, religious freedom in China has increased markedly in recent years, and the gap between China and Taiwan in this regard has closed somewhat.

Early Forces of Social Change

As noted earlier, the Chinese who emigrated to Taiwan several centuries ago had to adjust to a new environment, and the culture and social organization in the Chinese settlements evolved in response to an array of often harsh challenges presented by life in Taiwan: hostile Aborigines, ethnic feuds, civil unrest, violence, high crime rates, an imbalance in the sex ratio—societal traits that characterized "frontier areas" elsewhere in the world. The Chinese communities were thus organized more along ethnic lines and for defense and less like the farming communities they had been accustomed to in China.

Taiwan's Chinese population culturally also became more eclectic than most parts of China, being influenced by the mingling of customs, mores, and norms of the different ethnic groups, Western culture, and contacts with other peoples or nations in the region. Education and family origins did not remain the basis of class status as they had in China, or at least as much. The Chinese communities in Taiwan were confused about relations with China—and even about their roots. Their society and culture changed, yet they remained in many ways Chinese. However, a Taiwanese national identity did not develop. This helps explain why foreign influence on Taiwan's culture was considerable in ensuing years.[23]

Dutch rule brought significant social change to Taiwan, making Taiwan more cosmopolitan and Western, though its influence was limited to one generation and affected only a small portion of the population. The Dutch did, however, have a definite modernizing affect. Cheng family rule, which followed the Dutch period, generated a sense of local identity, but not among all Chinese living on the island and not for very long. Subsequent Chinese rule did not change Taiwan very much socially or culturally, and the Manchus (the rulers of China at the time) had little lasting influence in transferring their culture to Taiwan. However, Chinese culture was preserved on the island during this period; in fact, some aspects of Chinese society and culture that faded in China were retained in Taiwan.

After 1895, Japanese rule brought a new round of social change, both positive and negative. Tokyo abolished certain land use laws, namely the practice whereby the government granted permanent first title to land that was then transferred to secondary owners who, in turn, paid the first owners for its use and then cultivated or rented the land. Japan, as noted in Chapter 2, also got rid of the practice of buying servants and foot binding, along with a host of Chinese superstitions. Meanwhile, the building of a national economy created a new business class that included bankers and financial experts, not to mention entrepreneurs. The Japanese language was used in the education system and in official transactions, providing greater access to foreign—especially Western—technology and learning.

When Taiwan reverted to Nationalist Chinese control in 1945, Japanese social and other influences were eliminated by deliberate policies of the Nationalist government. The Japanese language was no longer used in government matters or in education, and Japanese newspapers, magazines, books, and movies were banned. Mainland Chinese dominated Taiwan politically and socially, forms of influence that were mutually reinforcing. The local, or indigenous, Chinese groups, as well as the Aborigines, had a difficult time adjusting. They had to learn Mandarin Chinese and the culture brought by the Mainland Chinese—difficult tasks considering there had been little contact between Taiwan and China for fifty years. They also had to adjust to a new legal and political system. In 1949, an influx of Mainland Chinese required housing, education, social services, and jobs—all of which were in short supply. They displaced many Taiwanese from their jobs, and they dominated the upper echelons of society via positions in the government and education. These developments, understandably, created further social instability and ethnic friction.

After 1945, social status in Taiwan depended largely on education and position in the government or the military and, of course, wealth. Success in business, except small businesses, depended to a large extent on connections with the government because much of the economy, especially large enterprises, was in the public sector. Non-Mainland Chinese had opportunities to rise socially, but only by learning Mandarin Chinese and establishing ties in government, business, and educational circles, or in the Nationalist Party. In all these realms, Mainland Chinese and their culture assumed a dominant role.

Taiwan's new rulers engineered broad and deep social change on the island from 1945 on in other ways. The most important factor fostering social progress in the post-1949 period in Taiwan, particularly in rural areas, was land reform. Rent reduction, the distribution of public lands, and the land-to-the-tiller laws, which were put in effect between 1949 and 1953, were its main components. Together, they increased the percentage of owner-farmers from about one-third of rural residents in 1948 to nearly 60 percent in 1953. Meanwhile, the amount of land cultivated by owners increased to more than 75 percent of the total land tilled. Among its most immediate social impacts, land reform undermined the feudal political and social structures that had existed in rural Taiwan for some time. This created more citizen participation and democracy in local government and benefited economic growth and the capitalist system. In China, Mao implemented land reform, but it had quite different results and was judged a failure.[24]

Land reform had other effects on the culture and society. Landlords, mostly Taiwanese, who were compelled to sell their land, were compensated in the form of bonds in government corporations. Not happy with this policy while perceiving that the bonds had no potential for growth, most landowners sold them. Also, because land prices dropped in anticipation of the effects of land reform, the land was worth less than expected when it was sold. As a result, many landlords not only got a depressed price for their land but also missed an economic windfall from subsequent increases in the value of the stocks they were given for their land. The socioeconomic position of the former landlords, an elite group in Taiwan's society, thus diminished dramatically. In short, land reform not only eliminated the landlord-tenant relationship that was a central part of the island's social system but it also reduced the landlord class to a small group with much less money as well as diminished social and political influence. This helped wipe out gross inequities in wealth in rural Taiwan; in fact, it contributed more than anything else to the leveling of incomes in Taiwan before the onset of industrialization.[25]

Land reform in Taiwan also brought secondary or delayed social changes or effects. It prompted the restructuring of rural society. The family no longer commanded the unquestioning loyalty of its members. The relationship between men and women changed, as did the practice of filial piety. The birthrate dropped. Agriculture became more efficient, leading younger people to seek jobs in the cities and farm families to decrease in size and number. Rural society became smaller and much more mobile.

The success of land reform and the resultant increases in agricultural productivity gave rise to rapid urbanization, as was noted in Chapter 1. The urbanization of Taiwan's population during the 1960s and after had a profound and lasting social impact. On the positive side, it fostered greater job specialization, created employment opportunities, promoted social equality, reduced social and class barriers, and vastly increased cultural opportunities. On the negative side, it weakened the family and engendered social alienation, giving rise to serious increases in crime rates, juvenile problems, and drug addiction. Meanwhile, a high but rapidly falling birthrate and an extremely fast decline in the death rate together caused Taiwan's population to grow rapidly and then to age quickly. These social problems remain serious, as will be seen in a later section of this chapter.

The United States was also a catalyst for social change in Taiwan, especially after 1949. At first, US influence was exerted through American economic and military assistance, plus the presence of a sizable number of US military personnel on the island. After aid was ended in 1964, trade links with the United States became just as important, as did American capital investment. Contacts with Americans brought ideas about democracy, social equality, and progress to Taiwan. American books and movies also had a noticeable social impact, as did the many students who returned to Taiwan after studying in the United States. (For some years,

Taiwan sent more students to colleges and universities in the United States than did any country in the world.) The United States also served as a model for social as well as economic and political change.[26]

Because of the importance of foreign policy and Taipei's claim to be Free China, the government was more responsive to and influenced by the global community than most countries. Furthermore, because economic growth was export driven, Taiwan's economic health and prosperity depended on friendly foreign markets, and as a consequence the island became increasingly penetrated by outside customs and ideas. Foreign travel, which became common in the 1970s and 1980s, helped make Taiwan's citizens global in their outlook. In short, Taiwan's society and culture were heavily influenced by the external world.

Underscoring the importance of the forces of change cited above, almost all of the social evolution (or devolution) that occurred in Taiwan after 1945 became permanent because the attendant modernization was embraced heartily by most of the population and was seen as either progressive or inevitable, or both. The key expediters of social change—economic growth, greater social and geographical mobility, expanded educational opportunities, and consumerism—were present in other places of the world. However, they fostered even greater change in Taiwan because many of the influencers of change were mutually reinforcing.

Economic Development and Social Change

Rapid economic growth has been a powerful force driving social and cultural change in Taiwan. Prosperity, in fact, has been the major "driver" behind the evolutionary—and in many ways "revolutionary"—social change Taiwan has experienced for the past six-plus decades. To understand both its speed and depth, it is helpful to examine some of Taiwan's economic data, particularly as they show how prosperity engendered social change. (Taiwan's economy is discussed in greater detail in Chapter 5.)

From 1953 to 1970, farm output in Taiwan grew rapidly—at two to three times the rate of population growth. Extremely large productivity increases in the agricultural sector and then in industry in the mid-1960s caused personal incomes in Taiwan to skyrocket—from about US$50 per year in 1950 to $200 in 1964 to more than US$3,000 by the mid-1980s and more than US$10,000 in 1992. During this period the average income of citizens in Taiwan increased two hundredfold.

Such rapid economic growth caused surplus labor to be quickly absorbed. Taiwan's unemployment rate (which was probably in the 20 percent range in the 1950s) fell to 5.2 percent in 1963 and to less than 2 percent in the 1970s—a level, economists say, that is needed to allow workers to change jobs or seek retraining. In subsequent years, unemployment remained consistently below 3 percent.[27] Low jobless rates caused base salaries—or the salaries of unskilled workers—to increase faster than others, markedly reducing the income gap between rich and poor. As a result, the income disparity ratio dropped from 15 (based on a comparison between the top 20 percent and the bottom 20 percent of the population) in 1952 to 4.9 in 1982 and to 4.1 a few years later. Taiwan's level of income inequality became not only one of the lowest among developing nations but fell below that of both Japan and the United States.[28]

Prosperity first had an impact on diet: from 1952 to 1981, caloric intake increased from an average of 2,070 per day to 2,830—a figure that exceeded that of any place in Asia. Protein consumption grew and a greater variety of foods were added to the diet. Next, it affected consumer buying. By 1986, 97.2 percent of families owned color television sets, 98.8 percent owned refrigerators, 78.5 percent had washing machines, 83.2 percent had telephones, 30.3 percent owned air conditioners, and 12.3 percent had automobiles. With the exception of automobiles, these figures were comparable to data for the United States and advanced Western European countries. By the mid-1980s, the number of color TVs, refrigerators, and washing machines per family in Taiwan was higher than in the United States. During this time, almost 80 percent of families in Taiwan became homeowners—one of the highest percentages in the world.[29] In other words, growth with equity benefited almost everyone, causing Taiwan to become a mass-consumption society.

This growing affluence affected Taiwan's society in important ways. A decline in the birthrate, an aging population, and rapid urbanization have already been discussed. The impact on education will be assessed in the next section of this chapter. The changing structure of employment and a new interest in politics will be discussed in subsequent chapters. Here, however, special attention will be given to changes in the social structure—both rural and urban, social classes, the status of women, the family, and leisure and travel.

In rural Taiwan, as a result of the economic boom (which, as noted earlier, the agricultural sector experienced first because of land reform), the social structure changed from a family- or kinship-based society to an "associated" one. In other words, the interactions among friends and associates became relatively more important than contacts among relatives. Rural society became less authoritarian and more democratic. The "leveling effect" of economic growth also led to the creation of new social and political organizations that were generally much bigger and involved more diverse memberships. In the words of sociologists, social organizations became horizontal rather than hierarchical in structure. They also became more political. Paternal and kinship relationships were replaced by mutual-benefit relations, while friendships or collegial relations supplanted family ties in the daily lives of rural citizens. Societal leadership saw Confucian academics and the traditional gentry replaced by successful businesspeople, professionals, educators, heads of farmers' associations, community affairs leaders, politicians, and others.[30]

With increases in rural incomes came electrification, which made it possible for farmers to lead more active lives simply because they could stay up later. The popularity of radio and television that followed brought new forms of culture. Schools became more the locus of social interactions and cultural activities. Meanwhile, higher crop yields and increases in the planting of cash crops linked farmers to the marketplace, thus cementing ties between farmers and the government through crop improvement efforts, subsidies, and farmers' co-ops. These relationships integrated rural Taiwan more fully into the national economy and broke down barriers between rural and urban Taiwan. This helped a national culture emerge.

In the cities, traditional culture broke down even faster and more completely. As a result of Taiwan's rapid industrialization, people formed new bonds based on friendship, work, business, and school ties. The importance of family links declined. Many found new opportunities to change their social status. Professional groups grew in importance. Even more than in rural Taiwan, in the cities people looked to the government for solutions to their problems. Western culture became much more widely accepted. Differences between rich and poor decreased, yet wealth became more important.

These developments heralded the creation of a large middle class in a society that had once been bifurcated into high and low classes. By the 1980s, when asked about their social-class status, three-fourths of the population in Taiwan said they were middle class—a 20 percent increase over the 1950s. More precisely, more than two-thirds of the population (according to a poll taken in 1986) ranked themselves between 4 and 7 on a social strata scale of 10. During this same period, over 60 percent said that their social position was higher than their parents, an indication that, for the majority of the population, social change was positive. Social transformation resulting from economic growth had still other ramifications: The effect of a father's occupation on his son's became small—about the same as it was in the United States. Profession became a more important indicator of class status (as self-defined, at least).[31]

Because of Taiwan's economic prosperity, women's roles changed markedly, especially in marriage and employment. Arranged marriages became a thing of the past, though arranged meetings, wherein either party had the right to refuse or reject the other, became common. Love came to be regarded as a desirable incentive to marry rather than a dangerous diversion from family arranged pairings. Women also began marrying later: at an average age of 26.1 in 2000 compared to 22.2 in 1971. In 2010, 37 percent of women in Taiwan aged 30–34 and 21 percent of those aged 35–39 were single.[32]

The number of women joining the labor force likewise increased very rapidly. In the past, women worked in the home, a situation that began to change significantly in the 1950s. By 1961, 35.8 percent held jobs outside the home. In 1990, the figure was 44.5 percent and in 2000, 46 percent—about the same percentage as in the United States and the countries of Western Europe. Perhaps even more telling was the large percentage of married women who began to work or stayed in the workforce after marriage. In 2008 almost half of adult women were working full-time.[33]

The social status of women, of course, improved markedly, though it was never as low as many Westerners have perceived it to be. Women in Chinese societies traditionally had much more control over their husbands and broader authority in the family than is generally assumed. Thus the transition to a modern society was not as difficult as it may have appeared. Today, women in Taiwan are active in politics, form their own companies, and own or control a significant portion of the national wealth—more, proportionately, than women in the United States. They also travel alone more and are less frequently victims of crime and abuse compared to women in the United States. Global surveys confirm the positive changes in the status of women in Taiwan. In one, Taiwan ranks number twenty in the world in the UN Gender-related Development Index and number four in the Gender Inequality Index.[34]

Women do, however, report difficulties in their new roles. For example, many married women say they are burdened by working while retaining the primary responsibility for keeping the family together and raising the children. They complain that they cannot maintain close bonds with their children because they must put them in child-care centers or with relatives during the day. Many women complain that they are severely discriminated against if they divorce. A large number of women say they do not enjoy the opportunities available to men in business and politics. Many more women now suffer from stress and say they cannot cope with social change. This notwithstanding a number of laws and other government actions recently put in place to address these concerns.[35]

Economic and social change have wrought a profound transformation in the family structure in both rural and urban Taiwan. The extended family, which was the rule in the past, is now less common. By the early 1980s, more than half of families were nuclear, less than a quarter were extended, and more than 5 percent were single-parent households. Meanwhile, family size decreased from an average of 5.9 persons in 1951 to 4.0 in 1990. A large part of the shift was accounted for by the fact that Taiwan was no longer an agricultural society. By 1996, less than 11 percent of the working population was employed in agriculture. Most of those who quit farming went to the big cities to live. Soon 50 percent of the population lived in the four largest cities. These statistics reflect the continuing weakening of the family.[36]

Still another facet of social change associated with economic growth, and one that seems to be more pervasive than all others, is the generation gap. Most older citizens in Taiwan have a rural background; the majority of younger people do not. Social change is accepted by the younger generation more than by older people, who feel they have not been able to keep up. The youth, say elders, espouse "odd" views of society and the world and espouse different standards of morals and behavior. Many elders complain that respect for age has been diminished by economic progress; they believe their children, and young people generally, have abandoned them for a different world.[37]

There are other major differences in life experiences between the older and younger generations. Older people remember the period of Japanese colonization, Japan's defeat in World War II, and the beginning of Nationalist Chinese rule. Younger people do not. Older people recall many hardships. Younger people have not known poverty or deprivation; instead they "suffer" from affluence. The younger generation is much more Westernized. Even the early period of Nationalist rule is seen differently by those who experienced it and those who have only heard about it. Older people recall the serious problems that developed when the Nationalists came, and they remember when US aid was critical to Taiwan. Younger people do not know about these things from personal experience. Some of Taiwan's youth even think the United States has become a failed country where a large percentage of the population is poor—a view that seems all the more real when they see Americans coming to Taiwan looking for jobs and sometimes begging on the streets. Older Taiwanese identify with the Japan of the past. Older Mainland Chinese remember their life in China before Communist rule. Even Taiwan's political elite is split between those with traditional views and education and those holding foreign degrees, particularly PhDs from top American universities.

Economic progress has fostered still other social and cultural changes. As Taiwan became affluent, recreation became more important. Mountain climbing and walking in the parks are common spare-time activities. Kung Fu and archery, which were traditional sports, are still practiced, but baseball, basketball, soccer, tennis, and golf have become more popular. Talking in the teahouses and visiting museums are common recreations, as are listening to music (in music halls or discos), karaoke, and dancing. Most people engage in recreational activities at home or close to home so as to avoid traffic and other problems. Many people spend a good portion of their free time watching television, videotapes, or discs—about the same amount of time spent by people in the United States and Japan. The advent of new cable stations in recent years has made television more popular. Yet many young people complain that they do not have as much leisure time as their counterparts in Western countries because they spend much more time studying and preparing for college entrance examinations or tests to study abroad.

The age factor also connects to the question of whether Taiwan should be independent or should reunite with China. Years of separation have created in Taiwan a unique society very different from that of the People's Republic of China. Aware of the political extremism and poverty in China under communism, most young people in Taiwan came to identify socially and politically with the United States, Japan, and, to a lesser extent, Western Europe. They did not understand or identify with China very much and saw themselves—and Taiwan—as a part of the international community and not part of China.[38]

Recently there has been a proliferation of people from Taiwan visiting China and vice versa. In 1992, 4.2 million people made trips overseas, more than one-third of those visiting China. In 1993, the number reached 4.6 million, an increase of 10 percent. In 2001, 7.2 million traveled abroad. One would conclude from the number of trips that more than one-fourth of the population travels abroad each year. Recently it has been said that the percentage of Taiwan's population that engages in foreign travel is one of the highest in the world. The large proportion of Taiwan's citizens visiting other countries makes the population quite worldly and affects the population's view of Taiwan's place in the world, including whether Taiwan is part of China or is a separate country.

Cross-strait contacts have altered the attitudes of the people of Taiwan in complex ways. Still, there are differences among Taiwan's ethnic groups regarding Taiwan's relationship with China. Taiwanese do not favor ties with China as much as Mainland Chinese and see Taiwan's future linked more to Japan and the United States. To some extent, they fear China. They are opposed to Chinese immigration. Mainland Chinese see more hope in a "Greater China," Hakkas are in between. Aborigines are less concerned about the issue. There are also divisions by profession. Businesspeople favor ties with the Mainland to enhance commercial opportunities and profits and, more than others, see Taiwan as part of a Pacific Basin or Greater China bloc.

Education

Education has long played a special societal role in Taiwan. In the past, one's education correlated closely with his or her class status more than it did in most other places in the world, except China. In recent years, education has afforded an avenue for social mobility and social-class change, while it has also made the population more cosmopolitan and conscious of events elsewhere in the world. It has been a source for many new interactions and opportunities, and it has helped promote culture, economic growth, a sense of national unity, and democracy.[39]

Before the Japanese period, the educated portion of the population was small. Upon making Taiwan a colony, Tokyo promoted mass education, and, within a few years, 70 percent of children attended elementary school. As a result, a basic education did not convey the elite status it once did.[40] Mass education had other effects: a broadly educated population fostered social change and helped facilitate economic growth. Still, only a small portion of the population received higher education and, as noted in Chapter 2, few studied law, the humanities, or the social sciences. The best students went to Japan to study, leaving the second best to form student organizations in Taiwan that had less social impact than would have otherwise been the case. Under the Japanese, the Chinese classics fell into disuse, and knowledge of the Chinese language and literature deteriorated.

The reestablishment of Chinese rule in 1945 brought continued support for educating the general population. The Constitution of the Nationalist government contained special provisions concerning education, including the right to education and a promise that education shall be provided free by the government to all children up to the age of twelve and to older people who have not received an adequate education. The Constitution also allocated 15 percent of the budget of the national government, 25 percent of the provincial government's budget, and 35 percent of municipal governments' budgets to education and culture. These constitutional provisions were fairly rigidly adhered to, and only defense accounted for a bigger portion of government spending.

Because of a tradition that emphasizes education and, more recently, strong public support for economic development (thought to be closely linked to improving the skills of the workforce), upgrading educational standards, keeping young people in school, and spending more money to do this had strong public approval. There was also support at the top. Chiang Kai-shek and the government under him viewed schooling as one of the most important tools for building social consensus and unity as well as a means of promoting economic, social, and political progress.

Early on, the national government not only set about upgrading schools but also planned the restructuring of the educational system. The Ministry of Education followed Sun Yat-sen's suggestions: that there should be compulsory education for six years (increased to nine years in 1968 and twelve years in 2011), that scholarships should be available to enable intelligent but poor students to attain further education, that education should be job oriented, and that teaching must be guided by government policies (to advance patriotism, national unity, and the like). Confucian learning was de-emphasized while Sun's writings, military strategy, and science and technology were accorded a higher place in the curriculum. In short, education was made more practical and goal oriented.

Some specific policies that were part of the government's educational reform program deserve special mention. To prevent cramming, examinations for entry to middle school were dropped. Girls were encouraged to go to school; thus, gender bias was removed from education. The government gave more financial support to vocational schools, which taught subjects that the economy and the job market required. Government actions thus further linked education to employment. Teacher training and parent-teacher organizations received government support, as did schools that taught night and specialized courses.[41]

Textbooks and curriculum, approved by the Ministry of Education, were upgraded. Grade levels, curriculum, and the academic calendar were adjusted to follow the US system. Unlike the United States, however, Taiwan used national competitive examinations in order to restrict the number of college students and, to a considerable degree, determined their majors. For most students, passing the entrance examination to college or university was very difficult, although getting through courses and remaining in school to graduation was less difficult than in the United States.[42]

From the early 1950s on, there was a phenomenal increase in the number of students at all grade levels. In primary schools, the number of students enrolled increased from less than 1 million in 1950 to nearly 2.5 million in 1985. The number of high school students rose even more dramatically: from 67,000 to more than 1.7 million, an increase from 8.8 percent of the student population to 44.6 percent. In 1950, 80 percent of school-age children attended school; by 1979, it was 99 percent.[43] In the meantime, the number of colleges rose from 7 to 105, and the number of students pursuing higher education increased from 6,665 to 412,381. In short, the student population of Taiwan overall increased markedly. In 1950, there were 139.6 students per 1,000 people; by 1979, the number was nearly double, and more than 25 percent of the population attended school.[44]

The social impact of greater educational opportunities was evident at both ends of the spectrum. At one end was illiteracy. Although Taiwan's illiteracy rate was the second lowest in Asia (after Japan's) in 1950, it was still a concern to the government and the citizenry. By 1962, illiteracy fell to 24.8 percent of the population over age six. By 1990, it was reduced to 6.8 percent; now it is just over 2 percent.[45] At the other end of the spectrum, more people attained higher education. In 1990, over half of those receiving an education got some secondary education, and Taiwan was rated one of the top countries in the world by the percentage of the population enrolled in college or university.[46]

The quality of education also improved. By the 1980s, compared with countries at a similar level of development, Taiwan's quality of education was six times higher. UN statistics indicated that its standards exceeded those of all major underdeveloped and developing nations, an achievement that reflected the tremendous improvements in education in Taiwan over the previous three decades. Taiwan was even able to compete with developed countries in the educational attainments of its citizens. For example, before the end of the 1980s, there were twice as many college students in Taiwan per capita as in Great Britain.[47] By the 1990s, Taiwan was gaining accolades around the world for its educational system. In a survey assessing knowledge of science and mathematics among thirteen-year-old children, Taiwan ranked first in the world. One author attributed Taiwan's excellent educational system to standardized instruction, intense competition, more time in class, more homework, more exams, and special schools.[48] The high status of teachers and their professionalization were also an important factor.

Still another aspect of education in Taiwan that is important when assessing its societal impact is its globalization effect. At the college level, many of Taiwan's best students study abroad: between 1954 and 1989, 115,000 went, 30 percent earning engineering degrees.[49] Since then the number has increased—especially to the United States (33,881 in 2010, 46 percent of the total).[50] However, fewer are now going for advanced degrees because of the improvements made in local colleges and universities and the proliferation of graduate degree programs. Also, because Taiwan's primary and secondary schools are so much more demanding than Western high schools and because going abroad now is affordable, younger but less outstanding students have been going to the United States and elsewhere to study.

Another aspect of the internationalization of Taiwan's education can be seen in what Taiwan's students have done after going abroad. During the 1950s and 1960s, few of these students returned home after receiving their degrees. But this "brain drain" turned around in the 1970s and 1980s as a result of Taiwan's prosperity and the job opportunities that economic growth created (and, at the same time, unemployment became a serious problem in the United States). This reverse brain drain contributed immensely to Taiwan's research capabilities and to the growth of knowledge-intensive industries. Returned students also stimulated political and social change as they began to assume various leadership roles.

Meanwhile, Taiwan has attracted a sizable number of foreign students to its colleges and universities. In 1996, 5,432 students from more than fifty countries were studying the humanities (most studying Chinese) in various institutions in Taiwan.[51] Taiwan has thus had considerable influence on Western Sinology, having long provided language training and research facilities to foreign students and scholars. Even more important is the large number of Overseas Chinese students who have enrolled in Taiwan's schools. From 1951 to 1992, 63,000 Overseas Chinese students graduated from Taiwan's educational institutions. In recent years, more than 10,000 have attended various schools at any one time.[52] In the last decade plus, students from the People's Republic of China have studied in Taiwan, and some students from Taiwan have studied and even pursued degrees in China. The numbers have been small, but they have increased steadily. Researchers have also crossed the Taiwan Strait in both directions.

The political impact of foreign higher education can hardly be overestimated. In the 1990s, 70 percent or more of cabinet members had been educated abroad, and 60 percent or more typically held doctoral degrees. Taiwan's top echelon of government was often described as the world's most educated. With a change in ruling parties in 2000, less stress was placed on education—notably educational qualifications for government jobs. Nonetheless, standards remained high compared to those in most countries of the world.[53]

Because of the rapidly expanding demand for education for a number of years, private educational institutions flourished. In the 1950s, almost all schools were public. In contrast, in the 1990s, private schools accounted for 23 percent of the nation's students, including 55 percent of all college and university students.[54] Today the ratio remains about the same. Private schools were, and still are, generally affiliated with a church or religious organization. The best schools, especially colleges and universities, however, remain public, although the best kindergartens and specialty schools are private.

With the expansion of educational opportunities, the number of college students has increased markedly in recent years as more colleges and universities have been built. Now few students who want to attend college cannot go. In fact, in recent years, there have been more slots in colleges and universities than applicants. As a result, more students who attend college drop out or fail to earn degrees. Some say, as a result, there has been depreciation in respect for college learning and a devaluation of the college degree. In 1992, 43.8 percent of graduating high school students went to college or university; in 2002 it was 80 percent. In 1992, Taiwan had 50 universities with 278,000 students; by 2002, this had increased to 148 universities (89 of them private) and 780,000 students.[55]

During the Chen era, the government put much emphasis on revising textbooks to teach Taiwan's history rather than China's, while using education to promote localism and a Taiwanese identity. Critics said education was used to promote a political agenda rather than teach. Teachers were demoralized as a result of this as well as the government ending Teachers Day, a holiday recognizing the importance of teachers (also Confucius's birthday). The government also did not try to resolve the problem of too many universities and the process of cheapening education that had been under way before 2000. Meanwhile, "Taiwanization" alienated many Overseas Chinese, who found going to Taiwan for an education less attractive than studying in China. Finally, unlike previous years, none of Taiwan's universities were rated in the top one hundred in the world, compared to six in China (three in Hong Kong), two in Singapore, five in Australia, four in Japan, and one in Korea.[56]

It seems likely that educational policies will be changed to fix these problems. Most college and university presidents believe that Taiwan should open up to students from China and that Taiwan should try to attract more Overseas Chinese students to improve the quality of education in Taiwan.[57] Others suggest many more ways. The Ma administration has decried the decline of educational standards and has implemented means to foster improvements such as offering government scholarships to go abroad, strict evaluations of colleges and universities, e-learning, and more.

Social Welfare

Welfare has an interesting history in Taiwan. Social programs were in evidence on the island when it came under Chinese rule in the seventeenth century. They consisted mainly of special aid to the poor, to women, and to children.[58] Under Japanese rule, social welfare was expanded considerably in scope. Japanese colonial governors used welfare programs as a means of facilitating their political control. Indeed, this strategy was quite effective: Tokyo enhanced its popularity by eliminating poverty, equalizing incomes and wealth, and engaging in charity work—all in the name of the emperor. The Japanese later used the term "social enterprises" to include education and research as well as social relief and economic assistance programs of various kinds.

After Nationalist China incorporated Taiwan in 1945, Governor-General Ch'en Yi, who regarded the welfare system as a tool used by the Japanese to destroy Chinese culture and render the population dependent, eliminated much of it, leaving intact only relief for the poor, medical care for the impoverished, and famine and disaster relief organizations.[59] However, when the Nationalist government moved to Taiwan in 1949, it took several social welfare programs with it. Need at the time also dictated both the expansion of existing programs and the creation of new ones. The aforementioned areas of welfare that were in operation in the late 1940s were expanded. New efforts focused on soldiers. Newly arrived Mainland Chinese were given help in finding housing and jobs while Taiwanese who had been displaced from jobs or had suffered during the economic hard times of the previous half decade were provided assistance.

In the 1960s and 1970s, as Taiwan began to prosper economically, the scope of welfare efforts grew to include vocational training, labor security, health, and public housing. New government agencies were created and the number of social workers increased accordingly. The government at this time also assumed a new responsibility: child welfare. Taiwan received funds from the United States and from the United Nations and its related agencies for some of these efforts. But government spending also increased by large amounts. Expenditures from all levels of government soared from 2.8 percent of budgets in the early 1950s to over 10 percent in the early 1970s.[60]

In the 1980s, the government and the ruling Nationalist Party embarked on a variety of formerly untried social welfare projects and again increased government spending on welfare. The motives were unique: the government faced a problem of legitimacy after the United States severed diplomatic relations in 1979 and established its embassy in Beijing. As disaffection with the government grew, many leaders perceived that they needed to take steps to defuse this potentially explosive situation. Officials thought that increases in welfare spending would make the government popular both at home and abroad, inasmuch as welfare would alleviate poverty and convey the impression that the government cared for its citizens. Increased welfare outlays would also send the message that the country was democratic and that the voters, even poor voters, had an input in formulating government policies. In the late 1980s, the opposition Democratic Progressive Party

pressured the government to further expand welfare and made specific suggestions. The government enacted many of them in an effort to pre-empt an important part of the DPP's platform. Finally, it was widely perceived that the country
could afford more social welfare.

At this time the thrust of social welfare also changed. Previously, it had been
aimed at groups considered vital to maintaining political stability: the military, labor, and government employees were the main beneficiaries. It now shifted to help
anyone who needed it. In the early 1980s, the government passed three pieces of
legislation that reflected this change: the Aged Welfare Law, the Handicapped
Welfare Law, and the Social Assistance Law. It also enacted laws to help youth and
launched a new insurance program for teachers and administrative staff in private
schools. In 1985, the Bureau of Labor Insurance was ordered to work on a program for giving farmers health insurance. In 1987, the government announced its
intention to establish a national health insurance program.

All of this caused social spending to increase by large amounts during the 1980s.
Welfare expenditures at the national level, which were under 2 percent of the gross
national product in 1980, passed 3 percent by 1990. Spending at all levels of government was around 3 percent in 1980, and by 1990 reached more than 4.5 percent of gross domestic product. Social welfare expenditures peaked in 1996 and
fell after 2001 for a few years.[61]

One of the items that caused social welfare spending to balloon was health care.
In 1995, the legislature adopted the National Health Insurance (NHI) system that
incorporated thirteen existing health insurance plans while extending coverage to
an additional 7.5 million people. Participation was mandatory under the Health
Insurance Law. The main beneficiaries were those who did not have insurance: the
elderly, children, students, and housewives. A fierce debate soon raged about who
would pay: the government, employers, or individuals. It was finally decided that
employers would pay 60 percent of the cost, employees 30 percent, and the government 10 percent. Citizens over seventy paid no premiums. Between 70 and 95
percent of costs were covered for patients admitted to hospitals and somewhat less
for those seeing a doctor in an office or clinic.

Although widely praised, Taiwan's NHI has not been without problems. The
program's reputation was sullied early on when better doctors demanded additional money for their services or refused to accept the scheduled payments. Over-
use resulted in much higher costs than anticipated, while the program's
effectiveness measured by increases in life expectancy and reduced health disparity among social classes was marginal. The Nationalist Party took credit for giving
health insurance to virtually all citizens, but it did not win many kudos because of
the attendant controversies and the fear that the increased tax burden it created
might make Taiwan's exports noncompetitive in the world market.[62]

More recently critics of the system cite doctors who complain of having to see
too many patients and thus suffer from overwork and health problems themselves.

They also say that they don't have time to keep up in their field and improve their skills and that medical students now select their specialty according to the NHI's compensation schedules and the time they have to spend seeing patients.[63] It is also reported that many of Taiwan's very best doctors have left to take up residence and practice elsewhere, including Hong Kong and China.

Meanwhile, the government got into new realms of social welfare. Added to the list of welfare causes were child protection services, campaigns against drug abuse, youth counseling and guidance, women's education, women's services networks, divorce counseling and aid, elderly day care, special services for the aged, help for the disabled, low-cost housing, and assistance to the Aborigines. In 2002, the government launched a program to help older citizens who received no pension or other such benefits. In mid-2007, the legislature passed the National Pension Act, which was inclusive for all citizens age twenty-five to sixty-four who did not already participate in a program.[64]

Very recently social welfare spending has again seen fairly large increases. The budget for 2012 exceeded $13 billion and constituted 21 percent of the central government's spending. For the first time it was the largest item in the budget, passing spending for the military and for economic development and reflecting a 10.6 percent increase from the previous year. Most of the increase was accounted for by higher expenditures by the National Health Insurance plan plus the National Pension System and the Labor Insurance Annuity launched in late 2008 and 2009.[65] Taiwan's aging society has caused welfare spending to increase and portends to make the situation worse in the future.

The proliferation of welfare initiatives and the costs associated with them have their critics. Many say that welfare has contributed to undermining and even destroying the family. Others contend that welfare has weakened the nation's work ethic and has hurt its competitiveness in the global marketplace. Some worry that the polity is evolving from a capitalist to a socialist one, a nanny state, and that welfare is "breaking the bank" of the country. The controversy intensified in 2001 when unemployment benefits and other welfare costs skyrocketed because of an economic recession and the worst earthquake ever that struck the island.[66]

The issue of social welfare generally also has its political side. The DPP, which had long stood for helping the poor and disadvantaged, had to cut social welfare because of a poor economy soon after it became the ruling party in 2000. As a result, the party's poor and disadvantaged constituencies were alienated. Meanwhile, many citizens in Taiwan noticed that China, after adopting free market reform beginning in the late 1970s, cut welfare spending and subsequently boomed economically. Not only that but China hollowed out and even destroyed many of Taiwan's industries that could not compete because of higher taxes and labor costs. This engendered a debate about whether Taiwan's generous welfare compromised its ability to compete with China and, if so, whether China might use its economic might to force Taiwan to unify with China.

Other Social Problems

A number of Taiwan's "social ills" have not been cited; some of these deserve further discussion. A few are serious; others are new or unique. Taiwan's rapid economic growth and its vast political and social changes account for most of them.

Some say the most hapless group in Taiwan is veterans. Around 150,000 soldiers came to Taiwan with Chiang Kai-shek and the Nationalist Party and government in 1949. They were promised land in China when they returned and were even given titles or deeds. These, of course, proved worthless. The large proportion was men of low socioeconomic status who could not find wives and had no family. Now many are in their eighties or older and need care but have little money, and their veterans' benefits have not kept up with inflation. Also, because government welfare budgets are now stretched and focus on numerous other groups, soldiers, as a consequence, receive less than they need. Veterans thus suffer from alienation and serious adjustment and health problems. Many commit suicide.[67]

Still another social problem is a housing shortage in some cities and the fact that houses and apartments are too expensive for many people to afford. The rate of home ownership in Taiwan is high, but in recent years—because of the very fast appreciation in the value of land and property—many people who want to buy, especially for the first time, find it difficult or impossible. During the 1989 election campaign, the so-called snails without shells (or people who could not afford housing) staged massive protest demonstrations in exclusive areas of Taipei. The government at various levels has intervened and has built more public housing while also providing low-cost loans to workers and first-time buyers. In 2010 the government calculated that the average family needed to save 100 percent of its income for 9.2 years to buy an average house. President Ma promised action as part of his "Golden Decade" plan and provided government land to some builders and offered government housing for lease for 70 years.[68]

Related at least indirectly to the housing problem is the matter of low-income households and individuals. Although poverty has been virtually eliminated in Taiwan owing to the economic miracle and the ease with which most people find employment, families with children still have difficulty making ends meet because of high rents and Taiwan's rapidly growing cost of living. The society's fast aging is also a contributing factor. In response, in 2011 the government raised the poverty line, relaxed income thresholds to qualify to receive financial assistance, and enacted new taxes (including a recent one on the turnover of luxury homes) to pay for aid to the poor.[69] Still some people are missed. Meanwhile, a number of people, out of pride, do not wish to collect government welfare.

Crime is a social problem that has appeared rather suddenly in recent years and is now regarded as quite serious by many of Taiwan's citizens; indeed, crime has consistently been among the top issues of concern, as reflected in public opinion surveys in recent years. Higher crime rates are generally considered the result of urbanization and the social alienation it has created, materialism, a weakening of the family structure, permissiveness, and Westernization. Some say democratization brought about lax law enforcement and less severe punishments and that this accounts for dangerous streets and high crime rates.

The significant growth in crime occurred in the late 1960s and increased even faster in ensuing years. Increases were especially large in violent crimes and juvenile offenses. Violent crimes rose from 7.4 percent of the total in 1981 to 10.9 percent in 1990, and juvenile crimes went up from 12.8 per 10,000 in 1970 to 27.6 per 10,000 in 1990. In the late 1990s, violent and juvenile crimes declined, but people were still alarmed. The total number of crimes committed in Taiwan in 2000 was eight times what it was twenty years earlier. Larcenies increased nearly sixfold, robberies by about that, and rape by more than three times. In 2001, recession caused the crime rate to shoot up—12 percent overall and 40 percent for violent crimes.[70]

In the past few years, crime in Taiwan, including crimes in almost all categories, has declined. This is attributed to better law enforcement, more public vigilance and confidence in the police, and government programs to deal with the causes of crime. It is also the product of an agreement signed in June 2005 with China to fight narcotics smuggling, money laundering, economic crimes, and telecom fraud and cooperation in apprehending and repatriating fugitives.[71]

Meanwhile, sensational crimes in recent years have made headline news, thereby making the crime problem appear much more serious while causing public alarm. The children of very wealthy citizens have been kidnapped and murdered. There is also growing public concern about gangs in Taiwan and their ties to politics and religion. It has been estimated that 15 to 20 percent of local township and county councilors are *heidaoren* or people "of the black way" (bad people or criminals), more common in rural central and south Taiwan. Some even serve openly in the Legislative Yuan. Many people believe gang influence began in the early 1980s with the lottery in Taiwan that provided the opportunity to get big money.[72]

Connected to increases in the crime rate is the rapid growth in drug use in Taiwan. Although still low by the standards of Western countries, the number of drug users and the amounts sold and consumed have escalated rapidly in recent years. Arrest statistics reflect the seriousness of drug abuse. In the past, drug-related crimes were about 5 percent of the total, but this rose to 13 percent in 1991 and to 32 percent in 1993. In 1994, drug offenders and drug-related crime accounted for 63 percent of prison inmates, the largest of any category. In 1993, convictions for drug crimes increased 70 percent. That same year, the amount of marijuana seized by the police increased 133 percent. Meanwhile, heroin seized increased twenty-three-fold from 1989.[73]

Drug use and related crimes declined in 1995 after the government took stern measures to control the flow of drugs and their use in Taiwan. Specifically, several laws were passed to prevent smuggling and money laundering, resulting in Taiwan being taken off the blacklist of transshipment countries by the US Department of State in 2000. Nevertheless, the drug problem is still seen as a very serious social ill. Some say drugs became a problem after the lifting of martial law, when sentences were reduced and pushers were seldom executed. Others say it is the product of modernization and Westernization. Still others relate it to organized crime and politics.

Another social problem that is a cause of concern is the increase in the divorce rate and accompanying family dislocation. The divorce rate in Taiwan has increased 10 percent or more a year, contributing to a nearly sevenfold increase in the forty-year period beginning in the 1950s. From 1985 to 2006, the rate of divorce more than doubled.[74] The rate has since continued to increase. Recently it has been estimated that 25–30 percent of marriages end in divorce. There are a number of side effects; for example, single-parent families account for 60 percent of child abuse. Some say the high divorce rate is the product of new laws, democracy, and a diminished loyalty to the family.[75]

Child abuse, regardless of the cause, has become a social problem of serious proportions, at least in perception. The number of cases reported more than doubled between 1993 and 1996. Physical abuse was the most common complaint (40.9 percent), followed by neglect (24.3 percent), and substandard parenting (19.1 percent). The Children's Welfare Law was enacted in 1973 and was subsequently revised in 1993 to deal with this problem. The approach is both unique and severe. Names of offenders are published, and fines can be as high as $11,000. Men have been most frequently charged under this law. Interesting to foreigners, child abuse has a broader definition in Taiwan: women are punished for smoking, drinking, taking drugs, and chewing betel nuts while pregnant. The government has taken serious legal steps recently to deal with the problem. Still, the data show that child abuse increased 30 percent from 2005 to 2009. The causes listed were lack of parenting skills, negligence, alcohol, and lack of anger management.[76]

Rape, child prostitution, and other sex crimes are also attracting increasing attention in Taiwan. Although the frequency of these crimes is much lower in Taiwan than in most other countries, these problems have generated grave concern among Taiwan's populace because they are widely reported in the press and cause alarm. Many people blame society for becoming too permissive and for lax law enforcement.

Another problem is a sudden increase in the number of both men and women who do not want to marry. In the twenty-year period between 1980 and 2000, the percentage of men in the eligible age range each year who marry had fallen from 6.7 percent to 4.65 percent. For women, it dropped from 9.19 percent to 6.37 percent. Taiwan in this respect seems to be following similar trends evident in Japan and some other countries, where more people don't want to marry or at least don't marry. Some observers feel this trend will make the society unstable, threaten the family, and cause a further decline in population growth.[77]

Suicide has become a serious social problem, recently being rated the ninth leading cause of death in Taiwan and the second cause of death among the youth. The death rate from suicide is 18.8 per 100,000 people with 70 percent occurring in the age group 20 to 50. Unemployment is cited as one of the top reasons. Youth suicide is reported to stem from emotional and interpersonal problems. It used to result from academic stress, but recently this has been the cause of only 3 percent of young people killing themselves. Elderly people also commit suicide more than they do in other countries. It is reported that one-fourth of gays and lesbians considers suicide even though Taiwan is considered a place that is not hostile toward either.[78]

Still another problem in Taiwan is obesity. Various data indicate that a fast-growing number of both adults and children are overweight. A recent study shows that the percentage of overweight children (age 2–18) has increased from 6 to 25 percent in the past ten years and is close in seriousness to the rates in the United States. Sedentary lifestyles and a poor diet are seen as the main causes. In 2009 the government considered enacting the world's first tax on junk food. Recently various groups have called on the government to "declare war" on obesity.[79]

Although Taiwan's social problems are not as serious as those found in the modern Western democracies, they seem to be worse because they have appeared so suddenly. This very abruptness might lead to quicker, better solutions; in fact, Taiwan may be able to solve these problems as efficiently as it has dealt with so many others. The alternative is a worsening social environment that will adversely affect the society.

Notes

1. The most detailed anthropological studies on Taiwan are to be found in Emily Martin Ahern and Hill Gates, eds., *The Anthropology of Taiwanese Society* (Stanford, CA: Stanford University Press, 1981).

2. Chen Kang Chai, *Taiwan's Aborigines: A Genetic Study of Tribal Variations* (Cambridge, MA: Harvard University Press, 1967), 43.

3. See Chiao-min Hsieh, *Taiwan—Ilha Formosa: A Geography in Perspective* (Washington, DC: Butterworths, 1964), 127–131.

4. See Edwin A. Winckler, "Roles Linking State and Society," in Ahern and Gates, *Anthropology of Taiwanese Society*, 63–65.

5. Edgar Wickberg, "Continuities in Land Tenure, 1900–1940," in Ahern and Gates, *Anthropology of Taiwanese Society*, 212.

6. See Arthur P. Wolf, "Domestic Organization," in Ahern and Gates, *Anthropology of Taiwanese Society*, 341–361.

7. Murray A. Rubinstein, "Taiwan's Socio-Economic Modernization," in *Taiwan: A New History*, ed. Murray A. Rubinstein (Armonk, NY: M. E. Sharpe, 1999), 388–389.

8. See Hill Gates, "Ethnicity and Social Class," in Ahern and Gates, *Anthropology of Taiwanese Society*, 241–282.

9. For data on the Aborigines, see *The Republic of China 2011 Yearbook* (Taipei: Government Information Office, 2011), 30.

10. Denny Roy, *Taiwan: A Political History* (Ithaca, NY: Cornell University Press, 2003), 6.

11. Some say the Hakkas constitute a buffer between the Mainland Chinese and the Taiwanese. Others say they identify with the Fukien Taiwanese but favor a government of Mainland Chinese. Hakkas have done very well in politics in Taiwan, and many hold top positions in various police organizations.

12. Hu Ching-hui, "Most Hoklo, Hakka Have Aboriginal Genes, Study Finds," *Taipei Times*, November 21, 2007, 1. According to the author, 85 percent of both groups have Aboriginal genes, though the study also indicated 90 percent have some Vietnamese ancestry stemming from their family origins on China's southeast coast, as do the Chinese living in that part of China now.

13. See Gates, "Ethnicity and Social Class," 61. Gates notes that one of the main reasons for this is that Mainland Chinese took houses evacuated by Japanese after 1945.

14. For further information on this topic, see Kuo-shu Yang, "Transformation of the Chinese People," in *Contemporary Republic of China: The Taiwan Experience, 1950–1980*, ed. James C. Hsiung (New York: Praeger, 1981), 268–281. In recent polls, nearly 40 percent of those asked said they were both Chinese and Taiwanese as compared to less than 30 percent in 1995. Also, the number saying they were Taiwanese decreased from nearly 50 percent to under 40 percent, and the number calling themselves Chinese fell from nearly 25 percent to just over 15 percent during the same time period. See "Cross Strait Breakthrough," *Topics* (November 1998): 13.

15. For details about the languages used in Taiwan, see *The Republic of China 1998 Yearbook* (Taipei: Government Information Office, 1998), chapter 3.

16. See Tse-han Lai, Ramon H. Myers, and Wou Wei, *A Tragic Beginning: The Taiwan Uprising of February 28, 1947* (Stanford, CA: Stanford University Press, 1991), 93–97.

17. See Anthony Kubek, *Modernizing China: A Comparative Analysis of the Two Chinas* (Washington, DC: Regnery Gateway, 1987), 187–189.

18. For details on the number of followers of the various religions in Taiwan, see *Taiwan Yearbook 2006* (Taipei: Government Information Office, 2006), 339.

19. *Taiwan Yearbook 2007* (Taipei: Government Information Office, 2007), 251–252.

20. "Dalai Lama visits Typhoon Morakot victims," *Daily Telegraph*, August 31, 2009 (online at telegraph.co.uk).

21. *Taiwan Yearbook 2007*, 460.

22. Ibid., 252.

23. A Taiwanese national identity did not develop to any degree at this time because there was no central government and little communication between or among the Chinese on the island. See, for example, Christopher Hughes, *Taiwan and Chinese Nationalism: National Identity and Status in International Society* (London: Routledge, 1997), chapters 1 and 2.

24. Land reform is also discussed in Chapter 5. For details on its impact on landowners and social change, see Thomas B. Gold, *State and Society in the Taiwan Miracle* (Ar-

monk, NY: M. E. Sharpe, 1986), 37–38, 65–67. Also see Kubek, *Modernizing China,* chapter 3.

25. John C. H. Fei, Gustav Ranis, and Shirley W. Y. Kuok, *Growth with Equity: The Taiwan Case* (Washington, DC: International Bank for Reconstruction and Development, 1979), 38.

26. For some assessment on Taiwan's political leadership, see Wen-hui Tsai, *In Making China Modernized: Comparative Modernization Between Mainland China and Taiwan* (Baltimore: University of Maryland School of Law, 1993), 118.

27. For background and further details on this topic, see Hung-mao Tien, *The Great Transition: Political and Social Change in the Republic of China* (Stanford, CA: Hoover Institution Press, 1989), chapter 2; and Yu Tzong-shian, *The Story of Taiwan: Economy* (Taipei: Government Printing Office, 2001), 50. For recent per capita income data, see "Taiwan Claims Economy Grew a Robust 5.46 Percent," *Earth Times,* December 27, 2007 (online at earthtimes.org).

28. For details, see Fei, Ranis, and Kuok, *Growth with Equity.*

29. See Beatrice Liu, "Housing Crisis Grows Worse," *Free China Journal,* May 25, 1989, 7.

30. See Peter Chen-main Wang, "A Bastion Created, a Regime Reformed, an Economy Reengineered, 1949–1970," in Rubinstein, *Taiwan: A New History,* 320–338.

31. For a comparison between Taiwan and other Asian countries, see the chart in Yuan-li Wu and Kung-chia Yeh, eds., *Growth, Distribution, and Social Change: Essays on the Economy of the Republic of China* (Baltimore: University of Maryland School of Law, 1978), 42–43.

32. "The Flight from Marriage," *Economist,* August 20, 2011 (online at economist .com).

33. "More Women Participating in the Work Force," *China Post,* October 13, 2009 (online at chinapost.com.tw). For details on women in the workforce, see Catherine Farris, Anru Lee, and Murray Rubinstein, eds., *Women in the New Taiwan: Gender Roles and Gender Consciousness in a Changing Society* (Armonk, NY: M. E. Sharpe, 2004).

34. Pat Gao, "Promoting Gender Parity," *Taiwan Review,* September 1, 2011 (online at taiwanreview.gov.tw). Taiwan, of course, is not a member of the UN; these rankings are derived by plugging statistics on Taiwan into the UN lists.

35. *Republic of China 2011 Yearbook,* 184–185.

36. *Taiwan Yearbook 2007,* 171.

37. For details, see Yui-chun Yu and Peter Miller, "The Generation Gap and Cultural Influence—a Taiwan Empirical Investigation," *Cross Cultural Management: An International Journal* 10, no. 3 (2003): 23–41.

38. *Taiwan Yearbook 2007,* 82.

39. For general background information on education in Taiwan, see *The Republic of China: Educational System* (Taipei: Kwan Hwa, 1980).

40. Mark Mancall, ed., *Formosa Today* (New York: Praeger, 1964), 2.

41. *Republic of China 1998 Yearbook,* 297.

42. Ibid.

43. *Taiwan Yearbook 2007,* 200.

44. Ibid.

45. *The Republic of China Yearbook—Taiwan 2002* (Taipei: Government Information Office, 2002), 101. The literacy rate in Taiwan is now 98.12 percent.

46. *Republic of China 2011 Yearbook*, 221.

47. Kubek, *Modernizing China*, 157.

48. Fei-yun Wang, "Solving Problems," *Free China Review* (January 1994): 42.

49. Chong-pin Lin, "China's Students from Abroad: Rates of Return," *American Enterprise* (November–December 1994): 14.

50. *Republic of China 2011 Yearbook*, 230.

51. See "The Combative Cabinet," *Taipei Review* (April 2002): 4–9. Sixty-two percent of cabinet members currently have foreign degrees and 42 percent have PhDs.

52. Kelly Hu, "In Pursuit of Excellence," *Taiwan Review*, December 1, 2002.

53. *Republic of China 1998 Yearbook*, 298.

54. *Republic of China Yearbook—Taiwan 2002*, 296.

55. See Hu, "In Pursuit of Excellence."

56. *Asiaweek* has rated the universities, and Taiwan does not make the top ten list. See http://www.cnn.com/ASIANOW/asiaweek/features/universities2000/. Recently, more than 80 percent of high school graduates taking their college or university entrance examinations passed. See "465 Places Still Vacant in Taiwan's Universities," *China Post*, August 10, 2002, 4.

57. See Jenny W. Hsu, "College Presidents Back PRC Students: Poll," *Taipei Times*, May 15, 2008 (online at taipeitimes.com).

58. For details, see Yeun-wen Ku, *Welfare Capitalism in Taiwan: State, Economy and Social Policy* (New York: St. Martin's Press, 1997).

59. Ibid., 36–37.

60. Ibid., 41.

61. *Republic of China 2011 Yearbook*, 178.

62. For details, see Chi Pang Wen, Shan Pou Tsai, and Wen-Shen Isabella Chung, "A 10-Year Experience with Universal Health Insurance in Taiwan: Measuring Changes in Health and Health Disparity," *Annals of Internal Medicine* (February 2008): 258–267.

63. Kelly Her, "Doctors' Talk," *Taiwan Review*, May 1, 2012 (online at taiwan review.gov.tw).

64. Ibid. Also see Pat Gao, "The State of Welfare," *Taipei Review*, March 2001, 6.

65. Pat Gao, "Strengthening the Safety Net," *Taiwan Review*, December 1, 2011 (online at taiwanreview.gov.tw).

66. See Chien-Hsun Chen, "Taiwan's Burgeoning Budget Deficit: A Crisis in the Making," *Asian Survey*, May/June 2005, 383–396.

67. Y. C. Ku, Y. F. Tsai, Y. C. Lin, and Y. P. Lin, "Suicide Experience Among Institutionalized Older Veterans in Taiwan," *Gerontocracy*, December 2009 (online at ncbi .nim.nih.gov).

68. Jim Huang, "Real Property, Real Problems," *Taiwan Review*, April 1, 2012 (online at taiwanreview.gov.tw). Taiwan's home ownership is 80 percent compared to between 50 and 70 percent for most developed countries.

69. "Promoting a Just Society," *Taiwan Review*, December 1, 2011 (online at taiwan review.gov.tw).

70. Ibid., 142–143. Also see "It's Time to Face the Crime Problem," *China Post*, July 22, 2002, 2.

71. See Jerome A. Cohen and Yu-jie Chen, "Cross Strait Cooperation in Fighting Organized Crime," *U.S. Asia Law Institute*, July 5, 2011 (online at www.usasialaw.org). Data on crime in Taiwan can be found at the National Police Agency's website (npa.gov.tw).

72. Jonathan Adams, "Gangster Life: Taiwan's Real Life Sopranos," *Global Post*, May 4, 2010 (online at globalpost.com).

73. *The Republic of China 1994 Yearbook* (Taipei: Government Information Office, 1994), 350; *Republic of China 1998 Yearbook*, 320. See also "War Against Drugs Posts Some Success," *Free China Journal*, March 3, 1995, 7. This article was based on a speech by Minister of Justice Ma Ying-jeou.

74. *Republic of China Yearbook—Taiwan 2002*, 325. The later figure is in *Taiwan Yearbook 2007*, 27.

75. "Taiwan's High Divorce Rate Signals Social Problems," Chinese Women's Research Network, April 13, 2012 (online at en.wsic.ac.cn).

76. "Reports of Child Abuse Increasing Significantly," *China Post*, April 3, 2010 (online at chinapost.com.tw).

77. See "Who's Afraid of Marriage," *Taipei Review* (February 2002): 14.

78. "Suicide Rate Climbing as Economy Falters," *China Post*, July 16, 2006, "Youth Suicide Rate on the Rise," *China Post*, September 21, 2010 (online at chinapost.com.tw); Steve Hsu, "Groups Call for Gay Rights Protection and Awareness," *Taiwan News*, April 18, 2012 (online at taiwannews.com.tw).

79. "Taiwan Mulls World's First Junk Food Tax: Report," AFP, December 21, 2009 (online at afp.com); "The Government Should Declare War on Obesity," *China Post*, December 20, 2009, "Youth Need More Support to Overcome Weight Obsession," *China Post*, May 21, 2012 (online at chinapost.com.tw).

4

POLITICAL SYSTEM

TAIWAN'S POLITICAL HISTORY IS A complex one. Its political culture finds its origins in local family rule, Western colonialism, China's bureaucratic system, and Japanese feudalism, with one or another prevailing during certain periods. Governance over the island changed several times in the recent past. After a brief period as a Dutch colony in the seventeenth century, Taiwan enjoyed a short interval of self-governance before two centuries of Chinese rule. The island had no effective central government, however, until it was colonized by Japan in 1895. After World War II, Taiwan's political system, which was transplanted from China by Chiang Kai-shek, was based on Sun Yat-sen's writings and his goal of establishing republicanism in China. It was democratic in form and constitutional. In practice, the system was authoritarian, based on one-party rule, a strong executive, and highly effective police control. In the 1950s, local elections produced the basis for "democracy from the bottom up." Beginning in the 1960s, Taiwan saw the growth of a free-market economic system, political reform in both local and national politics, and the beginnings of democratic change. In the 1970s and 1980s, more Taiwanese taking positions in government, the rise of new political parties, competitive elections, the expansion of political and civil liberties, and a concern for Taiwan's image in the international community produced a budding democracy. Some even referred to Taiwan's rapid and peaceful democratization as a "political miracle." In 2000, Taiwan experienced what was said to be its "democratic consolidation," when Chen Shui-bian of the opposition Democratic Progressive Party was elected president. But Chen's poor leadership, an economic slowdown, and massive corruption engendered serious public disappointment with his administration. As a consequence, the KMT won several subsequent elections, culminating in a big legislative victory in January 2008 and Ma Ying-jeou winning the presidency in March. In 2012, the KMT won another legislative election, and President Ma was re-elected.

Political Culture and Tradition

The political culture that evolved in China over many centuries—transported to Taiwan by early immigrants and later by officials who were sent to govern the island from the late 1600s to 1895—was elitist: it did not assume or favor mass participation. Yet it was comparatively egalitarian, because class was not a barrier to attaining a high position in government, as it was in most places in the world at the time, although lack of education was (and attaining education required leisure time and money). Chinese political tradition was authoritarian, even though individualism was part of the culture, and it was highly humanistic and moralistic (political decision-making being seen as involving ethical choices).[1]

Early in China's history, its political culture and its political system were influenced by the need to control water and maintain roads and other public projects. Their construction and maintenance required sophisticated levels of political organization and administration. When public works were not kept in repair, flooding and crop failure resulted, and often thousands—even millions—of people died. Thus, the bureaucracy wielded considerable power; arms and money were not the main sources of authority in China as they were in most political systems. An emperor and a scholar-official class that was synonymous with a powerful ruling bureaucracy governed China.[2]

In theory, China had a unitary political system; in fact, however, political power was decentralized. Local government officials, nominally responsible to the emperor, were in reality largely autonomous. Officials sent by the emperor to govern provinces and lower units of government checked on local administrators and advised them; but, because these emissaries usually did not know the language (dialect) of the regions they served and were rotated at regular intervals, they seldom became entrenched or powerful. A kind of balance of authority between the central and local governments was also the product of physical distance and the lack of modern transportation and communications as well as other limits on centralizing political control, with centrifugal tendencies being dampened or contained by the cohesive force of Chinese culture.

China's bureaucratic tradition was taken to Taiwan, though in many ways it did not fit. The control of water and the maintenance of public works were not critically important in Taiwan. Taiwan was much more geographically fragmented, and the livelihood of its population depended more on fishing, hunting, and, later, trading, than on farming. In addition, owing to Taiwan's good soil, moderate climate, and more regular and predictable rainfall, working the land was less risky than in China. Therefore, peasants on the island did not need government-built public works. Finally, Taiwan's early cosmopolitanism and foreign influences affected its political tradition. Thus, Chinese political culture could not be totally transplanted to Taiwan, and it took root there only partially.[3]

Throughout most of its history, there was not much government at the top in Taiwan, even in theory. Today, centralized political authority in Taiwan is quite feasible, given the small size of the island and the efficient means of transportation and political communications available to its rulers. But a free-market economic system, political party competition, constitutional limits on the authority of the national government, and strong local governments all prevent the centralization of political power. Also militating against the concentration of political authority are concerns about political freedoms, Chinese individualism and distrust of political authority, and the lessons afforded by Mao's radical efforts in China to concentrate political power at the center and control all aspects of life. In contrast, geographic size and a huge population limit the effectiveness of a central government in China.[4]

Taiwan's political culture was affected, in some ways irreversibly, by Japanese rule from 1895 to 1945. In the Japanese political tradition, arms and money were the crucial ingredients of political power; the bureaucracy was less important. Japanese rule thus reinforced the already present feudal nature of Taiwan's political culture and its political system. Japanese control over Taiwan was also notable for its legalism because the establishment of a framework of laws and regulations facilitated its colonial rule. Finally, obedience and loyalty were esteemed in Japanese political thinking, while individualism was not.

Tokyo administered Taiwan efficiently and, in many ways, with fairness and justice; but, as noted earlier, it never treated its subjects as equals. Exclusionist and racially discriminatory policies—notwithstanding economic and social gains—led to the creation of an identity among the Chinese in Taiwan not unlike that fostered by colonialism in other parts of the world. Indeed, Japanese rule marked the beginning, however weak, of a sense of community and nationalism in Taiwan. Toward the end of the period of Japanese governance, in a last-ditch effort to prevent defeat in war, Tokyo promised self-rule to many of the territories under its control, including Taiwan. But this effort was not very sincere, and the population was not prepared for it, although it did create expectations.

Finally, Taiwan's political culture bears the imprint of Nationalist China. Sun Yat-sen (1866–1925), the first president of China and founder of the Nationalist Party, or Kuomintang (KMT), spent some time in Taiwan, where he discussed politics and China's future. Loyal supporters spread his political ideals in ensuing years, even after the Japanese colonized the island in 1895. Many in Taiwan also knew of Sun through their relatives and contacts in China. In 1945, when the Nationalist Chinese government assumed political control over Taiwan, Sun and his teachings were thus familiar to a significant segment of the local population. Sun's writings subsequently provided Taiwan with a political philosophy and a formula for political development.[5]

Although there was a rebirth of Chinese culture in Taiwan after World War II, economic development strategies implemented in Taiwan in the 1950s and thereafter diluted its elitist nature, as did democratic reforms. Success in business and the professions, meanwhile, afforded political careers to newcomers. Authoritarianism persisted because the ruling elite demanded it, the nation was at war (in a state of readiness and perceiving that a conflict with the People's Republic of China was likely), and the population of Taiwan felt a need for a strong leader (though in recent years democracy and the advent of party politics have weakened this facet of Chinese political culture). A strong concern for moral behavior in politics reflected the survival of Confucian ethics. Subsequently, democracy in some respects amplified concern about good government.

From the 1960s on, Taiwan became suffused with Western political ideas. Political rights as practiced in the West became idealized, especially among younger Chinese. As the free market expanded and foreign trade grew, democracy came to be seen as a necessity, especially because the free flow of information (which the authoritarian system impeded) came to be viewed as essential to the acquisition of technology and to sustaining economic growth. Thus, Taiwan's political culture absorbed new democratic components.

In the 1970s and after, as Taiwan became diplomatically isolated, the desire of both the government and the population to protect Taiwan's (or the Republic of China's) national sovereignty inspired both national unity and democratization. Threats from Beijing and the need for Taiwan to impress the international community with its political modernization clearly impacted Taiwan's political culture and political system. Taiwan's economic accomplishments, societal change, and growing cosmopolitanism, all of which stimulated feelings of national pride and uniqueness, also contributed to its political culture.

In sum, Taiwan's political culture has been shaped by a rich diversity of influences, most recently democratization.[6] The culture differs, however, from that of the West in being more conservative and favoring society over the individual. The term "Asian democracy" may describe this kind of polity: a democracy (though some Western observers hesitate to use that word) that sees a danger in permissiveness, that puts a high value on hard work and social stability, that views the family as the basic social institution, that pays deference to the elderly, and that is less bureaucratic and less costly than Western democratic systems. Asian democracy seems to be what most people in Taiwan want.

The Constitution

Another place to begin an assessment of Taiwan's political system is its Constitution. Chiang Kai-shek brought the Republic of China's Constitution to Taiwan after World War II. This document evolved from a draft constitution written in May 1936 that became moot (or nearly so) when Japan invaded China the next year. Another effort was made to write a constitution at the end of World War II, even though a civil war between the Nationalists and the Communists followed on the heels of peace with Japan. The effort succeeded and a final document was approved in late 1946. After elections in 1947 and 1948 (held in only part of the country because of widespread fighting between Communist and Nationalist forces), the document became the basis of constitutional government in areas controlled by the Nationalists, including Taiwan.[7]

The framers of the Constitution designed a republican-style representative democracy. The system was mixed, though, and included cabinet, presidential, and parliamentary features. It set forth neither executive nor legislative supremacy (though in practice the former prevailed). The system was unitary, though it had many characteristics of a federal system, such as allowing local government a number of special prerogatives.[8] The Constitution guaranteed citizens a broad range of political and civil rights. It contained broader provisions for the separation of powers and checks and balances than are in most Western nations' constitutions.

The Constitution, in fact, was unique in that it established five branches (*Yuan*) of government rather than three, as is typical of Western systems. In addition to the executive, legislative, and judicial branches are the examination and control branches. The former three were accorded powers and functions similar to those in most Western democracies, while the latter two reflected the importance given to the recruitment of government officials and the need to keep a check on the bureaucracy to ensure its competence and honesty (as the Censorate did in the traditional Chinese political system). Designed to rule a very big country, the president and the vice president were elected by the National Assembly rather than by the electorate directly. The framers of the Constitution anticipated that political parties would perform many of the responsibilities relating to the functioning of democratic government, such as measuring and reacting to public opinion, responding to special interests, recruiting administrators and political leaders, and designing alternative policies. However—as in the US Constitution—political parties are not mentioned in the document.

Because of the war with the Communists and the ethnic tension that accompanied the rebellion that broke out in Taiwan in 1947, the Constitution was amended (or its implementation delayed, depending on one's interpretation) by the Temporary Provisions Effective During the Period of National Mobilization for Suppression of the Communist Rebellion enacted in 1948. The Temporary Provisions gave the president emergency powers to deal with threats to national security as well as financial and economic crises. Based on this authority, in 1949, the executive branch of government pushed through the legislature a bill called *chieh yen fa* (literally "vigilance measures law," but generally translated as "emergency decree" in Taiwan and "martial law" by the Western media), which remained in effect until July 1987.

The emergency decree (or martial law) gave the military and intelligence agencies a special role in politics, making it legal for Chiang Kai-shek to keep in place an authoritarian regime notwithstanding the democratic Constitution. The Temporary Provisions banned the formation of new political parties, nullified the two-term limit on the president (Article 47 of the Constitution), and empowered the president to set up ad hoc organizations to mobilize and control the population and to appoint delegates to the elected organs of government. The National Assembly, which was controlled by the ruling Nationalist Party, was authorized to amend or abrogate the Temporary Provisions. However, it took no steps to do so until President Chiang Ching-kuo ordered it to much later.

Those who argued that the process of democratization in Taiwan was too slow condemned the Temporary Provisions. Others, however, contended that Taiwan successfully attained democracy precisely because the Temporary Provisions held back the democratization process until social and economic conditions were right (that is, until there was a large middle class and the population was sufficiently educated and otherwise able to participate intelligently in democratic government). The public in Taiwan was certainly aware of the failure of premature democratization in many developing countries during the 1950s and 1960s.[9] But Taiwan's populace also believed that the country had to democratize to accommodate to Taiwan's rapid economic development, the rise of a middle class, and its rapid social change. Moreover, after Taipei lost its seat in the United Nations in 1971 and Taiwan was forced to engage in a struggle to win international support for its sovereignty (which China sought to undermine), it was widely thought that the implementation of democracy forthwith would help that cause.

The Constitution contains provisions guaranteeing citizens basic rights similar to those found in Western countries: freedom of speech, belief, residence, publication, assembly, association, and the right to privacy. Arrest, trial, and punishment must be carried out according to constitutional provisions. In the past, critics charged that the Temporary Provisions undermined or seriously weakened these basic freedoms, especially guarantees of political and civil rights. In particular, they cited the role intelligence organizations played in censorship, the use of military courts to try civilians, and restrictions on forming political organizations. In response, the government lifted many restrictions in these areas in the 1970s and early 1980s. In 1986, President Chiang Ching-kuo announced he would lift martial law and did so in 1987. All of this went far to change the authoritarian nature of Taiwan's political system.

However, sentiments still ran deep among opposition politicians for more change. Though pleased by the progress democratization was making, they complained about obstacles to competitive elections, such as the practice of retaining old members of the government's elected bodies (called the senior parliamentarians) who had been chosen when the government was on the Mainland or appointing their replacements, the advantages possessed by the Nationalist Party in election campaigns because of its ownership or control of much of the media, and the KMT's close links with the government.

Compared with Western democracies, constitutional guarantees of freedom of assembly, speech, and press in Taiwan were somewhat weaker (though the press was more representative of the populace in age, gender, political views, and place of birth generally than its counterparts in Western countries). Citizens in Taiwan, however, note that the expression of civil and political liberties is conditioned by the political culture, and, given the greater respect for political leaders in Chinese political culture and the values placed on stability, freedom of speech has not necessarily been more limited than in Western democracies. For example, most people in Taiwan do not consider it proper to criticize officials using vulgar language. In any event, in recent years, there seems to be little difference in the practice of basic rights by citizens of Taiwan as compared to most Western democracies. In some ways Taiwan has gone further. Citizens and the media assail and castigate political leaders with a verve that often surpasses Western polities.

Religious freedom is considered broader in Taiwan than in most Western nations because few religious organizations (other than the Presbyterian Church) have become involved in politics and because social problems seldom provoke religious debate. Also, few people discriminate against others for reasons of religion. Taiwan's lower crime rate affords greater freedom of movement. Freedom of association and privacy are guaranteed at about the same level as in Western nations. Taiwan's respect for basic rights and political and other freedoms is ranked high by various organizations, in marked contrast to the authoritarian tendencies of the People's Republic of China and many Third World countries.[10]

The Constitution provides citizens with the right to vote and the powers of recall, initiative, and referendum. Elections are held in Taiwan more often than in Western countries; indeed, political elites as well as many citizens complain they are too frequent. Campaigns are shorter than those in the West, and campaigning is more limited by election rules than in most Western countries (though the new trend is toward fewer campaign restrictions).

Written with the intent to legitimate rule over a heterogeneous nation when the Nationalists ruled China (or all of China), the Constitution contains protections for the rights of the various minorities. These provisions are so strong and specific that government officials sometimes dub them "affirmative action" provisions. For example, if they are not elected in sufficient numbers, the Constitution allocates seats in the elective bodies of government to racial and ethnic minorities, women, labor, and other groups. Few Western constitutions have gone this far in guaranteeing representation of minorities or the underprivileged.[11] The Constitution also specifies certain policies and goals in the areas of national economy, defense, foreign policy, social security, and education not usually found in Western constitutions. Some say these provisions have facilitated government planning, especially long-range planning, in these areas. Critics say it is unnecessary to have these things in the Constitution.

In early 1991, in an extraordinary session, the National Assembly abolished the Temporary Provisions and adopted ten amendments, or "additional articles," to the Constitution. Observers said that these articles created genuine constitutional rule in Taiwan. The amendments ended the representation in Taiwan's elected bodies of government—the National Assembly, the Legislative Yuan, and the Control Yuan—of delegates representing areas on the Mainland. The political system was also changed to include the election of a national constituency in the National Assembly and the Legislative Yuan based on proportional representation, with at-large seats granted to the political parties (including a provision for a small number of delegates to represent "Chinese who reside abroad"). Constitutional revisions also provided for laws to handle matters arising from the increasing contacts between Taiwan and China. Finally, provisions were made for the election of a new National Assembly in December 1991 that would enact further amendments.

In May 1992, the second National Assembly met as a kind of constitutional convention and added eight more amendments to the Constitution. These articles provided for the following changes in Taiwan's political system: the election of the National Assembly every four years, the direct election of the president (though the details were to be worked out later) every four years, the appointment of members of the Control Yuan (instead of their being chosen by indirect election), the implementation of reforms in provincial and local government, guarantees of state support for science and technology, provisions for environmental protection, the equivalent of an equal rights amendment for women, and safeguards for the handicapped, disabled, and the Aborigines.

In July 1994, the National Assembly revised and consolidated the eighteen amendments, reducing them to ten. Some new provisions were added. One of these set forth the details for the direct election of the president and vice president, beginning in 1996. Another one restricted—and nearly canceled—the power of the premier to countersign presidential appointments and dismissals. The National Assembly was also given more political power through provisions added for a speaker and yearly meetings. Other minor changes were made.

In the summer of 1997, the Constitution was amended once again with eleven more "additional articles." Important provisions in these articles, made necessary by democratization and multiparty politics, changed the nature of the relationship among the branches of the national government. As a result, the president now appoints the premier without approval of the Legislative Yuan and can dissolve the latter. The Legislative Yuan, however, can render a vote of no confidence in the premier. The Legislative Yuan was also given the power of impeachment. One amendment all but eliminated the provincial government. Various local government offices were turned into appointed positions in order to reduce the impact of vote buying and other kinds of corruption.[12]

In 2003, the Legislative Yuan passed the Referendum Act, which defined this term (used in the Constitution). The act did not allow referendums to be called to decide the national territory, and thus referendums could not be used to deal with the matter of independence. It did, however, allow the electorate to decide issues relating to national defense, and President Chen used this to add two referendums to the ballot during the 2004 presidential election that related to Taiwan's status as part of China or not. The referendums failed. In 2005, the Constitution was amended to abolish the National Assembly and transfer its power to ratify the Constitution to the Legislative Yuan and the people. Another amendment changed the electoral system from a single, nontransferable vote in multimember districts to a single constituency, two-ballot system (one vote for a candidate and one for a political party).[13]

Notwithstanding numerous constitutional amendments, Taiwan's political system remains a mixed one. Many officials and scholars believe the Constitution should be amended further in order to create clearly either a presidential or a parliamentary structure. In the past, this did not matter, because the Nationalist Party controlled both the executive and legislative branches of government. But divided government after May 2000 showed the political system was patently in need of repair. Nationalist Party victories in a legislative election in January 2008 and a presidential election that March made this a moot point for the time being.

The National Assembly and the Presidency

The Constitution (before it was amended) provided for an elected National Assembly, members of which were chosen for six-year terms to represent counties, municipalities, and areas of equivalent status. The National Assembly's most important functions were to (1) elect the president and vice president, (2) recall the same if necessary, (3) amend the Constitution, (4) make provisions to exercise initiatives and referendums, and (5) approve appointments made by the president. The first National Assembly was elected in 1947 before the Nationalists fled to Taiwan. Until 1991, no full election of the National Assembly was held. The official reason for this was that the "Communist rebellion" on the Mainland precluded a nationwide election. Cynics, however, charge the Assembly was "frozen in time" in order to impede both democratization and Taiwanization.

Critics of the National Assembly voiced several other complaints: that it met only once every six years (therefore its members did not earn their pay); that it was too large to deliberate effectively; and that it was composed largely of delegates without significant political experience or qualifications, most of whom were too old to do much work. In addition, opposition politicians charged that the National Assembly was little more than a rubber-stamp body for approving decisions made by the ruling Nationalist Party.

As democratization gained momentum in the 1980s, pressure grew to "fix" the National Assembly. In January 1989, the Legislative Yuan passed the Law on Voluntary Retirement of Senior Parliamentarians in the hope of persuading the elder members of the National Assembly and Legislative Yuan to step down. But only a few resigned. The Nationalist Party then tried to induce its older members to quit, but with little effect. In June 1990, the Council of Grand Justices (a group of justices that serves as a constitutional court) made a ruling that they had to retire before December 1991. This measure succeeded.

In December 1991, a second National Assembly was elected to a four-year term. The new National Assembly, democratically chosen and representing the population of Taiwan almost exclusively, became a true democratic body of government. In 1994, the National Assembly's powers were expanded through changes in the Constitution. However, because the president and vice president were now to be elected directly, the Assembly lost its most important function. At the time, it was uncertain whether it would become a second "chamber" in a bicameral legislature, whether it would be abolished, or whether it would become simply an electoral college.[14]

As the 2000 presidential election approached, the future status of the National Assembly became the subject of considerable and often intense debate. The Democratic Progressive Party, which had long advocated abolishing the Assembly, made an issue of its providing high-salaried sinecures for its members, thus constituting, it said, a form of political corruption. Court decisions regarding its future elections and James Soong forming the People First Party after the election (and the prospect of his drawing KMT members of the National Assembly away), paved the way for a KMT-DPP deal to settle the National Assembly issue once and for all. In April, its members voted to reduce the National Assembly to an ad hoc body. As a result, it virtually ceased to function. However, it retained its powers to ratify constitutional amendments and to vote on a presidential impeachment. To do either, though, a new National Assembly would have to be constituted when called upon, and that would no doubt complicate these functions and probably make forming a National Assembly infrequent. In 2005, an ad hoc National

Assembly ratified an additional article of the Constitution that included a provision to abolish itself.[15]

Unlike the National Assembly, the Office of the President has considerable authority that derives both specifically from the Constitution and that has evolved through practice. As chief of state, the president is formally responsible for state functions such as promulgating laws, declaring martial law, appointing officials, granting amnesty and commutations, and conducting foreign relations, including making treaties and executive agreements. He or she also commands the armed forces and can declare war or peace. Finally, the president is responsible for resolving disputes among the five branches of government and for exercising emergency powers.

The president, in addition, has powers that derive from his or her leadership position in the ruling party (if the president is of that party), though this authority has not been institutionalized. (Yen Chia-kan, who became president when Chiang Kai-shek died, was not a strong president because he did not lead his party. Chen Shui-bian gave up his party posts after he became president because his presidency was weak resulting from his party's failure to achieve a majority in the Legislative Yuan.) This "derivative power," when the president has it, strengthens the authority of the presidential office considerably, and it is in this instance not unlike similar powers enjoyed by presidents in Western democracies. The presidency has been bolstered further as a result of the perceived need for strong leadership and also because Taiwan's past presidents have been a major force behind successful economic and political reform. Symbolic duties and the president's role in representing the nation in the international community have similarly enhanced the power of the office.

The Office of the President consists of a secretary-general, senior advisers, national policy and military strategy advisers, and military aides. The secretary-general to the president manages the general affairs of the Office of the President, supervises staff members, and controls the president's time in a manner similar to that of the White House chief of staff in the United States. Bureaus under the president perform or oversee functions in three general areas: The First Bureau is responsible for the executive functions of the president, including promulgating laws and orders and keeping confidential and secret documents; the Second Bureau transmits military orders and maintains liaison with the military; the Third Bureau handles protocol and administrative duties.[16]

In 1967, the National Security Council was established within the Office of the President to coordinate national strategy. In 1990, the National Unification Council was founded to bring various groups and individuals together to discuss and implement the unification of China. Academia Sinica, the nation's foremost think tank or association of scholars, and Academia Historica, a historical research center and document-preservation organization, were already under presidential administration.

In 1994, the details were worked out, following the passage of a relevant constitutional amendment, for the direct election of the president and vice president. The first such election was held in 1996. Lee Teng-hui won re-election, and, because it was a direct election, he gained a stronger mandate and enhanced political power. Meanwhile, a constitutional provision reduced the authority of the premier, thereby making Taiwan's political system, according to many observers, more clearly presidential. Other constitutional provisions, however, such as the Legislative Yuan's expanded powers—especially its power to initiate impeachment of the president and the vice president—suggested otherwise. In any event, the lines of authority between the president and the legislature were in some important respects still in need of clarification.[17]

Chiang Kai-shek was president from 1950 until his death in 1975, having been elected in 1972 to a fifth six-year term that he did not complete. The Temporary Provisions enhanced Chiang's presidential powers, as did martial law and the fact that he held undisputed control over the ruling party, the military, and the police. He was thus an "authoritarian president." When Chiang died, Yen Chia-kan, a former governor of Taiwan Province and vice president from 1966 to 1975, succeeded him. Yen, however, was not a strong president. Premier Chiang Ching-kuo, Chiang Kai-shek's son, controlled the ruling Nationalist Party and wielded considerable political influence elsewhere, notably with the police, the military, and the intelligence community. This did not create an untenable situation because Yen and Chiang Ching-kuo were not political opponents and because the Constitution was at this time ambiguous about whether the system was presidential, parliamentary, or cabinet. In addition, Yen announced early on that he would not be a candidate for president in the next election and thus was viewed as an interim president. Chiang Ching-kuo de facto ran the government from his position as premier.

Chiang Ching-kuo was elected president in 1978 and inherited many of his father's powers. But he sought strenuously to make Taiwan a democracy and did not rule so much in an authoritarian way; in so doing, he weakened the powers of the presidency somewhat. He was re-elected in March 1984 for a second six-year term. Shieh Tung-min, the first Taiwanese to attain such a high office, was Chiang's first vice president. Chiang chose Lee Teng-hui, the former governor of Taiwan Province, also Taiwanese (Hakka), as his second vice president and heir apparent in 1984. In January 1988, Chiang died in office.

Upon Chiang Ching-kuo's death, Lee Teng-hui became president. For a time, there was talk that Lee might be a figurehead president because he did not have the power base or popularity of Chiang. It was also widely speculated, because of the hold on power by Taiwan's Mainland Chinese, that Lee's powers would be circumscribed. But Lee had earned respect both in the Nationalist Party and among the populace because of his foreign education (in Japan and the United States, including a PhD from Cornell University), his years of outstanding government service, and his many years of close ties with Chiang Ching-kuo. Lee also possessed considerable political acumen. Democratization, which many said required a Taiwan-born leader, also favored Lee, as did his election in a direct vote in 1996. Lee was nevertheless confronted by manifold challenges—many of which stemmed from Taiwan's rapid democratization and the transition to Taiwanese majority rule. He also had to deal with changes in the political system and the political culture, not to mention opposition politics and splits in his party. Still, he proved to be a strong, able, and generally popular leader.

In May 2000, Chen Shui-bian, a member of the opposition Democratic Progressive Party, became Taiwan's fifth president. He had been a legislator and was mayor of Taipei from 1994 to 1998. Almost immediately after his inauguration, the now-opposition Nationalist Party, in cooperation with James Soong's newly formed People First Party, through their control of the legislature engaged in a power struggle with President Chen that in part focused on the authority of the president. The gridlock that followed showed that presidential and legislative prerogatives should have been delineated more clearly in the Constitution and that amendments were needed to do this. The problem of divided government persisted throughout Chen's presidency, explaining in large measure why President Chen accomplished very little, though Chen also showed a lack of leadership at times, did not manage the economy well, and became woefully corrupt. He also exacerbated ethnic ill will to enhance his governance, which sullied his presidency.

In 2008, Ma Ying-jeou, a former minister of justice and Taipei mayor, was elected president, representing the Nationalist Party. Ma won the largest number of votes and the biggest percentage of the popular vote since direct elections of the president began. With the KMT having won a solid victory in the legislature two months earlier, Ma did not face a divided government and seemed destined to be a stronger and more effective president than Chen had been. In many ways Ma returned the presidency to what it had been before 2000. In 2012 Ma was reelected.

The Five-Branch Government

As noted earlier, Taiwan's central government is patterned after the US three-branch system, with the addition of two more branches. It was thought that a five-branch government would ensure greater division of power and more effective checks and balances. It had other advantages as well (though also some disadvantages). At the time the Constitution was enacted, it was considered by officials and citizens of the Republic of China to be a uniquely Chinese system.

Of the five branches of government, the Executive Yuan has always been the most powerful. The reason, of course, is that the president controls this branch of the government. The Executive Yuan early on was also efficient and responsive to public opinion, taking big strides in that direction after Chiang Ching-kuo took measures to reform the government in the late 1970s. In fact, before the retirement of the "elder parliamentarians," the Executive Yuan was regarded as more sensitive to the public pulse than the Legislative Yuan. In some respect, it still is.

The premier is chosen by the president to head the Executive Yuan. Under the premier are a vice premier and eight important ministers (interior, foreign affairs, defense, finance, education, justice, economic affairs, and transportation and communications) also appointed by the president. These ministries perform functions similar to those of their counterparts in other political systems. Attached to the Executive Yuan are a number of other important ministerial-level bodies.[18]

In 2010, the Legislative Yuan passed bills to restructure and streamline the executive branch of government to be implemented during the period of January 1, 2012, to December 31, 2014. The Executive Yuan was slated to consist of fourteen ministries, four councils, three independent agencies, and four additional organizations. The next year legislation was enacted to transform certain state-run organizations into independent bodies. These included the Chung-Shan Institute of Science and Technology, the National Sports Training Center, the National Science and Technology Center for Disaster Reduction, and the National Science Council.[19]

The numerous government organs that are part of the Executive Yuan reflect its broad authority for policy formulation as well as its host of administrative duties. In fact, this is where most bills or laws are drafted and political decisions implemented. Officials of the Executive Yuan work closely with the president and top leaders of the ruling party who, as a matter of practice, take the initiative to make policy and exercise strong influence broadly on the political agenda.

Decisions made by the Executive Yuan are checked by the Legislative Yuan, which has the power to interpret, reject, or alter them. In the past, these checks were rather feeble, owing to a weak legislature and the fact that the Nationalist Party dominated the setting of policy goals. The Legislative Yuan gained power as it became more representative of the population and more active, coinciding with Taiwan's rapid democratization in the 1980s and 1990s. After Chen Shui-bian was elected president in 2000, the Legislative Yuan became even stronger and aggressively impeded many of his actions and policies and put forth its own agenda.

When Chiang Ching-kuo became premier in 1972, that office became more powerful. When he was elected president in 1978, Sun Yun-suan became premier and served until May 1984. Sun had a technical background, and, though his critics claimed he did not have a sufficiently broad political base, he was highly respected and considered a superb leader. Before he suffered a stroke, many considered him the likely successor to Chiang Ching-kuo. Yu Kuo-hua, who had been head of the Central Bank, succeeded Sun. Yu was an effective—though not popular—premier.

In 1989, President Lee Teng-hui appointed Lee Huan, then secretary-general of the Nationalist Party and a popular political figure, as premier. However, a year later, in 1990, President Lee called on Hau Pei-stun, then minister of defense, to be premier. Some said Lee sought to win the support of the military, where he had little influence, and needed Hau.

But relations between the president and Premier Hau turned sour after a short time. Many said their difficulties reflected ethnic politics in Taiwan, because President Lee was Taiwanese and Premier Hau was Mainland Chinese (the same having been said also of the relationship between President Lee and Lee Huan). There were also disagreements between the two about policies and party issues. A systemic crisis resulted because of the ill-defined relationship between the premier—who was appointed by the president but who could not be fired by him or her—and the president. The crisis was, in practice, resolved after the 1992 Legislative Yuan election, when Premier Hau resigned. As noted earlier, the Constitution has since been amended to clarify the authority of the president and the premier in favor of the former. Since then premiers have not been as important.

Taiwan's unicameral Legislative Yuan is the lawmaking body of the national government, often called the parliament or senate. In addition to its legislative functions, it confirms emergency orders, approves budgets (submitted by the Executive Yuan), and proposes amendments to the Constitution. The Legislative Yuan approves Executive Yuan policy statements and reports and serves as a check on the Judicial Yuan, the Control Yuan, and the Examination Yuan. It may, as noted earlier, also initiate impeachment proceedings against the president and vice president. It has some lesser powers as well, such as providing grants-in-aid to provincial government organs and settling disputes between the national government and units of local government.

Legislative Yuan members elect a president or speaker and vice president and endorse his or her appointment of a secretary-general. Members of the legislature make their own rules regarding procedures for debating and passing laws and bills as well as for dealing with members who misbehave or violate ethical standards, although such responsibilities also belong to the Control Yuan. Much of the work of the Legislative Yuan is done in its standing committees.

The Legislative Yuan originally numbered 225 members (enlarged by 61 seats before the December 1998 election); it was made up of 176 delegates who represent electoral districts (mostly multimember districts of varying size), and 49 at-large senators (41 of whom represent a national constituency and 8 of whom represent Chinese overseas). Recently it has been downsized (as will be discussed below).

Currently, the Legislative Yuan convenes two sessions each year: one from February to the end of May, the other from September to the end of the year. It may hold extraordinary sessions, called by its president, at any time. A simple majority passes resolutions, with some exceptions specified in the Constitution. Legislative Yuan members have immunity from being sued or indicted for most crimes while in office, though the scope of this exemption has been narrowed in recent years because of abuse.

Like the National Assembly, the Legislative Yuan, when first formed, represented all of China, the Mainland as well as Taiwan, and continued to do so after the government moved to Taiwan in 1949. It became more representative of Taiwan after 1969, when new members were elected. Subsequently, as elections brought in more new blood and Mainland representatives grew older, younger members elected to represent Taiwan, who were mainly Taiwanese, dominated work in the Legislative Yuan. Still, critics protested that not all members of the Legislative Yuan were elected and that it unrealistically claimed to represent China. As in the case of the National Assembly, defenders pointed out that if the Legislative Yuan stopped representing districts in China, Taiwan would be de facto adopting a two-China policy and Beijing's leaders had promised to use military force against Taiwan to prevent Taiwan's legal independence. This issue became moot after the "elder parliamentarians" stepped down and a plenary election was held in 1992.

The Legislative Yuan traditionally had much less decision-making authority than the Executive Yuan. This changed with the nation's democratization. Nevertheless, the antics that went on in legislative sessions and the bad behavior of some of its members aroused public ridicule and satire in the press at home and abroad. Known—indeed famous—criminals winning election to the legislature and the underworld ties of many other members, not to mention frequent cases of corruption, also brought dishonor to the body.[20]

A number of reforms have consequently been enacted to enhance the prestige and effectiveness of the Legislative Yuan. In 1993, the legislature improved its image somewhat when it passed a "sunshine bill" that required members to disclose their personal wealth. In 2004, the Legislative Yuan voted 217 to 1 (in the context of 70 percent public support according to public opinion polls) to halve the number of seats to 113, increase the terms of members to four years (so that elections would coincide with presidential elections), and change the electoral system for the legislature. The new legislature seated in January 2008 contained 73 directly elected members and 6 seats reserved for Aborigines, plus 34 seats filled by the parties, half of which must be women. There was considerable debate at the time concerning whether this would improve the efficiency of the legislature and the quality of and respect accorded its members.[21]

The Judicial Yuan functions much like the judicial branches of government in other nations, although structurally it is somewhat different. It is composed of a president, a vice president, and fifteen justices. All are appointed by the Office of the President, originally with the approval of the National Assembly, but now the Legislative Yuan.[22] The Judicial Yuan is organized into a Council of Grand Justices, three levels of ordinary courts (the Supreme Court, high courts, and district courts), administrative courts, and a Committee on the Discipline of Public Functionaries. The Council of Grand Justices, which meets twice weekly, interprets the Constitution in a fashion that resembles the process of judicial review in Western systems. An interpretation of the Constitution requires a three-fourths vote from the members present and a quorum of three-fourths of members; a simple majority can make other decisions. Government agencies and individuals can call for an interpretation of the Constitution.

The Supreme Court is the highest of the three levels of ordinary courts. It hears appeals in civil and criminal cases, motions to set aside decisions of the high courts, and special cases. The Supreme Court is divided into several civil and criminal "senates" (at present eight and twelve, respectively). Each senate includes a presiding judge and four associates. Because of this division of work, the Supreme Court can hear more cases than would otherwise be possible and thus avoids backlogs and delays. Because the Supreme Court decides only issues of law, not of fact, its proceedings are primarily documentary; also, because few of its proceedings are oral, the system is less adversarial than Western legal systems.

The high courts hear cases of appeal from district courts, criminal cases involving rebellion and treason, cases involving other nations, and election lawsuits. District courts hear original civil and criminal cases involving juvenile, family, traffic, and financial cases and other less contentious matters. Administrative courts handle suits against the government and cases involving violations of citizens' rights by administrative actions of the government. The Committee on the Discipline of Public Functionaries serves as a check on decisions of the Control Yuan involving impeachment, dismissal, and the like.

Taiwan is a civil law society; thus the judicial system places an emphasis on statutes rather than on case law. Its legal culture has several historical origins in addition to its design based on the Constitutional structure just cited. Business and high tech have influenced the system in recent years, as has legal education modeled on that in the United States.

In terms of how the legal system operates in court, Taiwan's judicial system has been moved in recent years from a "judge-centered, inquisitorial system" (the German model) to an "attorney-based, adversarial system" (like that of the United States) in response to growing public interest in lawsuits and lawyers becoming more activist. There was concern that making this change would lead to a glut of legal cases in the courts; this, however, has been alleviated by a number of means including prosecutor plea bargaining.[23]

Critics of the Judicial Yuan have argued that it is not as strong as a judicial body of government should be and not sufficiently independent of ruling party influence. This charge was often leveled at the KMT when it was in power, but subsequently also at the DPP. Some observers complain that judges are government employees recruited through a government examination and are thus not impartial.[24] Defenders point out that the 1980 Separation of Trial from Prosecution Reform Act made the Judicial Yuan more independent and maintain that it should not be given excessive power because it is not an elected organ of government. Furthermore, they say that public distaste for instituting legal proceedings lessens the need for a strong judicial body. Taiwan is a less litigious society than the United States and other Western countries, though this has been changing in recent years.

Citizens' confidence in the judiciary suffered considerably during the Chen administration. The president promised judicial reform, but because of his administration's standoff with the Legislative Yuan and the paralysis that caused, plus corruption in the administration, little happened. Also, critics accused the Chen administration of making judicial appointments for purely political reasons. In fact, the street protest against President Chen and the DPP in 2006 was in part prompted by the fact that it was widely perceived that Chen controlled the judiciary and the prosecutors and that they, in turn, protected a corrupt administration. Confidence was to some extent restored when prosecutors indicted Chen's son-in-law and the president's wife for various crimes when Chen Shui-bian was serving as president.[25]

Under President Ma Ying-jeou, the judicial system underwent quite intense criticism related to its handling of former president Chen Shui-bian's indictment and sentencing for corruption, accepting bribes, misusing state funds, and money laundering. The criticism focused on the fact Chen was held in detention for some time without charges and on frequent leaks to the media about the case when it was in progress.[26] Part of reason for the controversy was that many people believed him innocent even of the crimes to which he confessed, while others wanted to use the trial to embarrass him and disgrace his political party.

The Control Yuan was originally a special branch of government patterned after the Censorate in Imperial China, which functioned as a watchdog body similar to the Government Accountability Office in the United States. Provincial and municipal councils elected its twenty-nine members. Because of scandals that arose over the buying of seats and a decline in the number of important cases it heard, among other reasons, the status of the Control Yuan was changed dramatically. In February 1993, the Control Yuan became a body of government appointed by the president with the approval of the Legislative Yuan. Its basic functions were truncated so it is no longer a parliamentary (elected) body and has lost many of its supervisory functions.[27] The Control Yuan is now best described as a quasi-judicial oversight branch of government designed to check on officials.

The Control Yuan retained the powers of impeachment, censure, and audit—though the authority to impeach the president or vice president was taken away in 1997. It may investigate the Executive Yuan and its subordinate agencies. It may censure public officials. It oversees the Ministry of Audit—one of its main functions. It approves presidential appointments (by a secret vote in a plenary session) and has the power to investigate and hear complaints from the public.

In 2004, President Chen submitted a list of Control Yuan appointees that the Legislative Yuan declined to approve. The legislature asked for a new list, but Chen did not submit one, and the Control Yuan, for all intents and purposes, ceased to function. Some observers said it was a casualty in the power struggle between the president and the opposition. Critics said that the president did not want it to investigate corruption in his administration. It would certainly have played a role when President Chen's wife was indicted, and it may have taken action against President Chen.[28]

The Examination Yuan is responsible for writing and administering the equivalent of civil service examinations in Western political systems. In the Chinese political tradition, the examination function was of such importance that a special branch of government was created to conduct and oversee it. Today, the Examination Yuan administers four kinds of special examinations to recruit and screen applicants for government service. It also deals with job qualifications, job security, and retirement issues. The Examination Yuan is organized into a council, a secretariat, and two ministries: the Ministry of Examination and the Ministry of Personnel. The president appoints members of the Examination Yuan.

There has been considerable public debate about the structure of the government in Taiwan. Various noted individuals and leaders of the political parties have proposed abolishing the Control Yuan and the Examination Yuan and establishing a three-branch system of government. If this were done, the functions of the two would be transferred to the Executive and Legislative Yuans. The relationship between the executive and legislative branches of government and the relationship of both to the president are also the subject of considerable debate.

Local Government

As stated earlier, Taiwan's political system is a unitary one (meaning that the central government is the dominant political authority), though it has some of the characteristics of a federal system (meaning that local government has first or primary jurisdiction in certain realms).[29] There is also overlapping authority. That was particularly true in the past in the relationship between the provincial government and the central government. External threats and advances in transportation and communications in recent years have expanded the role of the central government, as have its ability to make quick responses to problems associated with rapid economic and political change.[30] Finally, the ruling party and most top government officials both past and present have favored keeping power at the center.

Local government, on the other hand, gets a great deal of credit for political reform and democratization. Many argue that democracy evolved in Taiwan "from the bottom up," meaning that democratic change came first to local politics. Global trends also favor the decentralization of political authority, because governments must maintain cost-efficiency. Another factor that favors local government is that Taiwan's political system allows local politicians to gain experience and name recognition, thus providing them with an avenue by which they can move up to positions in the national government; indeed, local government remains strong, and its various offices find talent more easily because of those opportunities. Local officials who rise to the top also favor keeping the functions and powers of local government intact. Finally, there has been and remains a strong interest in local politics on the part of the citizenry of Taiwan.

The organization of local government is based on provisions in the Constitution for local self-government that created provincial and county governments in addition to metropolitan, city, town, and village borough systems. Although units of local government report to officials or sections of government at a higher level, all are given some powers and responsibilities that do not relate to other units of government and do not depend on higher authority, as in federal systems.

The provincial government, the highest level of local government in Taiwan, was established in May 1947, following mass unrest and violence directed at the central government. It replaced the despised Office of the Governor-General. However, in 1949, after the Nationalists fled to Taiwan, Taiwan Province came almost totally under the control of the central government. Because the latter had jurisdiction over nearly all the land and population now constituting the Republic of China, many provincial government functions and duties overlapped with those of the central government. In these areas, the national government usually dominated.

Below the provincial government were sixteen counties, where most of the work of local government was performed. County governments were divided into urban or rural categories, the former being subdivided into boroughs and the latter into villages. Two metropolitan governments were established later: Taipei and Kaohsiung. In many ways, these became more important than the county governments and more powerful than even the provincial government (before it was downsized) because of the number of people under their jurisdiction, the many difficult but important tasks they performed, and their close relationship with the national organs of government.[31]

The top level of local government was originally the popularly elected Provincial Assembly, composed of members who served four-year terms, and an appointed governor. The main policy-making body of the provincial government was the Provincial Government Council, which consisted of twenty-three of the seventy-nine members of the Provincial Assembly, specially selected by the Executive Yuan and the governor. The Provincial Government Council served as a cabinet. Though the powers of the Provincial Assembly were not broad, the body mirrored public opinion more accurately than elected bodies of the national government because the former was elected in full every four years and represented only Taiwan.[32]

For some years, many who demanded more democracy in Taiwan—especially those who rejected the ruling Nationalist Party's claim to represent China—

advocated a greater role for the provincial government. In particular, they sought to give broader responsibilities and powers to the Provincial Assembly and grant it greater independence from the national government. However, after plenary elections democratized the National Assembly and the Legislative Yuan, this criticism subsided.

In 1992, the legalization of local autonomy was realized by constitutional amendment and had a major impact in strengthening local government.[33] In the process, Quemoy, Matsu, and the parts of the Pratas and Spratly Areas under Taipei's control were granted local autonomy. They had been under military jurisdiction. Quemoy and Matsu now have county governments. At this time, the provincial governor was made an elective office, and in 1994 Taiwan's voters elected James Soong governor.

As noted earlier, in 1996, President Lee Teng-hui convened a gathering of officials, scholars, and politicians (called the National Development Conference) to discuss political reforms and additional constitutional amendments. One of the main topics at the meeting was downsizing or eliminating the provincial and village levels of government. The duplication of functions by the national and provincial governments was said to be expensive and made government less efficient. The opposition Democratic Progressive Party, as well as many scholars and government officials, supported Lee's proposals. The National Assembly subsequently acted, and, in 1997, made constitutional changes to shrink the provincial government drastically. In December 1998, the Provincial Assembly was virtually eliminated, along with the elected governorship and most other organs of the provincial government.

When the National Development Conference recommended that the provincial governor once again be made an appointed job, James Soong resigned. His resignation was not accepted, however, and he remained on the job until the end of 1998. In the meantime, his relationship with President Lee, which was once very close, deteriorated, and the two became hostile toward each other. Many disputes associated with downsizing the provincial government, such as where its assets and personnel would go and who would control them, were aired in public.

In the meantime, in 1967 Taipei was made a "special municipality" followed by Kaohsiung in 1979. As a result, the mayors of Taiwan's two largest cities were thereafter appointed by the national government. The official reason given was that the size of these two cities made it necessary for their executive heads to coordinate policies and actions with the national government—a seemingly logical explanation given that Taipei was the seat of the national government and Kaohsiung was Taiwan's major port city. However, opposition politicians claimed that the national government sought to inhibit the development of democratic government in these cities and eliminate a political base for popular Taiwanese politicians. In any event, the mayorships of these two cities were made elective offices again, and in December 1994 the two mayors were chosen by their respective electorates. The mayors of the two cities, but especially the mayor of Taipei, have been important and very visible political figures. Former president Chen was mayor of Taipei from 1994 to 1998; President Ma Ying-jeou was mayor of Taipei from 1998 to 2006; Frank Hsieh was mayor of Kaohsiung from 1998 to 2005.

In 2010, three new metropolitan cities were created: New Taipei City, which was originally Taipei County; Taichung City, formed by a merger of Taichung City and Taichung County; Tainan City, formed from Tainan City and Tainan County; Kaohsiung City, expanded by adding Kaohsiung County; and Taipei City, which remained the same. Taoyuan County, the site of Taipei International Airport, was made a provisional special municipality effective January 2011.[34]

According to the Constitution before it was amended, below the provincial government (except for the two municipal governments just mentioned) were county, town, and village governments. These units of local government operated with considerable autonomy and authority. This was true even though, as noted earlier, the political system of Taiwan is designed to be a unitary one. Local leaders had considerable say over budget issues and some other matters that do not relate directly to national policy.

The National Development Conference, in addition to proposing that the provisional government be scrapped, recommended the elimination of another level of government: village government. Again, efficiency was the main consideration, but reducing vote buying was also a reason. In fact, the National Development Conference's suggestion was made into another constitutional amendment, and village government was virtually eliminated. Some say it came at the expense of local democracy; others contend it made for better, more efficient, and more honest government.

Shortly after the Nationalists arrived in Taiwan, they held provincial and local elections. Contrary to expectations, the Kuomintang did not try to suppress democracy locally; rather, KMT officials encouraged it. Because of strong opposing factions in local politics and potent centrifugal forces, the KMT could play a mediator role and control or effectively play off local factions against one another while bringing many local leaders into the ruling party, thereby stemming the growth of a political opposition. On the other hand, many KMT leaders genuinely wanted to create a democratic system in accordance with Sun Yat-sen's teachings and felt that the existing local government was not sufficiently democratic.[35]

Many local officials did not share the KMT's view about local politics and believed that they could build the foundations for democracy locally, and later they said they did. Their view was that democracy came from "the bottom up." They argued that because democracy had been practiced locally for thirty years in the form of regular elections, the first competitive election in national politics in 1980 and national elections after that were successful. Interestingly, voter turnout has been higher in local elections than in national elections, which suggests that the electorate sees more—or at least more meaningful—democracy locally than it does at the national level. Part of the explanation, however, is that the electorate, like that in Japan and France (but unlike the United States and most other Western democracies), tends to identify with local issues. Voters also perceive that their votes are more important in deciding local matters than national ones, and they are generally better informed about candidates for positions in local government.

When it was founded in 1986, the Democratic Progressive Party attracted leaders and even candidates for high office that, for the most part, made their mark in local politics. In the 1990s, especially after the DPP won a major victory in local elections in 1997, there was talk that the DPP may come to control local politics and the KMT would continue to run the national government. While this did not happen, DPP officials have performed well in local offices and can claim to be better at it than the KMT.

Political Parties

To grasp how political power is exercised in Taiwan, one must understand the functions and roles of political parties, how they are organized, and how their leadership works, especially in the Nationalist Party and the Democratic Progressive Party. It is likewise essential to grasp the nature of Taiwan's party structure, how it has changed in some important respects in recent years, and what kind of system is evolving.

The Temporary Provisions, discussed earlier in this chapter, made it unlawful to form new political parties in Taiwan. Thus, until 1986, in addition to the KMT, only two other parties, the Young China Party and the China Democratic Socialist Party, which were established before the Temporary Provisions were enacted, campaigned or sponsored candidates in elections. But because these two parties were small and were in large measure controlled by the KMT, they had little real political power or influence. Taiwan thus had a de facto one-party system. In fact, for many years, the Nationalist Party almost alone carried out the functions of recruitment and training, interest articulation, and interest aggregation. It also made decisions and policies that the government adopted pro forma, typical of one-party states.[36]

The Nationalist Party traces its origins to several political organizations founded by Sun Yat-sen, the first being the *Hsing Chung Hui,* or the Society for Regenerating China, set up in Hawaii in 1894. In August 1912, the *Tung Meng Hui,* or the Revolutionary Alliance, which Sun had established in Japan in 1905, merged with other groups to form the Nationalist Party or Kuomintang (KMT). In February of the next year, the KMT won a victory in China's first parliamentary elections. Meanwhile, however, Yuan Shih-kai, an adviser to the former imperial

A farmer drying rice in a courtyard.

Rice-harvesting time. Machines relieve backbreaking work.

Fourth- and fifth-grade students on a field day.

The computer is Taiwan's key to future economic growth and is an important tool in education.

Nuclear plants provide a large portion of Taiwan's electricity, but nuclear power is controversial.

Soldier guarding Taiwan's outpost on Quemoy.

In Taiwan, athletic shoes of every kind and style are produced mostly for export.

The textile industry in Taiwan is large, but its importance is declining.

A tollgate on an expressway. Such highways link all of Taiwan's major cities.

Commuting to work.

Religion and scenic vistas meet in Taiwan.

Central Taipei—the heart of a modern city.

The Presidential Palace during Nationalist China's celebration of Double-Ten Day (October 10), similar to July 4 in the United States. On October 10, 1911, Sun Yat-sen's supporters overthrew the Manchu dynasty.

Minority groups in native dress.

The Peking Opera is popular in Taiwan, where the government tries to preserve Chinese culture.

Buddhist ceremony at the Temple of Guanyin.

The Presidential Palace in downtown Taipai—built by the Japanese.

Hsinchu Science Park—Taiwan's Silicon Valley.

President Ma Ying-jeou.

Vice President Wu Den-yih.

government, seized the reins of power in Peking and threatened battle with Sun's supporters in the south. The standoff seemed likely to ignite a civil war, so Sun abdicated. Yuan subsequently suppressed KMT activities and established himself as a virtual dictator. But the KMT survived, and, after Yuan's death in 1916, Sun made several unsuccessful attempts to establish a democratic form of government with the KMT serving as his power base.

Sun died in 1925. After a brief power struggle, Chiang Kai-shek, with the military as his base of support, took over leadership of the KMT. Chiang, mainly through the military and the KMT, ruled China until 1949 when the Communists defeated his armies. The Nationalist Party, along with the government and the military, fled to Taiwan. Chiang headed the Nationalist Party until his death in 1975.

Chiang's son, Chiang Ching-kuo, was unanimously elected chairman of the Central Committee of the party—and thereby head of the Nationalist Party—after his father's death. He remained chairman of the party until he died in January 1988. President Lee Teng-hui then became acting chairman of the KMT; he was formally elected chairman at the Thirteenth Party Congress in July 1988. Lee was pressured to resign as head of the party after its defeat in the presidential election of 2000, and he stepped down. Lien Chan replaced him. Ma Ying-jeou was elected party chairman in 2005 and held that office until 2007.

Owing to the influence of Soviet advisers, Sun's perception that the West had not adequately supported him and his calls for democracy in China, and the need for strong organization, the Nationalist Party took its organizational structure from the Communist Party of the Soviet Union. Thus, many refer to it as a "Leninist party," which is an accurate description of the KMT's structure. The National Party Congress is theoretically the highest decision-making body in the KMT, but it is too large to deliberate on issues efficiently and was, until recent years, generally a rubber-stamp body. To a large extent, it still is. When not in session, the KMT delegates authority to its Central Committee as well as its thirty-some-member Central Standing Committee, which analysts have long regarded as the center of political power (before 2000 and after 2008). As with other Leninist parties, the secretary-general of the party, in concert with the chairman and other top-ranking members, make policies and even specific decisions. The Central Committee then confirms their decisions.

The KMT differs, however, from Leninist parties in some important ways. For example, unlike the ruling parties in Communist countries (including China), the KMT is more a mass party than an elite party. In the 1990s, the KMT claimed a membership of 2.1 million, or about 10 percent of the population.[37] Also, in contrast to the Chinese Communist Party, it did not create a centrally planned economy or attempt to completely mobilize and control the population. Furthermore, it never gave such high importance to ideology. Finally, the KMT changed its organizational structure and decision-making process to keep up with the nation's political modernization. Successful efforts to democratize the KMT were undertaken at the Thirteenth Party Congress as well as at subsequent congresses.[38]

Various departments in the KMT carry out party work: Organization Affairs, Mainland Operations, Overseas Affairs, Cultural Affairs, Social Affairs, Youth Activities, Women's Activities, and commissions dealing with financial affairs, party history, and discipline. Party activities are broad and involve such matters as welfare, recruitment for government jobs, and guiding or promoting government policies. This is further evidence the Nationalist Party is much more a Western-style political party than other Leninist parties.

In the past, the KMT operated numerous profit-making business enterprises, including several in the media and cultural fields. Critics contended that the KMT monopolized many areas of business and controlled the media. Its past influence over the news, publishing, and movie industries did, in many respects, amount to media control, but that changed with democratization. In recent years, the KMT has sold many of its enterprises and has cut its ties with certain media organizations. It still owns some businesses, but so does the DPP.

The KMT was financially well off. With assets of at least $2 billion (some say it is much more), it was for some time labeled the richest political party in the world.[39] Its assets naturally have been an advantage for the party in running campaigns and in many other respects. But its wealth has also been a handicap in the context of the evolution of popular democracy, especially when the opposition claims that the KMT buys elections and thus undermines good government. When running as the KMT's nominee for president in the 2000 election, Lien Chan pledged to put the party's assets in trust. Still the DPP and President Chen continued to talk about the KMT's money and how it got it, suggesting it did so by illegal means. Both repeatedly called for investigations into the matter. The DPP even put the issue before the voters in a referendum in January 2008, but it failed to win sufficient votes. In the meantime, DPP corruption became a more serious issue, and this and the depletion of the KMT's financial resources resulted in a different view of whether the KMT is a rich party that thrives on money politics.

In the past, because most important political decisions in the Republic of China were made by and within the party, the Nationalist Party to a large extent controlled or manipulated the government. In the minds of most citizens, the KMT was the government or was synonymous with it. Others described Taiwan as a "corporate state" because of these connections.[40] However, beginning in the 1980s, party leaders sought to change the KMT's image by breaking ties between it and the government—a necessary process if the party was to avoid being blamed for mistakes made by government officials and if the country was to evolve into a two-party or multiparty system.[41]

Meanwhile, beginning in the 1960s, as Nationalist Party leaders began to change their attitude about the need for party competition, the government allowed a number of opposition politicians to run in elections as independents. In the 1970s, a loose political organization called the *tangwai*, or "outside the party" (meaning the KMT because it was the only significant party), began to become active. It "sponsored" candidates in various local elections and began to recruit and train political leaders. In the national election in 1980—a watershed election in terms of the growth of party competition and contested elections in Taiwan—the *tangwai* supported candidates who openly opposed those of the Nationalist Party.[42]

After 1980, Taiwan continued to witness the rapid growth of opposition politics. In the 1983 national election, the *tangwai* developed "party goals" and campaigned as an "organization." Observers called it a virtual party or proto–political party. It had a platform that included issues upon which the opposition generally agreed: placing more seats up for election in the National Assembly, the Legislative Yuan, and the Control Yuan; holding popular elections for the governor of Taiwan and the mayors of Taipei and Kaohsiung; appointing more Taiwanese to high government posts; allowing new political parties to form legally; expanding the scope of freedom of the press, speech, and assembly; loosening restrictions on campaigning; abolishing the Temporary Provisions; reviewing trials that had resulted in the jailing of political prisoners; and demanding that the KMT relinquish powers and prerogatives that should belong to the government, not to a political party.

However, the *tangwai* suffered from factionalism and did not immediately mature into a viable, competitive political party. In particular, it was plagued by differences between radicals and moderates and by personality disputes among its leaders. Many of its members also made unrealistic demands for more extensive reforms of the political system than the public wanted or were feasible at the time. Thus, it did not perform as well as hoped at the polls or in recruiting new members.

In early 1986, President Chiang Ching-kuo appointed a twelve-member committee made up of party leaders and government officials, among others, to discuss the termination of martial law, ending the ban on forming new political parties, and making other reforms in government. In September, in a unilateral (and technically illegal) move, a group of *tangwai* politicians met and announced the formation of the Democratic Progressive Party (DPP). Chiang Ching-kuo ordered the government not to take any legal or administrative actions to block this move because the restriction on forming new parties was going to be lifted.[43]

The newly formed DPP announced a platform that closely resembled that of the *tangwai*'s. A slate of candidates campaigned in the December election with a DPP party flag and party slogans. Meanwhile, most *tangwai* members and many independents joined the DPP. The electorate, as well as most observers, viewed the 1986 campaign and election as a two-party contest.

The DPP won support among Taiwanese, workers, city dwellers, the poor, and people who did not like the KMT or the government (some say from 10 to 15 percent of the population cast a protest vote). Because Taiwanese generally reside more in rural areas where the KMT was well organized and had strong support (stemming from its successful efforts in land reform), building a rural base of support was problematic for the DPP. A platform to attract workers with its welfare or socialist agenda also failed. For the same reasons, the DPP alienated many Taiwanese businesspeople who might otherwise have provided money and talent for the DPP. The DPP's frequent use of street demonstrations, disruptive tactics, and violence in Legislative Yuan sessions meanwhile hurt its image. These tactics conflicted with the basic Chinese desire for stability.[44]

The DPP, like the *tangwai,* also suffered from factionalism and from fundamental differences in views on some important political questions. One of the most divisive issues was support of Taiwan's independence. Many DPP members supported independence or permanent separation from China, while many considered it premature, dangerous, or both. Another controversial matter was the party's relationship with the KMT. Some argued that the DPP had little chance of carrying out its agenda unless it cooperated with the KMT, at least at times. Others regarded the KMT as "the enemy" and found any compromise unacceptable. Still another issue was whether to welcome Chinese residents of other countries to return to Taiwan and whether those not born in Taiwan should be allowed to vote or run for political office.[45]

The DPP nonetheless succeeded in attracting new members and running well-known, popular, and qualified people for office and winning at the polls. It adopted a host of fresh issues, many of which it promoted successfully between elections, and won broad public support on many of them. In addition, it exploited KMT weaknesses and capitalized on the public's desire for democratization, which required, it said, party competition. It also used its underdog status and what some called the Taiwanese feeling of victimhood to win votes. And, last but not least, it learned quickly and became adept at democratic politics.[46]

The DPP performed well in national elections in 1989 and 1992 as well as in local elections in 1997. (See section on elections below.) After election victories, pundits regularly voiced the opinion that the DPP was the only real opposition party. Some said it would not be long before it was in power. This prediction indeed proved accurate. In 2000, the DPP's candidate, Chen Shui-bian, was elected president. Subsequently, the DPP was designated the "ruling party," even though it did not control a majority of the seats in the Legislative Yuan. In 2001, however, the DPP became the largest party in the Legislative Yuan, and at that point the term "ruling party" seemed undeniable.

Interestingly, the DPP is organized in much the same way as the KMT and, for that reason, may also be called a Leninist party. It holds party congresses, and its delegates pick a central committee, which then selects a core leadership—just as the KMT does. Its leadership, however, has not been very stable, especially during the several years immediately after its formation. Party leaders said this made the party's decision-making process more democratic. The DPP is a mass party, like the KMT, which it intended to be from the beginning. Thus it has engaged in energetic recruitment efforts (though new members have to be recommended by current members, and there are some other requirements to attain membership). After Chen Shui-bian was elected president in March 2000, the DPP was much more successful in attracting new members.[47]

The DPP, on the other hand, was not the only opposition party to arrive on the political scene during the 1980s and 1990s. Six new political parties appeared in 1987, and several more in 1988. In February 1989, when the formation of new political parties became legal, sixteen parties registered. Leading up to the 1991 election, Taiwan had sixty-seven registered political parties, though only seventeen ran candidates, and only two besides the KMT and the DPP supported enough candidates to qualify for television time. Before the 1992 election, there were seventeen political parties but only fourteen fielded candidates, and only two other than the KMT and the DPP met the requirements for TV time.[48] Because it is easy to form a political party in Taiwan and because typically several parties register and run candidates in election contests, until very recently some observers described Taiwan's party system as a multiparty one.[49] However, there were few serious contending political parties. There are other reasons—including election laws that favor big parties and the US model, which has an attraction in Taiwan—to believe Taiwan was, in fact, a two-party system or was evolving in that direction.

In 1992, the KMT became badly divided between "mainstream" (pro–Lee Teng-hui) and "nonmainstream" factions (mostly Mainland Chinese who supported Premier Hau Pei-tsun). In 1993, a number of members of the nonmainstream faction left the KMT to form the New China Party, which later changed its name to the New Party (NP). Supporters of the New Party charged that the DPP was a party composed only of ethnic Taiwanese and separatists, or champions of Taiwan's independence. They further complained that the KMT under Lee Teng-hui had moved to the left to co-opt many of the tenets of the DPP and, like the DPP, did not support the reunification of China. Interestingly, many members of the New Party and the nonmainstream faction of the KMT (not all of its members joined the New Party) had been hard-line anti-Communists but now supported better relations with the People's Republic of China and the idea of "Greater China." The New Party performed well in two elections but experienced a disaster in the 2001 Legislative Yuan election.

The DPP has experienced similar problems with party splits, though the results have been very different. Perceiving the DPP had "surrendered" to the KMT on the issue of independence, a number of DPP members and some top leaders left the party. The party's 1996 presidential candidate, Peng Min-ming, called the DPP's independence view weak and, after losing the election, formed the Taiwan

Independence Party (Chienkuotang or "nation-building party" in Chinese). Some other DPP members and former heads of the party departed for other reasons, including opposition to independence. Some formed new parties. This, however, has not fatally hurt the DPP because these parties have had serious problems in recruiting and raising funds and have not performed well in elections. Also, most voters believed the DPP stands for an independent Taiwan even though it has moderated its stance on this issue.

In 2000, immediately after the presidential election, James Soong formed the People First Party (PFP). Though he had little money and not much grassroots organization, he was able to attract KMT members into his party, including members of the Legislative Yuan. Being a political star, Soong gave the party broad appeal. Those who questioned whether the PFP would grow and survive called it a "one man" party (meaning it was Soong's personal party). The party performed very well in the 2001 legislative election and was subsequently considered a viable and active party.

During the 2001 Legislative Yuan election campaign, former Interior Minister Huang Chu-wen formed the Taiwan Solidarity Union (TSU) with former president Lee Teng-hui's blessing and backing. Lee was angry about being removed from the chairmanship of the KMT and was upset that the KMT was going in a pro-unification direction under Lien Chan. He also opposed Lien's cooperation with James Soong to block President Chen Shui-bian's legislative agenda. Lee hoped to entice some members of the KMT into the TSU and win over some independents; he found some success in this effort. On the issue of independence, the TSU took a noticeably stronger position than the DPP. The TSU performed well in the election that year, especially for a new party, and was subsequently considered an important political party and a force in Taiwan politics.

After the 2001 election, Taiwan had what many called a "two-bloc" party system. The KMT, PFP, and the New Party jointly opposed the Chen administration and through their control of the legislature blocked Chen's policies and set forth their own agenda. Observers called them jointly the "blue team" or "pan-blue." The TSU supported President Chen and the DPP's agenda, and the two were referred to as the "green team" or "pan-green." After changing the electoral system in 2004, pundits speculated that the two blocs of parties would likely be transformed into two parties as a result of the new electoral system that greatly advantaged large parties.

Some speculated at this time that pan-green would become the dominant force in Taiwan politics as the KMT had been in the past and that the system was evolving toward a new dominant one-party (or bloc) system. However, following the 2004 legislative election and subsequent local elections, this view was rarely heard. In fact, during 2006 and 2007, when the Chen Administration and the DPP suffered from falling public support due to poor governance—especially the perception of terrible corruption in the Chen administration and the party—this view ceased to be heard. Following big defeats in the January 2008 legislative election and in March in the presidential election, many pundits predicted the KMT would be the majority for some time.

In the January 2008 legislative election, the KMT did very well; the smaller parties and independents fared very poorly. At this point Taiwan's political party system seemed to be evolving into a two-party one although there was some question as to whether the DPP would survive, given former president Chen's corruption and lawbreaking that seriously damaged the party's reputation. In any case, the DPP revived, won some local elections, and did well enough in the 2010 metropolitan elections and the dual presidential and legislative election in 2012 to quiet this speculation. The view is commonplace now that Taiwan has a two-party or two-bloc system.

Elections

Elections have played a vital role in Taiwan politics locally since 1950 and nationally since 1980. They have been instrumental in bolstering the political parties, helping formulate policy, and democratizing the polity. Thus, grasping how elections have evolved to become a central part of the political process and how they work is essential to understanding politics in Taiwan.

Under Japanese rule, in 1935, elections were held for some town, county, and prefectural offices. Although these elections were unprecedented, they were of limited significance because the number of officials elected had to be balanced by an equal or larger number of appointed Japanese officials. Other elections followed. However, there was no island-wide election in Taiwan during the Japanese colonial period.

This situation changed little in the years immediately after 1945 because the Nationalist Chinese government was at war with the Communists and considered Taiwan's affairs to be a low priority.[50] On the other hand, after 1949, when the Nationalist government moved to Taiwan—realizing that its failure to implement democracy on the Mainland was an important reason for its defeat by the Communists—the attitude of ruling party leaders changed. In particular, it shifted after the United States extended to Taiwan military protection in 1950, thus affording a secure environment in which to hold elections. That year, local election contests were held for county and city councils and for magistrates and mayors in sixteen counties and five cities. Smaller townships and villages elected councils and village or town chiefs. Voter turnout was high, and the electorate was knowledgeable about the qualifications and the views of candidates.[51]

Since then, local elections have been held regularly. Owing to the nature of Taiwan's political system as noted earlier, many locally elected officials moved to higher positions, including top offices in the central government. Voter turnout in local elections was high and has remained so—rarely below 70 percent of eligible voters and, in some elections, above 85 percent. For the most part, qualified individuals ran for office, and the electorate was aware of issues and enthusiastic about the process. In short, local elections made a major contribution to Taiwan's democratization.

In December 1951, an election was held for the Taiwan Provincial Assembly; it was the first island-wide election ever. However, the Provincial Assembly was not an important organ of government because it was subordinate to the Legislative Yuan and many of its functions overlapped with those of the central government. Nevertheless, it operated democratically and was the locus of considerable political debate. Subsequently, Provincial Assembly elections were held regularly.[52]

There were no meaningful elections at the national level at this time. The stated reason was that the central government represented the population of "all of China," and elections could not be held on the Mainland because it was under Communist control. Government leaders, of course, feared that democratizing too quickly would create political instability. Most government officials also thought that a too-hasty approach was not in keeping with Sun Yat-sen's plan to institute democracy in stages. Finally, the government, composed primarily of Mainland Chinese, was concerned that democratization done too fast would engender ethnic tensions and would threaten their political power and status.

A competitive national election, to be Taiwan's first, was scheduled for December 1978, but it was canceled when the United States broke diplomatic relations with Taipei. The election was subsequently rescheduled for December 1980. In the meantime, under President Chiang Ching-kuo's leadership, agreements were worked out with *tangwai* leaders, independents, and other opposition politicians so that they could genuinely compete with KMT candidates for seats in the legislature.

Thus, 1980 was a turning point: Taiwan held its first competitive national election. The campaign was the most lively and interesting one to date; in fact, it was more exciting than any subsequent campaign. In a milieu of freedom and openness, opposition candidates said things publicly they had never enunciated before. The public was, to say the least, surprised—flabbergasted or amazed would be better words.[53] But the election went smoothly. Cynics said the election was for show and that such free and open campaigns would not be allowed again. But another open and competitive election was held in 1983, and this skepticism faded. In both of these elections, the KMT performed well against competition it had never had before. This success gave party leaders confidence.

In December 1986, after *tangwai* politicians founded the Democratic Progressive Party, Taiwan witnessed its first two-party election. Because no Chinese nation had ever had a two-party election contest, this election was another watershed event. Even though it faced formal competition, the KMT performed well. Opposition politicians, however, said the KMT still controlled the government and the media and enjoyed many other advantages. Others noted that the ruling party had changed and that concessions made to the opposition were meaningful; this meant that the KMT had true support from the electorate.[54]

Subsequently the Democratic Progressive Party learned from its defeats while the KMT became too self-confident. In the 1989 election, the DPP performed much better than it had in 1986. Major newspapers called the DPP's performance a "victory" and a "breakthrough." Many spoke of Taiwan as now having a true two-party system. DPP leaders, while celebrating the victory, were quick to point out that, because the election was only supplemental and because so many delegates representing the Mainland were still in office, the opposition could not win control of the parliamentary body of government even if it won a majority of the popular vote. Some declared with confidence that, if a plenary election were held, the DPP would rule.[55]

Before the 1991 National Assembly election, the "elder parliamentarians" resigned; thus a nonsupplemental, or plenary, election was held. Deploying their superior organizational skills and benefiting from the DPP's unwise strategy of making Taiwan's independence a major issue, and also having learned from an election setback in 1989, the KMT won a big victory on what many said was a "level playing field."[56] The KMT could now claim a popular mandate it had not enjoyed before. Significantly, it won three-fourths of the seats, thus ensuring its ability to amend the Constitution without interference by the opposition. Last but not least, with countries throughout the world tossing out ruling parties in the context of profound global change that seemed to make parties in power almost by definition unpopular, the KMT's win seemed even more impressive.

However, the KMT did not repeat its stellar performance in what was a more important Legislative Yuan election in 1992. DPP candidates learned from their defeat the previous year, and more talented DPP candidates entered this race. (Many had refused to run in the National Assembly election because they had argued that this body of government was superfluous and should be abolished.) Though the KMT won a comfortable majority in seats and the popular vote, it was accustomed to winning by wider margins; the tallies therefore represented gains and a "victory" for the DPP. Its leaders spoke of "ruling the country in three to five years."[57]

Subsequent local elections, though, did not see the DPP's upward trend continue. The first election for the governor of Taiwan and the revived elections for the mayors of Taipei and Kaohsiung in late 1994 were something between a KMT win and a split decision. The DPP won the mayorship of Taipei but lost the other two offices, and it performed only marginally better in the Taiwan Provincial Assembly, Taipei City Council, and Kaohsiung City Council contests.[58]

In the 1995 Legislative Yuan election, in the context of charges of corruption that stuck, a weak economy (for Taiwan), and other problems, the KMT performed poorly. However, the DPP's internal difficulties, along with the Beijing government's intimidation (conducting missile tests in the Taiwan Strait during the summer and threatening just before the election to invade Taiwan if it declared independence), minimized the DPP's gains. The New Party, in contrast, more than tripled its seats. After the election, Taiwan pundits talked of an evolving three-party system and future party coalitions.[59]

In 1996, the Republic of China held its first direct election for its president and vice president. Incumbent President Lee Teng-hui and his vice presidential running mate, Lien Chan, won handily, getting over 54 percent of the popular vote against three other pairs of candidates: the Democratic Progressive Party's candidates and two sets of independents (although one set tacitly stood for the New Party). The election was lauded by the Western media and was seen by many observers as a defining event in the history of Taiwan's democratization. Even Taiwan's critics acknowledged that Taiwan was now a genuine democracy. The election was the first of its kind in Chinese history. The Nationalist Party emerged with a big victory, though the DPP and the NP made marginal gains in the concurrent National Assembly election.[60]

Offsetting this KMT win, the Democratic Progressive Party scored a momentous victory in local elections in November 1997: it captured county and city executive offices, which put the DPP in a position of running local governments with jurisdiction over more than 70 percent of the population. In subsequent local elections, however, the DPP did not do so well, and in the 1998 Legislative Yuan and metropolitan mayor and city council races, the Nationalist Party won significant victories, including taking back the Taipei mayorship, with Ma Ying-jeou defeating incumbent mayor Chen Shui-bian.

Taiwan's second direct presidential election in March 2000 was an earthshaking event. Several months before the voting, the KMT split when President Lee supported his vice president, Lien Chan, to be the party's presidential candidate. Lien was eminently qualified, but former governor James Soong enjoyed higher poll ratings and had strong support in the party. There was hope that Soong might lead the ticket, but Lee nixed that. Thus, Soong decided to run on his own as an independent. A few months before the vote, a KMT legislator released documents suggesting that Soong, when he was secretary-general of the party, had diverted party money to his own and relatives' accounts. Lee even called Soong a thief. Although Soong was later exonerated, he had difficulty answering the charges, and his popularity—which had been double Lien and Chen Shui-bian's in many polls—dropped precipitously. Meanwhile, Chen ran an astute campaign. He played down his pro-independence views while painting the KMT as a corrupt party with ill-gotten money and ties to criminal elements. Chen convinced voters he could manage the economy and, because of increasing interest in the environment and other issues, the KMT did not find promoting economic growth as good a campaign issue as it had been in the past. With the help of the Nobel Prize winner and head of Academia Sinica Lee Yuan-teh and several important business leaders, Chen peaked just days before the voting. China's Premier Zhu Rongji's warning to Taiwan's voters not to vote for Chen evoked a backlash that also helped him.[61]

Although Chen did not get a majority of the vote and won just over 2 percent more of the popular vote than James Soong, many observers said his election marked the "consolidation" of Taiwan's democracy. The KMT had ruled the country for more than half a century. Now the opposition was in office after a peaceful transition of power. Chen proved a sharp politician and was as charismatic as president as he was as a candidate, at least among the Fukien Taiwanese who voted for him (the other ethnic groups did not).

In the subsequent December 2001 Legislative Yuan election, not only did the KMT lose its majority, but the DPP made big gains and became the largest party in the legislature. Former President Lee's TSU performed fairly well and helped Chen gain a near majority. James Soong's PFP, however, also turned in a stellar performance and, together with the KMT, kept a slim majority for the "blue team." Although this election helped President Chen and gave him a better environment in which to govern after the election, it did not reflect a shift in voter preference. Moreover, the DPP's election victory was tainted by ethnic appeals and by the undemocratic practice of allocating votes (telling voters to cast ballots for weaker candidates instead of their favorites so more party candidates would win).[62]

President Chen and Vice President Lu were re-elected in the spring of 2004 in a very close election that Chen's critics charged they stole. Chen and Lu were both shot the day before the voting, and President Chen used this as justification for ordering the military and police, who would have voted mostly pan-blue, to stay at their posts. There was also a sympathy vote from pan-green's base. In view of the fact that the polls, gamblers' odds on the election, and the stock market all predicted a pan-blue win, the view that Chen would not have otherwise won seemed correct.[63]

In any event, the DPP lost the next several elections. It was defeated in the legislative election in late 2004 and two subsequent local elections. The KMT won the metropolitan mayoral and city council races in 2006, except for the mayorship of Kaohsiung.[64] The DPP suffered a serious setback in the January 2008 legislative election; the KMT won two-thirds of the seats (controlling three-fourths with party allies). The Chen administration's poor management of the economy and its rampant corruption were the reasons. The KMT's Ma Ying-jeou won the March 2008 presidential election for the same reasons and by a large margin—capturing more of the popular vote than any candidate ever.

This put the KMT strongly back in power. In ensuing months the DPP won some local and replacement elections but lost the 2010 metropolitan mayoral races. In 2012, for the first time elections were held concurrently for the legislature and the president and vice president. President Ma (running with Wu Den-yih, Vice President Vincent Siew having declined to run again for health reasons) was reelected by a comfortable margin, while the KMT won the legislative election handily. Convincing voters they would better manage the economy, maintain social stability, and promote better relations with China and the United States facilitated their victories. Ma won more votes than the DPP's candidate Tsai Ing-wen among every ethnic group, both men and women, and every age group.[65]

Ideology, Modernization, and the Future

To understand Taiwan's politics, it is essential to comprehend its philosophical and ideological underpinnings. Both have influenced the political culture, the nature of the political system, how it works, and much more. Both have been impacted by the search for a national identity, about which there are conflicting views, and many other core issues that are often the subject of debate. Both have evolved in recent times rapidly and profoundly.

Before looking at these matters, it is necessary to explain where Taiwan came from ideologically and the basic political thinking of its population. There was historically no systematic "Taiwanese" political philosophy espoused by the local population (other than certain ancient tenets of political philosophy taught by Confucius, Mencius, and others, and some elements of Japanese political philosophy). When the Nationalists moved to Taiwan, their political ideology—Sun Yat-sen's Three People's Principles (nationalism, democracy, and people's livelihood)—was easily transplanted. This process was facilitated by Sun's earlier visits to Taiwan that had given him a following on the island and by the fact that people knew about his teachings and writings. Finally, his ideas were not generally at odds with those of the ancient sages (though Sun's philosophy was in some ways antitraditional). On the other hand, ethnic enmity created some reluctance on the part of Taiwanese to accept what they considered a Mainland Chinese ideology.

Sun's Three People's Principles emphasized nation building (because China was traditionally more a culture than a nation), democracy (mass participation in politics to emulate what many—certainly Sun—saw as successful Western democratic systems), and economic development (to make the nation rich and powerful and the people prosperous). Sun, however, taught that democracy would have to develop in stages because the people were not yet trained or ready to accept their responsibilities as citizen-participants. There would be a period of "political tutelage" before full democracy could be realized. Sun's political ideals provided the KMT with an ideology and a basic blueprint for government, and his teachings and writings were widely propagated in Taiwan after 1945.[66]

Political opposition groups in Taiwan for the most part did not offer alternative ideologies; rather, most embraced Sun's teachings. Early on they actively promoted them—especially the second and third principles—and argued for some time that the KMT was not trying hard enough to carry out Sun's ideals for democratic government. Later the *tangwai* and the DPP called for increased spending for welfare and other programs based on Sun's concept of "people's livelihood."

Sun was unique in that he saw an intimate relationship between economic and political development; indeed, some say he was the first political theorist to see a causal link between the two.[67] He believed that economic growth would spur social change and political modernization and thus lead to democracy. In other words, economic development should precede political change. Most people in Taiwan accepted this premise. In the 1970s and 1980s, however, critics warned that the lag between economic development and political modernization in Taiwan created an explosive or revolutionary situation. But the gap closed, and observers now speak of Taiwan's combined approach to economic and political modernization as a model. Some have called this the "Taiwan political miracle."[68] Clearly, various countries, including China (though not usually openly), have emulated this aspect Taiwan's political experience.

In the early days, the KMT promoted anticommunism as one of its core ideological tenets, along with the cause of returning to the Mainland, liberating it from communism, and establishing Sun's teachings and a republican system of government there under Nationalist rule. Taiwan's populace never found communism appealing, but neither were most Taiwanese persuaded by the government's anti-Communist propaganda. The masses in Taiwan, likewise, never enthusiastically accepted the government's policy of reconquering the Mainland. Most, particularly the young, identified with the West when they thought about Taiwan's future. During the 1960s and 1970s, the KMT appeared to be giving up hope of liberating China even though returning to the Mainland remained its official policy until the 1990s.

Early on, opposition politicians paid lip service to the return to the Mainland policy and the government's anticommunism, or they didn't talk about either. More outspoken oppositionists chided the policy of liberating China as being unrealistic and even silly, while labeling it a pretext for the "Chiang clique" to maintain its dictatorship and resist democratic reform. Some opposition stalwarts in private advocated a Taiwan legally separate from China but did not express this openly because advocating independence was treason. Many instead called for self-determination and argued that the people of Taiwan should decide Taiwan's future.

The Kuomintang embraced free-market capitalism and free trade as important ideological tenets, though they were not an important part of the party's political lexicon during the early years. Taiwan had a large public-sector (some say socialist) economy until the late 1950s, when the private sector grew in importance. Thus, free-market capitalism evolved under Nationalist rule, and so did free trade.

KMT leaders linked free-market capitalism to democracy, while most party members identified with the West and its political cum economic ideology.

Opposition politicians, though they opposed neither capitalism nor free trade, advocated more welfare, better pay for workers, and what would be described in the West as a liberal agenda. Some DPP leaders called for Taiwan to adopt policies that resembled European social democracy, though this did not become a "DPP ideology." Moreover, because the KMT instituted rather broad social and other welfare programs in the 1980s and 1990s and because most of the population remained supportive of capitalism and a free market, the opposition's liberal and socialist ideas did not appeal broadly to the populace. Opposition leaders pushed environmental protection, but so did the KMT. Opposition politicians advocated unemployment insurance and national health care, and the KMT adopted these policies in large measure. The government and the opposition advocated quite similar policies regarding such problems as traffic, public transportation, land use, water control, and crime. Some opposition politicians appealed to ethnic identity (namely Taiwanese) and class issues (promoting causes of the poor) during election campaigns. Though ethnicity and economic status were important influences on voting, these appeals were only at times effective.[69]

In the 1970s the ideological gap between the KMT and the opposition began to close. This was especially noticeable as both tried to appeal to a bigger segment of the voting population. The *tangwai* became more moderate as it participated seriously in elections. From its inception in 1986, the DPP took pragmatic positions on many issues that public opinion polls showed to be concerns among the electorate. It gradually abandoned its more radical positions as its candidates won office and had to make policy decisions and manage government offices and programs. The DPP's "ideology" (if one can call it that) focused mainly on rapid democratization and other political reform and the idea of local nationalism and a Taiwanese consciousness or local identity. However, most observers said the basic philosophical principle of the KMT and the DPP, as well as the PFP and the TSU, was pragmatism.[70]

In power after 2000, the Democratic Progressive Party made no serious effort to develop a new political philosophy or ideology for Taiwan. Sun's teachings and other tenets of the KMT's ideology were played down and sometimes criticized, and, some might say, they were even discarded. But nothing was substituted for them. For a time, President Chen praised British sociologist Anthony Gidden's "third way"—which offered a moderate leftist perspective but was supportive of global capitalism. To some this seemed an effort to construct a DPP ideology. But it never developed into anything more than a few headlines.[71] Some DPP leaders referred to their party as a liberal party, some even making comparisons with the Democratic Party in the United States. The problem with this was that the DPP took an aggressive stance on Taiwan's independence that often provoked China and, because of this, needed military support from the United States. The US Republican Party favored using military force to defend Taiwan much more than the Democratic Party.

The blue and green blocs differed, and still do, on the issue of Taiwan's national identity (whether Taiwan is part of China or not) and whether Taiwan's history, culture, and the like should be more locally focused, and this may be said to constitute a philosophical divide. Pan-green favored localization. The blue camp advocated more links with China and favored the idea of "Greater China." Yet both sides generally saw independence versus unification as a future problem more than an issue to be resolved immediately. The two camps espoused differences concerning foreign policy, Asian democracy versus Western democracy, taxes, welfare, and a number of other issues. But these differences can hardly be called ideological, and it has been noted that neither party has implemented policies that were "ideologically based." One might conclude that Taiwan's political culture and the pragmatism of its people preclude the success of any ideology.

When Ma Ying-jeou was elected president in March 2008, there appeared to be a revival of some of the KMT's political ideas. One can say that he is a strong supporter of free market capitalism, globalism, Western democracy, and a generally conservative agenda. Yet Ma has exhibited little concern over ideology; rather he has shown that he is pragmatic.

Notes

1. For a discussion of China's political culture, see June Teufel Dreyer, *China's Political System: Modernization and Transformation* (Boston: Allyn and Bacon, 1996), chapter 2; Kenneth Lieberthal, *Governing China: From Revolution Through Reform* (New York: W. W. Norton, 1995), chapter 1; James R. Townsend and Brantley Womack, *Politics in China* (Boston: Little, Brown and Company, 1986), chapters 1 and 2; and James C. F. Wang, *Contemporary Chinese Politics: An Introduction* (Upper Saddle River, NJ: Prentice-Hall, 1999), chapter 1.

2. See Karl Wittfogel, *Oriental Despotism: A Comparative Study of Total Power* (New Haven, CT: Yale University Press, 1957).

3. Little has been written in detail on the subject of Taiwan's political culture. For some discussion on this topic, see *Area Handbook for the Republic of China* (Washington, DC: US Government Printing Office, 1982), chapter 16; Christopher Hughes, *Taiwan and Chinese Nationalism: National Identity and Status in International Society* (London: Routledge, 1997), chapter 1; Gary Klintworth, *New Taiwan, New China: Taiwan's Changing Role in the Asia-Pacific Region* (New York: St. Martin's Press, 1995), chapter 1; and Alan M. Watchman, *Taiwan: National Identity and Democratization* (Armonk, NY: M. E. Sharpe, 1994), chapter 1.

4. For details, see John F. Copper, with George P. Chen, *Taiwan's Elections: Political Development and Democratization in the Republic of China* (Baltimore: University of Maryland School of Law, 1984), chapter 2.

5. For details, see A. James Gregor, with Maria Hsia Chang and Andrew B. Zimmerman, *Ideology and Development: Sun Yat-sen and the Economic History of Taiwan* (Berkeley: University of California Center for Chinese Studies, 1981).

6. See Lucian W. Pie, *Asian Power and Politics: The Cultural Dimensions of Authority* (Cambridge, MA: Harvard University Press, 1985), 228–236.

7. For details on Taiwan's constitution, see Zhao Suisheng, *Power by Design: Constitution-Making in Nationalist China* (Honolulu: University of Hawaii Press, 1996).

8. For details, see Ray S. Cline and Hungdah Chiu, eds., *The United States Constitution and Constitutionalism in China* (Washington, DC: US Global Strategy Council, 1988).

9. For details, see John F. Copper, *A Quiet Revolution: Political Development in the Republic of China* (Lanham, MD: University Press of America, 1988), chapter 2.

10. Amnesty International ranks Taiwan one (the highest possible rating) in political rights and two in civil liberties—the same rating as France, Germany, Italy, and Japan. It is called a "free" nation. China is ranked seven (the lowest number possible) in both categories and is labeled "not free." The US Department of State and several other organizations paint a similar picture (see www.worldaudit.org for further details).

11. In allocating seats in the elected bodies of government for women if they are not elected, the Republic of China's Constitution is unique.

12. Yeong-kuang Ger, *The Story of Taiwan: Politics* (Taipei: Government Information Office, 1998), 45–48.

13. *Taiwan Yearbook 2006* (Taipei: Government Information Office, 2006), 68–69.

14. Jaushieh Joseph Wu, *Taiwan's Democratization: Forces Behind the New Momentum* (Hong Kong: Oxford University Press, 1995), 129–132.

15. *Taiwan Yearbook 2007* (Taipei: Government Information Office, 2007), 66.

16. See *The Republic of China 1994 Yearbook* (Taipei: Government Information Office, 1994), 101–102.

17. For the background of this situation, see Harvey J. Feldman, ed., *Constitutional Reform and the Future of the Republic of China* (Armonk, NY: M. E. Sharpe, 1991).

18. Among them were the Mainland Affairs Council; the Department of Health; the Council for Cultural Planning and Development; the Government Information Office; the Council for Economic Planning and Development; the National Youth Commission; the Research, Development, and Evaluation Commission; the National Science Council; the Atomic Energy Council; the Council of Agriculture; the Fair Trade Commission; the Environmental Protection Administration; the Council for Labor Affairs; the National Palace Museum; the Central Bank; the Central Election Commission; the Vocational Assistance Commission; the directorate general of Budget Accounting and Statistics; and the Central Personnel Administration. Recent additions include the Public Construction Commission, the Council for Aboriginal Affairs, the National Sports Council, the Coast Guard, the Council for Hakka Affairs, and the National Communications Commission.

19. *The Republic of China Yearbook 2011* (Taipei: Government Information Office, 2011), 60.

20. See John F. Copper, "Taiwan in Gridlock," in *Taiwan in Troubled Times: Essays on the Chen Shui-bian Presidency*, ed. John F. Copper (Singapore: World Scientific, 2002).

21. See Steve Chan, "Taiwan in 2005: Strategic Interaction in Two-Level Games," *Asian Survey* (January–February 2006): 67.

22. For background on Taiwan's judicial and legal system, see Hungdah Chiu, "Legal Development in the Republic of China, 1949–1981," in *China: Seventy Years After the*

1911 Hsia-Hai Revolution, ed. Hungnam Chiu and Shao-chuan Leng (Charlottesville: University Press of Virginia, 1984), 287–331.

23. Brian Kennedy, "Modified Adversarial System Proposed," *Taipei Journal*, November 30, 2001, 6; Margaret K. Lewis, "Taiwan's New Adversarial System and the Overlooked Challenge of Efficiency-Driven Reforms," *Virginia Journal of International Law* (Spring 2009): 651.

24. This is also the practice in some other democracies, such as France.

25. See John F. Copper, *Taiwan's 2006 Metropolitan Mayoral and City Council Elections and the Politics of Corruption* (Baltimore: University of Maryland School of Law, 2006), 28–34. For details on problems in the judiciary, see Brian Kennedy and Elizabeth Guo, "The Verdict on Judicial Reforms," *Topics*, October 2006, 21–28.

26. Jonathan Adams, "Taiwan: Spotlight on the Young Democracy's Judicial System," *Christian Science Monitor*, May 21, 2009 (online at csm.com).

27. See Hung-mao Tien, *The Great Transition: Political and Social Change in the Republic of China* (Stanford, CA: Hoover Institution Press, 1989), 152–153, regarding the decline in cases heard by the Control Yuan.

28. "'Defunct' Control Yuan," *China Post*, February 20, 2008 (online at chianpost.com .tw).

29. Much less has been written on local government in Taiwan than on other aspects of its politics. For a brief discussion of the topic, see *Area Handbook for the Republic of China*, 188–190; and Tien, *Great Transition*, 128–132. The workings of local government and various changes made are described in various editions of *The Republic of China Yearbook*.

30. See Tien, *Great Transition*, 131.

31. The population of these two cities is about one-fifth of the nation's population. The two mayors are members of the Executive Yuan. A host of other reasons can be cited for the importance of these metropolitan governments.

32. For a thorough, though now somewhat outdated, study on the Provincial Assembly, see Arthur J. Lerman, *Taiwan's Politics: The Provincial Assemblyman's World* (Washington, DC: University Press of America, 1978).

33. Yung-mao Chao and Michael Y. M. Kay, "Local Government and Political Development in Taiwan," *In Depth* (Winter 1993): 17.

34. *Republic of China 2011 Yearbook*, 63.

35. See Copper, with Chen, *Taiwan's Elections*, 40–46.

36. For background and details on the history and organization of the Nationalist Party and its rule of Taiwan, see Peter R. Moody Jr., *Political Change in Taiwan: A Study of Ruling Party Adaptability* (New York: Praeger, 1992); and Stephen J. Hood, *The Kuomintang and the Democratization of Taiwan* (Boulder, CO: Westview Press, 1997).

37. *The Republic of China 1998 Yearbook* (Taipei: Government Information Office, 1998), 109.

38. For details, see John F. Copper, "The KMT's 13th Party Congress: Reform, Democratization, New Blood," in *Modernizing East Asia: Economic and Cultural Dimensions of Political Change*, ed. Cynthia Chenault (New York: St. John's University Press, 1989); John F. Copper, "The KMT's 14th Party Congress: Toward Unity or Disunity?" *Journal of Chinese Studies* (October 1994); and John F. Copper, *The KMT's 15th Party Congress: The Ruling Party at a Crossroads* (Baltimore: University of Maryland School of Law, 1997).

39. See Julian Baum, "The Money Machine," *Far Eastern Economic Review*, August 11, 1994, 62–64.

40. For further details, see Edwin A. Winckler and Susan Greenhalgh, eds., *Contending Approaches to the Political Economy of Taiwan* (Armonk, NY: M. E. Sharpe, 1988).

41. See Tien, *Great Transition*, 90.

42. See Copper, with Chen, *Taiwan's Elections*, chapter 5.

43. Shelley Rigger, *Politics in Taiwan: Voting for Democracy* (London: Routledge, 1999), 126.

44. For details, see Wu, *Taiwan's Democratization*, especially chapter 4.

45. See Alexander Yale Lu, "Political Opposition in Taiwan: The Development of the Democratic Progressive Party," in *Political Change in Taiwan*, ed. Tun-jen Cheng and Stephen Haggard (Boulder, CO: Lynne Rienner, 1992). The DPP currently has a membership of around four hundred thousand, compared to the KMT's nearly one million.

46. See Shelley Rigger, *From Opposition to Power: Taiwan's Democratic Progressive Party* (Boulder, CO: Lynne Rienner, 2001).

47. See ibid., 61–66.

48. See John F. Copper, "The Role of Minor Parties in Taiwan," *World Affairs* (Winter 1993).

49. John F. Copper, "The Evolution of Political Parties in Taiwan," *Asian Affairs* (Spring 1989).

50. See Copper, with Chen, *Taiwan's Elections*, chapter 4.

51. Ibid.

52. Ibid.

53. Fifteen were added to the National Assembly, eleven to the Legislative Yuan, and two to the Control Yuan. For further details, see ibid., 50, and chapter 5.

54. See John F. Copper, *Taiwan's Recent Elections: Fulfilling the Democratic Promise* (Baltimore: University of Maryland School of Law, 1990), chapter 3.

55. Ibid., chapter 4.

56. John F. Copper, *Taiwan's 1991 and 1992 Non-Supplemental Elections: Reaching a Higher State of Democracy* (Lanham, MD: University Press of America, 1994), chapter 2.

57. Ibid., chapter 3.

58. John F. Copper, *Taiwan's Mid-1990s Elections: Taking the Final Steps to Democracy* (Westport, CT: Praeger, 1998), chapter 2.

59. Ibid., chapter 3.

60. Ibid., chapter 4.

61. John F. Copper, *Taiwan's 2000 Presidential and Vice Presidential Election: Consolidating Democracy and Creating a New Era of Politics* (Baltimore: University of Maryland School of Law, 2000).

62. See John F. Copper, *Taiwan's 2001 Legislative, Magistrates and Mayors Election: Further Consolidating Democracy* (Singapore: World Scientific/Singapore University Press, 2002). Voter allocation undermines the democratic processes since voting results do not reflect how popular certain candidates were, not to mention the issues they stood for.

63. John F. Copper, *Taiwan's 2004 Presidential and Vice Presidential Election: Democracy's Consolidation or Devolution* (Baltimore: University of Maryland School of Law, 2004).

64. John F. Copper, *Taiwan's 2006 Metropolitan Mayoral and City Council Elections and the Politics of Corruption* (Baltimore: University of Maryland School of Law, 2006);

and John F. Copper, *Taiwan's 2012 Presidential/Vice Presidential and Legislative Elections: Assessing Current Politics and Charting the Future* (Baltimore: University of Maryland School of Law, 2012).

65. John F. Copper, *Taiwan's 2008 Presidential and Vice Presidential Election: Maturing Democracy* (Baltimore: University of Maryland School of Law, 2008).

66. See Paul M. A. Linebarger, *The Political Doctrines of Sun Yat-sen* (Westport, CT: Hyperion Press, 1973).

67. See Gregor, with Chang and Zimmerman, *Ideology and Development*, chapter 1.

68. This writer has used this term. See John F. Copper, *The Taiwan Political Miracle: Essays on Political Development, Elections and Foreign Relations* (Lanham, MD: University Press of America, 1997).

69. Although more Taiwanese than Mainland Chinese support the DPP, in all national elections in Taiwan, the KMT has won more than half the Taiwanese vote.

70. See Alan M. Wachman, *Taiwan: National Identity and Democratization* (Armonk, NY: M. E. Sharpe, 1994), 65–68.

71. Su Lin Chieh-yu, "Chen Greets the British Sociologist Who Inspired His Election Success," *Taipei Times*, April 16, 2002 (online at www.taipeitimes.com).

5

THE ECONOMY

THROUGHOUT ITS HISTORY TAIWAN EXPERIENCED periods of economic boom and decline. Several centuries ago, Taiwan was for a time a center of trade and commerce in East Asia. Then this ended. In the late 1800s, as a part of China, for a brief time, Taiwan witnessed impressive economic progress. Under Japanese control from 1895 to 1945, Taiwan thrived economically, surpassing by most standards all of East Asia except for Japan. Immediately after World War II, Taiwan's economy deteriorated. Moreover, Taiwan did not appear to have good prospects for economic development. Predictions at that time were pessimistic because of the island's lack of resources, an unfavorable land-to-population ratio, a shortage of capital, and a discredited political leadership. Some even called Taiwan a "basket case"—meaning that it had little or no hope of developing economically. In the mid-1960s, however, Taiwan's economy took off and its rapid growth soon became the envy of the world. Many used the term "miracle" to describe Taiwan's economic success. Its economic boom engendered vast social and political change, producing a large middle class, consumerism, Westernization, democratization, and more. It also created a huge economic gulf between the island and China, dampening the desire on the part of its political leadership, not to mention its citizens, for unifying with China. In the 1990s, its growth slowed, the economy having matured; but Taiwan continued to do well economically—even through the so-called Asian economic meltdown in 1997. In 2001, Taiwan experienced a severe recession caused partly by the US and global economic slowdown and partly by political gridlock and the Chen administration's poor economic management. Subsequently, Taiwan's economic performance improved but was still viewed by most citizens as mediocre or worse when compared to the other "Asian dragons" (South Korea, Hong Kong, and Singapore) or China, the benchmarks for most people in Taiwan. Taiwan's economy was hit hard by the 2008 global recession but by the end of 2009 was doing well. China's booming economy meanwhile attracted Taiwan's investment and its entrepreneurs; this changed a significant portion of the population's views about China. Currently, with Taiwan's exports to the United States, Europe, and Japan in relative decline and exports to China increasing fast, many perceive that links with China are the only way for Taiwan's economy to grow and remain dynamic.

The Economy to 1950

Centuries ago, although Taiwan's economy was defined as one in a primitive state of development, the Aborigines engaged in commerce with other areas in the region, and Taiwan was more prosperous than most of East Asia. By the 1500s, however, Taiwan's external trade had all but disappeared. At the time Chinese immigration to the island began, the economic activities of the Aborigines were generally limited to hunting, fishing, berry picking, and some farming. The mountain Aborigines mainly engaged in the former three pursuits, while the lowland Aborigines cultivated some of the level land on the island. Taiwan subsequently became the base of operations for Chinese and Japanese pirates, who engaged in various forms of trade in the area before and during the time of the arrival of the Europeans.[1]

In the seventeenth century, the Dutch introduced oxen and farm implements to the island, created a cash economy, and launched modern forms of commerce and trade. The Dutch East India Company, which managed the economy, promoted the exports of rice, sugar, and deerskins and the imports of silk, porcelain, and other goods from China for re-export. The Company also encouraged the immigration of Chinese, who came in large numbers and who revolutionized farming by bringing new crops as well as the more advanced cultivation and irrigation techniques used in South China.

Under Chinese rule from the late 1600s to 1895, Taiwan's economy experienced some economic modernization. Owing to an increase in the Chinese population of the island, agricultural production expanded markedly; land under cultivation grew from a very small area to nearly all the island's flatlands. Trade also increased, and significant quantities of rice and sugar were shipped to China. The mining of coal and other minerals also became a part of the economy—coal primarily because it was exported and because Taiwan became a coaling station for steamship traffic in the region in the nineteenth century. Still, the island's economy was largely agricultural. Improvements in the economic infrastructure and the growth of business enterprises saw modest progress.

In the late 1800s, significant economic advances were made as a result of Peking's appointing better governors that adopted new policies to improve the economy of the island. As noted in Chapter 2, the best was Liu Ming-ch'uan, whom Peking made governor of Fukien Province (of which Taiwan was a part) in 1884. Liu, a close friend of China's modernizer, Li Hung-chang, was given a mandate to extend to Taiwan the "self-strengthening" movement popular in China at this time so as to improve economic conditions there. The island still lacked modern transportation and communications facilities, and its industries were few and mostly small and inefficient. Education was poor and not standardized.[2]

Liu moved the capital from Taiwan City in the south to Taipei and renamed the former Tainan. He expanded telegraph lines built by a former governor and oversaw the construction of harbors and railroads. He conducted an extensive land survey and improved the island's transportation system. Liu also adopted policies to improve the production of camphor, which quickly became a major export product. He then made tea production a priority. Rice and sugar production were increased. Liu built harbors and opened new mines. In a few years, he transformed Taiwan from one of China's most backward provinces into an advanced one. Although much of what Liu did, particularly at first, was aimed at strengthening Taiwan militarily in order to fend off foreign encroachments, his efforts had a positive effect on the economy overall.

But Liu's efforts were short-lived. The powerful families in Taiwan felt threatened by Liu's modernization efforts and used various means to undercut him. Liu then contracted malaria. Finally, his support in Peking waned. As a result, in 1891, Liu left Taiwan without accomplishing much of what he had hoped for. Most of Liu's economic improvements would have had little lasting effect had Taiwan not soon become part of the Japanese empire. Many projects had to be completed later by the Japanese.[3]

Although Taiwan experienced impressive economic progress before Japan colonized the island, its economic structure remained quite similar in many ways to that of the provinces of coastal southern China. There were vast discrepancies in income and wealth, and most people were poor. Yet Taiwan differed economically from China in some significant ways. Taiwan did not have a history of frequent famine caused by floods and crop failures. Fishing provided a more important food source than it did in China, especially inland China. Crop yields were better than China's because of Taiwan's richer volcanic soil and its heavier and more even rainfall. The island's economy was also much more heavily involved in trade. Finally, capitalism, which was brought to Taiwan earlier by the European colonial powers, was more in evidence.

Serious economic modernization in Taiwan began shortly after the island became a Japanese colony in 1895. Important progress in four areas laid the foundation for Taiwan's later growth: (1) the building of an economic infrastructure, including roads, railroads, port facilities, and electrification; (2) the establishment of local industries (such as food processing) and an export-oriented economy; (3) the organizing and training of the labor force; and (4) the opening of banking and other economic institutions.

Japan's colonial leaders concentrated first on agriculture. Tokyo provided capital investment, technology, and management skills. Crops were improved by the introduction of new farming techniques, irrigation, and fertilizers. Rice and sugar were given the highest priority, and both were shipped to Japan in significant quantities. From 1910 until World War II, agriculture spearheaded Taiwan's economic development, which overall exceeded population growth by about threefold. Agriculture also made a major contribution to capital formation throughout this period and aided the subsequent growth of other sectors of the economy.[4]

A decade or so later, Japan started building factories in Taiwan in significant numbers, marking the beginning of Taiwan's industrial revolution. The decline of European trade during World War I and Japanese policies aimed at making Taiwan's economy more industrial, along with the infusion of large amounts of Japanese capital into the island's economy, contributed to the process. World War II, which started in Asia in the 1930s, further stimulated Taiwan's industrialization and contributed to even faster economic growth.

Japan's management of Taiwan's economy during the fifty years before the end of World War II contributed immensely to its economic development and growth, but the island and its population were also exploited. Although the Chinese population's standard of living saw unprecedented increases, it lagged far behind rises in productivity and economic growth. As evidence of its colonial status, Taiwan exported considerably more to Japan than it imported.[5]

Before and during World War II, Japan used Taiwan as a base of operations and invested in industries there, including some heavy industry. Taiwan's economy thus thrived. Because US bombing during the war was generally restricted to military targets and oil storage depots, Taiwan sustained less damage to its economy than other Japanese-controlled areas of East Asia. Meanwhile, Japan and China suffered considerable war damage. Hence, Taiwan was in much better shape economically when the war ended than either Japan or China.

From 1945 to 1949, however, Taiwan's economy suffered several severe shocks. The first was caused by the sudden withdrawal of Japanese administrators and businesses. Lack of attention to the economy by the Nationalist Chinese government in the immediate postwar period made the situation worse. In fact, ruinous economic policies resulting from Nationalist leaders' preoccupation with the war against the Communists on the Mainland caused serious economic harm. Finally, Ch'en Yi's efforts to create a state-managed socialist economy on the island were disastrous. In short, for several years after World War II, Taiwan suffered economically almost as if it were a country at war.

Economic activity declined precipitously during this period, as measured by the output of nearly all goods and services. By 1946, just a year after Taiwan was turned over to Nationalist China, economic production had fallen to less than half of what it had been.[6] Subsequently, the economy declined even further. Many consumer products became scarce or unaffordable. Poverty and disease followed. The education system and public services deteriorated commensurately. Because China's monetary system was used in Taiwan, inflation decimated many commercial enterprises. In a period of just over one year (from November 1945 to the beginning of 1947), the price of food rose 700 percent, fuel and construction materials 1,400 percent, and fertilizer 25,000 percent.[7] In short, Taiwan's economy was severely traumatized by the Nationalist government's policies—or, in many cases, lack of policies—and its bad economic oversight.

An additional economic shock came in 1949 in the form of approximately 1.5 million Chinese immigrants arriving from the Mainland. This influx of people caused severe dislocations in housing, employment, and the already heavily taxed infrastructure. On top of this, preparations to defend the island against an invasion from the Mainland diverted precious resources that might have been used to revive the economy. At this time most citizens in Taiwan, as well as Western observers, were extremely pessimistic about Taiwan's economic future.

Economic Recovery and Boom: 1950–2000

In the 1950s, Taiwan's economy began to recover. At the onset of the Korean War and a consequent shift in US policy favoring Chiang Kai-shek and his government, the US Navy provided Taiwan a secure environment for economic planning. US economic and military aid helped Taipei make up for a serious foreign exchange shortfall and allowed it to divert funds from defense spending to economic rebuilding. The huge pool of administrative and other human talent that came from China in 1949 with Chiang Kai-shek and the desire of the population for economic growth coincided with the implementation of good economic development ideas.

Because of concern over feeding Taiwan's rapidly growing population and the realization that peasant support had been a major factor in the Communists' success on the Mainland, economic planners in Taipei decided to focus first on the agricultural sector, a choice that comported with advice they received from US aid personnel. It turned out to be a very wise decision.

Land reform was the first important measure taken to foster growth in the agricultural sector.[8] It was carried out in three stages: (1) rent reduction in 1949 (from around 50 percent to 37.5 percent of the main crop); (2) the sale of public lands in 1951 to tenant farmers at 2.5 times the value of one year's crop (resulting in 96,000 hectares of public land going to 156,000 tenant farm families); and (3) the "land-to-the-tiller" program, which forced landlords to sell land they did not farm themselves, except for 2.1 hectares of paddy field and double that amount for dry land.

The Joint Commission on Rural Reconstruction (JCRR), composed of two US and three Chinese commissioners, planned and carried out these decisions. After land reform was completed, the JCRR created farmers' associations, initiated a government program to exchange fertilizer for rice, and sponsored other activities that helped farmers. Nearly all the commission's efforts were successful—so much so that Taiwan's land reform program was and still is emulated today by economists in developing countries.

Individual initiative and hard work on the part of the farmers, who could now realize profits from their efforts, and flexible government planning that encouraged the planting of new crops and innovative farming techniques were critical to increasing agricultural productivity. Taiwan's agricultural sector also responded to markets abroad. In the early 1950s, when Japan lifted restrictions on banana imports, Taiwan's farmers doubled their yield in two years and took most of the Japanese market. Farmers began asparagus cultivation and canning in 1954, increasing production almost one hundredfold in the next fifteen years. Mushroom growing and canning became major enterprises in the 1960s. By 1971, asparagus and mushroom exports had earned $82 million in foreign exchange.[9]

Taiwan's average annual real growth rate in agricultural production during the 1950s was an impressive 14 percent. But by the 1960s, farming had nearly reached its full potential. Growth in the agricultural sector of the economy dropped to 4.5 percent annually at this time. Forestry was the slowest, while livestock, fish farming, and fruit production surpassed the average. Expansion of the agricultural sector overall was around 3 percent in the 1970s and 2 percent from the mid-1980s to the early 1990s.[10]

In short, agriculture's contribution to Taiwan's economic development occurred mainly in the early years but was a significant contribution. During the 1950s and early 1960s, agricultural exports supplied half the nation's foreign exchange earnings. Taxes collected from rural Taiwan, farmers' savings (40 percent of capital formation in the 1950s), and their purchases of goods from Taiwan's fledgling factories greatly facilitated Taiwan's industrialization. Even more important, rural Taiwan, because of rapid increases in agricultural productivity, was able to supply nearly half the new labor to nonagricultural production from the 1950s to the 1970s. Meanwhile, by the mid-1960s, Taiwan's farmers had provided the population a level of food consumption superior to that of any country in Asia except Japan; in caloric content, Taiwan even eclipsed Japan a few years later.

Though farmers continued to enjoy an improved standard of living, they suffered from relatively declining incomes—down to about 70 percent of nonfarm income by 1992. Farmers' buying power fell, and, in turn, agricultural work became less attractive. In addition, soaring labor and land prices, an aging workforce, foreign competition, and environmentalism beset farming. The result was that the agricultural sector's contribution to the nation's gross national product (GNP) fell from over 32 percent in 1952 to just 1.7 percent in 2000, while the farm population fell from more than one-third of the total population to 15 percent during the period from 1975 to 2005.[11] Taiwan joining the World Trade Organization in January 2002 had a further negative impact on agriculture in Taiwan, forcing the country to cut tariffs on food products that had protected farmers.[12]

Taiwan's farmers adjusted to a changing economic situation by reducing the production of some crops and increasing others. Production of sugar, sweet potatoes, rice, and other grains was cut; production of soybeans, tea, fruits, and vegetables was expanded. Hog and chicken growing increased. When fishing was affected by fewer catches in proximate waters, fishermen shifted to other endeavors: deep-sea fishing (farther and farther away from Taiwan's shore), marine aquaculture, and on-land fish farming. Recently, Taiwan's farmers have increased the production of flowers, fruits, tea, and aquaculture.

Meanwhile farmers became more politically active: in 1988, they engaged in a mass street demonstration to draw the government's attention to their plight.[13] In response, the government rezoned farmland so that it could be sold for other uses. This decision pleased many farmers but did not help agriculture overall. The government helped farmers mechanize and diversify, but this had only a limited effect. Because of participation in international agreements on free trade and, in particular, joining the World Trade Organization, the government cannot subsidize agriculture (except to help it adjust to different situations). Thus the future of agriculture in Taiwan is not promising. The latest statistics on agriculture, published in 2010, reflect that clearly: a decline of 0.16 percent in its share of the GDP and a 0.58 percent decline in the value of its output.[14]

After the late 1950s, industry became the engine driving Taiwan's economic growth. In the late 1950s, annual growth in the industrial sector of the economy was around 12 percent; it exceeded 17 percent during the 1960s and rose even faster in the 1970s. Factories, especially around Taiwan's cities, proliferated so rapidly that, by 1977, the industrial index had increased more than twenty-eight times the level in 1950. In fact, Taiwan's industrial sector grew at a rate seldom equaled anywhere at any time in history.[15] Comparisons with other countries are instructive: during the 1960s and early 1970s, industry's share of Taiwan's gross national product grew by 18 percent, double the pace of Britain and Japan during their industrial takeoffs. Even compared to other booming East Asian countries, Taiwan's industrialization was considerably faster. As a result, Taiwan was more industrialized by the mid-1970s than any other country in Asia except Japan.[16]

What accounted for this lighting pace of industrialization? The key factors were (1) the expansion of industrial employment; (2) increases in labor productivity; (3) US economic assistance; (4) privatization; (5) a high rate of local savings and considerable foreign investment; (6) a solid economic infrastructure, including transportation and port facilities; and (7) excellent planning by the government and the business community. The contribution of each needs some elaboration.

The industrial labor force in Taiwan grew from virtually nothing in 1950 to 850,000 by the mid-1960s and to more than 2 million by the mid-1970s. The increases were especially large in manufacturing and construction. Taiwan's rapid population growth and the movement of workers out of the agricultural sector owing to mechanization and other increases in farming efficiency were the main reasons for the large numbers of new entrants into the industrial labor force. From 1952 to 1968, workers employed in industry increased from 16.9 percent to 41.5 percent of the total workforce.[17]

Labor productivity in industry, not initially high, began to increase rapidly in the early 1950s and continued to rise sharply thereafter. Initially, Taiwan's industrial sector benefited from low labor costs, a relatively high level of skills and education among workers (particularly compared to labor costs), and a strong work ethic. Later, rising labor productivity came from the efficient organization of labor, laborsaving devices, and the rapid capitalization of production.

In the early years, US economic aid and advice were as important to Taiwan's industrial progress as they were to its agricultural growth. From 1951 to 1964, the United States injected nearly $100 million annually into Taiwan's economy, money critically needed to build Taiwan's new factories. As a matter of record, from the early 1950s to 1960, US aid provided 40 percent of Taiwan's capital formation, most of it helping the industrial sector. Few underdeveloped nations at that time or since have benefited as much from economic growth generated by foreign aid. Although US help ended in 1964, it had by then stimulated Taiwan's industrial progress such that the island's economy was able to sustain its rapid growth. In short, Taiwan's economy had "taken off." Taiwan later was applauded for being the only country in the world to experience increasing economic growth after the termination of US aid.[18]

Privatization also spurred Taiwan's industrial growth. In 1945, the government assumed management over most of the large manufacturing enterprises left by the Japanese. It also created or kept in place government monopolies it had created on the Mainland to provide sources of needed tax revenues. Top government leaders at that time believed that large industries must be government owned because of their size and importance to the economy and for reasons relating to national security. In 1954, only 43.4 percent of industrial production was privately owned.

Subsequently, government economic planners changed their view and the government sold many public companies. By the early 1960s, industrial production in the private sector was over 50 percent and growing fast. It reached 80 percent by 1972 and nearly 90 percent by the mid-1980s.[19] Subsequently, even compared with the other successful capitalist, free-market countries in Asia, a larger portion of Taiwan's enterprises was privately owned—due both to government privatization and the proliferation of small family-owned businesses, a hallmark of Taiwan's economy.[20]

A high rate of domestic savings and large inputs of foreign investment also helped Taiwan's economic development. During the 1950s and 1960s, growth in the agricultural sector and US economic assistance were the primary sources of capital accumulation. In the mid-1950s, new investment laws made it possible for foreign firms to import plants and equipment and sell their products in the domestic market to make profits and generate additional capital. Tax incentives were added in 1959 to attract foreign capital. Special laws were passed that included a maximum tax rate of 18 percent and a tax-exempt "holiday" lasting as long as five years for some new investors. In the mid-1960s, export processing zones (EPZs)—a Taiwan invention according to some economic historians—were established, giving foreign companies special set-aside zones to build factories where they enjoyed free-port status for imports and exports, relief from government red tape, and access to good harbors. Taiwan's EPZs were extremely successful in attracting foreign companies that invested and created jobs while also training workers and upgrading labor skills. Interestingly, the People's Republic of China later copied this concept.

These policies resulted in a marked increase in foreign capital input in Taiwan: from a total of $20 million from 1952 to 1959 to more than $950 million between 1966 and 1973. Amazingly, foreign investment in Taiwan's economy increased by almost fiftyfold during the 1960s and the early 1970s. Most of it came from the United States, Japan, and Overseas Chinese (especially from Southeast Asia); most was private investment. By the mid-1980s, Taiwan was absorbing more than $500 million in foreign capital annually.[21] Meanwhile, by the 1970s, the rate of individual and company savings had risen rapidly—to about 25 percent annually—providing further funds for investment. Personal savings were also increasing. In 1987, individual savings reached 40 percent—the highest in the world. The main reasons for this high rate of savings were favorable interest rates, individual frugality, and optimism about future economic growth.[22]

In the 1990s, the rate of savings in Taiwan fell to the high 20 percent range for private savings and company investment. The main reason for the decline was that Taiwan now had a capital surplus. Also, because of high labor costs, environmental problems, and a host of other factors, Taiwanese entrepreneurs and industries began to invest elsewhere. Still, a high level of capital accumulation helped Taiwan to continue to transform the economy into one based on capital- and knowledge-intensive companies. Foreign investment in Taiwan remained high, and, though it was not now as vital as it had been in fostering economic growth, it did aid the development of new industries and the inward transfer of technology while it bolstered commitments to Taiwan among countries that were economically and politically important to Taipei.

A good economic infrastructure also helped Taiwan's economic growth. In the early years, the government offered help in the form of cheap electricity and easy access to ports, good roads, and a well-trained labor force to domestic businesses and foreign enterprises. Later, transportation, energy, and banking were improved to further upgrade the economic infrastructure.

In 1973, the government launched ten projects at a cost of $5 billion. Beginning in 1975 and for the next ten years, it spent $2.7 billion on transportation projects, including an island-long freeway, railroads, airports, harbors, and ports. More projects were begun even before these were completed. In addition to these transportation projects, a steel mill, a shipyard, a petrochemical facility, and a nuclear power plant were built. In 1978, fourteen more large projects were started, including housing construction and farm mechanization. In 1985, an additional fourteen were added at a cost of $3 billion. Finally, in 1991, more than seven hundred other projects were approved as part of a six-year development plan. The cost of this last group of projects was projected to be more than $300 billion. The government boasted at the time that these infrastructure improvements would ensure continued economic growth and make Taiwan one of the top twenty countries in the world in per capita income by the year 2000. Meanwhile, the government helped finance the Asia-Pacific Regional Operations Center to make Taiwan a "hub" for business in the region, a $16 billion-plus high-speed railroad, energy development, and other infrastructure projects.[23]

Finally, astute planning lay behind Taiwan's economic success. This included research, forecasting, and planning done by the Ministry of Economic Affairs; the Research, Development, and Evaluation Commission; the Economic Planning Council (now the Council for Economic Planning and Development), and other organs of government coordinated by the premier. Although Taiwan does not have a planned or command economy and business is less regulated even compared to other similar free-market nations—including Japan, South Korea, and Singapore—the government has consistently given direction to the economy. The business community, farmers, and others have benefited greatly from government forecasts about the economic climate (including both opportunities and difficulties). Government policy, in fact, has played such an important role in Taiwan's economic miracle that it warrants further attention.[24]

Economic Growth Strategies

Taiwan's economic system is a capitalist one and ranks as one of the freest economic systems in the world by various key yardsticks: trade policies, taxation, monetary policy, wage and price controls, property rights and regulations, foreign investment, and banking. Taiwan has also been one of the most successful economies in the world.[25]

Creating Taiwan's miraculous economic growth, the government advocated—and created—an open market economy. The reasons behind favoring capitalist development were many, though four deserve special mention: (1) Japan had bequeathed the Nationalist government a capitalist economy; (2) the February 28 Incident in 1947 engendered public hostility toward government monopolies; (3) socialist planning and a socialist economy were associated with former governor Ch'en Yi; and (4) the world had split into two camps—communism and capitalism—and Taiwan was in the latter, aligned with the United States.[26]

Nevertheless, as noted above, the government has guided, and in some respects designed, economic growth. Government planners altered development strategies several times (radically at one point) and fine-tuned the nation's development strategies periodically. An examination of the work of these planners is essential in any assessment of Taiwan's economy as is an understanding of their attitudes about a free-market economy and the limited, yet critical, role of government.

In the late 1940s, the first task of Taiwan's economic planners was to stabilize the economy and reduce inflation, which was around 500 percent annually at that time. In early 1949, because of the defeat of the Nationalist regime on the Mainland, it was a horrendous 3,000 percent. The government, in response, legislated and enforced currency reform. Specifically, government officials imposed regulations on the financial system to control the money supply to prevent a resurgence of inflationary pressures. Finally, economic planners adopted conservative fiscal policies that required balanced budgets, reduced government spending, and controlled interest rates.[27]

These policies worked. Skyrocketing inflation was curtailed. The inflation index fell from 300 percent in 1950 to 30 percent in 1951–1952 and subsequently dropped to a reasonable 10 percent annually. In addition to stabilizing the economy, anti-inflationary policies benefited industrialization in two important ways: they encouraged labor-intensive production and, at the same time, made small factories and businesses compete. Reduced inflation meanwhile made economic planning easier and facilitated growth in general.[28]

In 1953, the government expanded its role in managing the economy when it launched a four-year plan, setting goals and guidelines for overall economic development. The objectives were stated in general terms, but planners were also specific about the government's role, thereby giving the business community clear signals concerning the economy's direction. The Ministry of Economic Affairs and the Ministry of Finance, under the general supervision of the premier, provided the leadership; other government organs and agencies followed. The business community gave the government high marks for its efforts and, in ensuing years, increasingly looked to government planners for guidance. Concrete government development plans lasting four or six years followed.

With respect to generating economic growth in the industrial sector, in the early 1950s Taiwan's development strategy was based on a policy of import substitution. Several conditions dictated this choice: Taiwan's Japanese market for food products had been cut off, capital and technology were in short supply, the currency was overvalued, and the bureaucracy was an obstacle to implementing a policy of promoting exports. Thus, the best economic growth strategy available was to aid the development of local industries by guaranteeing them special access to the domestic market. This approach, it was perceived, would help absorb excess labor, stabilize prices, and conserve foreign exchange. Industries such as textiles, food processing, fertilizers, and chemicals benefited from this policy. Finally, the import-substitution policy facilitated Taiwan's continued efforts at controlling inflation and stabilizing the economy.[29]

In accordance with the government's import-substitution strategy, in the next several years Taiwan's currency was overvalued, tariffs were high (doubling from 20 percent in 1948 to 40 percent in 1955), and import quotas and other controls were rigidly enforced—all measures that blocked or discouraged the purchase of foreign goods. Imports of flour and yarn, for example, fell from 70 and 80 percent, respectively, to less than 5 percent of local consumption, while synthetic yarn and bicycles fell from 100 percent to 1 percent. Selected businesses or producers, of course, quickly grasped the opportunity to produce and market these items. In 1951, a system of multiple exchange rates was established that discriminated in favor of certain industries. Also, special laws and regulations provided selected producers with favored treatment in acquiring credit.

Taiwan's import-substitution policy was quite successful. Between 1952 and 1959, various chosen industries grew at a rapid rate—sufficient to increase by 6 percent industry's share overall of the gross national product. Over 70 percent of the industrial sector's new production came from food (including tobacco), cotton and wool textiles, leather goods, and chemicals (including rubber goods, plastics, and petroleum)—all favored industries. Government policies also helped other industries. Factories making sheet glass, nonmetal mineral products, machinery, equipment, and rayon managed to gain a foothold and grew at this time.

Although the government deserves high marks for adopting an import-substitution policy at the proper time and for making it work, thus promoting economic growth, it probably warrants more applause for realizing that it had to be a temporary strategy. Otherwise, many industries would have become accustomed to protection and grown weak and noncompetitive. Taiwan's leaders thus resisted long-term reliance on the import-substitution policy—unlike planners in most developing countries then and now.

During the late 1950s, the government made a major shift in economic strategy when, for several reasons, it decided to scrap the import-substitution policy in favor of an export-promotion policy: First, the domestic market for the protected industries had become saturated and there was little room for expansion. Second, some of Taiwan's industries had gained sufficient experience and efficiency to be internationally competitive. Third, the workforce had improved. Finally, Taiwan now enjoyed a competitive advantage over Japan in some industries because of rising labor costs there.

Thus, in 1959, in order to transform Taiwan's economy into one that was export led, the government abolished its dual exchange-rate system and devalued the currency. It reduced tariffs and established laws and regulations favoring export companies. Taxes, interest rates on loans, and regulations on the importation of raw materials were altered, as were laws regulating foreign investment. Later, as noted above, export-processing zones were established.

The industries picked as "leading" export industries were chiefly those that produced consumer goods: textiles, processed food products (mostly canned), leather goods, wood products, and paper products. These industries, almost exclusively labor-intensive ones using small-scale production facilities, accounted for nearly 60 percent of the increase in exports during the early 1960s.

Taiwan's export policy was a big success. The industries slated to sell abroad did so. During the first half of the 1960s, the value of exports rose nearly 20 percent a year. Export companies absorbed considerable excess labor, generated needed foreign exchange, and attracted more foreign investment. Companies that aimed at specific foreign markets, in particular, contributed to growth, propelling the gross national product to record double-digit annual increases. As a result, by the 1970s, Taiwan had become a "newly industrializing country," or NIC.

Continued growth required more policy adjustments. The decade of the 1970s saw Taiwan's economic development strategy shift dramatically again in the use of labor and capital. The nation's labor surplus had become a labor shortage, and labor costs rose dramatically. This situation, and the availability of large quantities of investment capital, made it logical to promote capital-intensive industries such as electronics, electrical products, chemicals, machinery, instruments, and metal products. Textiles continued to do well because the industry turned to high fashion and a better grade of textiles; cheap textiles soon became only a memory. In other words, the export-oriented policy of the 1960s continued, but the quality, sophistication, and price of Taiwan's exports changed.

Taiwan's economy continued to boom. Though it suffered a severe shock during the 1973–1974 oil crisis, economic planners quickly adjusted to higher energy costs. They diversified energy sources, encouraged conservation, and tried to promote less energy-intensive industries. Taiwan also needed to store more energy—and did so. To justify keeping large stores of petroleum, planners facilitated the start-up and, later, growth of Taiwan's petrochemical industry, which soon became one of Taiwan's largest industries.

During the first half of the 1980s, Taiwan's economy encountered even higher domestic labor costs and faced more intense international trade competition. But, with high standards of education, which enhanced the quality of Taiwan's human resources, and a quick start in such areas as computers and electronics, Taiwan had—or appeared to have—a comparative advantage internationally in knowledge-intensive industries.[30] Government planners, therefore, favored the computer and other knowledge-intensive businesses.

Meanwhile, Taiwan had accumulated valuable experience in selling in the global marketplace. The quality of Taiwan-made products rose quickly such that in the late 1980s and early 1990s, the government began to promote Taiwan's best companies in order to build an international reputation for high-quality goods. Taiwan became increasingly conscious of standards for export products, even prohibiting the export of certain inferior goods. Innovation was crucial, and government policies shifted accordingly. The government meanwhile encouraged the growth of financial services companies and sought to make Taiwan a regional distribution hub.

Government planners, working with business and labor, continued to attract foreign capital and expertise, put more money into education as well as research and development (double-digit or near double-digit increases), kept taxes low (13 percent of gross domestic product, compared to 30 percent in the United States and much higher figures in Europe), helped build a good infrastructure (especially roads and railroads), wisely regulated banking and financial institutions, and maintained social and political stability. Together, these efforts earned Taiwan a favored position among analysts who rank countries for investment potential and risk.[31]

Key Industries and the Taiwan "Economic Miracle"

A brief survey of Taiwan's successful industries—including several that played a major role during the import-substitution policy period, then in Taiwan's export-led economic growth policy, and later during its efforts to move to upmarket and to capital- and knowledge-intensive industries—sheds considerable light on the origins and nature of Taiwan's economic miracle. Some industries were important only in the past, while others have become, and remain, world leaders.

For a number of years, textiles constituted Taiwan's largest industry when measured by the value of production and employment. Taiwan got its start with two textile mills at the end of World War II. By 1980, two hundred cotton and wool mills were operating on the island. The industry was helped both by import-substitution and export-promotion policies. Later the industry was hurt by high labor costs and a decline in productivity. However, for a number of reasons the industry remained viable. Today Taiwan is a large producer of synthetic fibers, the industry has become highly integrated, factories have moved offshore, and factories have been automated. Meanwhile, Taiwan has specialized in high-end products, and the industry imports from and exports to other producers, including China. In fact, in 2012 there was a rebound in production for export. Textiles now are the fourth-largest trade-surplus industry while accounting for just over 4 percent of Taiwan's exports.[32]

Beginning in the 1960s, the electrical equipment and electronics industries appeared to have a bright future, and did. These industries soon blossomed, beginning with electric fans, integrated circuits, and other labor-intensive products. As labor costs escalated, factories went upscale to produce household appliances, communications equipment, and consumer electronics. In a few years, Taiwan became a major producer of radios, tape recorders, televisions, videocassette recorders, stereo equipment, calculators, and video games, not to mention parts and accessories and electrical equipment.

Information products (mostly computer products) followed and saw the biggest growth of any sector of Taiwan's economy. Taiwan soon ranked number one in global market share for the production of liquid crystal monitors, motherboards, and notebook computers. In 2006, sales amounted to $88.6 billion. And although a large share of Taiwan's production was for foreign companies, Taiwan's own brands, such as Acer, took a growing market share (especially in Third World countries), even though they are not yet widely known elsewhere. Related to the success of computer production is the semiconductor industry. Taiwan had two of the world's two largest contract semiconductor companies—Taiwan Semiconductor Manufacturing Company Ltd. and United Microelectronics Corporation. The value of chips and related products produced in 2006 was $37.2 billion.[33]

But many of Taiwan's electronics, computer hardware, and chip factories have moved elsewhere because of high labor costs in Taiwan. Many moved to China for that reason and for the attraction of the huge China market. These industries are now highly specialized and fit into a global chain in which Taiwan is a link among other countries involved in research, design, and production. In fact, Taiwan is now proportionally more involved in research and design, with many of its factories now producing hardware in China instead of at home.[34]

The petrochemical industry in Taiwan was also promising. Beginning in the 1970s, government planners foresaw Taiwan's comparative advantage in petrochemical products. Twenty years later Taiwan became one of the world's largest producers of petrochemicals and the world leader in ethylene production. In 2006, the total value of production of its petrochemical factories was $39.1 billion. Taiwan's petrochemical companies exported and also produced for domestic use the ingredients for plastics, synthetic rubber, textiles, and more. Plastics, in fact, for some time was one of Taiwan's strongest industries. Plastic products were exported and went into many of the goods Taiwan exported. Rising labor costs and environmental problems, as well as public protest against new factories, however, confronted the petrochemical industry with serious problems, and many factories moved; new ones were built elsewhere, especially in China. Production in Taiwan has declined since the mid-2000s, though some of Taiwan's companies are doing well in China.[35]

In the late 1970s, Taiwan got into the production of steel, opening a blast furnace in 1977. The decision seemed questionable for a time because of tough competition in the world market, especially from much larger Japanese steel plants. Initially, the only customer of any importance was China Shipbuilding Corporation, which itself was not a growth company. But Taiwan's China Steel Corporation also built offshore drilling platforms (though this market did not expand at the time) and moved into ship breaking for scrap iron (which did grow). Both aided the steel industry, as did the rise of the Japanese yen. Subsequently, the auto industry and shipbuilding saw better growth, providing markets for Taiwan's steel. Later, however, China Steel suffered losses. Currently the industry is facing stiff competition globally and must specialize and find a niche in the global production chain, which again involves moving some facilities to China or linking up with the Chinese production chain.

Meanwhile, the production of aluminum, copper, and other metals grew, spurred by the growth of an aviation industry and extensive building construction. Today, though Taiwan's metal industry is healthy, in large part because it has gone upscale and has diversified, it is also suffering from higher labor costs, a more expensive Taiwan dollar, foreign competition, and environmental concerns.

Taiwan also launched a shipbuilding industry in the 1970s. In 1973, it completed a dockyard that had a capacity of 1.6 million tons of construction and 2.5 million tons in repairs. But the timing was bad because of the surplus of tankers and other ships on the world market at the time. Beginning in the 1980s, Taiwan's shipbuilding industry was hit by a global decline in fishing fleets and foreign competition. As a result, the China Shipbuilding Corporation was not profitable for some years. Consequently, it diverted a considerable amount of its productive capacity to offshore drilling rigs, nuclear power plant equipment, steel structures, and the like. Meanwhile, Taiwan developed a world-class yacht industry. But in the 1980s, the yacht industry fell on hard times because the US market contracted.

Taiwan's vehicle industry was and is an important one in the value of its production and the number of employees, though production has been declining in recent years. An automobile industry was launched in 1953, but overprotection prevented it from becoming competitive enough to export. Beginning in the mid-1980s, with a local buying boom, auto production increased markedly, although most of this came from foreign companies operating factories in Taiwan. In 2006, the value of auto production was $14.5 billion. Meanwhile, Taiwan became a world leader in car parts, motorcycles, and bicycles. The island even became the world's largest manufacturer of bicycles in the 1980s.[36]

A number of other industries are worth mentioning for their role in the Taiwan economic miracle or for their promise of future growth. In the 1980s, Taiwan experienced quite impressive expansion in telecommunication equipment, precision tools, optical machines and supplies, and sporting and fitness goods. The construction business has and is doing well because of higher standards of living, which led many people to seek better housing, and because of the nation's ambitious public works projects. Less strong are food processing, tobacco, alcoholic beverages, fertilizers, pharmaceuticals, rubber products, cement, glass products, nonferrous metals, wood products, and paper products. Tourism is a major industry, though a decade or more ago its halcyon days seemed to be over because of high prices in Taiwan. Tourists from China and government help and encouragement may revive the industry.

Taiwan produces some state-of-the-art weapons, including a jet fighter plane and missiles. (For further details, see Chapter 6.) Although its arms industry may contribute to modernizing the economy because of a certain amount of spin-off, it is doubtful Taiwan will become globally competitive in arms, as it will not likely be able to develop markets abroad. It got into the high-end weapons business because of concerns about China's pressure on other countries not to sell weapons to Taiwan and because of the fact that Taiwan was able to acquire US weapons technology. It is difficult to say whether Taiwan will remain in the business of producing arms and, if it does, to what degree.

Currently the government is supporting six "emerging industries." They are biotechnology (including R&D, drug testing, and a biotech incubation center), tourism (especially high-end tourism), green energy (photovoltaics, LED lighting, wind energy, hydrogen fuel cells), medical care (medical tourism, long-term care, improving rural care), high-end agriculture (organic farming and agritourism), and cultural and creative industries (filmmaking, pop music, new designs in entertainment). Some special projects include computerizing government agencies, building electric vehicles, promoting green architecture (integrating electronics and computers into construction), and patent commercialization.[37]

The government will rely mainly on private investment to start new industries and decide which current industries will remain competitive. Taiwan's planners have also spoken of "five pillars" of its economic planning for the future: attracting foreign talent, boosting higher education, ensuring energy security, promoting industrial innovation, and implementing trade liberalization.[38]

The Labor Force

Labor deserves special attention for its role in the Taiwan economic miracle; after all, Taiwan has almost no natural resources of commercial value. Its only resource of any importance is its human talent.

The expansion of the workforce was, in the early years after World War II, an especially important factor in the country's economic growth. Because of Taiwan's rapid population increase between the early 1950s and the early 1970s, the labor pool more than doubled. Employment rose from 2.89 million in 1953 to 5.5 million in 1974. By 1987, it had reached 8 million. Today, it is more than 11 million. The percentage of the population in the workforce—58.07 percent of those over age fifteen and below sixty-five—is high by international standards. In this category, Taiwan is on par with Western nations.[39]

The skill and education levels of Taiwan's workers have been high, particularly relative to labor costs. In fact, this has been a critical factor in the nation's competitiveness and its rapid economic growth. Even more important, the labor skills and the education levels of workers have increased at rapid rates and have developed according to the changing needs of the economy. Worker flexibility, including the willingness to change jobs or acquire new skills, has also been high.

As a result of the success of Taiwan's industrialization and the upscaling and maturing of the economy, there has naturally been a huge shift of employment from agriculture to industry and to services. In 1952, the mix was 52.1 percent agriculture, 20.8 percent industry, and 27.7 percent services; in 1962, the percentages were 45.9, 22.5, and 31.6, respectively; and in 1972, 33.0, 32.1, and 34.8 percent. By 1988, the number of employees in agriculture had shrunk to a quarter of what it was in 1952. Meanwhile, industry's portion had increased to 41.5 percent and services to 40.9 percent. Now the labor force is approximately 1.6 percent agriculture, 35.9 percent industry, and 58.8 percent services.[40] Most new jobs are now being generated in the service sector.

Unemployment, in double-digit figures in the 1950s, dropped markedly from the 1960s on. During the economic crisis of the early 1970s, Taiwan boasted the lowest unemployment rate in the world.[41] During the 1980s and early 1990s, the rate hovered below 2 percent and was among the lowest in the world. The Asian economic crisis, which started in mid-1997, caused it to increase a bit, though it remained below 3 percent. In fact, many companies complained of difficulties in hiring and retaining workers and sought to solve the problem by increasing automation, transplanting factories to other countries, and hiring foreign workers.[42] However, as a result of the 2001 recession, the rate of unemployment exceeded 5 percent the next year and remained above 4 percent for the next three years. It spiked again in 2008 and went above 5 percent in 2009; in 2012 it was around 4 percent.[43]

Wages increased very rapidly with economic growth, especially for unskilled workers, who earned around $5 to $10 monthly in the 1950s. Salaries rose quickly, especially in the mid-1960s and after. In 1985, the average monthly income for workers in eight primary industries was $368 per month. In 1999, the average wage was $1,263 and $1,421 for service workers. Currently the average monthly wage for workers is $1,318 (before bonuses, which are considerable).[44]

The minimum wage in Taiwan is $636 per month. Clearly the days of cheap labor are long gone, and Taiwan's business community must adjust to even higher labor costs in the future.

Laborsaving methods and equipment, increased specialization, and better labor organization helped increase productivity, which offset some of the increases in labor costs. In addition, labor and management both realized that labor costs have to be kept from increasing too quickly if many of Taiwan's products are to remain competitive in the international marketplace. In order to adjust to rising labor costs, the government pressures businesses to invest in research and development and to phase out labor-intensive production.

The quality of labor, however, remains high in Taiwan, and the labor force is hardworking. The average worker puts in nearly 200 hours per month (196.8 hours in the industrial sector and 183.7 in the service sector)—which is high even compared to other East Asian countries.[45] Many economists say the Confucian ethic of "work hard and don't complain" has made labor a major positive contributor to Taiwan's economic miracle and explains why Taiwan's labor force is considered one of the finest in the world. In a recent study Taiwan's workforce was rated third in the world for quality.[46]

There is a host of other reasons for labor's contribution to the economy, such as labor laws, labor organizations, and government regulations. During the period of Taiwan's rapid industrialization, workers were generally not organized. The formation of labor unions was discouraged—actually pre-empted—by the government and the ruling Nationalist Party. Strikes were forbidden under martial law. Although much has changed over the past few years, labor unions in Taiwan do not wield much clout compared to their counterparts in most Western countries. The main reason is that a large portion of the labor force is employed in small or family businesses. Also, many workers work in factories that sell to large foreign companies. Workers in these factories have little bargaining power.

After martial law was lifted in 1987, however, labor became more active. Within a year, new unions began to organize and compete with the government-controlled Chinese Federation of Labor. Soon, nearly twelve hundred industrial unions and twenty-four hundred craft guilds had formed.[47] Subsequently, new laws were written to cover bargaining, strikes, and other issues. Partly because of the numerous labor organizations, but for a variety of other reasons, labor did not become a supporter of a particular political party. In late 1987, the Labor Party formed to represent workers; in March 1989, the Workers Party was founded. Both failed. The Democratic Progressive Party made numerous appeals to labor organizations and took up workers' causes, but it was seen by labor as too preoccupied with Taiwanese independence and other ideological issues. The KMT was seen as probusiness, though it had and continued to get some labor support. It seems likely labor will remain uncommitted to any political party.

Though labor is not as active or as militant as it is in most other countries, the rate of union membership is high. Unionized workers constitute more than a third of union-qualified labor. This percentage is around triple the United States and much higher than Japan and other East Asian countries. If labor organization is defined broadly to include all kinds of workers' groups, such as craft guilds and other such organizations, over half of Taiwan's labor force is organized. However, the reason for the high rate of union participants is that legislation requires it in factories employing more than a small number of workers. Most workers thus consider union membership pro forma and the main benefit of membership to be labor insurance rather than bargaining strength through organization.[48]

Workers in Taiwan have been guaranteed the right to negotiate, organize, and strike. In 2010, the legislature amended labor laws allowing teachers to unionize and, subsequent to that, caregivers. Some people now complain that unionization is too broad and that in some cases compulsory membership is an infringement on workers' rights.[49]

In 1945 the government of the Republic of China brought with it to Taiwan laws and regulations that affected labor. Subsequently many more laws were enacted. In 1958, the Labor Insurance Act was passed. The most important piece of legislation, however, went into effect in 1984: the Labor Standards Law. It provided comprehensive guarantees and rights to workers and defined many unclear provisions in labor-management relations. In recent years, the government has expanded the coverage of the Labor Standards Law to include contracts, wages, work hours, leave, and more. The legislature has also enacted the Employment Insurance Act that provides pay for workers who are unemployed—60 percent of their salary for up to twelve months. In 1994, the legislature passed the Labor Safety and Health Law, which regulates hazardous jobs, and the Sexual Harassment Prevention Act aims to prevent bad behavior toward the opposite sex on the job.[50] The more recently enacted Labor Pension Act and the National Pension Act provide for retirement benefits for workers.[51]

Meanwhile, in 1992, the Employment Services Act legalized the employment of foreign workers in Taiwan. This law was passed in the context of a shrinking labor force caused by a slowdown in the birthrate for more than two decades. Also, more people were pursuing advanced education and thus staying out of the labor force for extended periods. Hence, the number of foreign workers recruited by employers in Taiwan soared; by 2001, it had reached 325,000, or 3.3 percent of the workforce. Some 54 percent were employed in manufacturing and 11 percent in construction. There were also many foreign workers in the nursing and caretaking fields, and many more worked as maids. Most of Taiwan's foreign workers came from Thailand (43 percent), Indonesia (27 percent), the Philippines (26 percent), and Vietnam (3 percent). A significant number of foreign workers came from several other countries, notably China, and were employed in Taiwan illegally.[52]

Most labor organizations oppose foreign workers for fear they will depress wages. Members of the Democratic Progressive Party have expressed concern that workers from China might alter the ethnic balance in Taiwan. During the 2000 election campaign, presidential candidate Chen Shui-bian promised to cut the number of foreign workers. The following year, the Chen administration reduced the number by 15,000 immediately and promised to cut the number by 5 percent yearly after that. Subsequently, though, foreign workers increased in numbers, reaching 367,119 by April 2008, up 5.75 percent from a year earlier. The largest portions were from Indonesia. Most were employed in industry, followed by caregiving and construction.[53]

In 2010, the number of foreign contract workers in Taiwan was 380,000.[54] The Council of Labor Affairs, the organ of government responsible for labor issues, tried to balance labor and management interests. Safety, working hours and conditions, and workers' rights have also been major concerns of foreign workers and their employers. Fringe benefits and workers' rights have similarly attracted the attention of labor, business, and government.

Trade, Investment, and Energy

Foreign trade, foreign investment, and imported energy are three special factors that help explain not only the nature of Taiwan's economy but also its economic success. All three deserve special attention.

Although Taiwan has traditionally engaged in foreign commerce, the growth of trade over the past six or so decades has been momentous by any standard. In 1953, Taiwan's imports and exports totaled only $320 million. Trade began to increase rapidly in the late 1950s and, especially, in the early 1960s, with the launching of Taiwan's export-oriented growth policy. In fact, trade grew at the astounding rate of more than 22 percent a year from 1959 to 1965, and it reached an annual value of more than $1 billion and continued to grow to $3 billion by 1970.[55] Not only did Taiwan's industrialization and its upscaling production further accelerate exports, but also both caused the value of exports to continue to skyrocket. By 1984, two-way trade totaled $52.4 billion, making Taiwan the tenth-largest exporting nation in the world and the fifteenth-largest trading nation. And the boom continued: in 2010, the value of Taiwan's trade exceeded $526 billion.[56]

Clearly, Taiwan's trade growth was by design. Having almost no resources and facing a serious population-to-land ratio disadvantage, the government early on calculated that Taiwan had to trade to survive. When the nation's import-substitution policy of the 1950s was abandoned in favor of an export-led growth strategy, foreign commerce became crucial. The surplus of well-trained laborers meant that the economy could grow by exporting Taiwan-produced goods. Taiwan was burdened by foreign debt, yet the country needed more foreign capital to improve the infrastructure and build new factories. Finally, Taiwan's economic planners anticipated economic benefits by specializing and selling in the global marketplace, and they perceived that certain of Taiwan's industries were globally competitive and that more such enterprises could be built.[57]

Being a small nation with a small domestic market and realizing the importance of trade, the relative size of Taiwan's trade soon outpaced that of Japan's: by the 1980s, its imports and exports amounted to more than 85 percent of its gross national product compared to Japan's 30 percent. Taiwan exported well over half of what it produced. Moreover, because most of its exports—over 75 percent—went to developed Western countries, Taiwan became very sensitive to the trade and other policies of the capitalist industrial nations, particularly of the United States and Japan, which, in the late 1980s, accounted for more than 40 and 30 percent, respectively, of Taiwan's foreign trade.[58]

The scope and the direction of Taiwan's trade by the 1970s, and even more clearly by the 1980s, might have set off alarm bells had economic planners in Taipei believed in "dependency theory." Planners in many Third World nations were apprehensive about tying their economies to Western nations, thinking they would lose control over their economies and that Western countries would impede their nations' economic development. But Taiwan's planners did not. Instead they calculated that participating in international trade was much more of an advantage than a disadvantage; so, they did almost precisely what critics said was potentially ruinous. Some writers subsequently argued that Taiwan, by directing such a large portion of its exports to Western countries and benefiting from doing so, disproved dependency theory.[59]

In fact, Taiwan experienced quite a different set of problems. Its exports found so many customers in the United States that Taiwan soon developed a large trade surplus with the United States. This surplus grew throughout the 1970s and 1980s—peaking at $16 billion in 1987. In fact, the United States then ended special tariffs for Taiwan under the Generalized System of Preferences (GSP). In a few cases, the United States took legal actions against Taiwan for dumping. In response, Taipei adopted measures to cut its trade surplus with the United States: sending buying missions, limiting or even banning the purchase of certain goods from other countries, and giving US exporters various kinds of preferences.

In contrast, Taiwan had a big deficit in its trade with Japan—its second largest trading partner. Taiwan took various steps to increase its exports to and cut imports from Japan, but these measures had only marginal success. Trade with other Asian countries, excluding Japan, accounted for about 15 percent of Taiwan's foreign trade in the 1970s and 1980s, with neither surpluses nor deficits constituting serious problems. Western Europe accounted for 10 percent of Taiwan's foreign commerce, and the Middle East another 10 percent, largely from oil purchases.

Taiwan carried a trade surplus with most Western European countries and a deficit with Middle Eastern countries. These patterns largely obtain today.

In the 1980s, Taiwan began trading with Eastern European Communist countries and the Soviet Union, though this trade did not become economically significant. Taiwan also began trading with China, indirectly (through Hong Kong). Taiwan's China trade skyrocketed, with exports leading imports by a huge margin; hence the Mainland became an important market for Taiwan in the early 1990s. Soon, China was competing with the United States as a market, and, by 2000 Taiwan's exports to the two were almost the same.[60] Some saw this development as natural; others expressed concern that it would tie Taiwan to China economically and politically. Still others said that, if it wanted to remain economically healthy, there was nothing Taiwan should or could do.

Several factors accounted for the rapid growth of trade across the Taiwan Strait. First, Taiwan's products had a particularly good reputation in China for their quality and style. Second, beginning in the early 1980s, Beijing encouraged the purchase of Taiwan-made products and exempted them from tariffs by labeling them "domestic," though this policy was later revised because of the excessive demand for Taiwan-made goods and a shortage of foreign exchange in China. Third, Chinese economic planners noted that Taiwan's trade surplus with China provided Taiwan's companies with profits, which they invested in China; thus, the trade deficit did not really matter. Fourth, Taipei took the position that although trade with China was illegal, it was not practical to try to control where its products were sold. Still, trade remained primarily indirect—mostly through Hong Kong. Taipei, meanwhile, allowed imports from China, but also only through third countries.

This changed quickly after 2000. By 2002, China had become Taiwan's largest export market, and, by 2006, its sales to China exceeded that to any other country. By 2010 exports to China were almost fourfold exports to the United States or Europe. Japan, ASEAN, and Europe followed as Taiwan's biggest export markets. Taiwan's imports came from Japan, China, the Association of Southeast Asian Nations (ASEAN), the European Union, and the United States.[61] It was amazing how quickly and to what degree China had become important to Taiwan economically and how the United States had ceased to be.

Over the years, the kinds of products Taiwan exported have also changed dramatically. In 1952, industrial goods accounted for only 8 percent of Taiwan's foreign sales; agricultural products were Taiwan's main export items. Within just a decade, manufactured goods accounted for 94 percent of Taiwan's total foreign sales. Agricultural exports, meanwhile, became insignificant. During this period, the portion of capital-intensive, high-tech, and knowledge-intensive products in the manufactured goods category increased as Taiwan's exporters went upmarket. Currently, Taiwan's main exports are electronics, precision instruments, plastic and rubber products, chemicals, machinery, and iron and steel products. A large share of Taiwan's exports became part of a networking chain that included many nations, but especially China. In 2010, more than half of Taiwan's export orders were filled by its companies operating in China.[62]

Over the years Taiwan's economic growth was facilitated by capital inputs, mostly from large quantities of foreign investment. In the 1950s, Taiwan's main source of foreign capital was US economic assistance. Later, Taiwan attracted foreign firms and private investors that provided large sums of needed capital. Most foreign funds went into manufacturing; indeed, close to 10 percent of investment in companies in the manufacturing sector came from foreign sources during the 1960s and 1970s—a very high figure when compared to the percentages in other developing countries. And this made a mark: in 1979, 795 foreign firms accounted for more than 8 percent of Taiwan's gross national product. At this time, the exports of foreign firms accounted for 20 percent of the nation's exports.[63]

Foreign investors contributed to Taiwan's economic growth in still another important way, namely, by facilitating technology imports. Nonlocal firms brought new production techniques to Taiwan while stimulating research and providing training for workers. Because Taiwan's educational system was geared toward training young people to learn new technologies, the rate of technology absorption and use was high and accounted in considerable measure for Taiwan's rapid growth. Among less-developed nations, for some years, Taiwan enjoyed the world's highest proportion of growth through the addition of new technologies.[64]

Government policies were in large part responsible for the large inputs of foreign investment. Legislation provided for start-up periods when foreign companies were exempt from most taxation. Government agencies recruited and trained workers for foreign investors. Foreign firms benefited in particular from Taiwan's export processing zones, which, as noted earlier, afforded foreign companies freedom from taxes and many regulations. Finally, private businesses often sought foreign partners and usually worked well with them.

In 1995, when foreigners were allowed to invest in Taiwan's stock market, considerable funds flowed in from abroad. During the Asian economic crisis that began in 1997, Taiwan's stable economy attracted capital from other countries in the region. In 2006, foreign investment in Taiwan was almost $14 billion, and it reached $15 billion in 2007. Most of it came from offshore banking sources, the Netherlands, the United States, Singapore, Japan, and the United Kingdom. The favorite areas attracting foreign capital were electronics, financial services, and venture capital.[65]

Recently Taiwan has been the recipient of much less foreign investment and instead is investing large sums abroad. In 2010, Taiwan took in $3.91 billion in foreign investments (not including money that went into Taiwan's stock market), while its outward investments totaled $15.05 billion. Almost a third of the inbound investments went into the banking and insurance industries. More than 80 percent of Taiwan's outbound investments went to China. Electronics and information technology products were the big areas.[66]

Beginning in the 1970s and up to the present, Taiwan has had a favorable balance of trade. This and its high rate of savings made it possible for Taiwan to accumulate large amounts of foreign exchange. As of mid-2012 Taiwan was the world's fourth-largest holder of foreign exchange (after China, Japan, and Russia).[67] Its large reserve of capital meant that the government did not have to pay off a debt and could keep taxes low, which were advantages in terms of competing in global trade, increasing research and development, and encouraging entrepreneurship.

As might be deduced from Taiwan's economic success and the rapid rise of living standards that has accompanied it, Taiwan has been a quickly growing energy user. From 1954 through 1985, energy consumption increased at an average rate of 9.2 percent per year—faster toward the end of the period. Subsequent increases in energy use fell behind growth in the gross national product but skyrocketed nonetheless. As a consequence of the growing consumption of energy, combined with limited indigenous supplies, Taiwan became a major importer of energy. In the mid-1950s, Taiwan produced more than 80 percent of the energy it used, and cheap hydroelectric power helped the growth of industry. By the late 1960s, only half of Taiwan's energy was derived locally. In 1972, that amount fell to 34 percent. Today it is 1.8 percent.[68] Consequently, Taiwan has become extremely dependent on foreign energy sources.

Although cheap foreign energy early on was a boon to Taiwan's economic development, this situation obviously did not last. After the oil crisis in 1973, and again in 1978, energy costs soared, and uncertainty about supplies caused anxiety for economic planners as well as the business community. Nevertheless, Taiwan could not do much about the quantity of energy it imported, nor could it reduce its reliance on foreign supplies. Its coal mines could not increase production and were closed. Taiwan has some natural gas and petroleum, but exploration so far has yielded disappointing commercial results. Petroleum and natural gas were found offshore, but not in significant quantities—though there is some hope this will change. So far Taiwan's situation of energy import-dependency persists.

On the other hand, the government has been quite successful in diversification. In the early 1970s, Taiwan imported oil, its main source of energy, mainly from Saudi Arabia and Kuwait. Those countries remained the main suppliers for Taiwan, and 80 percent of its supply came from the Middle East. After the oil crisis, Taiwan began buying petroleum from Indonesia, Malaysia, Brunei, several Latin American countries, the United States (Alaska), and some other countries. It also began buying coal. During the 1950s and until the mid-1960s, the use of coal had declined rapidly for environmental and cost reasons, accounting for only 13 percent of the total energy used in 1979. Now, however, owing to better burning techniques, Taiwan began importing a considerable amount of coal, and suppliers are not generally the same countries from which Taiwan buys oil: the United States, Australia, Canada, South Africa, and China. Taiwan has also begun importing liquid natural gas, mostly from Indonesia. Currently, petroleum accounts for 49 percent, coal 32.1 percent, and natural gas 10.2 percent of Taiwan's energy use.[69]

Meanwhile, in the late 1970s, Taiwan became a user of nuclear power. The first plant was opened in 1978. With the building of more nuclear plants, Taiwan soon became a major consumer of nuclear power. Taiwan currently has six nuclear units (in three plants) that produce 17 percent of the nation's electricity. A fourth nuclear plant is under construction. As a result of the nuclear power plant accident in Japan in 2011, opposition to nuclear power grew in Taiwan. In 2012, President Ma pledged to apply new safety equipment and standards to the new plant and phase out the older plants. Thus the future of nuclear power in Taiwan is uncertain.[70]

In the 1980s Taiwan began to experiment with solar, wind, and thermal power. The government also pushed conservation. In 2010, Taiwan ranked number three in the world in per capita solar energy use. That year green energy accounted for 6.8 percent of Taiwan's energy use and generated $10.97 billion in production value. At that time the government planned to invest $838 million in renewable energy promotion and $635 million in research and development.[71]

Taiwan's energy use has also changed markedly over the years. As the industrial sector became a major part of Taiwan's economy, it became the consumer of the lion's share of energy. In 1972, it took 61 percent of the nation's energy. This proportion subsequently declined with Taiwan's economy shifting to less energy-intensive and more knowledge-intensive enterprises and to a service economy. Industry's share of energy use is now around 58.7 percent. Meanwhile, transportation's share rose from 8 percent in 1972 to 15.5 percent today. Agriculture dropped from 4 percent to 1 percent during that same period, while residential use rose from 9 percent to 12 percent, and commercial use from 2 to 11.1 percent.[72]

Although both Taiwan and China are energy deficient and import large quantities of energy, there is considerable room for cooperation, and Taiwan can benefit from this. Already Taiwan is importing a significant amount of coal from China, its third-largest supplier. Taiwan has more experience in civilian nuclear power use and can help China. There is also room for cooperative efforts to develop potential oil and gas reserves in the Taiwan Strait and near the Senkaku Islands. China has invited Taiwan to invest in and work on China's exploration and development of its offshore areas. Finally, China has become one of the world's most advanced nations in the use of wind and solar energy, and Taiwan can benefit from links with China in these areas. In 2008, the government announced a plan to increase renewable energy to 8 percent of Taiwan's total usage (from less than 1 percent). In 2009, Taipei took steps to expand cooperation with China to accomplish this. Because of lessening tension with China, this holds considerable promise.[73]

A Model of Economic Development

Taiwan's economic development has been so successful that referring to it as an "economic miracle" is hardly an overstatement. What it accomplished in engineering economic growth has made it a model—for economists, scholars, and leaders of developing nations. This, in fact, warrants further discussion.[74]

First, it is necessary to recapitulate a bit and look at Taiwan's economic growth over the past four decades. During the 1950s, the island's economy grew at a healthy rate of 8.2 percent annually; expansion in the 1960s averaged 9.2 percent annually. Taiwan was hit hard by the oil crisis in the early 1970s, but it quickly adjusted and turned slow growth back into "miracle" growth after a two-year hiatus. After the adjustment, Taiwan's economy grew even faster than it had before the oil crisis—notwithstanding much higher energy prices. In fact, during the 1970s, Taiwan's GNP grew at an average annual rate of 10.2 percent. In the 1980s, the rate was 8.2 percent. Taiwan's economy slowed down a bit more in the 1990s; after all, Taiwan was now a developed—or mature—economy.

For three decades, Taiwan had more years of double-digit growth than any nation in the history of the world. For a decade and a half, its growth was approximately double Japan's and triple that of the United States. Taiwan's per capita income, which was nearly the same as China's in the 1950s, by the 1980s was twenty times that on the Mainland. When economists rank nations' growth records, they usually mean increases in the gross national product over two or three decades. By that criterion, at the close of the twentieth century Taiwan could claim to be number one in the world.[75]

Not only are Taiwan's growth numbers fantastic, but early on the expectations were low and the handicaps formidable. In the 1950s Taiwan was a very poor place. Many experts considered its economic prospects dismal and even called Taiwan hopeless. In short, Taiwan succeeded against what seemed to be very long odds. To repeat, these were an unfavorable land-to-population ratio, almost no natural resources, little capital, the loss of its markets in Japan and China, a discredited government, the influx of 1.5 million people, and the need for high defense spending owing to the threat of invasion from the People's Republic of China.

In addition to defying the odds, Taiwan's leap into prosperity was mostly free of the side effects that usually attend rapid growth. It had low inflation, no price instability, and no increase in income disparity; in fact, income disparity decreased during Taiwan's period of rapid growth to become one of the lowest in the world. Taiwan also avoided some of the other pitfalls of high growth rates: a large external debt, serious dislocations in certain sectors of the economy, and political instability.

What Taiwan accomplished was incredible. No wonder its economic success has attracted the attention not only of economists and political leaders in other countries but also of political scientists, risk analysts, and others. In fact, those who view Taiwan's accomplishments as instructive and worthy of the label "economic miracle" span a large gamut. Yet, most important among those who admire Taiwan's economic development are the many leaders of developing countries who see Taiwan as a place to study in planning their own economies. Some have even come to believe that what Taiwan did needs to be copied wholesale. Others point to specific lessons: that the capitalist model of growth does not necessarily mean income disparity, as many have thought, and that the Confucian work ethic is the way to go. Most have been convinced that a free-market economy and an emphasis on exports are the formula for economic success.

There are some more specific lessons gleaned by development economists from Taiwan's economic success: agriculture first; import substitution, but only for a short period; export-led economic growth based on comparative advantages in international trade; and a free market. Government planning, forecasting, and advice to guide the economy and to help the decisions of farmers, owners of small companies, and business leaders are also important. In addition, foreign investment in the initial phases of growth is crucial, a high savings rate is to be encouraged or forced, productivity must exceed wage increases, noncompetitive sectors of the economy must be pressured to restructure or close, the populace must be made aware of economic goals and plans and must support them, economic planning decisions must reflect changes in the world economy, taxes must be kept low, political and social stability are crucial, and welfare dependency and crime are to be kept to a minimum.

Some less noticed points can also be taken from Taiwan's economic success. One is that foreign aid can promote economic development—if both donor and recipient sincerely regard growth as their goal and work together to accomplish it. Taiwan's US aid had a major positive impact at a critical stage in the island's economic development. Most nations fail to use aid well because of poor planning, corruption, a lack of cooperation between recipient and donor, and the absence of a commitment on the part of the citizenry. This is still true. Taiwan has also been adept at going upmarket as labor costs increased and at building a reputation for quality control. It has likewise invested a large portion of the governments' (at all levels) budgets in education, which it tailored to meet the needs of business.

Comparing Taiwan's style of capitalism with other successful East Asian nations is also instructive. Japan and South Korea enjoyed exemplary economic development and, along with Hong Kong and Singapore, are considered among the world's shining examples of economic modernization. Japan and Korea, however, have far more large companies and more heavy industries than Taiwan. Hong Kong and Singapore, also high-growth countries, have almost none. In short, the role of big business and heavy industry varies considerably among these countries, as does the closeness of ties between government and business (greater in Japan and Korea, less in Hong Kong and Singapore). Nevertheless, all four "little dragons" and Japan are major trading nations and have adopted strategies that emphasize exports and the use of comparative advantage in the world market. A strong work ethic can be found in all five, while a free market has encouraged innovation and initiative and has helped keep government small and efficient. Social and political stability are important goals. There is another difference to note: unlike Japan, which has protected its manufacturing sector from foreign competition, Taiwan let its industries move out and encouraged global economic integration. The recent growth rates of the two suggest Taiwan's approach has worked better.

Taiwan may be the best model for economic development there is. It is usually considered a better model for Third World developing economies than Hong Kong and Singapore, which are little more than cities. Some also consider Taiwan a more relevant prototype than Japan, which industrialized before World War II and benefits from economies of scale and low defense spending—strategies most developing nations cannot adopt. Finally, Taiwan is more highly regarded than South Korea because the latter's economic system is modeled after Japan's. Taiwan is small and comparable to most developing countries in population, climate, and so on. Taiwan's growth has also been more recent than that of the Western industrial nations and Japan and started from a lower base. Finally, most of Taiwan's planning and economic development strategies have been assessed in studies done by foreign and local economists and can be used by developing nations (and they are using them—even China). Although an exact duplication may not be possible, most developing countries can in large part replicate Taiwan's success.

The Economy Under Chen Shui-bian and Ma Ying-jeou

In 2001, Taiwan's economy fell into recession. The proximate cause was the Chen administration's fight with the opposition parties in the legislature over the construction of Taiwan's fourth nuclear plant, which President Chen and the DPP opposed. The opposition won the fight and President Chen's image was hurt with the business community, which worried about future energy supplies. Chen's critics meanwhile charged him with poor leadership and mismanagement of economic affairs. The economic downturn was caused, Chen said, by the world recession, which had adversely affected high-tech industries, and the opposition's stubbornly blocking his economic agenda; he was partly right.[76]

In any case, by the end of the year, the stock market had lost 50 percent of its value, defaults on loans reached new highs, and private investment fell dramatically as capital fled to China (triple the amount a year earlier) where the business climate was better. The Council for Economic Planning and Development reported that Taiwan's "economic fitness index" had fallen ten points to the lowest point since it had begun keeping records.[77] By midyear, the stock market had fallen by another 40 percent and unemployment topped four hundred thousand, or 4 percent of the workforce (both forty-year highs). The media reported that the business community lacked confidence in the Chen administration and many chose to leave. "China fever" (investing and/or doing business in China) in Taiwan, it was reported, was fifty to eighty times what it was in Japan and the United States. By year-end, unemployment went up to 5 percent, and the gross national product contracted 2 percent.[78]

In response, the government took funds from the National Stabilization Fund and labor insurance and pension reserves to prop up the stock market, adding NT$350 billion to the national debt. The Chen administration pressured banks to help companies facing bankruptcy, which diverted funds that otherwise would have been available to help start-up companies and finance growth by healthy enterprises. The stock market and Taiwan's currency fell further. According to a poll conducted at this juncture, 60 percent of the population lacked confidence in Chen's economic policies. The president then established the Economic Development Advisory Council to give him recommendations on fixing the economy, but many business leaders refused to participate, citing the poisonous political atmosphere while fearing that Chen was seeking to pass blame for his situation.[79]

In 2002, the economy showed signs of recovering from the recession. But it did not perform up to the expectations of most citizens. The gross national product grew by only 3.5 percent, and unemployment remained a high (for Taiwan) 4 percent. The Chen administration tried various other means to stimulate growth and employment. It cut taxes, which meant programs to help the poor had to be pared. The government sold state assets and increased fees and fines, sometimes to very high levels. Chen proposed making Taiwan a "gateway to China" for foreign business, but this idea failed to gain traction. There were two obstacles. First, many in his party opposed the idea, as it would mean expanding commercial relations with China, making Taiwan dependent; former president Lee Teng-hui and Vice President Annette Lu both issued public warnings about dependency. Second, China did not cooperate and promoted Shanghai as the place to operate from in doing business in China.

The economy continued to grow, but still at what citizens in Taiwan considered an anemic rate. Unemployment, foreign investment, and stock market figures did not provide evidence of a good recovery. The Chen administration continued borrowing to the point that public debt by the end of President Chen's second term was 45 percent of the gross national product (GNP)—if hidden debt were counted, it was perhaps 90 percent. The media and Chen administration critics cited bad economic news with regularity. For example, in 2002, Taiwan's economy measured by the GNP was the sixteenth-largest in the world, but in 2006, it ranked twenty-second—dropping six places. During that same period Taiwan declined from 30 percent of China's economy to 18 percent. When Chen Shui-bian became president, South Korea's per capita income was two-thirds of Taiwan's; in 2006,

South Korea was higher. In 2000, Kaohsiung was the second busiest port in Asia; six years later it ranked seventh.[80]

In early 2007, Bloomberg reported that Taiwan's stock exchange had devalued 18.5 percent in US dollars during President Chen's tenure—the worst of ninety indexes it tracked. Shortly thereafter, the World Competitiveness Report showed Taiwan fell one place in the past year while China rose three slots—to pass Taiwan for the first time ever. The directorate general of Budget, Accounting and Statistics announced that the wages of workers increased 1.77 percent in 2007; this was below the rate of inflation. In other words, workers' buying power had declined.[81]

When Ma Ying-jeou ran for president in 2008, voters were attracted by the KMT's previous economic record and Ma's plans to restore economic growth. After he won the election, the stock market rose, as did Taiwan's currency, housing values, and other indicators. Observers expected Taiwan to continue to see better times again. But that was not to be. The global recession that year hit Taiwan hard. The economy contracted by more than 8 percent in the last quarter of the year, and for the year growth was under 2 percent. This was followed by a more serious economic downturn in 2009: the GDP's growth was negative in the first quarter by 9 percent and in the second quarter by nearly 7 percent. The year ended with negative growth of almost 2 percent.

In response to the crisis, the government launched a $5.6 billion stimulus plan equal to 3 percent of Taiwan's GDP. The stimulus provided financial incentives to businesses, including tax cuts. It focused on infrastructure, aid to small and medium-sized businesses, encouraging new investments, and building low-cost housing. Government planners also helped exporters seeking new markets. The plan was implemented quickly and efficiently, and in the last half of 2009 the economy was in a fast recovery mode, unlike most nations in the world. In 2010, the economy saw very rapid growth, ending the year with 10.5 percent rise in the GDP—a figure higher than China. The growth rate slowed in 2011 and 2012 because of the continued bad global economy, but Taiwan performed considerably better than most countries including the United States, Europe, and Japan, indicating Taiwan's economic fundamentals and its government planning were very good.[82]

There was another reason for Taiwan's good economic performance: in June 2010 Taiwan signed the Economic Cooperation Framework Agreement with China, which lowered the tariffs on a number of products (more on Taiwan exports), allowed for Chinese investment in Taiwan, raised the number of Chinese tourists permitted to visit Taiwan, and broadened other commercial relations. The agreement also gave Taiwan greater opportunities for trade with Southeast Asia, China having reached an agreement with ASEAN countries in January that created the first stage of a China-ASEAN common market.[83]

There was concern in Taiwan of becoming economically dependent on China. Networking and joining chains of production made this seem even more serious.

But most countries in Southeast Asia also worried about this. In any case, Taiwan had been through this with its commercial links with the United States in the past, and managed trade or protectionism did not seem to offer much in terms of a healthy economy. Further economic integration with China seemed inevitable.

Notes

1. For details about Taiwan's early economic history, see James W. Davidson, *The Island of Formosa: Past and Present* (New York: Oxford University Press, 1977).

2. For background on Taiwan's economy, see Samuel P. Ho, *Economic Development of Taiwan, 1860–1970* (New Haven, CT: Yale University Press, 1978). Also, see the introductory chapters of the books cited in the economy section of the bibliography of this book.

3. Samuel Chu, "Liu Ming-chuan and the Modernization of Taiwan," *Journal of Asian Studies* (November 1963): 37–53.

4. For details on capital formation during this period, see Teng-hui Lee, *Intersectoral Capital Flows in the Economic Development of Taiwan, 1895–1960* (Ithaca, NY: Cornell University Press, 1971), 19–20.

5. Cal Clark, *Taiwan's Development: Implications for Contending Political Economy Paradigms* (New York: Greenwood Press, 1989), 60.

6. Ho, *Economic Development of Taiwan*, 104.

7. See Anthony Y. C. Koo, "Economic Development of Taiwan," in *Taiwan in Modern Times*, ed. Paul K. T. Sih (New York: St. John's University Press, 1973), 402–406.

8. See Anthony Y. C. Koo, *The Role of Land Reform in Economic Development: A Case Study of Taiwan* (New York: Praeger, 1968); and Ho, *Economic Development of Taiwan*, for further details.

9. Walter P. Falcon, "Lessons and Issues in Taiwan's Development," in *Agriculture's Place in the Strategy of Development: The Taiwan Experience*, ed. T. H. Shen (Taipei: Joint Commission on Rural Reconstruction, 1974), 275.

10. *The Republic of China 1998 Yearbook* (Taipei: Government Information Office, 1998), 164, 199.

11. Yu Tzong-shian, *The Story of Taiwan: Economy* (Taipei: Government Information Office, 2001), 7; *Taiwan Statistical Yearbook 2007* (Taipei: Council for Economic Planning and Development, 2007), 84.

12. *Taiwan Yearbook 2007* (Taipei: Government Information Office, 2007), 102–103.

13. Ibid., 138.

14. *The Republic of China 2011 Yearbook* (Taipei: Government Information Office, 2011), 106.

15. See Yuan-li Wu, *Becoming an Industrialized Country: ROC's Development on Taiwan* (New York: Praeger, 1985), for further details on this subject.

16. Ibid. Moreover, Taiwan's agricultural sector did not experience the adverse effects that Britain's did during its industrial revolution.

17. "Farming Population Declines," *Free China Journal*, August 14, 1998, 4.

18. See Neil H. Jacoby, *U.S. Aid to Taiwan: A Study of Foreign Aid, Self-Help, and Development* (New York: Praeger, 1966), for details.

19. The data cited above are from Anthony Kubek, *Modernizing China: A Comparative Analysis of the Two Chinas* (Washington, DC: Regnery Gateway, 1987), 94.

20. More than 95 percent of registered companies in Taiwan are privately owned. See Chen Chien-jen, "ROC Looks to Future with a Vision," *Free China Journal*, April 10, 1998, 7.

21. See Wu, *Becoming an Industrialized Country*, 12, 48–49.

22. See *The Taiwan Development Experience and Its Relevance to Other Countries* (Taipei: Kwang Hwa, 1988), 25. Stanford Research Institute International prepared this study.

23. See *The Republic of China Yearbook—Taiwan 2001* (Taipei: Government Information Office, 2001), 216.

24. For details, see Wu, *Becoming an Industrialized Nation*, chapter 2.

25. See various issues of *The Index of Economic Freedom*, published by the Heritage Foundation and the *Wall Street Journal*.

26. See Wou Wei, *Capitalism: A Chinese Version* (Columbus: Ohio State University Press, 1992), 55.

27. See Clark, *Taiwan's Development*, 168.

28. Ibid.

29. See Wei, *Capitalism*, chapter 7.

30. Ibid., 39–40, 45–46.

31. See Richard Dobson, "New Report Contradicts AmCham," *Taipei Times*, May 6, 2002 (online at www.taipeitimes.com). Dobson cites Switzerland's Business Environment Risk Intelligence (BERI).

32. "Overview of Taiwan Textile Industry—2010," Taiwan Textile Federation, March 2011 (online at ttf.textiles.org.tw); "Taiwan Textile Industry's Production Value Expected to Exceed NT$530B in 2012," Yarn and Fiber Exchange, March 9, 2012 (online at yarnandfibers.com).

33. *Taiwan Yearbook 2007*, 105.

34. Many of Taiwan's factories that produce computers, chips, and other high-tech products have moved to China, and many more are expected to go soon.

35. "Taiwan Petrochemicals Report 2012," *Business Monitor International*, November 1, 2011 (online at marketpublishers.com).

36. *Taiwan Yearbook 2007*, 107.

37. *Republic of China Yearbook 2011*, 114–115.

38. Grace Kuo, "Ma's Five Pillars Initiative Wins AmCham Support," *Taiwan Today*, June 5, 2012 (online at taiwantoday.tw).

39. *Republic of China Yearbook 2011*, 178, 185.

40. Ibid., 105.

41. See Jan Prybyla, "Economic Development in Taiwan," in *China and the Taiwan Issue*, ed. Hungdah Chiu (New York: Praeger, 1979), 106. See also *National Economic Statistics of the Republic of China* (Taipei: Department of Budgeting and Statistics, 1985), 34.

42. See Yu, *Story of Taiwan: Economy*, 49–50.

43. "National Statistics: Republic of China (Taiwan) June 2012 (from the government's Statistics Bureau (online at eng.stat. gov.tw); *Taiwan Statistical Yearbook 2007* (Taipei: Executive Yuan, 2007), 19. This book is a collection of data prepared by the Council for Economic Planning and Development.

44. *Republic of China 2001 Yearbook*, 337; "Most Workers Unhappy with Salaries: Poll," *China Post*, May 23, 2012 (online at chinapost.com.tw).

45. *Taiwan Statistical Yearbook 2007*, 336.

46. *Republic of China 2011 Yearbook*, 185. The 2010 "Labor Force Evaluation Measure," a report done by the US Business Environment Risk Intelligence, is cited as the source.

47. *Republic of China 2001 Yearbook*, 343.

48. Jim Huang, "Behind the Numbers," *Taipei Review* (November 2001): 22–23; US Department of State, "Taiwan: Country Reports on Human Rights Practices, 2007," March 11, 2008, http://www.state.gov/g/drl/rls/hrrpt/2007/.

49. "Taiwan: Labor Union Law Amended, Giving Teachers Right to Unionize," News and Events (Library of Congress), n.d. (online at loc.gov/lawweb).

50. *Republic of China 1998 Yearbook*, 338.

51. *Republic of China 2011 Yearbook*, 187–88.

52. Pat Gao, "Adjusting Foreign Labor's Role," *Taipei Review* (November 2001): 10. Between 1990 and 1994, there were reportedly seventy-three thousand foreign workers illegally in Taiwan. See *The Republic of China 1995 Yearbook* (Taipei: Government Information Office, 1995), 388.

53. "Council Urged to Control Number of Migrant Workers," *China Post*, May 23, 2008 (online at chinapost.com).

54. *Republic of China 2011 Yearbook*, 186.

55. See Shirley W. Y. Kuo, Gustav Ranis, and John C. H. Fei, *The Taiwan Success Story: Rapid Growth and Improved Distribution in the Republic of China, 1952–1979* (Boulder, CO: Westview Press, 1981), chapter 6.

56. *Republic of China 2011 Yearbook*, 110.

57. See Wei, *Capitalism*, chapters 2 and 3, for further details.

58. The United States accounted for almost half of Taiwan's trade in the mid-1980s. New trade policies and efforts to expand trade elsewhere soon reduced this proportion to less than 40 percent.

59. For details, see Edwin A. Winckler and Susan Greenhalgh, "Analytical Issues and Historical Episodes," in *Contending Approaches to the Political Economy of Taiwan*, ed. Edwin A. Winckler and Susan Greenhalgh (Armonk, NY: M. E. Sharpe, 1988), 6–7.

60. For the reasons for this, see Hans H. Bass, "Export Dynamism in Taiwan and Mainland China, 1950s–2000," Institute for World Economics and Management (University of Breman), January 1999.

61. *Republic of China 2011 Yearbook*, 111.

62. Ibid., 110.

63. Chi Schive, *The Foreign Factor: The Multinational Corporations' Contribution to the Economic Modernization of the Republic of China* (Stanford, CA: Hoover Institution Press, 1990), 4.

64. Ibid.

65. "2000 Taiwan White Paper," *Topics*, May 2008, 10.

66. *Republic of China 2011 Yearbook*, 110. In 2010, foreigners, including Chinese, purchased $170 billion in Taiwan's stock and sold $161 billion.

67. "Taiwan Forex Reserves Down 1.5 Pct in May," *Currency and Forex News*, June 5, 2012 (online at xe.com).

68. For background details on Taiwan's energy problems, see John F. Copper, "Taiwan's Energy Situation," in *National Energy Profiles*, ed. Kenneth R. Stunkel (New York: Praeger/Holt, Rinehart and Winston, 1979). For details on the current situation, see *Taiwan Yearbook 2007*, 104.

69. "Energy Supply," Bureau of Energy of Ministry of Economic Affairs, cited in *Wikipedia*, accessed June 7, 2012.

70. Mo Yan-chih and Chris Wang, "Ma Unveils His Nuclear Energy Policy," *Taipei Times*, November 4, 2011 (online at taipeitimes.com).

71. Tomas Clancy, *Countries of the World: Republic of China* (n.p.: Create Space, 2012), 311; Oscar Chang, "Contributing to a Greener World," *Taiwan Review*, March 2010 (online at taiwanreview.nat.gov.tw).

72. For the early figures, see *Republic of China Yearbook—Taiwan 2001*, 166. For the recent data, see "Invest in Taiwan," Department of Investment Services. Data are for 2007 (online at investintaiwan.nat.gov.tw).

73. Hongyi Lai, "Taiwan-Mainland China Energy Ties: Cooperation and Potential Conflict," Taiwan's Energy Conundrum Asia Program Special Report (Woodrow Wilson Center), May 2012.

74. In this connection, see *The Taiwan Development Experience and Its Relevance to Other Countries* (Taipei: Kwang Hua, 1988).

75. See John M. Leger, "The Book: How Asians Started the 'Pacific Century' Early," *Far Eastern Economic Review*, November 24, 1994, 43. China, South Korea, Hong Kong, and Singapore rank in that order after Taiwan. The ranking is based on the period from 1975 to 1993. For the period 1968–1998, Taiwan ranks number one in the world in per capita growth in gross national product, but it was surpassed by Botswana, Oman, and South Korea in overall GNP growth. See Herman Pan and Elizabeth Hsu, "ROC Long-term Economic Growth 4th Largest; GNP Growth Highest," *China Post*, April 26, 1998, 14. The first two being very small countries economically that export raw materials, they may be considered of little importance. Because of South Korea's recent economic problems, Taiwan has again surpassed South Korea in GNP growth.

76. Yu-shan Wu, "Taiwan in 2000: Managing the Aftershock of Power Transfer," *Asian Survey* (January/February 2001): 47.

77. "Taiwan Economic Outlook Dim," *Economic News Daily*, March 20, 2001 (online at taiwanheadlines.com).

78. Ramon H. Myers and Jialin Zhang, *The Struggle Across the Taiwan Strait* (Stanford, CA: Hoover Institution Press, 2006), 70.

79. Yun-han Chu, "The Political Economy of Taiwan's Politics: Implications for Northeast Asia" (paper presented at the London School of Economics and Politics, May 12, 2007).

80. See David DeVoss, "Tear Gas and Running Dogs," *Weekly Standard*, December 4, 2006, 18–19.

81. See "The State of the Nation," *CommonWealth*, March 28, 2007 (online at cw.com .tw).

82. Clancy, *Countries of the World*, 308.

83. *Republic of China Yearbook 2011*, 115–116.

6

FOREIGN AND MILITARY POLICIES

TAIWAN HAS LONG BEEN, AND still is, a special player in international politics. It was the first ever Western colony in Asia to become independent. It was the launching pad for Japan's invasion of Southeast Asia at the onset of World War II. During the Cold War, on two or three occasions it was involved in conflicts with China that portended to explode into a global war. For twenty-two years, from 1949 to 1971, as the Republic of China, it represented China in the United Nations. Then it was expelled and quickly lost formal diplomatic ties with most nations of the world. In 1979, Taipei suffered a break in formal ties with its most important friend and ally, the United States. Yet Taipei resisted Beijing's efforts to isolate and delegitimize its government and carried on diplomacy by way of commercial, cultural, and other contacts. Taipei also adopted a "democratic" foreign policy. In 1991, Taipei officially terminated its war with the People's Republic of China. This and the end of the Cold War should have given Taiwan greater security; but Beijing lost an enemy (the Soviet Union) and, as a consequence, moved more of its soldiers and weapons to areas close to the Taiwan Strait. In addition, China's military power grew quickly as a product of its booming economy, making it a serious threat to Taiwan. In 1996, China intimidated Taiwan with missile tests close to Taiwan's shores; the United States sent aircraft carriers to protect Taiwan—precipitating a face-off between Washington and Beijing that by many accounts almost led to war. After 2000, President Chen Shui-bian made moves toward legal independence and in so doing angered China. He also upset the United States (which was focused on the war on terrorism); as a consequence, US-Taiwan relations deteriorated badly. Furthermore, Chen's policies were out of sync with both Taiwan's growing economic integration with China and his administration's reduced defense spending. President Ma Ying-jeou, elected in 2008, rejected independence (but also unification) and enjoyed cordial relations with China and the United States. But, whether the United States would continue to support Taiwan's separation became a more serious question, as defending Taiwan became viewed by some in the United States as a policy that could not be sustained, given China's military rise and America's decline.

Background

Before the era of Western colonialism, Taiwan engaged in interactions with several neighboring countries, though one would not equate these contacts to diplomatic relations that were being practiced in the West at the time. The island's merchants, meanwhile, maintained active commercial ties with trading centers in East Asia, including some in China. In the sixteenth century, both the Chinese inhabitants of the island and the Aborigines began to engage in diplomacy of a sort with the Western powers and Japan.[1]

While Taiwan was under Dutch colonial rule, its foreign relations were managed by the mother country. When the island was subsequently governed by China, Peking handled Taiwan's external affairs. China, however, did not adhere to modern diplomatic practices and at times made disclaimers to the United States, Japan, and other foreign countries about its responsibilities over Taiwan, giving rise to doubts about whether China claimed the island.[2] Between 1895 and 1945, while a Japanese colony, Taiwan's external relations were handled by Tokyo. Relations with other nations varied during this period, but they were generally more restricted during the later years of Japanese rule. Contacts with China at any time during this period were limited.

In 1945, responsibility for Taiwan's external affairs passed to the Nationalist Chinese government in Nanking, even though the issue of Taiwan's legal status was not decided.[3] In 1949, after its defeat by the Communists, the Nationalist government moved to Taiwan, at which time Taiwan and the Republic of China became virtually synonymous. The United States abandoned Chiang Kai-shek, but quickly changed its policy as a result of the Korean War and once again became Taiwan's protector.

Chiang contended Mao's government was illegitimate and would not last—a somewhat credible claim at the time because of internal instability in China, US antipathy toward the Communist regime, and the UN-inspired boycott of the People's Republic of China after its entry into the Korean War. Most Western countries—with a few exceptions, such as the United Kingdom (because of Hong

Kong)—accorded diplomatic relations to Taipei instead of Peking and supported Taipei's claim to represent the Chinese people in international affairs. The Republic of China occupied the China seat in the United Nations, including a permanent seat on the Security Council, notwithstanding Soviet protests. Soviet-bloc countries, of course, accorded diplomatic recognition to the People's Republic of China and established embassies in Peking.

Both Nationalist China's foreign policy and its defense strategy were founded on the premise that its military would counterattack the Mainland, defeat Mao's armies, and again rule China. But carrying out this plan with any real hope of success depended on help from the United States and/or a global conflict between the Communist and Western blocs. Neither happened.

The local population of Taiwan had little or no experience in making—or in even influencing—diplomatic decisions; thus, it would be conjecture to suggest to what extent public opinion supported the main tenets of Taiwan's foreign policy. It seems fair to say a majority of the populace did not favor a policy of liberating the Mainland, yet they clearly opposed Peking ruling Taiwan. They supported aligning with the United States, but the Nationalist government already had such a policy. In sum, the population's views on foreign policy were unclear and seldom articulated. Some spoke of independence, but this had no outside support.

Because the government of the Republic of China regarded Mao's Communist regime its enemy, links between Taiwan and the Mainland that had been established after 1945 were severed. Two Chinas thus emerged: Nationalist China and Communist China, or the Republic of China and the People's Republic of China. The two contended for legitimacy, influence in the world community, and the allegiance of the Overseas Chinese. Because it espoused capitalism and aligned with the United States, Nationalist China enjoyed advantages that offset its much smaller size and population.

Owing to Nationalist China's new situation—that is, its move to Taiwan and its greater dependence on the West, especially the United States—its diplomatic practices and policies shifted. The vestiges of traditional Chinese-style diplomacy were displaced by Western practices. The island's external policies also reflected its government-in-exile status and its reliance on America for economic and security support. The Republic of China's foreign policy did not, in any meaningful way, reflect Taiwan's or China's historical past practice of conducting foreign relations.

In the late 1950s, Taipei began to play down its policy of "liberating" the Mainland. In his 1959 New Year's speech, Chiang Kai-shek defined the Mainland recovery policy as 70 percent political. Many thought this remark signaled a change of strategy and believed the plan to return to China would eventually be scrapped.[4] Chiang's decision probably stemmed from the perception that the United States no longer supported Taipei's desire to liberate China, as demonstrated by Washington's stance during the two Offshore Islands crises of 1954–1955 and 1958. In fact, the US Department of State conveyed the message, emphatically after the second conflict, that it did not sanction efforts by Taipei to start a conflict with Peking and believed that two Chinese nation-states would become a permanent arrangement.[5]

Taipei also began to perceive the world differently as it became aware of the significance of détente between the superpowers and Sino-Soviet discord. In 1960, the rift between Moscow and Peking ended Soviet military support for China, a decision that reduced China's military capabilities and, thus, the likelihood that it would attack Taiwan. Taipei's underground and intelligence networks on the Mainland, meanwhile, no longer functioned as they had before; its personnel there had aged, some had defected, and many were captured. In the interim, the division of China became less a concern to the rest of the world. Hence Taipei's leaders had to design policies based more narrowly on Taiwan's national interests.

Nationalist Chinese leaders similarly understood that world opinion was shifting toward Peking in the battle for diplomatic recognition; in other words, Taipei could not continue to garner global support to represent all of China in various international forums and organizations. In the United Nations, Peking each year won more support on the issue of whether it or Taipei should represent China. Still, Chiang Kai-shek did not formulate a new policy agenda. Some argued at the time that Taipei should quickly abandon its claim to represent China and adopt a foreign policy that represented the reality of governing only Taiwan. Had it not been for the Vietnam War and the Cultural Revolution in the People's Republic of China, both of which played into the hands of hard-liners in Taiwan, a new foreign policy might have been forthcoming.

Some Western scholars as well as critics of the government in Taiwan have argued that in the early 1960s Taipei would have been successful in promoting a two-Chinas or a one-China, one-Taiwan policy, thereby avoiding the subsequent humiliation of being "expelled" (technically Taipei withdrew) from the United Nations in 1971 and the diplomatic isolation caused by the loss of recognition from a host of countries after that. Others, however, doubt this. They say Taipei could not forsake the one-China ideal because of ethnic tensions between the ruling Mainland Chinese and the Taiwanese, as such a change would have evoked demands by Taiwanese for a bigger political role too soon. Indeed, abandoning the one-China policy might have engendered domestic political instability that would have made Taiwan vulnerable to Peking's efforts to subvert and weaken it, while giving Mao a pretext for attacking Taiwan, as he had planned to do in 1950.[6] This is an interesting question though now a moot one.

Diplomatic Decline and Partial Recovery

In 1968, US voters elected Richard M. Nixon president of the United States with a mandate to get out of the Vietnam War with honor. To do this, Nixon needed to dramatically change US-China relations. In fact, he made this a central goal in American foreign policy. The US-China rapprochement that followed and Peking's (now spelled Beijing) ending its self-imposed isolationism were to Taiwan's detriment.

In 1971, Taiwan "lost" the China seat in the United Nations and, with it, membership in that important world body. Henceforth, Taiwan could no longer claim to represent the Chinese people in international affairs. This was a major foreign policy setback for Taipei. It resulted in the loss of diplomatic ties with a host of nations. By 1970, the number of countries recognizing each had already tipped in Beijing's favor, 68 countries to 53. Three years later, Beijing had more than twice as many: 85 to 39. In 1977, Beijing had 111 compared to Taipei's 23.[7] Fearing that diplomatic seclusion would make it vulnerable to Beijing's claim that Taiwan belonged to China and had to be returned, Taipei adopted a policy called "substantive diplomacy," in which it sought to substitute commercial and other ties for formal diplomatic links.[8]

Taipei suffered still another shock in December 1978, when President Jimmy Carter announced the termination of US diplomatic recognition effective on January 1, 1979, and the cancellation of the US–Republic of China defense treaty a year after that. Taipei reacted stoically. President Chiang Ching-kuo reiterated Taiwan's earlier declared "three no's policy": no contact, no negotiations, and no compromise (with China). He took important steps to democratize the political system and construct a "democratic foreign policy." This meant Taiwan could promote the view that it was democratic and China was not and that it, therefore, deserved to be considered sovereign and independent.

Beijing broached reunification (unification from Taipei's point of view because Taiwan had never been governed by the People's Republic of China) proposals to Taipei. On the surface, its offers seemed generous, but the bottom line was that Chinese leaders called on Taipei to surrender its sovereignty.[9] Taiwan's leaders did not consider China's proposals seriously. Nevertheless, the Western media often treated Beijing's gestures as reasonable while labeling Taipei's responses stubborn. Taiwan thus adopted new stratagems: making counteroffers that Beijing could not accept, publicizing Taiwan's wish (and its moral and legal right) to determine its own future, and stating its citizens' desire to remain separate.

In ensuing years, Taipei sought more energetically to cement as many contacts as possible of any kind with willing nations and global organizations to avoid being isolated. Taipei went a step further with its substantive diplomacy; it began to speak also about its "informal diplomacy," which emphasized various new kinds of ties. Though the number of countries having official relations with Taiwan remained low, many wanted to carry on commercial and various other kinds of informal ties with Taiwan. As a result, Taiwan's global status became in some ways more unique. Beijing denied that Taiwan was a nation-state or had sovereignty.

Although most nations of the world agreed there was only one China, few wanted to get involved in the matter of whether Taiwan was legally a part of China.

The 1980s saw another shift in Taiwan's diplomatic strategy. Taipei began to pursue a lowering of cross-strait tensions and a strengthening of economic and other ties with China. Although its leaders valued Taiwan's sovereignty, they perceived that they needed to pursue amicable relations with Beijing. Some thought that, ultimately, unification was likely and desirable. The People's Republic of China had in many ways become a new and different country following the death of Mao in 1976 and the ascendancy of Deng Xiaoping in 1978. Deng's economic policies brought prosperity, which gave rise to manifold political and social change in China. More important, China was on the way to becoming a global economic power that no one, especially Taiwan, could ignore.

The end of the Cold War and the appearance of a New World Order from 1989 to 1991 presented Taiwan with not only bigger diplomatic opportunities, but also more challenges.[10] The Tiananmen Massacre in June 1989 made the People's Republic of China a pariah nation in the eyes of many Western countries. Yet Taipei could not, or at least perceived it should not try to, isolate China or eschew contacts with Beijing. It had attempted this before. More important, China and Taiwan were in the same economic bloc in what many in Taiwan perceived was an evolving tripolar (the European Union, the North American Free Trade Association, and the Pacific Basin bloc) world.[11]

In January 1988, Lee Teng-hui became Taiwan's first Taiwanese president. He coined the term "pragmatic diplomacy" to describe Taiwan's approach to foreign affairs. Lee accelerated Taiwan's efforts to re-establish or maintain contacts with as many nations as possible—even those having formal diplomatic ties with the People's Republic of China. This included dual recognition, which Taipei had heretofore rejected. Taipei at this time adopted still another term—"flexible diplomacy"—that some called a multidirectional or omnidirectional approach to diplomacy. Accordingly, Taiwan sought trade and other relations with various former and current Communist nations. Taipei also made efforts to adapt to the New World Order and to take advantage of new rules and ideals in global politics, including the notion that no country or political entity should be barred from participating in the world community. In short, Taiwan's foreign policy makers quickly adjusted to a new global structure and became more assertive.

In 1991, Lee ended Taiwan's so-called period of mobilization, officially terminating the state of war with Beijing. In 1993, Taiwan "negotiated" (labeled talks) with Beijing for the first time. The meetings were predicated on Taiwan accepting the doctrine of one China, though Taipei could have its own interpretation of the meaning of "China." There followed a significant thaw in cross-strait relations. However, President Lee perceived China was closing Taiwan's "international space" and undermining its diplomatic status. Lee wanted to "break out." He visited the

United States in 1995, seriously souring relations with China. In 1999, President Lee announced a "two-state theory," again provoking China and causing his tenure to end on a low note in terms of cross-strait relations.

When Chen Shui-bian became president in 2000, he promised to improve relations with both the United States and China. Beijing took a wait-and-see stance toward Chen. Early in the Bush administration, US-Taiwan relations were reportedly better than they had been in a long time. But this soon changed, and relations with Washington deteriorated badly. The cause was 9/11. China joined the United States in fighting the war on terrorism. Washington perceived that Chen sought, with talk of independence, to provoke China for his own political gain while disregarding America's preoccupation with terrorism; thus, the Bush administration questioned whether Taiwan under the Chen administration was a faithful ally. The United States subsequently responded with anger to Chen's push for independence.[12]

Taiwan's relations with China worsened as Beijing came to see Chen as a determined proponent of independence. So China showed its clout. Taipei lost diplomatic relations with several countries despite Chen's boast that he could improve Taiwan's diplomatic situation. Efforts to win representation in the United Nations turned into embarrassment for Taiwan. The Chen administration's localism prompted many Overseas Chinese communities to switch sides to China when Beijing made a pitch for their loyalty. In short, under Chen Taiwan became more isolated and its foreign policy overall less successful.

In 2008, Ma Ying-jeou was elected president. Ma sought to lessen tension with China and improve relations with the United States. He succeeded in doing both. But Ma had to consider the reality that the population of the island wanted to preserve Taiwan's sovereignty, that China was a fast-growing power both economically and militarily, and that the United States was declining by both measures. Ma adopted a new policy that he called "viable diplomacy," which may be defined as pragmatism while using better relations with China to pursue Taiwan's diplomatic objectives elsewhere.

Domestic Affairs and Foreign Policy

The influence of domestic politics on Taiwan's foreign policy has increased markedly over the years for a host of reasons. Most relevant to this change, of course, was, and is, Taiwan's democratization. But even before this, domestic politics influenced Taiwan's foreign policy to a considerable degree. In the 1950s, Taiwan was a focal point in the bipolar global struggle. Its center-stage role in world politics and its permanent membership in the United Nations Security Council drew public attention to Taiwan's global importance. The KMT proclaimed that it rather than the Communist regime on the Mainland represented "Free China."

Hence officials in Taipei felt compelled to demonstrate that they had public support for the major tenets of Taiwan's foreign policy.

Public opinion thus influenced foreign policy. Most citizens felt that the government should be more concerned about domestic problems, especially economic development, than with overthrowing Mao's regime in China. This may explain why the leadership started playing down this policy. The government rationalized that Taiwan had to develop a strong economy (a policy that had strong public support) if it were to defeat communism.

The public strongly supported relations with the developed Western countries—especially the United States, because Washington guaranteed Taiwan's security and extended economic aid. Later, the United States and other Western countries (including Japan) provided capital investment for Taiwan's economic expansion. For these reasons and the popularity of the United States in Taiwan, neither the populace nor important government officials ever seriously considered questioning Washington's lead in international affairs. Likewise, they never regarded isolationism as an option, even as Taipei's global status declined.

During the 1960s, when Taiwan's economy began to boom (but when its diplomatic ties with most of the world began to look tenuous), foreign policy makers started to seek greater domestic support for their main external goals. Taiwan's leaders realized that time was not on their side in the struggle with Beijing for diplomatic recognition. Yet economic and other ties could be translated into support for Taiwan's sovereignty. Policy makers sought public approval for their economic and cultural diplomacy, and they got it.

In the early 1970s, public input into foreign policy making increased noticeably. Taipei's expulsion from the United Nations in 1971 engendered widespread public anxiety that the Republic of China was doomed to delegitimization and isolation. For the first time, serious public debate ensued over foreign policy. When Chiang Ching-kuo became premier in 1972, he ordered the Nationalist Party and the government to heed public opinion in making both domestic and foreign policy. Foreign policy decision makers often suggested that Taiwan's future should be determined in a democratic way, the implication being that Taiwan should remain sovereign and independent because its population wanted this. Taiwan's Mainland Chinese leaders had become increasingly comfortable with the idea of remaining on Taiwan and, with the exception of a few hard-liners, abandoned any hope of returning to China. Most, because of their bad experience negotiating with the Chinese Communists in the 1930s and 1940s and the bright economic prospects at home, saw little advantage in trying to reach some reconciliation with Beijing. The Taiwanese mostly favored separation in any case.[13]

With Taiwan's first national competitive election in 1980, a two-party election in 1986, and the termination of martial law the following year, opposition politicians became much more active, and their influence on foreign policy increased.

Their dissatisfaction with their government's foreign policy was often expressed in public. In response the Ministry of Foreign Affairs became more sensitive to public views. In fact, some say this gave rise to the term "public diplomacy." In one important respect, the public debate worked to the advantage of foreign policy decision makers: because of democratization, they could say the reason they resisted negotiating with Beijing about reunification was that the people did not want it, at least not now. They also pointed out that the Nationalist Party was no longer the only political party in Taiwan; thus party-to-party talks were inappropriate (which Beijing called for to avoid government-to-government contacts that would, China feared, give Taipei the status of a sovereign nation-state).

In 1979, after the United States broke diplomatic relations with Taipei, widespread debate on foreign relations again ensued. Many citizens questioned the wisdom of certain aspects of Taiwan's foreign policy. Opposition politicians became particularly vocal at this time. They advocated a more "democratically based" foreign policy lest, they said, Taiwan would not survive. The issue of Taiwan's independence was thus thrust into the foreign policy debate. There was a dilemma: advocacy of legally separating Taiwan from China was sedition according to the law, yet the government had abandoned its policy of liberating China. In addition, proclaiming an independent Taiwan was unnecessarily risky because it could provoke Beijing into using military force. And the United States opposed it. Yet because of democratization, the advocacy of independence could not be curtailed.[14]

The government, or at least the ruling Nationalist Party, found it convenient to argue that its policy was "moderate," because Beijing demanded reunification and Taiwanese independence advocates asked for separation and no ties with China. In fact, the KMT's status quo or "wait and see" policy looked reasonable and found broad support as reflected in opinion polls. In the early 1990s, the independence issue seemed in large part resolved, or at least defused, when, in 1991, the Democratic Progressive Party placed the issue of independence in its campaign platform and voters rebuffed it. The issue arose again after China conducted missile tests to intimidate Taiwan in 1995 and 1996, and independence gained considerably in popularity. But, with the resumption of talks between Taipei and Beijing in 1993, the issue receded a bit. Supporters of independence also did poorly in the December 1998 election.

Meanwhile, with so many citizens traveling to China and with trade and investment increasing rapidly at this time, attitudes regarding contacts with China began to change. Many people in Taiwan, especially businesspeople (including many Taiwanese), opposed government restrictions preventing more extensive commercial contacts. Many feared being left out of the "China boom." Also, with the advent of a New World Order, many citizens in Taiwan started to think about belonging to the same economic bloc as China and even began to consider the idea of a "Greater China."

In 1989, after the massacre of students and other protesters in Tiananmen Square in Beijing, Taiwan's pariah image evaporated; the People's Republic of China was now *the* pariah nation. These developments and an election victory by the opposition Democratic Progressive Party that year caused the Western media to treat Taiwan as a democracy and worthy of praise. Beijing's overtures and its pressure on Taipei to negotiate reunification lost credibility. At the same time, support from the population and the media gave the government more confidence and prompted it to take domestic public opinion more seriously.

Subsequently, concern for public opinion was widely cited in Taipei's efforts to participate in various international organizations.[15] Although Taiwan did not win support from any important nations in this effort, by citing its successful democratization and the wishes of Taiwan's citizens, it embarrassed various organizations that excluded Taiwan.

Public opinion also began to have an impact through the legislature in Taiwan. Lawmakers were sensitive to public views, especially organized groups. The legislature put pressure on foreign policy decision makers in a number of ways. The most noteworthy was the influence it used to push for expanding commercial relations with China and easier contacts across the Taiwan Strait. In 2003, the public was given a new venue by the Referendum Act passed that year.[16]

The government's promotion of its "democratic foreign policy" has also been reflected in its publication of treatises on defense and foreign policy. In 1992, the Ministry of Defense published its first white paper explaining in layman's terms Taiwan's strategic and defense problems and policies.[17] In early 1993, the Ministry of Foreign Affairs published its first-ever foreign relations white paper, presenting an easy-to-read but fairly detailed statement of foreign policy. Meanwhile, high officials who had spent time in the academic world wrote books and contributed articles on Taiwan's foreign relations and foreign policy.[18] Recently, reports and statements on defense and foreign policy have been issued regularly. It seemed clear that in the future, the media, opposition groups, political parties, lobbying and public interest organizations, and the public would have even more influence on foreign policy.

When Chen Shui-bian campaigned for president, he built the tenets of his foreign policy on public opinion surveys and the notion of public diplomacy. As president, Chen found that he could improve his image by making foreign policy pronouncements and personally taking charge of Taiwan's diplomacy while drawing public attention with foreign trips. Some even said that Chen was Taiwan's first "foreign policy president." But as his popularity waned, this did not work well; in fact, it created a disconnect between public sentiment and the conduct of foreign relations.

President Ma Ying-jeou has heeded (or used) the views of the public on various issues in making foreign policy decisions. His diplomacy with China, especially on the issue of unification, was based on the public's view that trade ties should go forward quickly but that political change should proceed slowly, if at all. He sought and found public support for the Economic Cooperation Framework Agreement negotiated with China in 2010 and other agreements to expand cross-strait relations. In fact, he won re-election in 2012 in some part because the public supported his foreign policy vis-à-vis China and the United States.[19]

Taiwan's National Security Policy

National security is the driving force that, to a large extent, molds Taiwan's foreign policy.[20] Almost without peers, Taiwan has been under threat by a much bigger power, in fact, now a truly global power: China. Taiwan's strategic thinking is thus dominated by how to deal with the China threat.

Some background will help put this in perspective. As noted earlier, shortly after the Nationalists fled to Taiwan in 1949, Mao made plans to "liberate" the island. Because of the Korean War, the United States not only stopped a People's Liberation Army (PLA) invasion but also became the guarantor of Taiwan's security. Yet Washington sought to limit Taiwan's offensive military capabilities by supplying it with defensive arms only. American advisors also tried to persuade Taipei to reduce its forces on Quemoy and Matsu—the site of two crises in the 1950s. The United States reasoned that they constituted a tinderbox and Taiwan's military units there were vulnerable to being cut off and destroyed by Mao's PLA forces. But Chiang Kai-shek was unwilling to do this because the Offshore Islands symbolized Taipei's links with the Mainland and its claim to be the legitimate government of China. Thus, Chiang kept approximately one-third of Taiwan's military manpower on these islands.[21]

Eventually realizing its military in terms of manpower was too small to attack China while gradually abandoning a military strategy in favor of a political one to liberate China, President Chiang bowed to US pressure and cut the size of Taiwan's military (which was large and costly for a small country) while he upgraded its professionalism and the quality of its weapons. From a peak of more than six hundred thousand, Chiang cut the standing army to below five hundred thousand.[22]

A serious problem related to improving Taiwan's military capabilities was that it could not obtain all of the weapons it wanted or raise the level of sophistication of its important weapons systems. In particular, it needed state-of-the-art fighter planes and antisubmarine warfare capabilities. The United States was Taiwan's only meaningful supplier of weapons, but it refused to sell Taipei all it wanted or needed. So Taiwan looked for other sources. The government did manage to purchase two submarines from Holland (delivered in 1988), but Beijing put such pressure on the Dutch government that it promised not to make any more weapons sales to Taiwan. Taiwan purchased weapons from other European countries but nothing significant. Israel was willing to sell weapons to Taiwan, but Taipei, with a few exceptions, eschewed buying weapons from Israel because of Taiwan's good relations with Saudi Arabia and its dependence on several Middle Eastern countries for oil.

Taipei was able to overcome this problem to some degree by obtaining US weapons technology, which was not covered in Washington's 1982 pledge to Beijing to cut arms sales to Taiwan. Such technology transfers made it possible for Taiwan to build a new high-performance jet aircraft called the Indigenous Defense Fighter or Ching Kuo (after the late president), a prototype of which was put into service in 1994. Meanwhile there was a breakthrough: in 1992, the Bush administration offered to sell F-16 fighter planes to Taiwan. At almost the same time, France proposed selling Taipei its Mirage fighters. The government bought both. This change in policy by two major arms producers seemed to reflect a consensus abroad, in the United States at least, that Beijing's increased defense spending and its purchasing more sophisticated weapons from Moscow after the breakup of the Soviet Union needed to be balanced.[23]

Subsequently, Taiwan's biggest concern became the short-range missiles Beijing placed in areas adjacent to Taiwan across the strait. Beijing's missile tests exposed Taiwan's vulnerability. Soon China had more than a thousand missiles aimed at Taiwan and was reportedly increasing the number by fifty to one hundred per year. In addition to the damage that a missile attack would do to military facilities and population centers, Taiwan also had to worry that Beijing would quarantine the island through verbal threats and military maneuvers (with missiles to back them up). China could shut off Taiwan's trade. In response, and coinciding with a continuing willingness on the part of the United States to sell arms to Taiwan, Taipei purchased antimissile defense systems (including the Patriot missile system), ships, and other weapons.[24]

The Chen administration moved toward a new strategy in dealing with the China threat. President Chen suggested an offensive policy to replace what had long been essentially a defensive posture when he announced a strategy called a "decisive offshore campaign." Chen's premier even spoke publicly of bombing Shanghai and Hong Kong in retaliation if China were to attack Taiwan. But President Chen had his detractors. Many felt that such "wild talk" would make Taiwan less secure. In any event, the United States and other countries did not support Chen's proposed shift of policy.[25]

The Ma administration in 2008 adopted a security policy of improving relations with China while upgrading Taiwan's military forces. This strategy was confirmed by changes in the makeup of Taiwan's military. The manpower of its military was cut to 275,000 with a reduction to 215,000 planned for 2014. Half of its personnel were now career military. Compulsory military service was cut to twelve months and will probably be ended in the near future. More funds were allocated to the air force and navy. More money was spent on military training and on high-tech weapons.[26] Yet, in most areas Taiwan was still not keeping up with China's military expansion. All of this suggests Taiwan intends its military to be a defensive force and that it seeks to be able to fend off a PLA attack for a short time until the United States can come to Taiwan's rescue—which has long been the basis of Taiwan's military strategy equation.

This leads to one question: What are Taiwan's other options? Clearly Taiwan cannot match China's military buildup with one of its own and must rely on the US military to deter China from attacking the island. But what else can it do?

One option for Taipei is to look for other allies. In the past one possibility was the Soviet Union. During the 1960s and 1970s, because of strained relations between Moscow and Beijing, there was reason to believe that Soviet leaders wanted to see Taiwan remain outside Beijing's control. The Soviet Union's Pacific Fleet indeed benefited from the Taiwan Strait being an open international waterway. Moscow gave some signals, including making references to Taiwan as a "nation" and giving Taipei information on Soviet naval maneuvers, that it wished to see the status quo in the area preserved.[27] But with the collapse of the Soviet Union and the fact that Russia now is pursuing good relations with China, this option no longer exists, if indeed it ever did.

Japan has also been considered a possible ally and still is. Many, probably most, policy makers in Tokyo prefer a separate Taiwan to one that is part of the People's Republic of China because of the importance of Japan's trade and investment ties with Taiwan, historical links, and Japan's possible interest in eventually extending its naval power farther south. In a joint communiqué with the United States in 1969, Tokyo referred to Taiwan as being "within its defense perimeter." In 1997, they signed an agreement whereby Japan promised to provide logistical support to the United States in "situations surrounding Japan"—presumably extending to Taiwan. Meanwhile, Japan's military spending is increasing, and its military power is growing.

However, Tokyo is restrained by pacifism at home. Also, the Japanese government faces the problem of apprehension and even fear among nations in the region about its growing military strength. Thus, even though Japan wishes Taiwan to remain independent, Tokyo is reluctant to translate this into policy. Japan is also highly unlikely to pursue a Taiwan policy that is at odds with that of the United States. Finally, increasingly Japan does not seek to challenge China militarily.

Yet Tokyo has some influence on Beijing's foreign policy that is to Taiwan's advantage. Japanese trade and investment are important to China. Beijing does not want to give cause for Japan to alter its defense policies. China's brandishing its military forces against Taiwan would, indirectly at least, threaten Japan and might serve as a catalyst for Japan to rearm quickly and perhaps even abandon its anti-nuclear weapons policy. Chinese leaders obviously do not want that.

Also, there is the issue of theater missile defense (TMD). The United States and Japan are working on such a system for Northeast Asia, nominally aimed at the North Korean missile (and nuclear weapons) threat. Some say, however, that TMD is also (primarily perhaps) directed at China, and Taiwan may join this project. Its leaders have hinted strongly that Taiwan would like to. If Taipei were to participate, Taiwan could better defend itself against the threat (and use of) Chinese missiles. In addition, Taiwan would benefit from an important psychological boost because its security would be linked to Japan's and the US commitment to defend Taiwan would be enlarged. For these reasons, China is adamantly opposed to TMD and is very hostile to the idea of Taiwan's joining.

Another option for Taiwan is to build nuclear weapons.[28] Because Beijing has them—and has never ceased to threaten to use military force against Taiwan—Taipei would seem to be justified in making its own. Taipei has done research on nuclear power and has the technology, the money, and the scientists to build nuclear bombs, probably within less than a year if it decided to do so. However, as noted earlier, in the 1970s, the United States pressured Taiwan to stop its nuclear weapons program, and Taipei obliged. It could, however, reinstate its programs, or it might purchase nuclear weapons. Perhaps, even worse, it could produce or buy chemical and biological weapons. Incidentally, Beijing claims that Taiwan could produce nuclear weapons easily and speculates that it already has chemical and biological weapons (although Taipei denies it).

Taipei has no defense against Beijing's nuclear weapons. Yet this might not be necessary. The 1968 Nuclear Nonproliferation Treaty signed by the United States and the Soviet Union guarantees nonnuclear nations protection from those with nuclear weapons. Although the signatories do not recognize Taipei diplomatically, Taiwan may still be protected from nuclear attack under the broad terms of the agreement. Beijing is also constrained by world opinion from using nuclear weapons against a nonnuclear country (or a province of China, in its view). It is also worthy of note that Chinese leaders have publicly stated that they will never use nuclear weapons on their own people. Finally, it has been rumored that Taipei concluded a secret agreement with the United States that affords Taiwan certain military guarantees in return for Taiwan's not developing nuclear weapons.[29]

Several other options are available to Taipei in the event of a conflict with Beijing. Taipei could cause considerable dislocation to trade and travel in the area by declaring a state of war or by delineating military zones and warning ships and planes to stay away. It might surrender islands it controls in the South China Sea to Vietnam or some other country in the region, thereby creating a diversion. It might allow or encourage citizens to flee to the United States and other countries, creating a refugee problem and thereby making the problem one of US and/or international concern. Taiwan might even threaten to bomb Chinese cities or dams (including the Three Gorges dam, which would cause tremendous losses in lives and property if hit).

Taipei's strategic planners have shown an interest in joining an East Asian security system or collective security organization—with or without Beijing. If an "Asian NATO" were to evolve, Taiwan might use it to bolster its security. Such an alliance system, however, seems a distant possibility, if one at all. A more realistic option for Taiwan is supporting a US-managed Asian balance of power system. Such a concept has been around for a few years. It offers the United States a way to cope with China's military expansion and America's decline. It also offers Japan, the countries of Southeast Asia, and India a means to counter China's growing military prowess.[30]

Taiwan and the United States

Of all the nations in the world, the United States has been the most important to Taiwan. This has a history going back to World War II when the United States was Nationalist China's ally. During the Chinese civil war that followed, the United States continued to support the Nationalists with arms and money. With the onset of the Korean War, the United States became Taiwan's protector, formalizing that role with a defense pact in 1954. US aid, which had been briefly terminated, was resumed. Up to 1965, it totaled $1.5 billion—more than the United States had given to any country not at war.[31] In ensuing years, the United States was Taiwan's leading trading partner and source of investment capital. Until 1971, Washington gave Taiwan political backing so that it could remain in the United Nations and represent China in the global community

Accordingly, Taipei cultivated close relations with the United States. During the early years, it maintained intimate ties with the China lobby in the United States, which supported closer US relations with Taiwan and opposed any US dealings with "Red China."[32] In the 1960s, foreign policy makers in Taipei realized they had to do more, given America's need and desire to establish contacts with the People's Republic of China.[33] Taipei thus sought other means of influence, which included sending outstanding diplomats to Washington, making efforts to impress US tourists visiting Taiwan, and expanding contacts with US military personnel stationed in Taiwan. Taiwan also hired top public relations firms in Washington.

In the early 1960s, a two-China policy began to evolve in the United States. After two Offshore Islands crises, the Eisenhower administration began seriously considering such a policy in an effort to preclude the outbreak of hostilities between Chiang Kai-shek and Mao Tse-tung that might ensnare the United States in an unwanted war. Scholars and policy wonks recommended a policy of either a separate Taiwan or one China and one Taiwan.[34] Meanwhile, especially after 1960 when the Sino-Soviet dispute became apparent, the foreign policy elite in the United States pressured US policy makers to stop trying to isolate China. A vocal minority of intellectuals and others meanwhile advanced the idea of granting China diplomatic recognition. But events intervened: the Great Proletarian Cultural Revolution resulted in China's self-imposed isolation, while an escalation of the war in Vietnam again increased hostilities between the United States and China.[35]

Then US policy toward China/Taiwan changed, dramatically so, during the Nixon administration. President Nixon was determined to get out of Vietnam and avoid involvement in another land war in Asia; he had to establish better relations with China to realize these goals. He faced another serious foreign policy problem. Because of diminishing public support for military spending at home and larger military outlays by the Soviet Union, the United States was losing the arms race. Nixon thus sought to establish strategic ties with China as a way to avoid having to continue to engage in a weapons-building contest with the Kremlin that the United States could not win, at least not in the short run. To Nixon's advantage, China's relations with the Soviet Union had deteriorated markedly following a war on their border in the spring of 1969. President Nixon thus employed what became known in the West as the "China card" (using closer ties with China to hold the Soviet Union in check); in the process, relations between Washington and Beijing improved markedly.

The United States could not allow the Taiwan issue to block a US-China rapprochement, and America's commitment to Taiwan and Taipei-Washington relations were affected adversely. But Taipei had no alternatives to its vital US ties and its reliance on Washington as its protector. Moscow was not a feasible option because economic ties to the United States were too important. And Taiwan was already evolving into a democracy solidly in the Western camp, both economically and politically. Although Taipei knew it could not prevent US-China relations from improving, it felt, or hoped, it could maintain good enough relations with the United States such that Washington would not abandon Taiwan.

Taipei adjusted by democratizing its political system along lines suggested by Washington, and, as it did so, it let Washington know. It paid more attention to human rights. As noted earlier, Taipei, at the request of the United States, terminated its plans to build nuclear weapons and promised never to go nuclear. In short, Taiwan still sought to maintain its friendship with the United States and the US government.

Taiwan survived the trauma of the United States severing diplomatic relations in January 1979 and terminating the US–Republic of China defense treaty a year later. The shock was softened by actions taken by the US Congress. Congress reacted to President Jimmy Carter's one-China policy and his "abandonment" of Taiwan by enacting the Taiwan Relations Act (TRA). This, the first-ever US law establishing guidelines for Washington's relations with another country, was signed reluctantly by President Carter in April 1979. In essence, the TRA reestablished Taiwan's status as a sovereign nation-state in allowing Taipei to continue to post representatives in the United States, have access to US courts, and retain diplomatic privileges. Finally, it provided Taiwan with security and economic guarantees.[36]

Some in Taiwan did not like the TRA. Throughout the document, the term "Taiwan" or "the people of Taiwan" was used rather than "Republic of China." This, some said, was demeaning. Others said it supported independence. Still, most government officials supported the act because it preserved the role of the United States as Taiwan's protector and put Taipei-Washington ties on a stable—albeit less formal—basis. Most important, the TRA did not acknowledge that Taiwan is part of China as was stated in President Carter's Normalization Agreement.[37]

In 1989, the US public and the American media began to seriously reassess US-Taiwan relations as a result of the Tiananmen Massacre in Beijing and an election that year in Taiwan that reflected its rapid democratization. An even more important event to policy makers occurred at this time: the Soviet bloc began to disintegrate and the Cold War drew to an end.

In 1992, as noted above, President George H. W. Bush approved the sale of F-16 fighter planes to Taiwan. The move reflected US concern that Beijing, by markedly increasing its defense spending and buying sophisticated weapons from Russia, had undermined the balance of forces in the Taiwan Strait. Washington also questioned why Beijing was expanding its military budget when other powers throughout the world were cutting theirs in response to the end of the Cold War. In any event, Taiwan's most serious strategic problem, air superiority over the island and part of the Taiwan Strait, was resolved in its favor.

When he became president, Bill Clinton seemed favorably disposed toward Taiwan. Clinton had made four trips to Taiwan when he was the governor of Arkansas, his purpose being to sell the state's products. He had not visited China. During his presidential campaign, he was very critical of Beijing for its human rights abuses, saying President Bush was not. In 1994, the Clinton administration reviewed US policy toward Taiwan and made adjustments that allowed senior officials to visit Taiwan, permitted Taiwan's leaders to make stopovers in the United States, and changed the title of Taiwan's diplomatic offices in the United States (from the Coordination Council for North American Affairs to Taipei Economic and Cultural Representative Office, which indicated who the office represented). He also promised support for Taipei's entrance into international organizations where statehood was not at issue.[38]

But Clinton's pro-Taiwan stance didn't last. He began tilting toward China, seeing the economic importance of China and a need to promote trade and job creation. In response Congress attached a provision to an appropriations bill stating that the Taiwan Relations Act had precedence over the communiqués negotiated with Beijing. President Clinton signed it. Congress also pressured the president to allow President Lee Teng-hui to visit the United States (which he did in June 1995) and began work on a bill called the Taiwan Security Enhancement Act to upgrade the defense provisions of the Taiwan Relations Act. Congress so acting assumed a role of protecting Taiwan against what it saw as a hostile State Department and White House.

In 1995 and 1996, the United States came to Taiwan's rescue when China conducted threatening missile tests near Taiwan's shores. In the latter case, President Clinton dispatched two US carrier groups to the Taiwan Strait to display US power and constrain Beijing's actions (though some say he did this in anticipation of Congress taking the initiative if he failed to act). In any event, this action constituted the largest display of US military power in Asia since the Vietnam War. Some said later that the United States and China nearly went to war.[39]

In the aftermath of the crisis, the White House spoke of ending America's policy of "strategic ambiguity" in US–China/Taiwan policy. Clinton's advisors also expressed concern that Taiwan's major opposition party, the Democratic Progressive Party, after a major election victory in November 1997, might seek to push Taiwan further toward formal separation from China in defiance of America's one-China policy. President Clinton sent officials to Taipei to "send a message." Washington also changed a major tenet of its Taiwan policy: no longer did it believe that the Taiwan issue was "a matter for the Chinese themselves to resolve" (as many US leaders had said). Rather, the crisis warranted US concern and intercession.[40]

In 1998, President Clinton traveled to China. There, he formally stated what became known as the "three no's" policy: no to two Chinas, no to one China and one Taiwan, and no to Taiwan's joining international organizations that required statehood for membership. This had been US policy, but no president had ever stated it in public, much less in China. The president also described the relationship of the United States with the People's Republic of China as a "strategic partnership." Both statements upset Taiwan as well as the US Congress. Congress forthwith passed several resolutions repudiating Clinton's idea of strategic ties with China and his ill treatment of Taiwan. Clinton's efforts to improve relations with China were undermined for another reason: his decision to pursue theater missile defense (TMD) in Northeast Asia (part of his national missile defense program) with Japan. Chinese leaders were angered by talk of Taiwan's participation because it would enlarge the area covered and Taiwan could help pay for it.

President George W. Bush took a decidedly more friendly line toward Taiwan during the campaign and initially adopted distinctly pro-Taiwan policies. He repudiated Clinton's strategic partnership idea. After a crisis in April 2001 that resulted from a midair crash involving a US reconnaissance plane and a Chinese air force fighter, called the EP-3 Incident, Bush said he would do "whatever it took" to defend Taiwan. He subsequently approved the largest arms sales purchase ever for Taiwan, save his father's F-16 sales. He allowed some high officials from Taiwan to visit or travel through the United State. Observers reported that US-Taiwan relations had not been better in many years.[41]

But Bush did not alter America's one-China policy or support Taiwan's independence. These mainstays of US-Taiwan policy remained unchanged. Then, after 9/11, the Bush administration's relationship with Beijing changed dramatically. This was largely due to the fact that China signed on as a partner in the war on terrorism. But the Bush administration also became convinced that President Chen was taking the United States for granted and disregarded US concerns when, for his own political reasons, he provoked China with talk of an independent Taiwan, despite his campaign promises to lower tensions in the Taiwan Strait. US policy makers concluded that Chen was dangerous, labeled him a loose cannon, and took various measures to express America's dislike of him and his policies. These included even questioning Taiwan's sovereignty (though this was a warning, not a shift in US policy) while limiting Chen and members of his administration from visiting the United States. The United States also openly opposed Chen's push for Taiwan's legal independence when he proposed a referendum to join the United Nations as Taiwan.[42]

When Ma Ying-jeou was elected president, the United States sent its congratulations and expressed a feeling of relief. Ma reduced tensions with China, which improved Taiwan's relations with the United States. Ma and his administration also showed a greater understanding of the United States, sent effective diplomats to Washington, and in a number of other ways engineered better relations.

Before he became president, Barack Obama said little about Taiwan. As president he focused on problems in the Middle East. His reference point in foreign affairs was Europe; he paid little attention to Asia. US relations deteriorated with China, but this had little or no impact on America's Taiwan policies. Hence, US Taiwan policy for some months remained what it was under the Bush administration. In 2010 President Obama, however, when on a visit to China concurred with Beijing that Taiwan was one of its "core interests," which was taken to mean Taiwan is territory that belongs to China. To many observers, Obama's words reflected the increasingly large debt the United States owed to China. In any event, Taiwan showed concern.

Subsequently the pro-Obama media and pro-Obama scholars and officials began to speak and write that the United States should consider abandoning Taiwan. Some military leaders contended Taiwan was not defensible in view of China's rapid military buildup. Some said Taiwan was not worth the problem it posed to US-China relations. However, when the United States subsequently announced its "pivot to Asia" and away from the Middle East, some saw Taiwan in a different light. At that point in 2012, US-Taiwan policy was unclear and confusing to many observers.[43]

Taiwan and the
People's Republic of China

As noted above, when Chiang Kai-shek and the Chinese Nationalist army and government fled to Taiwan in 1949, their stated policy was to counterattack, destroy the Communist "bandit" regime on the Mainland, and reunite China. Given the continuation of the Chinese civil war, albeit in a cold phase, political, economic, cultural, and all other ties between Taiwan and China were severed. The two opposing regimes were at war, and China was a divided nation.

In the early 1960s, détente between the superpowers further dimmed Chiang's hopes for "liberating" China. In the 1970s, Taipei lost two diplomatic battles with Beijing: one over representing China in the United Nations and the other in maintaining formal diplomatic ties with the United States. Subsequently, Beijing pressured Taiwan to reunify with China. Taipei resisted. Nevertheless, Taipei's harsh rhetoric appeared counterproductive and was changed. Taipei stopped using pejorative language like "Communist bandits" to describe the government in China. Taiwan sought to make a good impression on the United States and the world community and even expressed a willingness to talk with Beijing.[44]

In the early 1980s, China proposed to Taiwan what it called the "three links"—mail, trade, and transportation ties. Taiwan's response was cautious but not hostile. In 1986, a plane belonging to Taiwan's flag carrier, China Airlines (CAL), was hijacked and flown to China. In an unexpected move, CAL officials (with the approval of the government) offered to negotiate with officials from Beijing to get the plane back. This was the first time the two sides talked openly.[45] Not long after this, Taipei announced that its citizens could participate in conferences and its athletes go to games in Communist countries—including the People's Republic of China. Taipei's change of stance toward Beijing was influenced by the economic and political reforms launched by Deng Xiaoping in 1978 that dramatically changed China. But Taipei was also influenced by criticism abroad and by suggestions that its policies were too hard-line in view of the vast changes going on in the world.

In 1987, Taipei enacted a new policy allowing its citizens to travel to the Mainland. Contacts with China, including trade and investment relations, mushroomed as a result. The next year, at its Thirteenth Party Congress, the Kuomintang adopted a new "Mainland policy," formally scrapping Taiwan's harsh anti-Communist posture.[46] To manage its new policies, which some labeled détente, the government created the Mainland Affairs Council to coordinate efforts of government agencies and regulate exchanges across the Taiwan Strait. The council became an official organ of government in 1990. At this same time the National Unification Council was established in the Office of the President and given similar functions. Still another organization (this one private or semiprivate), the Straits Exchange Foundation, was created to manage unofficial relations.[47]

In the meantime, Beijing proffered the "one country, two systems" formula for resolving the "Taiwan issue" and unifying the country. Taiwan replied that the idea, which was the blueprint for Hong Kong's return to China, did not apply to Taiwan, as Taiwan had sovereignty and could defend itself. The opposition's reaction was different; it spoke of self-determination and the right of Taiwan's citizens to determine their future. In 1989, a member of the Legislative Yuan offered the idea of "one nation, two equal governments" as a framework for pursuing a more positive relationship with China. According to this formula, Beijing and Taipei both had sovereignty, but there was expressed hope they might unite to become one nation in the future. The government in Taiwan realized it had to formulate new policies on its relations with China, formal and otherwise.[48]

Cross-strait détente, however, was put on hold when Beijing blamed Taiwan for instigating the student protests that led to the Tiananmen Massacre in June 1989. Citizens in Taiwan were taken aback by the accusations and appalled by the brutal massacre that was followed by a sudden turn to the left politically (and to some degree economically as well) in China. Notwithstanding, Taipei took the view that, though the People's Republic of China had become a global pariah and was hostile toward Taiwan, Beijing would not likely adopt a self-imposed isolationist policy, as it had in the mid-1960s, and would continue to boom economically. Thus, Taipei still had to deal with Beijing.

In 1991, the National Unification Council adopted the Guidelines for National Unification, which amounted, some said, to a formal statement of Taiwan's China policy. The document said unification would have to be attained in three stages: first, establishing exchanges and reciprocity; second, building trust and confidence; and third, promoting consultations and unification. The timing for moving from stage one to stages two and three, it said, should "respect the rights and interests of the people in the Taiwan area and protect their security and welfare." Whether President Lee Teng-hui genuinely sought unification is uncertain. Government leaders held differences of opinion while the opposition was less supportive of cross-strait ties. The bottom line appeared to be that Taipei's policy was to wait and see and to maintain the status quo.

That same year, Taipei proclaimed an end to the war with the People's Republic of China and pledged that it would not use force to achieve China's unification. Although war between Taiwan and China was not really at issue, formally ending this policy had some salience. It seemed a friendly gesture toward China, though oddly Taipei's reversals on the Beijing government's legitimacy and on the policy of liberating China were construed as ending Taiwan's one-China policy and as another step in separating Taiwan from China. Taipei then announced its opposition to political negotiations until the "second stage" of relations had been reached. Additionally, officials in Taiwan stated that direct trade, postal, and transportation links would have to wait until Beijing ceased denying Taipei's existence and dropped its threats to use force to resolve the Taiwan question.

In April 1993, unprecedented "negotiations" were held between representatives from Taipei and Beijing in Singapore. The Koo-Wang (Wang-Gu in Beijing) talks, named after the heads of the unofficial organizations they represented (the Straits Exchange Foundation in Taiwan and the Association for Relations Across the Taiwan Strait in China), led to agreements on legalizing documents and establishing formal channels for communications between China and Taiwan. Although the agreements were not of great substance, the talks that produced them marked a significant breakthrough in cross-strait relations. In addition, both sides promised more significant talks in the future.[49] The meeting was thus called historic. Trade and investment contacts continued to flourish at this time, and Taiwan soon became the People's Republic of China's second largest source of investment capital (after Hong Kong), and China became one of Taiwan's biggest export markets.

But President Lee announced a "go South" policy to encourage Taiwan's business community to look for trade and investment opportunities in Southeast Asia instead of China because, Lee thought, Taiwan was becoming too economically dependent on the Mainland. He reiterated this policy in stronger language in 1995 in what was called his "no haste" policy. The government later formalized this policy with "guidelines," stating that no enterprise in Taiwan should invest more than $50 million in the Mainland or put money into infrastructure projects.

Better relations between Taipei and Beijing were subsequently hampered by the latter's hostile reaction to Taipei's attempt to rejoin various governmental and international organizations, including the United Nations and by actions Taipei regarded as part of Beijing's "scheme" to isolate Taiwan. A white paper on reunification, released in late 1993 by the People's Republic of China, contributed to further ill feeling,[50] as did an incident at the time in which some tourists from Taiwan were murdered in China, following which Beijing engaged in a cover-up.

Relations were further strained by Lee Teng-hui visiting the United States in 1995 in an effort to "break out" of the isolationism China had imposed on Taiwan. Beijing conducted missile tests in the Taiwan Strait in response and did even more provocative tests and military exercises in the spring of 1996 during Taiwan's first direct presidential election campaign. Taiwan's voters expressed their displeasure with Beijing by re-electing President Lee with more votes and a stronger mandate than he would have won otherwise.

Two years later, cross-strait relations witnessed improvements, with the United States encouraging and apparently pressuring both sides to resolve their differences through talks. In October 1998, the Koo-Wang talks were put back on track. Koo Chen-fu, head of the Straits Exchange Foundation, traveled to China to meet with his counterpart and, at the same time, talked with President Jiang Zemin. The meetings were cordial and seemingly productive. But in July 1999, President Lee Teng-hui, during an interview with a German radio station, announced that hereafter cross-strait relations must be considered state to state. Chinese leaders were incensed and castigated Lee in hostile public statements. Some observers said that Lee's pronouncement was a response to President Clinton's "three no's" statement made in China in 1998 that many considered hostile toward Taiwan. In any event, cross-strait relations again turned sour.

During the 2000 presidential election campaign in Taiwan, all of the major candidates adopted policies of pursuing better cross-strait relations. Chen Shui-bian, who had been a staunch advocate of independence, softened his views dramatically—many observers said for the purpose of winning the election because voters viewed him and his party as too radical on this issue. In his inauguration address, President Chen pledged that, as long as China does not use military force against Taiwan, he would not declare independence, change the national title, put former president Lee Teng-hui's state-to-state relationship idea in the Constitution, or promote a referendum to change the status quo regarding the question of independence or unification. He also promised not to abolish the National Reunification Council or nullify the National Reunification Guidelines. This statement was labeled Chen's "five no's" policy.[51]

But soon after this, in the context of political paralysis and President Chen's failed efforts at building a governing coalition, he played the "China card." Chen rebuffed Beijing's one-country, two-systems formula (except as a talking point) and repudiated the so-called 1992 consensus (both sides would espouse a one-China policy, though each could interpret this as they wished), which had made possible the Koo-Wang talks. This and Chen's previous advocacy of Taiwan's independence, his not-so-subtle pro-independence actions in other contexts, and the view that Chen was a weak president prompted Chinese leaders in Beijing to eschew dealing with him.[52]

In August 2002, President Chen, owing to continued strained cross-strait relations and Beijing's still shunning him, announced that perhaps Taiwan's future should be decided by a referendum. He also spoke of two sovereign states, one on each side of the Taiwan Strait. Beijing's reaction was hostile. In 2004, Chen had referendums put on the presidential election ballot dealing with Taiwan's future (as separate from China) that further provoked Beijing. After his re-election, he said he had a mandate to push for Taiwan's independence.

In 2006, Chen declared the National Unification Council and the unification guidelines defunct. Meanwhile, President Chen stated his intent to rewrite Taiwan's Constitution (obviously to remove the provision that Taiwan was a part of China) while advocating a referendum on participation in the United Nations as Taiwan. Beijing's response was multidimensional: China requested that the

United States "handle" Chen, promoted expanded commercial relations with Taiwan, and ignored Chen's provocations so as to avoid helping him politically.

Meanwhile, in 2005, in response to President Chen's provocations, China's parliament enacted the Anti-Secession Law that read that China would employ nonpeaceful means to prevent Taiwan from implementing legal independence. Taiwan's response understandably was negative. But the law did not specify any time limit and did not cite any specifics for enforcement. Soon Beijing invited leaders of the opposition in Taiwan to China, took a more friendly line on trade and some other issues, and, in 2006, offered pandas to the Taipei Zoo.

It was commonly said that Chinese leaders personally hated Chen Shui-bian and opposed all of his policies. He was no doubt a distraction to Beijing. Chen also apparently caused discord between China's civilian and military leaders. But there is another view on this issue: that Chinese leaders "appreciated" Chen because he mismanaged Taiwan's economy (making Taiwan economically dependent on China), ruined Taiwan's democratic image (with his policies of ethnic discrimination and declining press freedom and civil rights, and, more important, the chaos he created), and undermined Taiwan's relations with the United States (thereby strengthening Sino-US ties). Some even said Beijing viewed the Chen administration as having done more to bring Taiwan "into the fold" and make reunification more likely than had any leader in Taiwan.[53]

In any event, when Ma Ying-jeou ran for president in 2008, he promised to promote better relations with China. One of his campaign slogans was "no independence, no unification, and no war." Most voters agreed. Most wanted improved relations with China and increased trade. After Ma became president, the 1992 consensus was re-established as the basis of relations, and tensions across the Taiwan Strait subsided. Talks were resumed on a number of issues. Leaders of nations throughout Asia and elsewhere praised Ma for reducing the likelihood of conflict in the area.

In June 2010 the two sides negotiated the Economic Cooperation Framework Agreement (ECFA), which lowered the tariffs on a large number of items traded between the two sides. Provisions were also made to increase Chinese tourism and investments from both sides to the other, to reduce restrictions on academic contacts, and to establish the right for China to station permanent media representatives in Taiwan.[54]

Taiwan's exports to China increased 8.66 percent in 2011, a development largely attributed to the agreement. Tourism and other exchanges increased significantly. Meanwhile the "checkbook diplomacy" practiced by both Taipei and Beijing whereby they used foreign aid to attract diplomatic ties, a contest Taiwan had been losing, ended. When Ma ran for reelection in 2012, ECFA, the 1992 consensus, the retention of diplomatic partners, and much improved cross-strait ties helped him win votes.

Taiwan and the Rest of the World

Other than China, Japan is by far the most important country in Asia to Taiwan.[55] Even though the two countries have not had formal diplomatic ties since 1972, relations at various levels are extensive and meaningful. When Japan broke relations with Taipei, its government opened the Japan Interchange Association in Taipei, and Taiwan set up the Association of East Asian Relations in Tokyo. Both were designed to handle business formerly done by their embassies. Japan continued to trade with Taiwan and maintained other contacts generally without interruption, though most Japanese businesses renamed their operations in Taiwan. This became known as the "Japan Formula," and many other nations used it as a model when they shifted formal diplomatic ties to Beijing.

In 1992, Tokyo "upgraded" Taiwan's representative office in Japan, renaming it the Taipei Economic and Cultural Representative Office. The word "Taipei" made the title seem more official and eliminated any ambiguity that the organization represented Taiwan. Again, many nations followed Japan's lead on this name change.

For some time Japan was Taiwan's second-largest trading partner after the United States, and this trade relationship was important to Taiwan. However, leaders in Taiwan were concerned, and still are, about a large and persistent trade deficit with Japan. In addition, Japan was Taiwan's largest foreign investor. Finally, Taiwan's leaders believed Japan had a security interest in Taiwan and that Tokyo therefore favored Taiwan's continued sovereignty (though neither side said this openly). On the other hand, Taipei realized Japan was not in a position to challenge China militarily or in other ways and that Tokyo's Taiwan policy would not likely depart from US policy in any meaningful way.

Currently trade between the two continues to increase, with Japan still ranking as Taiwan's second-largest trading partner and Taiwan Japan's fourth. Other relations remain cordial. In the wake of the 2011 tsunami in Japan, Taiwan sent five hundred tons of relief supplies plus $200 million in cash, one of the largest donations Japan received. Recently former Japanese prime ministers have visited Taiwan.[56]

Taiwan long shared a bond with South Korea based on their strongly anti-Communist foreign policies (but now relaxed considerably in both). South Korea was one of the last important countries (and the last in Asia) with whom Taipei retained formal diplomatic ties, relations having been broken in 1992. Though the two are economic competitors, political and other relations are friendly. With the end of the bipolar world, Taipei made some contacts with North Korea; however, this did not affect relations with South Korea. In pursuing relations with nations who have formal ties with Beijing, Taiwan's diplomats have often cited the fact that China has formal relations with both North and South Korea (or a two-Koreas policy).

Taiwan's contacts with Hong Kong have long been important, though they have presented Taipei with unique challenges. The Nationalist Chinese cause once found many supporters (both anti-Communists and admirers of the Republic of China) among Hong Kong Chinese, and trade with the British colony was significant. Thus, the 1984 agreement between Beijing and London on Hong Kong's re-unification with China presented Taipei with a serious dilemma: whether to try to continue contacts with Hong Kong after July 1, 1997 (the date Hong Kong would revert to China), and, if so, in what fashion. Taiwan chose to maintain commercial and other links with Hong Kong. In fact, much of Taiwan's extensive trade with the People's Republic of China transited Hong Kong. Ironically, better relations between Taipei and Beijing (especially direct trade) hurt Hong Kong economically. Nevertheless, Taiwan's relations with Hong Kong remain friendly and economically significant.

Taipei maintains trade and other ties with every country in Southeast Asia, even though it has diplomatic ties with none. Taipei lost its diplomatic ties with most of the non-Communist countries in the 1970s and 80s. For some time, Singapore and Indonesia diplomatically recognized neither Beijing nor Taipei, but in 1990 both established formal ties with China. Relations with Myanmar (formerly Burma) were poor, however, because of the disruptive presence of Nationalist soldiers there after World War II (a problem not completely resolved to this day) and its government's close ties with Beijing.

In the 1980s, Taipei sought to balance its trade and other ties with Beijing by what it called a "go South" strategy aimed at forging closer economic ties with the countries of Southeast Asia. Taiwan became (if it wasn't already) a major trading partner with the capitalist countries in the region and a critical foreign investor in several. Taiwan imported natural resources from the area, including sizable quantities of oil from Indonesia. Foreign laborers from the area worked in Taiwan, most of them from Thailand, the Philippines, Vietnam, and Indonesia. This situation remains.

Until the 1990s, relations with the former Communist Indochina countries—Vietnam, Cambodia, and Laos—were all but nonexistent. As Taipei changed its policy of not dealing with Communist countries, relations changed with these countries—especially Vietnam, where Taiwan became a major investor. Relations remain cordial with these countries.

When Chen Shui-bian was president, his support of local nationalism, playing ethnic politics, and anti-Chinese (as opposed to Taiwanese) policies undermined Taiwan's relations with the Overseas Chinese communities in Southeast Asia. He was also viewed (in the eyes of most Southeast Asian leaders) as needlessly provoking Beijing, which increased tensions in the region. This and China's enlarged foreign aid and investments in the countries in the region badly undermined Taiwan's diplomatic efforts. Since 2008, good relations have been restored, and trade and other commercial ties have grown. The ASEAN countries collectively constitute Taiwan's second-largest export market and in 2009 became its third source of imports (behind China and Japan).[57]

Ties with the countries of South Asia have never been very meaningful to Taiwan, either politically or economically. Taiwan has not perceived the region as one where it has vital interests. On the other hand, Taiwan has a representative office in India, and trade and investment ties between the two countries are growing. There has been some speculation Taipei realizes that India plays a "balancing role" against China, and this may become more meaningful in the future, especially if US-Indian relations (particularly at the strategic level) improve, as has been the case. In other words, India may become part of an Asian balance of power that will have relevance to Taiwan.

Taiwan for some years had meaningful ties with several Middle Eastern countries, especially those that were strongly anti-Communist. That included diplomatic relations. But, over time, Taiwan lost formal relations with all of the countries in the area. In 1991, Taipei ended its diplomatic ties with Saudi Arabia—the most important nation in the world with which Taipei still had formal relations at the time and the last country in the region to still diplomatically recognize Taipei. Yet relations remained cordial with Saudi Arabia, and it is still Taiwan's largest supplier of petroleum. Kuwait is also a major source of oil for Taiwan, and relations between the two countries are good. Taipei, in addition, maintains friendly relations with other Middle Eastern countries. Taiwan's Middle East policy concentrates on maintaining reliable sources of petroleum (getting a large portion of its imports from the area), encouraging trade, and maintaining cultural contacts.

Taipei maintains informal—but in some ways important—ties with Israel. In 1949, Israel extended an offer of diplomatic recognition to the People's Republic of China, which Beijing did not accept. Taipei did not openly try to promote better relations with Israel because it did not want to endanger its relationship with Saudi Arabia and other Middle East countries. Nevertheless Taiwan trades with Israel and has purchased some of its weapons. For some time, observers saw Taiwan's position in the world as similar to that of Israel: located in the midst of an enemy or enemies that have support from the Third World; its pariah nation status among left-leaning countries; and its role as a successful, albeit controversial, regional actor (although Taiwan is certainly no longer a pariah).

In Western Europe, Taipei maintains formal diplomatic ties with only one nation—the Vatican. The good relationship with the Vatican has hinged mainly on strained relations between the Catholic Church and Beijing, which may or may not last. Taipei's contacts with other European nations are primarily commercial. Several Western European countries are important trading partners for Taiwan, the largest being Germany. Trade and other relations between Taiwan and the

European Union (EU) have increased appreciably in the last two decades. For some time the EU has been the number one investor in Taiwan. Taipei's major objectives vis-à-vis Europe are to increase and diversify its trade relations and also to expand nonpolitical ties that can bolster support for its sovereignty. It likewise seeks to increase its global political ties and win European help for its participation in various international organizations. The European Union has often supported Taipei's efforts to gain global status, especially in international economic organizations. After 2008 when Ma Ying-jeou became president, the EU praised his success in easing tensions in the Taiwan Strait and in 2010 applauded the Economic Cooperation Framework Agreement.

Taiwan has no diplomatic ties with any of the nations of Eastern Europe. Taipei established formal relations with Macedonia when it became independent after the breakup of the former Yugoslavia, but subsequently those ties were broken. After the collapse of the Soviet bloc in 1991, Taipei initiated informal contacts with several Eastern European countries that led to establishing trade and cultural ties. In fact, links with Eastern European nations have helped Taiwan diversify its imports and exports. Taiwan's "dollar diplomacy" (giving economic aid for increased political ties) produced results, though limited, in the region for a while. Taiwan's leaders have made some high-level visits to Eastern European countries.

Before 1990, as mentioned earlier, Taiwan had few formal contacts with the Soviet Union, though there were some reports of behind-the-scenes meetings in the 1960s as Sino-Soviet relations deteriorated. In April 1990, Taiwan ended many restrictions on contacts with the Soviet Union as part of its flexible diplomacy. Trade, which was minimal, increased very quickly. Currently, however, decision makers in Taipei have little hope of establishing more meaningful relations, especially political ties, with Russia because of closer relations between Moscow and Beijing.

After the breakup of the Soviet Union, Taipei sought to develop various contacts with members of the new Commonwealth of Independent States, though it did not think seriously of establishing formal diplomatic relations with any of them. In 1991, Taipei's China External Trade Development Council opened an office in Moscow, and in 1992 Taipei negotiated establishing a representative office there called the Taipei Moscow Economic and Cultural Coordination Commission, which it opened in 1993. In 1996, Russia established a similar office in Taipei.

In the 1960s, Taipei established and maintained formal diplomatic ties with some of the newly independent countries in Africa, notwithstanding its close relations with South Africa. Relations with South Africa were the most meaningful of any countries on the continent, and South Africa was, when it severed formal ties with Taipei in 1996, the most important nation in the world with which Taipei still maintained formal diplomatic relations at that time. Informal relations have been maintained since then. Taiwan still purchases uranium from South Africa, and other trade between the two is significant. Investments from Taiwan have diminished with the break in diplomatic relations, however.

Although Taipei lost its diplomatic ties with most other African states in the competition with Beijing for recognition in the 1960s and 1970s, many of these states established ties with Beijing mainly for symbolic reasons to support what was then considered a Third World cause. Few broke with Taiwan for other reasons. Some reestablished formal diplomatic ties with Taipei even after establishing them with Beijing; Taipei accepted dual recognition, but Beijing did not. Taipei maintained a good image in Africa—generally because of its economic successes and because Beijing, with its new cordial relations with the West, disappointed some African countries. In the 1980s China began taking the lion's share of loans and grants from various international financial organizations to the detriment of many African countries. Taipei has also won sympathy from African countries because it is a small nation bullied by a larger one—a familiar situation for many African nations. Taiwan's enlarged economic assistance program, called the International Economic and Cooperation Development Fund, established in 1988, enabled Taiwan to reestablish ties with several African nations and restore formal diplomatic relations with some of them.

In recent years, however, Taiwan has suffered repeated diplomatic setbacks in Africa due to China's increased interest in the area as a source of energy and raw materials needed to keep its economy booming. China also has big money to spend on aid and investments, which African nations sorely need. Taiwan has not been able to compete.

Taiwan maintains formal diplomatic ties with more nations in Latin America than anywhere else—mostly Central American and Caribbean countries. The reason for this is that most of these countries have simply lacked any motive for establishing relations with Beijing. Taipei's efforts to rejoin the United Nations (after 1993) and other international organizations were supported by some of these nations. However, like Africa, Taiwan's relations with nations in the region have recently been undermined by China's increased trade, investments, and aid.

In lieu of formal diplomatic relations, Taiwan has trade and cultural ties with Australia, New Zealand, and Canada. Relations have improved with all three in recent years, most noticeably with Canada, whose government was cool toward Taiwan for some years after it established diplomatic relations with Beijing in the 1960s. Australia is a major source of natural resources for Taiwan, and Taiwan has made sizable investments there. However, it is unlikely Taiwan can count on any of these nations for support for its legal separation from China.

Taipei maintains formal diplomatic ties with several South Pacific countries. Though aid competition with China in this region favored Beijing, Taipei was able to keep its ties with a number of these nations because it could concentrate aid in smaller countries. In any event, though the aid game has diminished since 2008, Taipei has maintained its ties there. However, these countries do not have much global influence and certainly won't impact Taiwan's status as a nation.

When the Chen administration left office in May 2008, only twenty-three countries, all minor ones, maintained formal diplomatic relations with Taiwan. This was half a dozen fewer than in 2000 when President Chen assumed office. He had promised to expand Taipei's formal relations when he campaigned for president, saying that he would establish ties as Taiwan rather than the Republic of China. In this effort, he failed. Some argue he thus damaged Taiwan's bid to be a sovereign nation, although Taipei's status as a nation-state had already diminished considerably before 2000.

Ties with International Organizations

The Republic of China was a founding member of the United Nations in 1945 and was one of the five big powers given a permanent seat on the Security Council.[58] When the Nationalist government fled to Taiwan in 1949, it retained the China seat mainly for two reasons: (1) the government of the Republic of China had survived, and (2) the newly founded People's Republic of China expressed hostility toward the Western rules of diplomatic practice as well as toward most international organizations, including the United Nations.

After China became an active participant in the Korean War, sending troops that did battle with UN forces, China's relations with global organizations worsened. In ensuing years, Taipei and many of its friends contended the Communist regime in China did not meet the UN Charter's requirement that member nations be "peace-loving." Meanwhile, Mao and other Chinese leaders made no serious efforts to counter this view and expressed no serious interest in joining the United Nations.

For the next two decades, given Peking's strongly anti–status quo foreign policy, it was obvious that China had no desire to join the world body. Moscow likewise did not appear to want the People's Republic of China admitted, though it consistently said it did. Taipei, on the other hand, wished to remain a member and represent China. The United States and many other Western countries continued to support Taipei's position.

As memories of the Korean War faded and global politics evolved away from a rigidly bipolar structure, and as the People's Republic of China established diplomatic ties with a significant number of nations around the world, Taipei gradually lost support to continue to represent China in the international community. As early as the 1960s, Taipei encountered some problems with the United Nations and other international organizations. In 1961, it was put in an awkward position at the UN when the Soviet Union proposed that Outer Mongolia be admitted. Taipei claimed Outer Mongolia was Chinese territory; furthermore, it did not want to see another Communist country admitted to the UN for fear of setting a precedent that might lead to the seating of the People's Republic of China. But the proposal was to admit Outer Mongolia and Mauritania simultaneously, and Taipei did not want to anger African nations by invoking the veto.[59] Taiwan, therefore, acquiesced. More such situations followed.

Meanwhile, the charge that the People's Republic of China was not a peace-loving nation began to fade as UN members committed frequent examples of less than peace-loving acts. Moreover, because universality was considered important, many nations felt it was wrong to isolate the People's Republic of China, the largest nation in the world in population. Hence, Taipei's supporters, rather than continuing to condemn the People's Republic of China, switched approaches, arguing that the issue of China's representation in the United Nations was an "important matter" that required a two-thirds vote. China was unlikely, Taipei reckoned, to get two-thirds of UN members to support its admission.

As a sidelight, in the 1960s Beijing sought to create a new "revolutionary" United Nations (in cooperation with Indonesia). The Cultural Revolution and the Vietnam War also hardened China's foreign policy. Nevertheless, throughout the decade, the UN vote on the issue of Chinese representation increasingly favored Beijing. In 1965, it was a tie: forty-seven for the People's Republic of China, forty-seven against, and twenty abstentions. China seemed destined to win the China representation battle. In 1970, Beijing got two more votes than Taipei when the issue of the China seat was considered. This margin was not sufficient, though. In 1971, after US National Security Adviser Henry Kissinger flew to Beijing and arranged for President Nixon's visit there to take place in February of the following year (a highly publicized event), a vote was taken on the two-thirds rule. The United States, which tacitly supported the rule (though it put little pressure on its allies to vote with the United States), lost.[60] The United Nations thereupon seated Beijing.

In the wake of losing the UN fight (actually withdrawing rather than proposing two China seats or a new seat for Taiwan or creating a crisis by claiming the right to veto), Taipei lost its representation in other international organizations. Subsequently Beijing sought Taipei's expulsion from all international public or governmental institutions, even demanding the exclusion of statistics on Taiwan from the United Nations and its affiliated agencies' publications. Its objective was to completely isolate Taiwan from the international community and thereby compel Taipei to negotiate reunification with Beijing. Taipei, of course, resisted.

Taiwan remained in the World Bank and the International Monetary Fund until the early 1980s, but it was eventually forced out of these organizations at Beijing's behest. By 1984, Taiwan belonged to but ten governmental international organizations, the most important of these being the Asian Development Bank (ADB). Taipei retained its membership in the ADB because it had different rules for membership; in addition, the United States supported Taipei's efforts to stay. Still, pressure mounted to admit the People's Republic of China, and a compromise reached in 1985 allowed representation of both in the bank. Meanwhile, in 1981, Taipei rejoined the International Olympic Committee under the name "Taipei, China." Although this term was humiliating to Taiwan (and was used also by the Asian Development Bank after Beijing joined), it reflected Taipei's flexible diplomacy and prevented Taiwan from being excluded from these two important international organizations.

During this period, Taipei remained active in many international bodies that were less important and/or were not overtly political (did not require statehood for membership). From 1979 to 1982, it increased its representation in nonpolitical or nongovernmental international organizations from 254 to 630. By the middle of the 1980s, Taiwan was represented in a host of nonpolitical organizations in which Beijing also participated.[61]

In the late 1980s, Taipei launched some new and creative efforts to rejoin some important international organizations, chiefly financial or trade groups. In 1990, Taipei formally applied for membership in the General Agreement on Tariffs and Trade (GATT); it was given observer status. The next year, it attained membership (together with the People's Republic of China and Hong Kong) in the Asia Pacific Economic Cooperation (APEC) group, using the appellation "Chinese, Taipei" while agreeing to be represented by its minister of economic affairs rather than its foreign minister. In 1992, Taipei was admitted to the South Pacific Forum using the name "Taiwan/Republic of China."

In 1991, the Legislative Yuan passed a motion saying that Taiwan should be allowed to rejoin the United Nations. Two years later, President Lee Teng-hui announced that Taipei would seek participation in the world body, after which the Foreign Ministry declared this a major goal of the Republic of China's foreign policy. Subsequently, seven Central American countries put this issue on the agenda of the General Assembly's fall meeting. Though the proposal did not succeed, supporters continued to speak for Taiwan's representation in the United Nations and UN-affiliated organizations. In ensuing years, Taipei failed in annual bids to "participate" in the United Nations, though the number of supporters increased from three in 1993 to seventeen in 1996. In 1996, the European Parliament passed a resolution stating that Taiwan deserved a seat in all major international organizations. Subsequently, the US Congress passed a resolution supporting the European Parliament's position.

In 1997, Taipei changed its strategy and asked its supporters to request that the UN General Assembly reassess Resolution 2758 (which, in 1971, unseated

Taipei and seated Beijing) and revoke it. The efficacy of such a tactic—or, for that matter, any other—however, was doubtful. Beijing remained adamantly opposed to Taipei's presence in the United Nations in any form and held veto power over its admission; it also had the support of the United States and many other countries for this position. On the other hand, the United Nations allowed non–nation-state representation, and it endeavors to be more universal, giving Taiwan some hope.

In January 2002, Taiwan gained membership in the World Trade Organization (WTO). Because the WTO is a prominent international organization, this was important to Taipei. However, it had to wait several years to enter because of an understanding that China would enter first. Also Taiwan had to accept the title "Customs Territory of Taiwan, Penghu, Kinmen, and Matsu." Some in Taipei said that Taiwan's membership would serve as the venue to negotiate with Beijing. This did not prove true.

In ensuing years Taipei charged that not being allowed a voice in the United Nations and other bodies is based on a "myth" (reminding one of the argument used by supporters of Beijing's application in the 1960s) that Taiwan does not exist. It contended that its exclusion was a violation of the human rights of its twenty-three million people and further claimed that its being denied membership was not consonant with the inclusive and nondiscriminatory ideals of these organizations. Finally, Taipei noted that it was a democratic nation and an upstanding member of the international community and did not deserve the treatment it had received from the world body. Certainly, reason suggested Taiwan be allowed membership in some global regulatory organizations, such as the World Health Organization and the International Atomic Energy Agency (because Taiwan is a major user of nuclear energy), as well as environmental, law enforcement (such as INTERPOL), and other such agencies.

In 2007, the Chen administration made a bid for Taiwan to participate in the United Nations as "Taiwan." But the UN rejected its bid. Many nations, including the United States, saw this as an effort by President Chen to grandstand and to provoke China for his own political reasons. The DPP presented the issue to the electorate in the form of a referendum, but this failed to pass. To some degree, this discredited Taiwan's effort to gain greater global recognition.

In 2008, the Ma administration took a different approach to participating in international organizations: avoiding conflict with China and in the process perhaps getting China's acquiesce. In May 2009 the World Health Organization secretariat invited Taiwan to send an observer to its annual assembly meeting. China did not object. Taiwan attended the meeting in 2010 and 2011. Some saw this as a breakthrough for Taiwan. At this point Taiwan looked forward to participating in more global organizations, though this ostensibly depended upon continued good relations with China and Beijing's concurrence.

Notes

1. See W. G. Goddard, *Formosa: A Study in Chinese History* (East Lansing: Michigan State University Press, 1966), 25. The author notes that in the year 1000, sugar, rice, tea, and dyes were exported to China in meaningful amounts.

2. See Denny Roy, *Taiwan: A Political History* (Ithaca, NY: Cornell University Press, 2003), 29–30.

3. For a detailed study of Taiwan's external relations for the three decades after 1949, see Chiao Chiao Hsieh, *Strategy for Survival: The Foreign Policy and External Relations of the Republic of China on Taiwan, 1959–79* (London: Sherwood Press, 1985). For a more recent analysis, see Yu San Wang, ed., *Foreign Policy of the Republic of China on Taiwan* (New York: Praeger, 1990).

4. Chiang's speech can be found in *The China 1959–1960 Yearbook* (Taipei: China, 1960), 947.

5. Thomas E. Stolper, *China, Taiwan and the Offshore Islands* (Armonk, NY: M. E. Sharpe, 1985), 88–90. Also see David M. Finkelstein, *Washington's Taiwan Dilemma: From Abandonment to Salvation* (Fairfax, VA: George Mason University Press, 1993). This agreement was formalized in a communiqué between Washington and Taipei. See "ROC-US Joint Communiqué, October 23, 1958," in *American Foreign Policy Documents* (Washington, DC: US Government Printing Office, 1962), 1184–1185.

6. This point is further argued in John F. Copper, "Taiwan's Strategy and U.S. Recognition of China," *Orbis* (Summer 1977): 261–276.

7. Ralph N. Clough, *Island China* (Cambridge, MA: Harvard University Press, 1978), 153–154.

8. See John F. Copper, *China Diplomacy: The Washington-Taipei-Beijing Triangle* (Boulder, CO: Westview Press, 1992), chapter 4.

9. For details, see Robert L. Downen, *To Bridge the Taiwan Strait* (Washington, DC: Council for Social and Economic Studies, 1984).

10. See John F. Copper, "Taiwan and the New World Order," *Journal of East Asian Affairs* (Winter/Spring 1995), for further details.

11. See John Fuh-sheng Hsieh, "Chiefs, Staffers, Indians, and Others: How Was Taiwan's Mainland China Policy Made?" in *Inherited Rivalry: Conflict Across the Taiwan Strait*, ed. Tun-jen Cheng, Chi Huang, and Samuel S. G. Wu (Boulder, CO: Lynn Rienner, 1995).

12. John F. Copper, "Why the Bush Administration Soured on Taiwan," in *U.S.-China Relations: Cooperation and Competition in Northeast Asia*, ed. Suisheng Zhao (London: Palgrave/Macmillan, 2008).

13. For details on Taiwan's security problems, see Dennis Van Vranken Hickey, *United States–Taiwan Security Ties: From Cold War to Beyond Containment* (New York: Praeger, 1994); and Martin L. Lasater, *The Taiwan Issue in Sino-American Strategic Relations* (Boulder, CO: Westview Press, 1984).

14. See "The Republic of China," *Wikipedia* (online at wikipedia.com). In addition, Taiwan had reserves totaling $3.87 million.

15. Clough, *Island China*, 118–120.

16. See Dennis Van Vranken Hickey, *Foreign Policy Making in Taiwan: From Principles to Pragmatism* (London: Routledge, 2007), 66–67.

17. See John W. Garver, "Taiwan's Russian Option: Image and Reality," *Asian Survey* (July 1978): 752.

18. See, for example, King-yuh Chang, *A Framework for China's Unification* (Taipei: Kwang Hwa, 1987); Parris H. Chang, "China's Relations with Hong Kong and Taiwan," *Annals* (January 1992); Parris H. Chang, "Beijing's Relations with Taiwan," in *If China Crosses the Taiwan Strait*, ed. Parris H. Chang and Martin L. Lasater (Lanham, MD: University Press of America, 1993); Frederick Chien, "A View from Taipei," *Foreign Affairs* (Winter 1991–1992); Bih-jaw Lin, "Taipei's Search for a New Foreign Policy Approach," in *The United States and the Republic of China: Democratic Friends, Strategic Allies, and Economic Partners*, ed. Stephen W. Mosher (New Brunswick, NJ: Transaction Publishers, 1992); and Yu-ming Shaw, "Taiwan: A View from Taipei," *Foreign Affairs* (Summer 1985).

19. John F. Copper, *Taiwan's 2012 Presidential/Vice Presidential and Legislative Elections: Assessing Current Politics and Charting the Future* (Baltimore: University of Maryland School of Law, 2012), 15–23.

20. See Dennis Van Vranken Hickey, *United States–Taiwan Security Ties: From Cold War to Beyond Containment* (New York: Praeger, 1994), 79–81.

21. See Clough, *Island China*, 64–66.

22. "Phasing Out Conscription Readies Army for a New Era," *Taiwan Journal*, August 29, 2008 (online at taiwanjournal.nat.gov.tw).

23. See Ralph N. Clough, *Reaching Across the Taiwan Strait: People-to-People Diplomacy* (Boulder, CO: Westview Press, 1993), 156–157, for further discussion of domestic politics and foreign policy. Also see Chapter 4 of this book.

24. See Jonathan D. Pollack, "Short-Range Ballistic Missile Capabilities," in *If China Attacks Taiwan: Military Strategy, Politics and Economics*, ed. Steve Tsang (London: Routledge, 2006), 57–72.

25. Michael D. Swaine, "Taiwan's Defense Reforms and Military Modernization Program: Objectives, Achievements, and Obstacles," in *Dangerous Strait: The U.S.-Taiwan-China Crisis*, ed. Nancy Bernkopf Tucker (New York: Columbia University Press, 2005), 156.

26. *The Republic of China 2011 Yearbook* (Taipei: Government Information Office, 2011), 96–97; Tomas Clancy, *Countries of the World: The Republic of China* (n.p.: Create Space, 2012), 294.

27. See Dennis Hickey, "Coming in from the Cold," *Issues and Studies* (October 1994): 101–102.

28. Various authors and publications have listed Taiwan as a potential nuclear power. There seems little question that Taiwan could build a nuclear weapon if it chose to do so.

29. See *ROC Foreign Affairs Report* (Taipei: Government Information Office, 1993).

30. Henry Kissinger broached this idea several years ago. See Henry Kissinger, *Does America Need a Foreign Policy?* (New York: Touchstone, 2001). Some observers perceived that President Clinton's efforts to improve relations with Japan and especially India indicated this was Washington's intention. Little was heard of it during the Bush or Obama presidencies.

31. For background details, see Jerome Alan Cohen, Edward Friedman, Harold C. Hinton, and Allen S. Whiting, *Taiwan and American Policy: The Dilemma in U.S. China Relations* (New York: Praeger, 1981).

32. See Nancy Bernkopf Tucker, *Taiwan, Hong Kong and the United States, 1945–1992: Uncertain Friendships* (New York: Twayne, 1994), 45–47.

33. Ibid., 122.

34. See Roderick MacFarquhar, *Sino-American Relations: 1949–1971* (New York: Praeger, 1972), 183–184.

35. A. James Gregor and Maria Hsia Chang, "Taiwan: The 'Wild Card' in U.S. Defense Policy in the Far Pacific," in *Asia and U.S. Foreign Policy*, ed. James C. Hsiung and Winberg Chai (New York: Praeger, 1981).

36. See Copper, *China Diplomacy*, chapter 2.

37. Ibid., 88–95.

38. For further details, see Robert G. Sutter, "Taiwan: Recent Developments and U.S. Policy Choices," CRS Issue Brief (Congressional Research Service, Library of Congress), January 23, 1995.

39. See John F. Copper, *Playing with Fire: The Looming War with China over Taiwan* (Westport, CT: Praeger, 2006), chapter 13.

40. See John F. Copper, "A U.S. Negotiating Role in Resolving Beijing-Taipei Differences," *Journal of East Asian Affairs* (Summer/Fall 1998).

41. See Nancy Bernkopf Tucker, "If Taiwan Chooses Unification, Should the United States Care?" *Washington Quarterly* (Summer 2002).

42. Hickey, *Foreign Policy Making in Taiwan*, 38–39.

43. See John F. Copper, "Will the United States Desert Taiwan?" in *China: The State of Governance*, ed. Wang Gungwu and Zhen Youngman (Singapore: World Scientific, 2012).

44. Premier Sun made this statement in a speech titled "The China Issue and China's Reunification" in June 1982. The Government Information Office in Taipei subsequently published this speech.

45. Taipei was represented by officials of China Airlines, but because CAL is the Republic of China's national carrier, talks were considered official.

46. See John F. Copper, "The KMT's 13th Party Congress: Reform, Democratization, New Blood," in *Modernizing East Asia: Economic and Cultural Dimensions of Political Change*, ed. Cynthia Chennault (New York: St. John's University Press, 1989).

47. For details on these organizations, see John F. Copper, *Historical Dictionary of Taiwan*, 3rd ed. (Lanham, MD: Scarecrow Press, 2007).

48. See Clough, *Reaching Across the Taiwan Strait*, 16.

49. For details, see Hungdah Chiu, *The Koo-Wang Talks and the Prospect of Building Constructive and Stable Relations Across the Taiwan Straits* (Baltimore: University of Maryland School of Law, 1993).

50. For details on Beijing's white paper and its policies toward Taiwan, see John F. Copper, *Words Across the Taiwan Strait: A Critique of Beijing's "White Paper" on China's Unification* (Lanham, MD: University Press of America, 1995).

51. Hickey, *Foreign Policy Making in Taiwan*, 100–101.

52. For details, see Lijun Sheng, *China and Taiwan: Cross-Strait Relations Under Chen Shui-bian* (London: Zed Books, 2002), chapter 4.

53. See John F. Copper, "China's Choice for Taiwan's Next Leader," *Taipei Times*, July 15, 2007 (online at taipeitimes.com).

54. *Republic of China 2011 Yearbook*, 85–89.

55. For details on Taiwan's relations with various countries, see *The Republic of China Yearbook—Taiwan 2002* (Taipei: Government Information Office, 2002), 130–138.

56. *Republic of China 2011 Yearbook*, 76–77.

57. Ming-tong Chen, "Taiwan in 2011: Focus on Crucial Presidential Election," *Asian Survey*, January/February 2012, 79.

58. For background, see Jerome Alan Cohen, "U.S. Policy Options: The United Nations, Diplomatic Relations, and the Status of Taiwan," in Cohen et al., *Taiwan and American Policy*, 156–166.

59. See Samuel S. Kim, *China, the United Nations and World Order* (Princeton, NJ: Princeton University Press, 1979), 189.

60. Ibid., 101–105.

61. *Taiwan Yearbook 2007*, 127.

7

THE FUTURE

IN THE PRECEDING CHAPTERS OF this book, the reader has learned how and why Taiwan's status is unclear and why it faces a future fraught with uncertainty. The crux of the situation can be summarized here in a few paragraphs.

The People's Republic of China, based on historical records and events, claims Taiwan is its territory—a province of China. Its view of recent history is that Taiwan was stolen by Japan and then "occupied by American imperialists" with Chiang Kai-shek's connivance. Underscoring China's feelings, its "century of humiliation" will not end until Taiwan is recovered. Worse still, China fears that if Taiwan goes its own way, Tibet and other parts of China may try to also. The disintegration of China might follow. The virulence of Chinese nationalism and irredentism that relates to the situation gives the Chinese military, which espouses an especially hostile view about Taiwan's current status, a growing voice in China. Hence, Beijing promises to use military force if necessary to resolve the matter.

The United States believes Taiwan should have the right to choose its future. It is a democracy. America created and nurtured that democracy. American leaders believe that if the United States were to abandon Taiwan, its role in promoting democracy throughout the world would become a hollow cause. Worse, America's credibility in Asia would be fatally damaged. Its allies would no longer trust the United States and would go their own way. The United States would cease to be an Asian power. Because Asia is a dynamic area of the world, Washington would likely see its global influence shrink, and the United States would become a second-ranking power.

These opposing views brought China and the United States into conflict twice in the 1950s and close in the 1960s. The last time, in 1996, they faced off and almost went to war. That is why the Taiwan Strait has been labeled the world's number one flashpoint, or the site where conditions might ignite a global war, which would involve the use of nuclear weapons and horrendous loss of life and damage.

In deciding Taiwan's future, the United States has been the kingpin. If Beijing were to invade Taiwan and the United States did not intervene, Taiwan would not survive; if the United States intervened on Taiwan's side, it would. But in the last three-plus decades much has changed. Currently China is a fast-rising power. America is in decline. The question is then: How long will the United States be able to defend Taiwan?

Some say what Taiwan wants must be considered. The majority in Taiwan prefers the status quo. More precisely, most people in Taiwan want separation from China for now, but they also favor cordial cross-strait relations and want their government to promote economic ties and avoid war. Obviously that does answer the question.

The international community regards Taiwan highly. Taiwan is democratic, has a fine human rights record, and has performed miraculously in economic development. It has provided extremely well for its citizens. To many it is a model. Furthermore, the principles espoused by the United Nations and other organizations would suggest they would support and defend Taiwan. But they have not. And there is little reason to think they will. Many perceive they hypocritically ignore Taiwan. Even worse, they are hostile toward Taiwan.

Hence, Taiwan's future will be decided by China, the United States, or both. Perhaps it should not be this way. But it is.

Beginning Assumptions

Neither Taiwan nor China's early historical records are very useful in ascertaining whether Taiwan is or should be part of China. There are no early written records in Taiwan. In China's case, the records are vague. China did not seem to think that Taiwan was part of China, but that was because China was a cultural rather than a political entity. Taiwan was not, at least for many centuries, considered civilized. Whether it would become so and become part of China was uncertain. One can only speculate about that. Yet no one else acted to make claim to Taiwan. In any case, historical arguments are generally not very effective in resolving territorial claims.

That said recent history does not help much, either. Taiwan was part of China for only four years in the twentieth century. For a longer period, Taipei, representing the Republic of China, claimed legal jurisdiction over all of China. Taipei formally and officially espoused a one-China policy, meaning that it considered Taiwan part of China but revealed over time that it meant this less and less. President Lee Teng-hui spoke of unification but acted for independence. The 2000 election appeared to change Taiwan's national identity and its future: President Chen Shui-bian had long been an ardent advocate of Taiwan's permanent separation from China. But the Chen government was inconsistent about this; indeed, some of its actions suggested its policy was independence, while others, especially Chen's promoting economic ties with China, did not. In the end, President Chen hurt the cause of independence more than he helped it.

Arguing from the perspective of international law, Taiwan arguably possesses sovereignty. Under traditional international law, there were four qualifications for nationhood: territory, population, government, and diplomatic ties. As noted in Chapter 1, Taiwan is as large in territory as nearly half the world's nations. The territory under its control has remained unchanged for more than a generation. Its population is larger than more than two-thirds of the member states of the United Nations. Its government is stable. Only Taiwan's diplomatic status is in doubt because of the small number of its formal diplomatic partners.

Meanwhile, according to modern practice, the qualifications for nationhood have been weakened so that former colonies, trust territories, and numerous small and Third World countries can qualify. There was, and is, a popular expectation that all the land territory in the world will become or join sovereign nation-states—most likely the former. In the wake of the Cold War, international institutions were supposed to be universal. The proliferation of nation-states in recent years, based on the idea of self-determination, is also pertinent. All of these factors appear to advantage Taiwan if it wants to be or remain a nation-state.

But Taiwan lacks a forum. It is not a member of the United Nations or any other global organization where it can effectively present its case. Most international organizations are focused on lesser issues, and this is unlikely to change. Most global institutions are not very daring. Ultimately, power politics trumps the legal and moral arguments. Indeed, Beijing has successfully pressured most nations of the world to eschew diplomatic relations with Taiwan and has blocked Taipei from entering international organizations where statehood is a qualification for membership. Thus, the international community, if the UN is its representative, does not view Taiwan as sovereign. Even if it did, it is not likely to challenge China on this matter. This situation is unlikely to change.

Over the last half century–plus, Taiwan has developed its own identity. This process was called Taiwanization or localization. The Mainland Chinese who came to the island after World War II promoted the island's Chinese heritage and its links with the Mainland; but, with democratization, the Taiwanese majority began playing a new and much greater role in education, social policy, the economy, and politics. From the growing influence of the locally born Chinese, there grew a "revisionist" history of the island. Taiwanese historians emphasized the island's uniqueness rather than its affinity to China. Taiwan's culture became more Taiwanese. Local "things," such as books, dance, songs, and much more, became more visible than Chinese "things."

However, in the last three and a half decades, these trends have been offset or even negated to a large extent by an increasing interest in China. Many people in Taiwan are now looking for their roots. They are proud of China. Many share a desire to see China restored to its once-dominant role in the world. Many recognize that Taiwan is too small to make an impact on world history. Many believe that if Taiwan were to become part of China, it would make a difference. Finally, if Taiwan is, as many in Taiwan and elsewhere suggest, a model that the People's Republic of China is applying in its economic and political development (which seems to have happened and is happening), there will doubtless be convergence and eventually the foundation laid for a smooth, peaceful reconciliation.

Meanwhile doubt has grown in Taiwan about its wholesale imitation of the United States and Europe. Unlike two or three decades ago, many in Taiwan today see much in the United States that is undesirable: crime, mistreatment of the aged, child abuse, juvenile delinquency, pornography, drugs, a decline in the quality of education, excessive freedom, unsustainable spending, unpopular and unworkable governments, and more. Most people oppose allowing these problems to "infect" Taiwan's society. Many are aware of racial discrimination against Asians, notably in America's best academic institutions, but also in America's immigration policies, which keep Asians out while ignoring millions of illegal immigrants from Latin America. Hollywood and the media, in the eyes of Asians, are biased against them.

There is a feeling in Taiwan that its experiment with American-style democracy went too far. Taiwan is the only Asian country that followed the American model in its quest for political modernization almost to the exclusion of others. Many in Taiwan are now thinking more of Asian democracy. Certainly America is not seen in Taiwan as a model as it once was. America is no longer viewed as an economic beacon. Rather the United States stands out for its economic mismanagement. In Taiwan many view American politics as chaotic. China is now seen as the success story to emulate.

Taiwan's populace also harbors similar if less impassioned feelings about contemporary Europe. Europeans are seen as lazy. People in Taiwan perceive Europe as increasingly uncompetitive, protectionist, and irrelevant in world affairs. Few in Taiwan now read or cite European authors or scholars. One hardly hears the word "model" together with the name of a European country anymore. Fewer students want to study in Europe, and there is less interest in learning European languages (with the exception of English).

For more than two decades, Taiwan's citizens have been visiting China in large numbers. Early on, such visits reinforced the belief in Taiwan's superior economic and political systems and its living standards and lifestyle. Clearly, China was not a country that the people of Taiwan admired. But recently that has changed. Now nearly 5 percent of Taiwan's population resides in China, and a much higher percentage of its workforce is there. A large proportion of Taiwan's entrepreneurs is in China or goes there frequently. There is a brain drain moving toward China. Fifteen percent of college students favor a career in China.

Important trends tell us more. What are these?

First, the economic trends. Up until 2001, when it was hit by recession, Taiwan was still being called a "miracle economy." That term was heard infrequently after that. Taiwan was struck by an economic downturn in 2008. It recovered quickly, but growth soon slowed with the sustained global low-growth situation.

Can Taiwan return to high growth? Given the ingredients that made Taiwan successful—planning, technology, research and development, and, perhaps most of all, human resources—one can logically anticipate solid, sustainable economic growth in the future. With Taiwan's high levels of savings and investment and its quality of labor, management, and innovation, the island's economic vitality will likely last for some years to come. Yet, the double-digit annual gross national product (GNP) growth of the 1960s through the 1980s is likely a thing of the past. GNP increases of the 1990s—from 5 to 7 percent—must be considered normal now. In short, one should expect that growth rates higher than the world's average can be sustained for some time, but there will be no return to "miracle" growth.

An important factor to consider when assessing Taiwan's economic future is the integration of Taiwan's economy with China's. Already many of Taiwan's companies are linked in terms of division of labor, research and development, and in a host of other ways to the companies they have built or helped build in China and to Chinese companies. This will no doubt continue. It will likely be enhanced by China's investment in companies in Taiwan, which is now a fast-growing trend. In short, Taiwan's economy is becoming integrated with China's.

Another trend is the development of an Asian, or at least East Asian, economic bloc. The area is dynamic and is experiencing good growth, while the United States and Europe are not. Asian countries are thus increasingly trading with each other and less with the United States and Europe. Many people believe this is the "new normal." Certainly it is likely to continue, as Taiwan's trade is more and more interregional. Taiwan's relations with other Asian countries will become more important; its relations with the United States and Europe will decline in importance.

Then there is the military equation. The rise of China's military power in recent years has not been met by Taiwan strengthening its military proportionally or in any way that might seriously counter China's threat. During the Chen era, Taiwan's military budget decreased as a proportion of the gross national product. Troop levels were cut. Taiwan bought only a small portion of the weapons the

United States allocated in 2001. Taiwan thus became very vulnerable to China's missile intimidation. It also became more dependent on the US military while relations with the United States plummeted. The Chen administration spoke of deterrence as central to Taiwan's military strategy. But most in Taiwan and elsewhere thought this was wrong thinking, had little chance of succeeding, and would hurt Taiwan's global image.

The reality is that Taiwan has no other choice than to assume the United States will defend the island. But there is serious worry in Taiwan that the US military is fast declining in strength because of budget problems and that the United States is retreating from East Asia or soon will. The 2011 US "Asia pivot" has not convinced many in Taiwan that Washington will rebuild its Asian military forces or even sustain them.

Taiwan may try to join an East Asian alliance system (one that includes China or not). But the likelihood of this providing a solution to Taiwan's defense problems seems distant at best. Such a system would require the cooperation and commitment of Asia's major powers and probably the approval of a majority of Asian countries. Currently this seems little more than a dream. A balance of power system seems more promising. Japan, ASEAN, and India have expressed grave concerns about China's rise, especially the growth of its military power.

But there is a big question: What role will the United States play in managing such a system? Will the United States manage it? Many, including China, would see a US-run balance of power system as little more than an effort to contain China. Then what might Taiwan's role be? Taiwan's active participation might be the cause for permanent US-China alienation. This is not desirable.

An alternative for Taiwan is a Greater China federation, confederation, or commonwealth. Such ideas have been broached in both Taiwan and China. One of them might become very attractive to both sides for a host of reasons. Beijing does not want to risk serious negative reactions from the United States (even short of military action) or the international community for using force against Taiwan. China is concerned about its global image and believes it relates to its economic development. Taiwan can resolve the matter of China's fatal attraction, or the contradiction of having intense economic relations with China with few political ties, by coming to some agreement about a Greater China organization. The sticky issue is Taiwan's sovereignty, which probably means that political arrangements will be difficult and will probably be slow in coming. Another problem is that many of China's leaders view these ideas as a plot to keep China split. They are suspicious.

The China Factor

It is undeniable that China has become a great economic power. For three-plus decades, its economy has boomed. Its economic performance is unmatched in human history. Never has a big country grown so fast.

China's economic growth has eclipsed that of any other world power; as a consequence the People's Republic of China has passed every other country in the world except the United States in economic output. An outcome of this is that, for nearly two decades, China's military spending increases have outpaced all competitors. Most other world powers have cut their military budgets. The rise of China economically and militarily inevitably impacts how others view Taiwan's status and also how Taiwan views China and sees its future.

Some, of course, cast doubt about whether China will continue to grow economically at a fast pace. That is not certain. China faces problems that could derail its economic growth. But there are better reasons for thinking that will not happen. Even if China's boom slows (which it inevitably will), it will likely still grow at a respectable pace and faster than most nations for some time. Considering the worst-case scenario, if China's economic growth stalls completely or nearly so, China will have an advantage over other countries because of its trillions of dollars in foreign exchange and money owed to it by other countries in the world.

Predicting China's economic future, one must consider the following. China was historically a rich country; it is in the process of returning to that state. China has followed the model and the growth trajectory of the four dragons (South Korea, Taiwan, Hong Kong, and Singapore); they continue to do well economically. Globalism, with its free markets and free trade, favors China and will continue to do so. China's inexpensive labor will continue to be an advantage for a while after that. China's high quality of education, innovation, and productivity all favor continued good growth. China's huge market gives it an advantage. On the less tangible side, Chinese are hardworking and are driven to succeed and make their country stronger and greater.

The real question to address here is how China views the Taiwan issue and how it will seek to resolve it. The crux of the matter is this: as noted, Chinese leaders in Beijing contest Taiwan's claim to nationhood and threaten to deploy their military against Taiwan under certain circumstances. Beijing says it will use the force of arms if Taipei (1) allows foreign bases on or foreign control of any or all of its territory, (2) builds nuclear weapons, (3) experiences internal turmoil, (4) declares independence, or (5) refuses to negotiate reunification over a long period. This casts serious doubt on the future of Taiwan's claim to sovereignty. Who is to challenge China on this matter now or in the future?

These conditions need to be assessed one by one. So do Chinese leaders' views about how serious any of them might become.

In the years immediately after 1949, Chinese leaders feared that some nation or nations might harbor territorial designs on Taiwan. The United States was first on the list. But America did not have any intention to colonize Taiwan or make it part of the United States. In any case, China was not powerful enough to change the situation. The Soviet Union was thought, after 1960, to have ill intentions toward

Taiwan. But if that true were at that time, it is no longer. Japanese leaders may well covet Taiwan and may want to govern it, but this will not happen under current or foreseeable circumstances. In short, Beijing had reason to fear outsiders had designs on Taiwan, but it does not now need to worry seriously that Taiwan will become the property of another nation or come under significant foreign influence. Given these circumstances, there appears to be no need for Chinese leaders to consider using force against Taiwan to keep it from falling into someone else's hands.

What about a foreign nation acquiring bases on Taiwan? That also seems improbable. The United States closed its bases in Taiwan after President Nixon's rapprochement with China, and it is not Washington's policy to re-establish them. The possibility of stationing US troops on Taiwan, at least temporarily, was broached during the 1996 missile crisis. But it did not materialize. If there is a conflict in the Taiwan Strait or an attack on Taiwan, the United States may well exercise this option. But, in this event, the conflict will have already started, so the issue of foreign bases would probably be little more than a minor irritant in a broad war with other much more serious consequences.

What about Taiwan going nuclear? As noted in Chapter 6, at one time Taiwan considered the "nuclear option." Washington's "abandoning" Taiwan under Nixon, Ford, and Carter caused the issue to gain resonance. The United States, however, took overt (brazen and illegal) actions to stop it—including kidnapping Taiwan's top nuclear scientists. Nothing much has been heard of the matter since. Even if Taiwan were to acquire nuclear weapons, it could not rationally engage in a nuclear war with China. Taiwan would lose. So why try? Both presidential candidates in Taiwan during the 2008 election campaign forswore seeking nuclear weapons. President Ma has since declared that Taiwan will not seek to acquire nuclear weapons. Thus, the likelihood is that Taiwan won't go nuclear; therefore, the People's Republic of China has no "nuclear reason" to attack Taiwan.

Internal stability, or the lack of it, in Taiwan cannot be easily defined, much less predicted. One can say, however, that Taiwan (as was noted in Chapter 4) has a good record of political and social stability, particularly given the vast economic, political, social, and other changes it has undergone in recent years. It has democratized smoothly and without bloodshed. Taiwan made a peaceful transition of executive power from the KMT to the opposition party in 2000. This produced less turmoil and uncertainty than a similar change of governments in most developing nations. In 2008, Taiwan's democracy was "consolidated again" when the KMT returned to power. Therefore, there is little reason to anticipate serious political instability or chaos in Taiwan in the future.

Taiwan has a potential for ethnic conflict. Notwithstanding equitable economic and social opportunities, considerable intermarriage, and other indicators, ethnic discord is still a problem. Candidates play the "ethnic card" during election campaigns. Tensions were particularly evident after Chen Shui-bian became president in 2000. Ethnic friction might erupt as a by-product of future debates about reunification with the People's Republic of China. It is a potential problem. Yet exacerbating ethnic ill will was part of the reason the DPP lost power in 2008. That year and in 2012 citizens voted for better ethnic relations, and ethnic tension is now less of a problem.

Other possible causes of political instability are crime, corruption, and some other (perceived at least) serious social problems. The public's alarm about crime has increased in recent years. However, while crime has become a more serious problem, it is not increasing now and has certainly not reached dangerous proportions. Corruption is a major concern to Taiwan's populace because it is viewed as bad for democratization and is related in the public's mind to crime (inasmuch as politicians and gangs have been associated). But it is viewed as a more serious problem than it really is—at least comparing Taiwan to other countries. Also it was a prime cause of the ruling party's fall from power in 2008. That was a good lesson, and corruption is now a less serious problem. Taiwan has other social problems, but they do not seem of such a magnitude as to cause the kind of serious instability that might justify Beijing's military intervention.

A declaration of independence by a political party or a top politician has long been considered a distinct possibility. Depending on how "declaration" is defined, it may be very likely or not likely at all. For years politicians, especially opposition politicians, discussed the issue of self-determination. They spoke in favor of it and even advocated it, citing provisions in the Atlantic Charter and the UN Charter that support it. This legitimated their bid for a government free from Nationalist rule and later a Taiwan separate from China. With democratization, self-determination came to mean, almost exclusively, separation from the People's Republic of China. Subsequently, independence, a more provocative term, was discussed in public, advocated by the main opposition party, and even put into the party's charter. Taiwanese politicians, while calling for independence, burned the flags of the People's Republic of China in public before television cameras and cursed Chinese leaders in Beijing. They then called them cowards for not invading Taiwan as they promised if anyone seriously advocated independence.

What then might constitute an "official" declaration, or one provocative enough to cause Beijing to attack Taiwan? If the ruling party were to issue a formal proclamation of independence or amend the Constitution to this effect, this might be viewed in Beijing as an "official declaration." President Chen and the DPP broached ideas like this. They, however, are no longer in power, and the DPP has dampened its advocacy of in independent Taiwan. A joint declaration of independence by two or more political parties might happen if Taipei becomes too isolated, feels excessively threatened, or becomes desperate for some other reason. This would likely provoke hard-liners in Beijing. A statement by the president or a future president unequivocally suggesting the permanent separation of Taiwan from China might be enough for the People's Liberation Army to call for military action. But these scenarios do not seem probable. Statements or actions, if made only by individual politicians, would not necessarily reflect broad support in Taiwan for independence and could easily be ignored in Beijing.

Finally, what constitutes refusing to negotiate over an extended period is very unclear. Chou En-lai (Zhou Enlai) once talked about Taiwan "returning to the fold" after fifty, one hundred, or one thousand years. Mao said something similar. Deng Xiaoping spoke of Taiwan as being a "back burner" issue that could wait until later—perhaps much later—to be resolved. Yet Deng also made quite different statements about Taiwan, no doubt under pressure from the military and in the context of nationalist sentiment that enveloped China during his rule. Jiang Zemin was subject to even greater pressure and spoke of resolving the "Taiwan question" earlier rather than later. In 1995 and 1996 Jiang ordered missile tests near Taiwan. Whether future leaders will be compelled to do something aggressive is difficult to say. Military-civilian relations in China are something to worry about.

However, concerning a time limit, one might query: As long as Taiwan does not declare independence and does not allow its territory to be used for bases or taken by another nation, why should there be a deadline? Anyway a deadline is not an ultimatum. Regardless, deadlines have been discussed—even set—and they have come and gone. Clearly, a long time may be, or become, acceptable. Chinese are known for their patience.

Another factor to consider is that Chinese leaders face some harsh realities regarding unifying China by incorporating Taiwan. At the moment, Beijing is more concerned about economic growth than anything else; many say, and Chinese officials confirm this, the survival of China's leaders depends on continued economic development. They have the strong support of the population on this issue. If Beijing were to obtain and govern Taiwan in the near future, the island's economy would likely decline because Taiwan has a different kind of economy and its global trade, upon which its economic health depends, would likely be disrupted, and it would become a burden to China, not an asset. Even talk of an invasion might precipitate a full-blown economic disaster, including the flight of Taiwan's valuable human capital. Money would also go. Taiwan would become a human rights case. For good reason, then, Chinese officials may find it to their advantage not to hurry the process of unification. In any case, economic and other relations between China and Taiwan currently are very good.

Making an even better case for patience, Chinese leaders have good reason to think that time is on their side. China will likely continue to grow faster economically than other world powers and faster than Taiwan. As mentioned earlier, globalism favors China. China's growing economic relations with other Asian countries means Taiwan must see its future as with China, not against it. The military balance in Asia is tilting in China's favor. China can simply wait.

In sum, it would clearly be best for China if Taiwan were to be incorporated based on economic ties and a voluntary affiliation with (and presumably an eventual integration into) China. This would be much preferable to military means. The latter would not only damage China's image abroad, undermine its relations with many countries, and hurt its image in the international community. In addition, it would likely give the military undue influence over foreign policy making for some time. China's civilian leaders do not want this.

The US Factor

As already stated, the United States is Taiwan's sole ally and its only important friend. Concerning future US-Taiwan relations, three salient questions need to be addressed: What exactly is current US policy toward Taiwan? Will it change? And what might those changes be? A brief review of US-China policy in this context is in order.

US-Taiwan policy, as suggested in Chapter 6, has been ambiguous for some time, some say by necessity. When President Richard Nixon visited Beijing in 1972, it was obvious that the United States could no longer ignore the People's Republic of China; nor could it contain or isolate China. It did so in the past, but that was because China was isolationist. It was not possible to contain China when Nixon was president.

Given the realities of international politics—in particular, the Soviet military buildup, which the United States could not alone challenge—it was Nixon's strategy to improve relations with China to counterbalance Soviet power. Just as important Nixon perceived that the United States had to get out of the Vietnam War. China could facilitate this effort and wanted to. Beijing and Washington thus ended two decades of enmity and became friends, perhaps even allies. Taiwan could not be allowed to obstruct the United States from forging a new relationship with China.

Yet President Nixon did not abandon Taiwan. Nixon did not declare that Taiwan was a part of China, but rather he said that the United States "does not challenge" Beijing's view—a very ambiguous statement. Other matters were dealt with obliquely or ignored. The issue of Taiwan was not (and ostensibly could not be) resolved at this time.

In concluding the Normalization Agreement of 1979, the Carter administration concurred with China, as Deng Xiaoping demanded, that Taiwan is part of China. Washington broke diplomatic relations with Taipei and gave notification of canceling the US–Republic of China mutual defense treaty. At this juncture, it appeared that the United States had decided to forsake Taiwan. But Carter's policy was reversed a few months later when Congress passed the Taiwan Relations Act (TRA). The TRA, for all intents and purposes, restored Taiwan's sovereignty in the eyes of the United States.

After that, the United States had, many said, two China policies: one made by the White House and the Department of State (pro-Beijing), the other made by Congress (pro-Taiwan). There were subsequently two forces at work in making US-Taiwan policy. This created a new and different form of ambiguity.

In 1982, the Reagan administration promised to end arms sales to Taiwan, but President Reagan said this agreement was predicated on a "peaceful solution only" of the "Taiwan issue," which Beijing supposedly pledged. But Deng Xiaoping said he had made no such promise. The communiqué was not signed; later the State Department said it "lacks status" in international law. More important, Reagan did not restrict military technology transfers, and he rejected Beijing's requests to pressure Taipei to negotiate with Beijing on reunification and other matters. Reagan's "six assurances" given to Taiwan at this time also seemed to directly contradict the communiqué.

The first Bush administration seemed to favor Beijing; but, with the breakup of the Soviet Union and the end of the Cold War, Washington no longer needed the "China card" as leverage against the Soviet Union. Almost coinciding with this sea change in international politics came the Tiananmen Massacre in June 1989, which caused China to become a pariah nation in America's eyes. Congress and Democrats assailed Bush's pro-Beijing policy.

In 1992, Bush suddenly adopted what seemed to be a pro-Taiwan policy, or at least a policy much more favorable to Taipei, in the security realm. He broke Reagan's agreement to cut arms sales to Taiwan and sold 150 F-16 fighter planes to Taipei. With these planes, Taiwan could protect its air space. The conventional view was that Taipei didn't need to negotiate with China and could remain separate and sovereign.

The Clinton administration was hostile toward China early on. President Clinton called Chinese leaders "butchers." He allowed the planes promised to Taiwan by the Bush administration to be delivered; he could have blocked the sale. He sold more weapons to Taiwan. In 1994, Clinton "upgraded" relations with Taiwan (as a part of a "Taiwan policy review"), making it possible for high US government officials to have contacts with government officials from Taiwan. President Clinton also accepted the position that the Taiwan Relations Act has precedence over communiqués signed with Beijing. In 1995, President Lee Teng-hui, with White House approval, was given a visa to visit the United States.

But all these decisions were made in the face of congressional pressure. In 1998, President Clinton traveled to China. There he spoke of a "strategic partnership" with the People's Republic of China and announced a "three no's" policy: no to independence for Taiwan, no to two Chinas or one Taiwan, one China, and no to Taiwan joining any organization for which statehood is a requirement. Clinton subsequently denied that he changed US-China/Taiwan policy or that he in any way had hurt Taiwan. Still, his pronouncements deeply troubled Taipei and the US Congress. Congress acted to override Clinton's anti-Taiwan policy change by voting overwhelmingly on resolutions favorable to Taiwan while expressing America's support for Taipei. The gap between executive- and legislative-branch views toward US-China policy, and especially toward Taiwan, widened.

Initially President George W. Bush was much more friendly toward Taiwan and tougher toward China than his predecessor. He denied that China, as President Clinton had said, was a strategic partner. He called China instead a challenger and a competitor and said he would do "whatever it took" to defend Taiwan. He increased arms sales to Taipei, including offensive weapons (submarines), even though the Taiwan Relations Act specified defensive weapons.

Yet President Bush did not alter the US one-China policy, nor did he hint that he supported Taiwan's independence—other than by allowing Taiwan's leaders to visit the United States. Also, as presidents before him, except faster, Bush moved away from a pro-Taiwan stance. He was influenced by America's preoccupation with the war on terrorism. China "signed on" and became an important US ally in that "war." At the same time the Bush administration came to view President Chen as a provocateur who would risk a war between the United States and China for its own domestic political benefit. President Bush ceased to view Taiwan as a loyal ally and even displayed anger and hostility toward President Chen.

In his first two years in office, President Barack Obama showed little interest in Taiwan. US-Taiwan policy remained unchanged from the Bush administration. The Obama administration was hostile toward China, but that did not influence its relations with Taiwan. Subsequently, as a realization of China's rise grew as did America's dependence on China's financial help and as Beijing adopted more assertive policies, the Obama administration showed signs of being willing to abandon Taiwan. In late 2011, however, with the US "pivot to Asia" and with an election approaching (and not wanting to appear too friendly with China), President Obama became more friendly toward Taiwan.

What is to be gleaned from all of this? US-Taiwan policy has shifted a number of times. It has confused, even vexed, China and China/Taiwan watchers. It has been impacted by the triangular relationship of Washington, Taipei, and Beijing, as well as the vagaries of world politics. It has been affected by differences of viewpoints among foreign policy makers and by power struggles between two branches of government, based on very different perspectives espoused by the White House and the Department of State on the one hand and the Congress on the other.

Recent history suggests the United States will intervene if China threatens Taiwan. The Taiwan Relations Act seems to legally obligate the United States to protect Taiwan. The Clinton administration acted with resolve during the 1996 missile tests in the Taiwan Strait. The record shows that the United States has consistently used military force when necessary to protect Taiwan.

But conditions have changed dramatically. Apparently China has become too big a power to face down. Also China is too important an ally. The war on terror is too important. The United States owes China too much money and needs more. Antiwar sentiment in the United States is strong. Taiwan is too much trouble. US officials have said Taiwan cannot be defended. Others have stated Taiwan should be "let go."

Clearly the trends in US defense spending indicate that the United States cannot expect to win a conflict with China ten or so years from now. It may be much sooner than that. Some say it has already happened.

This suggests the United States has little choice but to try to balance China's growing power. Constructing an Asian balance of power system will not be easy for the United States. America may not have the will or the wherewithal to do it. Asian countries have not been schooled in such a system and may not want to, or know how to, cooperate. Then what if it is tried and does not work? Washington may need to negotiate with China over Taiwan's future

With this in mind, views in United States about China have shifted dramatically in recent years. China is a challenger and a threat to Americans. The American public is hostile toward China. However, China now has strong support in the US business community that, to some degree, makes up a new "China lobby." In recent years, Beijing has also come to realize more and more that it needs influence in the United States, and its diplomacy in the United States in the last few years has, as a result, become more effective. How negotiating over Taiwan will play out is difficult to say.

Summing Up

Taiwan is special. Its history is unique. It was at the vortex of the East-West struggle and might have sparked a major, even global, war. In some ways nothing has changed. Though small, Taiwan was, and is, a critical player in international politics. What Taiwan accomplished in economic and political development is exemplary. This means something in terms of its future, but not as much as it should.

It seems most likely Taiwan will remain separate from China in the short run. China sees no good to be found in a quick solution. However, ties with China, especially commercial ones, will increase and will lead to other ties. It would seem that, because there is no symmetry in their size, population, and so on, China will decide Taiwan's future and not the other way around. Yet this may be too simple a judgment.

China's rise and its perceived threat to the United States may prompt America to see a separate Taiwan as still, or even more so, being in its national interest. But will

America retain the will and means to do what it has in the past? Likely not. Nevertheless America has friends and allies that fear and may oppose China's rise.

America's relationship with China is unusual. China is America's foremost enemy, but China is also its most important friend. This paradox will not likely end soon. US policy makers generally perceive that America cannot keep up with China's booming economy and its growing military power. Yet Washington may help China figure out what it wants from Taiwan and when.

In terms of its formal status, Taiwan will likely remain an anomaly for some time. Many say Taiwan is not a nation, but few can say what it should be called. Taiwan will remain diplomatically isolated, yet it will also remain an important player in international politics and economics. The Taiwan Strait will likely remain an area of possible conflict.

In short, political entities have ever been regarded simultaneously as a pariah and a role model, as a sovereign nation-state and a disconnected part of a major power. Few small entities have played such a key role in so many of the major dramas of modern history. Taiwan's future will no doubt remain an uncertain and interesting one.

SELECTED BIBLIOGRAPHY

General

Area Handbook for the Republic of China. Washington, DC: US Government Printing Office, 1983.

Chai, Weinberg, and May-lee Chai, eds. *Chinese Mainland and Taiwan: A Study of Historical, Cultural, Economic and Political Relations*. Dubuque, IA: Kendall/Hunt, 1996.

Chang, Cecilia S. T., ed. *The Republic of China on Taiwan, 1945–1988*. Jamaica, NY: St. John's University Press, 1991.

Chiu, Hungdah, ed. *China and the Taiwan Issue*. New York: Praeger, 1979.

Chiu, Hungdah, with Shao-chuan Leng, eds. *China: Seventy Years After the 1911 Hsin-Hai Revolution*. Charlottesville: University Press of Virginia, 1984.

Clancy, Tomas. *Countries of the World: The Republic of China*. N.p.: Create Space, 2012.

Clough, Ralph N. *Island China*. Cambridge, MA: Harvard University Press, 1978.

Edmonds, Richard Lewis, and Steven M. Goldstein, eds. *Taiwan in the Twentieth Century: A Retrospective View*. Cambridge: Cambridge University Press, 2001.

Feldman, Harvey, and Ilpyong J. Kim, eds. *Taiwan in a Time of Transition*. New York: Paragon House, 1988.

Han, Lih-wu. *Taiwan Today*. Taipei: Institute of International Relations, 1986.

Hsieh, Chiao-min. *Taiwan—Ilha Formosa: A Geography in Perspective*. Washington, DC: Butterworths, 1964.

Hsiung, James C., ed. *Contemporary Republic of China: The Taiwan Experience 1950–1980*. New York: Praeger, 1981.

Jo, Yung-hwan, ed. *Taiwan's Future*. Tempe: Arizona State University, 1974.

Klintworth, Gary. *New Taiwan, New China: Taiwan's Changing Role in the Asia Pacific Region*. New York: St. Martins, 1995.

Kubek, Anthony. *Modernizing China: A Comparative Analysis of the Two Chinas*. Washington, DC: Regency Gateway, 1987.

Long, Simon. *Taiwan: China's Last Frontier*. New York: St. Martin's Press, 1991.

---

* These books are published annually. The *Republic of China Yearbook* has been published for several decades, for a period under the title *Taiwan Yearbook*.

Mancall, Mark, ed. *Formosa Today*. New York: Praeger, 1964.
The Republic of China 2011 Yearbook. Taipei: Government Information Office, 2011.*
Shambaugh, David, ed. *Contemporary Taiwan*. Oxford: Clarendon Press, 1998.
Sih, Paul K. T., ed. *Taiwan in Modern Times*. New York: St. John's University Press, 1973.
Sutter, Robert G. *Taiwan: Entering the 21st Century*. Lanham, MD: University Press of America, 1988.
Taiwan Statistical Data Book 2011. Taipei: Executive Yuan, 2011.*

History

Andrade, Tonio. *How Taiwan Became Chinese: Dutch, Spanish, and Han Colonization in the Seventeenth Century*. New York: Columbia University Press, 2008.
———. *Lost Colony: The Untold Story of China's First Great Victory over the West*. Princeton, NJ: Princeton University Press, 2011.
Cline, Ray S. *Chiang Ching-kuo Remembered: The Man and His Political Legacy*. Washington, DC: US Global Strategy Council, 1989.
Copper, John F. *Historical Dictionary of Taiwan*. 3rd ed. Lanham, MD: Scarecrow Press, 2007.
Crozier, Ralph C. *Koxinga and Chinese Nationalism: History, Myth and the Hero*. Cambridge, MA: Harvard University Press, 1977.
Davidson, James W. *The Island of Formosa: Past and Present*. New York: AMS Press, 1977.
Davison, Gary Marvin. *A Short History of Taiwan: The Case for Independence*. Westport, CT: Praeger, 2003.
Edmonds, Richard L., and Stephen M. Goldstein. *Taiwan in the Twentieth Century: A Retrospective View*. The China Quarterly Special Issues, n.s., no. 1. Cambridge: Cambridge University Press, 2001.
Furuya, Keiji. *Chiang Kai-shek: His Life and Times*. New York: St. John's University Press, 1981.
Gilbert, Stephen P., and William M. Carpenter. *America and Island China: A Documentary History*. Lanham, MD: University Press of America, 1989.
Goddard, W. G. *Formosa: A Study in Chinese History*. East Lansing: Michigan State University Press, 1966.
Gordon, Leonard H. D., ed. *Taiwan: Studies in Chinese Local History*. New York: Columbia University Press, 1970.
Hung Chien-chao. *A History of Taiwan*. Rimini, Italy: Il Cerchio, 2000.
Kagan, Richard C. *Taiwan's Statesman: Lee Teng-hui and Democracy in Asia*. Annapolis, MD: Naval Institute Press, 2007.
Kerr, George H. *Formosa Betrayed*. Boston: Houghton Mifflin, 1965.
———. *Formosa: Licensed Revolution and the Home Rule Movement, 1895–1945*. Honolulu: University of Hawaii Press, 1974.
Knapp, Ronald G., ed. *China's Island Frontier: Studies in the Historical Geography of Taiwan*. Honolulu: University of Hawaii Press, 1980.
Lai, Tse-han, Ramon H. Myers, and Wou Wei. *A Tragic Beginning: The Taiwan Uprising of February 28, 1947*. Stanford, CA: Stanford University Press, 1991.
Lee Wei-chin, and Y. T. Wang, eds. *Sayonara to the Lee Teng-hui Era*. Lanham, MD: University Press of America, 2003.
Leng, Shao-chuan, ed. *Chiang Ching-kuo's Leadership in the Development of the Republic of China on Taiwan*. Lanham, MD: University Press of America, 1993.

Li, Laura Tyson. *Madame Chiang Kai-shek: China's Eternal First Lady*. New York: Atlantic Monthly Press, 2006.

Lou, Tsu-kiang. *Personal Legends of Formosa*. Pasadena, CA: Oriental Book Store, 1975.

Lumley, F. A. *The Republic of China Under Chiang Kai-shek*. London: Barrie and Jenkins, 1978.

Manthorpe, Jonathan. *Forbidden Nation: A History of Taiwan*. New York: Palgrave-Macmillan, 2005.

Phillips, Steven E. *Between Assimilation and Independence: The Taiwanese Encounter Nationalist China, 1945–1950*. Stanford, CA: Stanford University Press, 2003.

Rigger, Shelley, *Why Taiwan Matters: Small Island, Global Powerhouse*. Lanham, MD: Roman & Littlefield, 2011.

Riggs, Fred W. *Formosa Under Chinese Nationalist Rule*. New York: Macmillan, 1952. Reprint, New York: Octagon Books, 1972.

Roy, Denny. *Taiwan: A Political History*. Ithaca, NY: Cornell University Press, 2003.

Rubinstein, Murray A., ed. *The Other Taiwan: 1945 to the Present*. Armonk, NY: M. E. Sharpe, 1994.

———. *Taiwan: A History*. Armonk, NY: M. E. Sharpe, 1998.

———, ed. *Taiwan: A New History*. Armonk, NY: M. E. Sharpe, 2007.

Takekoshi, Yosaburo. *Japanese Rule in Formosa*. 1907. Reprint, Pasadena, CA: Oriental Book Store, 1978.

Taylor, Jay. *The Generalissimo: Chiang Kai-shek and the Struggle for Modern China*. Cambridge, MA: Harvard University Press, 2009.

———. *The Generalissimo's Son: Chiang Ching-kuo and the Revolutions in China and Taiwan*. Cambridge, MA: Harvard University Press, 2000.

Tsai, Shih-Shan Henry. *Maritime Taiwan: Historical Encounters with the East and West*. Armonk, NY: M. E. Sharpe, 2009.

Wang, David Der-wei, and Carlos Rojas, eds. *Writing Taiwan: A Literary History*. Durham, NC: Duke University Press, 2007.

Society and Culture

Ahern, Emily Martin, and Hill Gates, eds. *The Anthropology of Taiwanese Society*. Stanford, CA: Stanford University Press, 1981.

Aspalter, Christian. *Democratization and Welfare State Development in Taiwan*. London: Ashgate, 2002.

Brown, Melissa J. *Is Taiwan Chinese? The Impact of Culture, Power, and Migration on Changing Identities*. Berkeley: University of California Press, 2004.

Canquelin, Jovian. *The Aborigines of Taiwan*. London: Routledge, 2010.

Chen, Ya-chen. *Women in Taiwan: Sociocultural Perspectives*. Indianapolis: University of Indianapolis Press, 2008.

Ching, Leo T. S. *Becoming Japanese: Colonial Taiwan and the Politics of Identity*. Berkeley: University of California Press, 2001.

Clart, Philip, and Charles B. Jones, eds. *Religion in Taiwan: Tradition and Innovation in a Changing Society*. Honolulu: University of Hawaii Press, 2003.

Cohen, Marc J. *Taiwan at the Crossroads: Human Rights, Political Development and Social Change on the Beautiful Island*. Washington, DC: Asia Resource Center, 1988.

Cohen, Myron L. *House United, House Divided: The Chinese Family in Taiwan*. New York: Columbia University Press, 1976.

Corcuff, Stephane, ed. *Memories of the Future: National Identity Issues and the Search for a New Taiwan*. Armonk, NY: M. E. Sharpe, 2002.

Eberhard, Wolfram. *Moral and Social Values of the Chinese: Collected Essays*. San Francisco: Chinese Materials and Research Aids Service Center, 1974.

Gold, Thomas B. *State and Society in the Taiwan Miracle*. Armonk, NY: M. E. Sharpe, 1986.

Harrell, Steven, and Huang Chun-chieh, eds. *Cultural Change in Postwar Taiwan*. Boulder, CO: Westview Press, 1994.

Hsiao, Hsin-huang Michael, Wei-yuan Cheng, and Hou-sheng Chan, eds. *Taiwan: A Newly Industrialized State*. Taipei: Department of Sociology, National Taiwan University, 1989.

Kang, Peng-cheng. *The Story of Taiwan: Culture*. Taipei: Government Information Office, 2001.

Ku, Yeun-wen. *Welfare Capitalism in Taiwan: State, Economy and Social Policy*. New York: St. Martin's Press, 1997.

Lai Ming-yan. *Nativism and Modernity: Cultural Contestations in China and Taiwan Under Global Capitalism*. Albany: State University of New York Press, 2008.

Liao, Ping-hui, and David Der-wei Wang, eds. *Taiwan Under Japanese Rule 1895–1945: History, Culture, Memory*. New York: Columbia University Press, 2006.

Liu, Alan P. L. *Social Change on Mainland China and Taiwan*. Baltimore: University of Maryland School of Law, 1982.

Marsh, Robert M. *The Great Transformation: Social Change in Taipei, Taiwan Since the 1960s*. Armonk, NY: M. E. Sharpe, 1996.

Moser, Michael J. *Law and Social Change in a Chinese Community: A Case Study from Rural Taiwan*. Dobbs Ferry, NY: Oceana, 1983.

Moskowitz, Marc L. *Popular Culture in Taiwan: Charismatic Modernity*. London: Routledge, 2011.

Myers, Ramon H., ed. *Two Societies in Opposition: The Republic of China and the People's Republic of China After Forty Years*. Stanford, CA: Hoover Institution Press, 1990.

Rubinstein, Murray A., ed. *The Protestant Community on Modern Taiwan: Mission, Seminary and Church*. Armonk, NY: M. E. Sharpe, 1991.

The Story of Taiwan. Taipei: Government Information Office, 2000.

Thornton, Arland, and Hui-sheng Lin. *Social Change and the Family in Taiwan*. Chicago: University of Chicago Press, 1994.

Tien, Hung-mao. *The Great Transition: Political and Social Change in the Republic of China*. Stanford, CA: Hoover Institution Press, 1989.

Tsai, Wen-hui. *In Making China Modernized: Comparative Modernization Between Mainland China and Taiwan*. Baltimore: University of Maryland School of Law, 1993.

Wei, Jennifer M. *Language Choice and Identity Politics in Taiwan*. Lanham, MD: Lexington Books, 2008.

Weller, Robert P. *Alternate Civilities: Democracy and Culture in China and Taiwan*. Boulder, CO: Westview Press, 2001.

Wilson, Richard W. *Learning to Be Chinese: The Political Socialization of Children in Taiwan*. Cambridge, MA: The MIT Press, 1970.

Wu, Tsong-shien. *Taiwan's Changing Rural Society*. Pasadena, CA: Oriental Book Store, 1973.

Yip, June. *Envisioning Taiwan: Fiction, Cinema, and the Nation in the Cultural Imaginary.* Durham, NC: Duke University Press, 2004.

Government and Politics

Alagappa, Muthiah, ed. *Taiwan's Presidential Politics: Democratization and Cross-Strait Relations in the Twenty-First Century.* Armonk, NY: M. E. Sharpe, 2001.

Chao, Linda, and Ramon H. Myers. *The First Chinese Democracy: Political Life in the Republic of China on Taiwan.* Baltimore, MD: Johns Hopkins University Press, 1998.

Cheng, Chu-yuan, ed. *Sun Yat-sen's Doctrine in the Modern World.* Boulder, CO: Westview Press, 1989.

Cheng, Tun-jen, and Stephen Haggard, eds. *Political Change in Taiwan.* Boulder, CO: Lynne Rienner, 1992.

Chin, Ko-lin. *Heijin: Organized Crime, Business, and Politics in Taiwan.* Armonk, NY: M. E. Sharpe, 2003.

Ching Cheong. *Will Taiwan Break Away? The Rise of Taiwanese Nationalism.* Singapore: World Scientific, 2001.

Copper, John F. *Consolidating Taiwan's Democracy.* Lanham, MD: University Press of America, 2005.

———. *The KMT's Return to Power: Elections in Taiwan 2008 to 2012.* Lanham, MD: Lexington Books, 2013.

———. *A Quiet Revolution: Political Development in the Republic of China.* Lanham, MD: University Press of America, 1988.

———. *Taiwan Approaches the New Millennium: Essays on Politics and Foreign Affairs.* Lanham, MD: University Press of America, 1999.

———, ed. *Taiwan in Troubled Times: Essays on the Chen Shui-bian Presidency.* Singapore: World Scientific, 2002.

———. *The Taiwan Political Miracle: Essays on Political Development, Elections and Foreign Relations.* Lanham, MD: University Press of America, 1997.

———. *Taiwan's Democracy on Trial: Political Change During the Chen Shui-bian Era and Beyond.* Lanham, MD: University Press of America, 2010.

———. *Taiwan's Mid-1990s Elections: Taking the Final Steps to Democracy.* Westport, CT: Praeger, 1998.

———. *Taiwan's 1991 and 1992 Non-Supplemental Elections: Reaching a Higher State of Democracy.* Lanham, MD: University Press of America, 1994.

———. *Taiwan's Recent Elections: Fulfilling the Democratic Promise.* Baltimore: University of Maryland School of Law, 1990.

Copper, John F., with George P. Chen. *Taiwan's Elections: Political Development and Democratization in the Republic of China.* Baltimore: University of Maryland School of Law, 1984.

Dickson, Bruce J., and Chien-min Chao, eds. *Assessing the Lee Teng-hui Legacy in Taiwan Politics: Democratic Consolidation and External Relations.* Armonk, NY: M. E. Sharpe, 2002.

Feldman, Harvey J., ed. *Constitutional Reform and the Future of the Republic of China.* Armonk, NY: M. E. Sharpe, 1991.

Fell, Dafydd. *Government and Politics in Taiwan.* London: Routledge, 2012.

Ger, Yeong-kuang, *The Story of Taiwan: Politics.* Taipei: Government Information Office, 1998.

Greene, J. Megan. *The Origins of the Developmental State in Taiwan.* Cambridge, MA: Harvard University Press, 2008.

Gregor, A. James, with Maria Hsia Chang and Andrew B. Zimmerman. *Ideology and Development: Sun Yat-sen and the Economic History of Taiwan.* Berkeley, CA: Institute of Asian Studies, 1981.

Hood, Steven J. *The Kuomintang and the Democratization of Taiwan.* Boulder, CO: Westview Press, 1997.

Hughes, Christopher. *Taiwan and Chinese Nationalism: National Identity and Status in International Society.* London: Routledge, 1997.

Jacobs, J. Bruce. *Local Politics in Rural Taiwan Under Dictatorship and Democracy.* Norwalk, CT: EastBridge, 2008.

Lee, Wei-chin. *Taiwan's Politics in the 21st Century: Changes and Challenges.* Singapore: World Scientific, 2010.

Lerman, Arthur J. *Taiwan's Politics: The Provincial Assemblyman's World.* Lanham, MD: University Press of America, 1978.

Liu, Alan P. L. *Phoenix and the Lame Lion: Modernization in Taiwan and Mainland China, 1950–1980.* Stanford, CA: Hoover Institution Press, 1985.

Mendel, Douglas. *The Politics of Formosan Nationalism.* Berkeley: University of California Press, 1970.

Moody, Peter R., Jr. *Political Change on Taiwan: A Study of Ruling Party Adaptability.* New York: Praeger, 1992.

Rigger, Shelley. *From Opposition to Power: Taiwan's Democratic Progressive Party.* Boulder, CO: Lynne Rienner, 2001.

———. *Politics in Taiwan: Voting for Democracy.* London: Routledge, 1999.

Shaw, Yu-ming. *Beyond the Economic Miracle: Reflections on the Developmental Experience of the Republic of China on Taiwan.* Taipei: Kwang Hwa Publishing Company, 1988.

Tsai, Henry Shih-shan. *Lee Teng-hui and Taiwan's Quest for Identity.* New York: Palgrave/Macmillan, 2005.

Wachman, Alan M. *Taiwan: National Identity and Democratization.* Armonk, NY: M. E. Sharpe, 1994.

Wei, Jennifer M. *Virtual Missiles: Metaphors and Allusions in Taiwanese Political Discourse.* Boston: Lexington Books, 2001.

Wu, Joseph Jaushieh. *Taiwan's Democratization: Forces Behind the New Momentum.* Hong Kong: Oxford University Press, 1995.

Zhao, Suisheng. *Power by Design: Constitution-Making in Nationalist China.* Honolulu: University of Hawaii Press, 1996.

Economy

Berger, Suzanne, and Richard K. Lester, eds. *Global Taiwan: Building Competitive Strengths in a New International Economy.* Armonk, NY: M. E. Sharpe, 2005.

Chan, Steve, and Cal Clark. *Flexibility, Foresight and Fortuna in Taiwan's Development.* London: Routledge, Chapman and Hall, 1992.

Chang, Chun-Yen, and Po-Lung Yu, eds. *Made by Taiwan: Booming in the Information Technology Era.* Singapore: World Scientific, 2001.

Cho, Hui-wan. *Taiwan's Application to GATT: Significance of Multilateralism for an Unrecognized State.* Westport, CT: Greenwood Press, 2001.

Chow, Peter C. Y. *National Identity and Economic Interest: Taiwan's Competing Options and Their Implications for Regional Stability*. New York: Palgrave Macmillan, 2012.

———, ed. *Taiwan in the Global Economy: From an Agrarian Economy to an Exporter of High-Tech Products*. Westport, CT: Greenwood Press, 2002.

Clark, Cal. *Taiwan's Development: Implications for Contending Political Economic Paradigms*. New York: Greenwood Press, 1988.

Clark, Cal, and Alexander C. Tan, *Taiwan's Political Economy: Meeting Challenges, Pursuing Progress*. Boulder, CO: Lynne Rienner, 2012.

Fei, John, Gustav Ranis, and Shirley W. Y. Kuo. *Growth with Equity: The Taiwan Case*. New York: Oxford University Press, 1979.

Galenson, Walter, ed. *Economic Growth and Structural Change in Taiwan: The Postwar Experience of the Republic of China*. Ithaca, NY: Cornell University Press, 1979.

Greenhalgh, Susan M., and Edwin A. Winkler. *Approaches to the Political Economy of Taiwan*. Armonk, NY: M. E. Sharpe, 1987.

Ho, Samuel P. *Economic Development of Taiwan, 1860–1970*. New Haven, CT: Yale University Press, 1978.

Jacoby, Neil H. *U.S. Aid to Taiwan: A Study of Foreign Aid, Self Help, and Development*. New York: Praeger, 1966.

Koo, Anthony Y. C. *The Role of Land Reform in Economic Development: A Case Study of Taiwan*. New York: Praeger, 1968.

Kuo, Shirley W. Y. *The Taiwan Economy in Transition*. Boulder, CO: Westview Press, 1983.

Kuo, Shirley W. Y., Gustav Ranis, and John C. H. Fei. *The Taiwan Success Story: Rapid Growth with Improved Distribution in the People's Republic of China, 1952–1979*. Boulder, CO: Westview Press, 1981.

Kuo, Tai-chun, and Ramon H. Myers. *Taiwan's Economic Transformation: Leadership, Property Rights and Institutional Change, 1945–1965*. London: Routledge, 2011.

Li, K. T. *The Evolution of Policy Behind Taiwan's Development Success*. 2nd ed. Singapore: World Scientific, 1995.

Mai, Zhaocheng, and Jiansheng Shi. *Taiwan's Economic Success Since 1980*. London: Edward Elgar, 2001.

Poon, Teresa Shuk-ching. *Competition and Cooperation in Taiwan's Information Technology Industry: Inter-Firm Networks and Industrial Upgrading*. Westport, CT: Greenwood Press, 2002.

Reardon-Anderson, James. *Population, Politics and Foreign Intervention in Taiwan*. Armonk, NY: M. E. Sharpe, 1992.

Schive, Chi. *The Foreign Factor: The Multinational Corporation's Contribution to the Economic Modernization of the Republic of China*. Stanford, CA: Hoover Institution Press, 1990.

Simon, Dennis, and Michael Yin-mao Kao, eds. *Taiwan: Beyond the Economic Miracle*. Armonk, NY: M. E. Sharpe, 1992.

The Taiwan Development Experience and Its Relevance to Other Countries. Taipei: Kwan Hwa, 1988.

Wang, N. T., ed. *Taiwan Enterprises in Global Perspective*. Armonk, NY: M. E. Sharpe, 1992.

Wei, Wou. *Capitalism: A Chinese Version*. Columbus: Ohio State University Press, 1992.

Winkler, Edwin A., and Susan Greenhalgh, eds. *Contending Approaches to the Political Economy of Taiwan*. Armonk, NY: M. E. Sharpe, 1988.

Wu, Yuan-li. *Becoming an Industrialized Nation: ROC's Development on Taiwan.* New York: Praeger, 1985.

Wu, Yuan-li, and Kung-chia Yeh, eds. *Growth, Distribution, and Social Change: Essays on the Economy of the Republic of China.* Baltimore: University of Maryland School of Law, 1978.

Yang, Maysing H., ed. *Taiwan's Expanding Role in the International Arena.* Armonk, NY: M. E. Sharpe, 1997.

Yu Tzong-shian. *The Story of Taiwan: Economy.* Taipei: Government Printing Office, 2001.

Foreign Relations

Barnett, A. Doak. *U.S. Arms Sales: The China-Taiwan Tangle.* Washington, DC: Brookings Institution, 1982.

Bereuter, Douglas. *Taiwan, the PRC and the Taiwan Security Enhancement Act.* Collingdale, PA: Diane, 2001.

Blanchard, Jean-Marc F., and Dennis V. Hickey, *New Thinking About the Taiwan Issue: Theoretical Insights into Its Origins, Dynamics, and Prospects.* London: Routledge, 2012.

Bush, Richard C. *At Cross Purposes: U.S.-Taiwan Relations Since 1942.* Armonk, NY: M. E. Sharpe, 2004.

———. *Untying the Knot: Making Peace in the Taiwan Strait.* Washington, DC: Brookings Institution, 2005.

Chang, Cecilia S. T., ed. *U.S.-R.O.C. Relations: From the White Paper to the Taiwan Relations Act.* Jamaica, NY: St. John's University Press, 1984.

Chang, King-yuh. *A Framework for China's Reunification.* Taipei: Kwang Hwa, 1986.

———. *ROC-US Relations Under the Taiwan Relations Act: Practice and Prospects.* Taipei: Institute of International Relations, 1988.

Chang, Parris H., and Martin L. Lasater, eds. *If China Crosses the Taiwan Strait.* Lanham, MD: University Press of America, 1993.

Chase, Michael S. *Taiwan's Security Policy: External Threats and Domestic Politics.* Boulder, CO: Lynn Rienner, 2008.

Cheng, Tun-jen, Chi Huang, and Samuel S. G. Wu, eds. *Inherited Rivalry: Conflict Across the Taiwan Straits.* Boulder, CO: Lynne Rienner, 1995.

Chi, Su. *Taiwan's Relations with Mainland China: A Tail Wagging Two Dogs.* London: Routledge, 2009.

Chien, Frederick F. *Faith and Residence: The Republic of China Forges Ahead.* Houston: Kwan Hwa (USA), 1988.

Ching Chong. *Will Taiwan Break Away: The Rise of Taiwanese Nationalism.* Singapore: World Scientific, 2001.

Chiu, Hungdah. *Koo-Wang Talks and the Prospects of Building Constructive Relations Across the Taiwan Straits.* Baltimore: University of Maryland School of Law, 1993.

Chiu, Hungdah, and Karen Murphy. *The Chinese Connection and Normalization.* Baltimore: University of Maryland School of Law, 1979.

Cline, Ray S., ed. *The Role of the Republic of China in the International Community.* Washington, DC: US Global Strategy Council, 1991.

Clough, Ralph N. *Reaching Across the Taiwan Strait: People-to-People Diplomacy.* Boulder, CO: Westview Press, 1993.

Copper, John F. *China Diplomacy: The Washington-Taipei-Beijing Triangle.* Boulder, CO: Westview Press, 1992.

———. *Playing with Fire: The Looming War with China over Taiwan.* Westport, CT: Praeger, 2006.

———. *Words Across the Taiwan Strait: A Critique of Beijing's "White Paper" on Taiwan.* Lanham, MD: University Press of America, 1995.

Denise, Donald J., and Diane D. Pikcanas. *Can Two Chinas Become One?* Washington, DC: Council for Social and Economic Studies, 1989.

Downen, Robert L. *Of Grave Concern: U.S.-Taiwan Relations on the Threshold of the 1980s.* Washington, DC: Center for Strategic and International Studies, 1981.

Finkelstein, David M. *Washington's Taiwan Dilemma: From Abandonment to Salvation.* Fairfax, VA: George Mason University Press, 1993.

Frost, Michael S. *Taiwan's Security and the United States Policy: Executive and Congressional Strategies.* Baltimore: University of Maryland School of Law, 1982.

Gregor, A. James, and Maria Hsia Chang. *The Republic of China and U.S. Policy: A Study in Human Rights.* Washington, DC: Ethics and Public Policy Center, 1983.

Henckaerts, Jean-Marie, ed. *The International Status of Taiwan in the New World Order.* London: Kluwer Law International, 1996.

Hickey, Dennis Van Vranken. *Foreign Policy Making in Taiwan: From Principle to Pragmatism.* London: Routledge, 2007.

———. *Taiwan's Security in the Changing International System.* Boulder, CO: Lynne Rienner, 1997.

———. *United States–Taiwan Security Ties: From Cold War to Beyond Containment.* Westport, CT: Praeger, 1994.

Hsieh, Chiao Chiao. *Strategy for Survival: The Foreign Policy and External Relations of the Republic of China on Taiwan, 1959–1979.* London: Sherwood Press, 1985.

Kintner, William, and John F. Copper. *A Matter of Two Chinas.* Philadelphia: Foreign Policy Research Institute, 1979.

Lasater, Martin L. *The Changing of the Guard: President Clinton and the Security of Taiwan.* Boulder, CO: Westview Press, 1995.

———. *Policy and Evolution: The U.S. Role in China's Reunification.* Boulder, CO: Westview Press, 1988.

———. *Security of Taiwan: Unraveling the Dilemma.* Washington, DC: University Press of America, 1978.

———. *The Taiwan Issue in Sino-American Strategic Relations.* Boulder, CO: Westview Press, 1984.

———. *U.S. Interests in the New Taiwan.* Boulder, CO: Westview Press, 1993.

Lee, Bernice. *The Security Implications of the New Taiwan.* New York: Oxford University Press, 2000.

Li, Victor H. *Derecognizing Taiwan: The Legal Problems.* Washington, DC: Carnegie Endowment for International Peace, 1977.

Lilley, James R., and Chuck Downs, eds. *Crisis in the Taiwan Strait.* Washington, DC: National Defense University Press, 1997.

MacFarquhar, Roderick. *Sino-American Relations: 1949–1971.* New York: Praeger, 1972.

Myers, Ramon H. *A Unique Relationship: The United States and the People's Republic of China Under the Taiwan Relations Act.* Stanford, CA: Hoover Institution Press, 1989.

Myers, Ramon H., and Jialin Zhang. *The Struggle Across the Taiwan Strait: The Divided China Problem*. Stanford, CA: Hoover Institution Press, 2006.

Rawnsley, Gary D. *Taiwan's Informal Diplomacy and Propaganda*. New York: St. Martin's Press, 2000.

Romberg, Alan D. *Rein In at the Brink of the Precipice: American Policy Toward Taiwan and U.S.-PRC Relations*. Washington, DC: Henry L. Stimson Center, 2003.

Sheng, Lijun. *China and Taiwan: Cross Strait Relations Under Chen Shui-bian*. London: Zed Books, 2002.

———. *China's Dilemma: The Taiwan Issue*. Singapore: Institute of Southeast Asian Studies, 2001.

Snyder, Edwin, A., James Gregor, and Maria Hsia Chang. *The Taiwan Relations Act and the Defense of the Republic of China*. Berkeley, CA: Institute of International Studies, 1980.

So, Alvin Y., Nan Lin, and Dudley L. Poston. *The Chinese Triangle of Mainland China, Taiwan and Hong Kong: Comparative Institutional Analyses*. Westport, CT: Greenwood Press, 2001.

Stolper, Thomas E. *China, Taiwan and the Offshore Islands*. Armonk, NY: M. E. Sharpe, 1985.

Swaine, Michael D., Andrew N. D. Yang, and Evan S. Medeiros, with Oriana Skylark Mastro, eds. *Assessing the Threat: The Chinese Military and Taiwan's Security*. Washington, DC: Carnegie Endowment for International Peace, 2007.

Tan, Alexander C., Steve Chan, and Calvin Jillson. *Taiwan's National Security: Dilemmas and Opportunities*. London: Ashgate, 2001.

Tkacik, John J., Jr., ed. *Reshaping the Taiwan Strait*. Washington, DC: The Heritage Foundation, 2007.

Tsang, Steve, ed. *If China Attacks Taiwan: Military Strategy, Politics and Economics*. London: Routledge, 2006.

Tucker, Nancy Bernkopf, ed. *Dangerous Strait: The U.S.-Taiwan-China Crisis*. New York: Columbia University Press, 2005.

Wang, Mei-ling. *The Dust That Never Settles: The Taiwan Independence Campaign and U.S.-China Relations*. Lanham, MD: University Press of America, 2002.

Wang, Yu San, ed. *Foreign Relations of the Republic of China on Taiwan: An Unorthodox Approach*. New York: Praeger, 1990.

Wheeler, Jimmy W., and Perry L. Wood. *Beyond Recrimination: Perspectives on U.S. Taiwan Trade Tensions*. Indianapolis, IN: The Hudson Institute, 1987.

Wu, Hsin-hsing. *Bridging the Strait: Taiwan, China, and the Prospects for Reunification*. New York: Oxford University Press, 1994.

Zhao, Shisheng, ed. *Across the Taiwan Strait: Mainland China, Taiwan, and the 1995–1996 Crisis*. London: Routledge, 1999.

INDEX

CPSIA information can be obtained
at www.ICGtesting.com
Printed in the USA
BVOW09s0826080517

483398BV00005B/10/P